The Modernisation of Russia 1676–1825

This important new addition to the *New Approaches to European History* series is the first book to place Russia's 'long' eighteenth century squarely in its European context. The conceptual framework is set out in an opening critique of modernisation theory which, while rejecting its linear implications, maintains its focus on the relationship between government, economy, and society. Following a chronological introduction, a series of thematic chapters emphasise the ways in which Russia's international ambitions as an emerging great power provoked administrative and fiscal reforms with wide-ranging (and often unanticipated) social consequences. Russia's kinship-dominated peasant communities were not the casual detritus of government-inspired reform, but rather its direct consequence: the more the tsars tried to modernise their state, the more backward their empire became. Though social and political history are naturally crucial to such a study, the thematic treatment adopted here also permits an unusually full discussion of the intellectual developments that helped to give educated Russians a sense of cultural autonomy even as their minds were opened to an unprecedented range of Western influences. In order to help the reader further, a chronology and a critical bibliography are also provided to allow students to discover more about this colourful period of Russian history.

SIMON DIXON is Senior Lecturer in Modern History at the University of Glasgow. He has written a number of articles on the Russian Orthodox church and on Russian nationalism, and is editor of *Britain and Russia in the Age of Peter the Great: Historical Documents* (1998).

NEW APPROACHES TO EUROPEAN HISTORY

Series editors
WILLIAM BEIK *Emory University*
T. C. W. BLANNING *Sidney Sussex College, Cambridge*

New Approaches to European History is an important new textbook initiative, intended to provide concise but authoritative surveys of major themes and problems in European history since the Renaissance. Written at a level and length accessible to advanced school students and undergraduates, each book in the series will address topics or themes that students of European history encounter daily: the series will embrace both some of the more 'traditional' subjects of study, and those cultural and social issues to which increasing numbers of school and college courses are devoted. A particular effort will be made to consider the wider international implications of the subject under scrutiny.

To aid the student reader scholarly apparatus and annotation will be light, but each work will have full supplementary bibliographies and notes for further reading: where appropriate chronologies, maps, diagrams and other illustrative material will also be provided.

For a list of titles published in the series, please see end of book.

The Modernisation of
Russia 1676–1825

Simon Dixon

CAMBRIDGE
UNIVERSITY PRESS

CAMBRIDGE UNIVERSITY PRESS
Cambridge, New York, Melbourne, Madrid, Cape Town, Singapore, São Paulo

Cambridge University Press
The Edinburgh Building, Cambridge CB2 2RU, UK

Published in the United States of America by Cambridge University Press, New York

www.cambridge.org
Information on this title: www.cambridge.org/9780521371001

First published 1999

A catalogue record for this publication is available from the British Library

Library of Congress Cataloguing in Publication data
Dixon, Simon (Simon M.)
The modernisation of Russia 1676–1825 / Simon Dixon.
    p.   cm. – (New approaches to European history)
Includes bibliographical references.
ISBN 0 521 37100 7 (hc.) – ISBN 0 521 37961 X (pbk.)
1. Russia – History – 1613–1917.   I. Title.   II. Title:
Modernisation of Russia.   III. Title: Modernization of Russia
1676–1825.   IV. Series.
DK127.D59   1999
947 – dc21   98–46739   CIP

ISBN-13 978-0-521-37100-1 hardback
ISBN-10 0-521-37100-7 hardback

ISBN-13 978-0-521-37961-8 paperback
ISBN-10 0-521-37961-X paperback

Transferred to digital printing 2005

Contents

Maps

Preface

With the exception of peasant revolts and aspects of the reign of Peter the Great, the eighteenth century fared poorly in the hands of Soviet historians, to whom it seemed suspect as a time of foreign influence in Russian affairs. Following the fall of the USSR, the prospects have become more encouraging. Though there remains much about which we know nothing – an ignorance I have made no attempt to conceal – multi-national scholarship over the last generation or so, much of it in Russian archives, has allowed us to answer familiar questions in a fresh or better-documented way. In turn, such work has suggested new questions to ask of well-known evidence. This book attempts to draw the threads together in coherent and accessible form.

Though flashes of originality may be detected in my arguments, a book of this kind naturally draws heavily on the researches of others. I should like to have been able to acknowledge each debt individually. But whilst authors experience a frisson of conceit to see their reading recorded in copious footnotes (where its limits may be exposed), many readers merely shudder at the sight of such a cumbersome apparatus. Following the pattern of the series, I have kept references to a minimum: they identify quotations and mention works that might otherwise have escaped the bibliographical notes. To satisfy the book's anticipated readership, these highly selective reading lists are heavily slanted towards work in English, though it would have been impertinent to omit the most important Russian and continental scholarship. There is also a bias towards publications from the last two decades, not because I have confused novelty with excellence, but because recent works in turn refer to older ones, some of which are conveniently listed by P. Clendenning and R. Bartlett, *Eighteenth-Century Russia: A Select Bibliography of Works Published Since 1955* (Newtonville, MA, 1981). Dates are given in the Old Style – ten days behind the Western calendar in the seventeenth century, eleven in the eighteenth, and twelve in the nineteenth – except in the case of the events of the Napoleonic invasion where both Old and New Style dates appear. For the sake of simplicity, place names, subject to frequent change and some controversy, are given in their Russian form: so, for example, Belorussia not Belarus. A few common anglicisations are retained: thus, Archangel not Arkhangel'sk.

The Study Group on Eighteenth-Century Russia has offered a model of scholarly friendship to a relatively recent recruit. This book stands as testimony to the contribution its members have made to the field. I must thank, in particular, Tony Cross, Lindsey Hughes, L. R. Lewitter, and above all Roger Bartlett, whose detailed critique of much of the draft manuscript immeasurably improved it. My interest in the subject was awakened by Mr C. H. Eames at Bolton School, where another remarkable master, Mr Roy Waterhouse, taught me Russian and twice took me to Moscow. At Sidney Sussex College, Cambridge, I owe most to Derek Beales, my much-missed neighbour on E Staircase, and to Tim Blanning, an eagle-eyed editor, an inspired teacher, and a generous and patient friend. At the University of Glasgow, which granted me leave in order to complete the book, I am grateful to colleagues for their encouragement and company. If I single out Thomas Munck it is because he has read several chapters with particular care. I am conscious of having stretched the tolerance of Richard Fisher at Cambridge University Press beyond all reasonable bounds. His colleague, Vicky Cuthill, has managed the final stages of production with exemplary courtesy and efficiency. Karen Anderson Howes has been a reassuringly meticulous copy-editor. Students at Cambridge, Glasgow, and Keele have allowed me to experiment in lecture form. I am as grateful to them as I am to all those friends and colleagues who have saved me from error. Remaining mistakes are entirely my responsibility.

I cannot adequately express my debt to my wife, Stephanie, who has lived with this book almost as long as she has lived with me. I dedicate this book to her.

Chronology

As in the text, dates are Old Style, according to the Julian calendar, except for the events of the Napoleonic invasion where both Old and New Style (Gregorian) dates are given.

1676–82   **Fedor Alekseevich**
1676 29   January: death of Aleksei Mikhailovich
1678   Household census
1679   February: tax assessment by land replaced by assessment by household
1682   Abolition of *mestnichestvo*
  27 April: death of Tsar Fedor sparks Moscow rebellion
1682–1725   **Peter I (1682–96 joint ruler with half-brother, Ivan V)**
1682–9   **Regency of Sophia Alekseevna (Peter's half-sister)**
1682   26 May: ritual confirmation of tsars' joint rule
1686   'Eternal peace' with Poland
1687   V. V. Golitsyn's first Crimean campaign
1689   Second Crimean campaign
  September: *strel'tsy* revolt removes Sophia leaving Peter effectively in control
1694   25 January: death of Peter's mother
1696   29 January: death of Ivan V
1696–1725   **Sole rule of Peter I**
1697–8   Grand Embassy to the West
1698   July: *strel'tsy* revolt
1700–21   Great Northern War
    1700   November: Russians defeated at Narva
    1705   February: introduction of new recruiting system
    1709   June: Swedes defeated at Poltava
    1714   July: Russian naval victory at Hangö
    1721   September: treaty of Nystad
1700   Patriarchate suspended on death of Patriarch Adrian
1703   Foundation of St Petersburg

1707–8	Bulavin's revolt in Astrakhan'
1708–10	Reform of local government
1711–13	Russo-Turkish war
	1711 22 February: foundation of Senate
	July: Russians defeated on River Pruth
1714	23 March: law of single inheritance
1716	Military Regulation
1718	First administrative colleges founded
	Second reform of local government
	Poll tax decreed
	Death of Tsarevich Aleksei
1720	Maritime Regulation and General Regulation
1721	Spiritual Regulation
	Abolition of patriarchate and creation of Holy Synod
1722	14 February: Table of Ranks
1722–4	War with Persia
1725	Foundation of Academy of Sciences
1725–7	**Catherine I**
1726	February: creation of Supreme Privy Council
	Austro-Russian alliance
1727	May: death of Catherine I
1727–30	**Peter II**
1727	September: exile of A. D. Menshikov
1729	November: death of Menshikov
1730	January: death of Peter II creates succession crisis
	18–19 January: Supreme Privy Council seizes initiative and offers throne to Anna
1730–40	**Anna**
1730	25 February: Anna rejects D. M. Golitsyn's 'conditions'
1731	Repeal of law of single inheritance
1733–5	War of Polish Succession
1735–9	Russo-Turkish war
1739	September: peace of Belgrade
1740	October: death of Anna creates succession crisis
1740–1	**Ivan VI (Anna Leopoldovna as regent)**
1741	24–5 November: arrest of infant Ivan VI; accession of Peter I's daughter, Elizabeth
1741–61	**Elizabeth**
1741–3	Russo-Swedish war
1754	Noble monopoly on alcohol
1755	Foundation of University of Moscow
1756–62	Seven Years War

	1757	Prussia defeated at Gross-Jägersdorf
	1759	Prussia defeated at Kunersdorf
1757	Foundation of Imperial Academy of Fine Arts
1761	25 December: death of Elizabeth
1761–2	**Peter III**
1762	18 February: edict freeing nobility from obligatory service
	21 March: confiscation of church peasants
	28 June: Empress Catherine's coup
1762–96	**Catherine II**
1764	February: secularisation of church lands
	April: Russo-Prussian alliance
	October: abolition of Ukrainian hetmanate
1765	Foundation of Free Economic Society
1767	Publication of *Nakaz*
	Legislative Commission convened
1768–74	Russo-Turkish war
	1768	December: foundation of assignat banks
	1770	Russian naval victory at Chesme
	1774	July: treaty of Kutchuk-Kainardzhii
1772	August: first partition of Poland
1773–5	Pugachev revolt
1775	7 November: provincial reform
1779	Russian mediation at peace of Teschen
1781	Secret Austro-Russian alliance
1782	Commission on Public Schools
1783	Legislation to permit private publishing
	Russia annexes the Crimea
1785	21 April: Charters to the Nobility and the Towns
1787	Catherine's journey to the south and the Crimea
1787–91	Russo-Turkish war
	1789 July: Russian victory at Fokshani
	September: Russian victory on River Rymnik
	1790 November: Russian victory at Ismail
	1791 March: crisis over Ochakov (captured in 1788)
	December: treaty of Jassy
1788–90	Russo-Swedish war
1788	July: naval stalemate at Hogland
1790	June: Russian naval defeat at Svenskund
1790	Radishchev's *Journey from St Petersburg to Moscow*
1793	April: second partition of Poland
1795	Third partition of Poland
1796	6 November: death of Catherine II

1796–1801 Paul I

1797	5 April: law of succession
1798	Paul elected grand master of the Knights of St John of Jerusalem
1801	11–12 March: coup and assassination of Paul I

1801–25   Alexander I

1801	24 June: first meeting of Unofficial Committee
1802	8 September: decree establishing ministries
1803	February: Free Agriculturalists Law
1803–4	Reform of elementary education
1805–7	War of the Third Coalition against France

        1807   2/14 June: Russians defeated at Friedland

               13/25 June: first Tilsit meeting between tsar and Napoleon

               26 June/7 July: Russia allies with France

1807–12	Alliance with Napoleon

        1808   Russia invades Finland, incorporating it into the empire as a grand duchy

        1809   March: Alexander I promises the Finns constitution at the Diet of Porvoo

        1810   December: Russia abandons Napoleon's Continental System

1808–11	Speranskii's domestic reforms
1812	17 March: dismissal of Speranskii
1812	Napoleonic invasion of Russia

               11/23 June: Grande armée enters Russia

               26 August/7 September: battle of Borodino

               2/14 September: French troops enter Moscow

               11/23 October: Russian troops re-enter Moscow

               12/24 October: battle of Maloiaroslavets

1814	March: treaty of Chaumont; Russian troops enter Paris
1814–15	Congress of Vienna
1815	15 November: constitution of Congress Kingdom of Poland
1819–22	Siberian reforms under leadership of Speranskii, partially restored to favour
1825	19 November: death of Alexander I
	14 December: Decembrist revolt

Abbreviations

AHR	*American Historical Review*
CASS	*Canadian–American Slavic Studies*
CMRS	*Cahiers du Monde Russe et Soviétique*
CSP	*Canadian Slavonic Papers*
CSSH	*Comparative Studies in Society and History*
EHR	*English Historical Review*
FzOG	*Forschungen zur Osteuropäischen Geschichte*
HEI	*History of European Ideas*
HEQ	*History of Education Quarterly*
HJ	*Historical Journal*
HUS	*Harvard Ukrainian Studies*
JEcH	*Journal of Economic History*
JEurEcH	*Journal of European Economic History*
JfGO	*Jahrbücher für Geschichte Osteuropas*
JIH	*Journal of Interdisciplinary History*
JMH	*Journal of Modern History*
NS	new series
OSP	*Oxford Slavonic Papers*
P&P	*Past and Present*
RH	*Russian History*
RR	*Russian Review*
SEER	*Slavonic and East European Review*
SGECRN	*Study Group on Eighteenth-Century Russia Newsletter*
SIRIO	*Sbornik imperatorskago russkago istoricheskago obshchestva,* 148 vols. (St Petersburg, 1867–1914)
SR	*Slavic Review*
SVEC	*Studies on Voltaire and the Eighteenth Century*

1 Modernisation theory and Russian history

Modernisation theory

Loosely conceived, 'modernisation' may signify nothing more than a programme of reform required to bring an allegedly outmoded institution 'up to date' and fit to face the future. In Britain, for example, both the Labour Party and the Anglican church have recently been subjected to such campaigns, the one with more obvious benefit than the other. Modernisation, in this simple sense, has long appealed to historians as shorthand for the ways in which an apparently isolated and backward Muscovy – transformed into the Russian empire when Peter the Great (1672–1725) assumed the title 'Imperator' at the thanksgiving service for the end of the Great Northern War on 22 October 1721 – adopted Western standards in the eighteenth century in order to compete in the cut-throat world of the European international system. Scholars, however, have given modernisation explicit conceptual content, and it is in this sense, not always synonymous with Westernisation and sometimes directly contrary to it, that the term will be used in this book.

Modernisation theory takes as its principal economic transformation the shift from a network of predominantly rural communities, preoccupied by the needs of agrarian self-subsistence, to an increasingly urbanised, market-oriented society dominated by mechanised industry. A specialised workforce, distinguished by a division of labour unknown to traditional society, is supplied by a demographic revolution brought about by a fall first in mortality rates and later in fertility rates. Sustained economic growth, beyond the reach of traditional society, grants increased productivity to the modern state and a better standard of living to the majority of its population. Whereas traditional communities were stable hierarchies dominated by kinship networks, modern social mobility creates a more impersonal society in which national loyalties outweigh social ones. In this sense, nationalism generates nations, and not the other way around. Within the amorphous national mass, individuals have more choice than before, empowered not only by increased affluence but also by the spread of literacy. This allows the written word to replace face-to-face contact as the principal mode of communication. By popularising scientific discoveries, education helps to demystify the world, enabling modern man to spend more time contemplating his history than agonising about his future. Wider access to education makes traditionally restricted high culture publicly accessible and opens up careers based on talent rather than on lineage, leading ultimately to an increase in popular politicisation and political equality. However, there is a price to pay. Modern states, in which personal sovereignty is eclipsed by bureaucratic institutions governed by law, exert a tighter fiscal hold over their citizens than did their traditional predecessors and constantly seek to extend their regulatory tentacles. Further, autonomous individuals may become alienated from their fellows and are likely to be beset by doubt in a secular modern world.[1]

Derived from the ideas of Max Weber (1864–1920), and reformulated by English-speaking scholars in the 1960s, such a bold thesis could hardly be expected to pass without criticism. Its rigid categories are by definition incompatible with the shimmering world of postmodernism. Yet post-modernists who regard rationality as an elusive, not to say undesirable, goal are far from the only ones to question modernisation theory: conventional scholars have also attacked it. Its linearity is evidently misleading: historians of religion, for example, have convincingly rejected any straight-line claims for secularisation.[2] Recoiling from the excesses of concept-driven historical writing, Joanna Innes complains in the cause of authenticity that 'we obstruct our own efforts to understand the eighteenth century by imposing upon it a set of analytical dichotomies [industrial/pre-industrial, secular/religious and so on] with their roots in nineteenth-century

[1] This paragraph amalgamates several key statements of the theory. Important early formulations included C. E. Black, *The Dynamics of Modernization* (New York, 1967), and S. N. Eisenstadt, *Tradition, Change and Modernity* (New York, 1973). J. Goody and I. Watt, 'The Consequences of Literacy', in Goody, ed., *Literacy in Traditional Societies* (Cambridge, 1968), pp. 27–68, signified an interest in modernisation theory that was subsequently modified in Goody, *The Domestication of the Savage Mind* (Cambridge, 1977), and implicitly retracted in Goody, *The East in the West* (Cambridge, 1996). The central modernist interpretation of nationalism is E. Gellner, *Nations and Nationalism* (Oxford, 1983). Among recent reflections, see S. N. Eisenstadt, ed., *Patterns of Modernity*, 2 vols. (London, 1987); M. Adas, *Machines as the Measure of Men: Science, Technology, and Ideologies of Western Dominance* (Ithaca, NY, and London, 1989); J. A. Hall and I. C. Jarvie, eds., *Transition to Modernity: Essays on Power, Wealth and Belief* (Cambridge, 1992); C. Offe, *Modernity and the State: East, West* (Oxford, 1996). See also H.-U. Wehler, *Modernisierungstheorie und Geschichte* (Göttingen, 1975), and T. Nipperdey, 'Probleme der Modernisierung in Deutschland', *Saeculum*, 30 (1979).

[2] See S. Bruce, ed., *Religion and Modernization: Historians and Sociologists Debate the Secularization Thesis* (Oxford, 1992).

social science'.[3] And the modernist view of nationalism has recently sustained a damaging blow (though not a knock-out punch) from Adrian Hastings.[4]

In fact, modernisation theory has been vilified by both Left and Right. The Left took offence at the arrogance of the theory's Anglo-American liberal–capitalist assumptions and condemned it for making invidious comparisons between 'advanced' societies and so-called latecomers. It was in this way that modernisation became equated with Westernisation, which critics portrayed as 'a subtle form of "cultural imperialism"' discredited by its association with American expansionism.[5] By contrast, the Right, offended by modernity itself, has tended to dismiss modernisation as the Whig theory of progress dressed up in sociological jargon, and to condemn it for offering the sort of teleological historical education that imparted to Evelyn Waugh's unprepossessing Hooper 'a profusion of detail about humane legislation and recent industrial change' when it might instead have instilled in him a litany of glorious battles and respect for religious orthodoxy.[6]

Even its most distinguished proponents acknowledge weaknesses in modernisation theory. In striving for comprehensiveness, to borrow a phrase from the late Ernest Gellner, it sacrifices precision, so that the exact 'conditions of the exit' from tradition to modernity remain unclear.[7] Overexcited by the prospect of quantifying historical change in terms of economic growth, early theorists made modernisation synonymous with industrialisation. Long after their optimism had evaporated, Gellner continued to stress the qualitative influence of industrialisation, arguing that the mutual relationship of a modern culture and state were determined by the requirements of a modern economy. By contrast, E. A. Wrigley distinguishes *between* modernisation and industrialisation, seeing 'the twin, key notions' underpinning modernisation as 'rationality and self-interest', where rational behaviour is defined as action tending to maximise the decision-maker's economic returns, and self-interest is

[3] J. Innes, 'Jonathan Clark, Social History and England's "Ancien Regime"', *P&P*, 115 (1987), p. 177.

[4] A. Hastings, *The Construction of Nationhood: Ethnicity, Religion and Nationalism* (Cambridge, 1997).

[5] D. C. Tipps, 'Modernization Theory and the Comparative Study of Societies: A Critical Perspective', *CSSH*, 15, 1 (1973), pp. 209–10. Tipps's article is reprinted with other significant contributions to the debate in C. E. Black, ed., *Comparative Modernization: A Reader* (New York and London, 1976).

[6] E. Waugh, *Brideshead Revisited* (Harmondsworth, 1962), p. 15. The most aggressive spokesman for this point of view has been J. C. D. Clark, *English Society, 1688–1832* (Cambridge, 1985), and Clark, *Revolution and Rebellion* (Cambridge, 1986). See Innes's critique (above, n. 3).

[7] E. Gellner's *Plough, Sword and Book: The Structure of Human History* (London, 1988) is his most ambitious treatment of the subject.

interpreted in terms of individual monetary gain.[8] Cyril Black's definition of modernisation suggested that 'economic development depends
to a great extent on the intellectual and political aspects of the process,
the growth in knowledge and the ability of political leaders to mobilise
resources'.[9] A fourth variant, pioneered by Joseph Lee, defines modernisation as 'the growth of equality of opportunity', since 'this requires
that merit supersede birth as the main criterion for the distribution of
income, status and power, and this, in turn, involves the creation of
political consciousness among the masses, the decline of deference
based on inherited status, and the growth of functional specialisation,
without which merit can hardly begin to be measured'.[10] In the light of
these differing modulations, it is clear why Wrigley once confessed that
'a cynic might say that modernisation has come to be a term of
convenience used by those who are aware of the profound difference
between traditional and modern society, and need a word which can
convey their appreciation of its importance, but which does not commit
them to any one interpretation of the causes or the course of change'.[11]

According to its many detractors, then, modernisation theory, inherently disfigured by anachronism and ethnocentrism, is either too diffuse
or too rigid to be a useful conceptual tool. Confronted with such a
barrage of criticism, one can see why a scholar who 'stumbled upon the
debate unwittingly' instinctively wished he could 'stay out of it altogether'.[12] Why have so many historians of Russia persevered with a
concept which arouses such widespread dissent?

The first point to make is that modernisation theory is not the only
concept to prove 'a slippery thing susceptible of subtle massage and
rough manipulation alike':[13] the same could be said of any historical
model. If we place such models as templates over the past, expecting
them to correspond in every detail, then naturally we shall be disap-
pointed. Instead, it seems more appropriate to use models as prisms
through which to view any given historical society. Certain features will
doubtless be magnified or distorted; others may slip from view. Yet

---

[8] E. A. Wrigley, *Continuity, Chance and Change: The Character of the Industrial Revolution
     in England* (Cambridge, 1988), pp. 99–100. For Gellner's comments on Wrigley, see
     his 'On the Highway to Perpetual Growth', *Times Literary Supplement*, 11–17
     September 1987, pp. 980–2, a review of E. A. Wrigley, *People, Cities and Wealth: The
     Transformation of Traditional Society* (Oxford, 1987).
[9] Black, *The Dynamics of Modernization*, p. 20.
[10] J. Lee, *The Modernisation of Irish Society, 1848–1918* (Dublin, 1973), preface, n.p.
[11] E. A. Wrigley, 'The Process of Modernization and the Industrial Revolution in
     England', *JIH*, 3, 2 (1972), p. 228.
[12] D. H. Kaiser, *The Growth of the Law in Medieval Russia* (Princeton, 1980), p. ix.
[13] K. T. Hoppen, 'Ireland, Britain and Europe: Twentieth-Century Nationalism and Its
     Spoils', *HJ*, 34, 2 (1991), p. 505.

without some organising principle, however tacit, the historian's work would lack explanatory power. Rather than profess not to have inhaled an intoxicating substance, it has seemed sensible to begin by setting out some of our chosen model's salient side effects.

Yet, in the Russian context, the modernisation model can also claim curative properties. Most obviously, we can point to evidence that Peter the Great and his acolytes were themselves self-conscious modernisers, even though 'modernisation' was not a word they used.[14] Neither were they the last influential Russians to think in this way. The fact that 'the drive to modernise, begun around 1700 as the wish of a ruler, became by 1750–60 the cornerstone of the government's policies, an important ingredient of the political class's ethos, and finally a tradition of government'[15] helps to explain why modernisation remains central to most histories of Russia. Even two scholars who dismiss modernisation theory as 'a shopping list of traits identified with the industrialised West in the twentieth century' and prefer 'to discuss population growth or industrialisation in their own terms without reference to an illusory standard' nevertheless refer blithely – and accurately – to 'the modernisation efforts of Peter the Great and his successors'.[16]

If modernisation theory offers a way of understanding the motives of Russia's rulers as an 'attitude of mind' designed to encourage creativity and make full use of both intellectual and material resources,[17] then the 'analytical dichotomies' around which the theory revolves also have a particular resonance in the Russian context. Lotman and Uspenskii have insisted that the eighteenth-century opposition between rhetorics of 'new' and 'old' – generated when the autocratic ruler's commitment to innovation automatically branded those who resisted change as subversives – was symptomatic of a wider polar dualism integral to a culture that knew no neutral zone between heaven and hell, Christ and Antichrist, or Holy Russia and the sinful West.[18] Their model is no less vulnerable to charges of distortion than any other. In particular, it has provoked important attempts to re-emphasise the social and political significance of the 'grey zones and middle ground' for which these

---

[14] See first L. R. Lewitter, 'Peter the Great and the Modern World', in P. Dukes, ed., *Russia and Europe* (London, 1991), pp. 92–107.

[15] M. Confino, 'Traditions, Old and New: Aspects of Protest and Dissent in Modern Russia', in Eisenstadt, *Patterns of Modernity*, vol. II, *Beyond the West*, p. 17.

[16] P. M. Hohenberg and L. H. Lees, *The Making of Urban Europe, 1000–1950* (Cambridge, MA, 1985), pp. 178, 168.

[17] M. Raeff, *The Well-Ordered Police State: Social and Institutional Change Through Law in the Germanies and Russia, 1600–1800* (New Haven, CT, 1983), p. 120, n. 150.

[18] Ju. M. Lotman and B. A. Uspenskij, 'The Role of Dual Models in the Dynamics of Russian Culture (Up to the End of the Eighteenth Century)', in their *The Semiotics of Russian Culture*, ed. A. Shukman (Ann Arbor, MI, 1984), pp. 3–35.

Russian scholars found no room.[19] But this is not to deny the conceptual utility of binary oppositions whose cultural roots can be traced not to nineteenth-century German sociology but to native medieval eschatology. In that sense, there is nothing anachronistic about using them to interpret the eighteenth century.

The survival of apocalyptic imagery into the 1920s and 1930s, when renewed insecurity prompted peasants to identify the nascent Soviet régime with Antichrist,[20] warns against any simplistic interpretation of modernisation as a linear process. Neither was it only the collectivist, risk-averse peasantry who preserved elements of traditionalism. For all Peter the Great's rhetoric, not all his policies were new, and many of his innovations succeeded only because they relied on well-tried Muscovite methods. I shall also highlight tensions between economic liberalism and social conservatism, and between freedom of intellectual inquiry and the requirements of political stability that ultimately persuaded the state to doubt the value of ideas it had once encouraged. Nor was this the only paradox: taxes designed to fund modernisation ultimately consolidated serfdom. So, far from entrenching some Whiggish notion of linear progress, modernisation theory can be used to show not only that Muscovy needs to be taken seriously on its own terms, but that due weight must be given to its legacy in Russian history. Indeed, although Russia began to look increasingly backward from the middle of the nineteenth century, the survival of traditionalism did more to strengthen than to weaken it before 1825. What made Russia powerful in our period was the peculiar compound *mixture* of traditional and modern that, in varying measure, was also characteristic of its rivals: Austria, Prussia, Britain and France.[21]

This helps us to answer a question which has naturally exercised Russian minds in the aftermath of the Soviet Union's fall: did the Russian failure to embrace capitalism stunt its development as a modern state? A leading Russian scholar has recently argued that Muscovy

---

[19] Notably V. Kivelson, *Autocracy in the Provinces: The Muscovite Gentry and Political Culture in the Seventeenth Century* (Stanford, CA, 1996), quote from p. 266. See also E. K. Wirtschafter, *Structures of Society: Imperial Russia's 'People of Various Ranks'* (DeKalb, IL, 1994).

[20] L. Viola, 'The Peasant Nightmare: Visions of Apocalypse in the Soviet Countryside', *JMH*, 62 (1990), pp. 747–70; S. Davies, *Popular Opinion in Stalin's Russia: Terror, Propaganda and Dissent, 1934–1941* (Cambridge, 1997), pp. 80–1.

[21] For sophisticated use of the concept of modernity, see S. Schama, *Citizens* (London, 1989); P. Langford, *A Polite and Commercial People: England 1727–1783* (Oxford, 1989); T. C. W. Blanning, 'The French Revolution and the Modernization of Germany', *Central European History*, 22, 2 (1989), pp. 109–30; Blanning, *Joseph II* (London, 1994); and J. M. Roberts, *The Penguin History of Europe* (Harmondsworth, 1997).

overcame a 'crisis of traditionalism' at the end of the seventeenth century by a necessary programme of 'Europeanisation' that was fatefully diverted along a 'special path' by the failure to abolish serfdom.[22] Historians of Germany were once attracted by a related thesis. But the notion that the German *Sonderweg* was warped by the lack of a bourgeois revolution now finds little support. It has been undermined partly by research into the *Bürgertum* but principally by the recognition that there is no common standard from which to diverge.[23] I shall not attempt to deny Russian history its distinctive identity. But by using modernisation theory as a comparative analytical framework rather than as a measure of normative development, we shall also be able to see important parallels with the Western states against which it became locked in deadly rivalry.

Some critics, as we know, regard such comparisons with distaste. Eighteenth-century Russians would have been surprised to hear it. They knew that they were lost if they could not compete with their neighbours. Population size, the impact of fiscal change on social structure, the rational ordering of administration, and the capacity to harness scientific knowledge to productive economic activity – all crucial elements in modernisation theory – were also among the indices by which eighteenth-century European states measured their relative strength. I shall follow their example in a series of thematic chapters. However, let us begin by tracing Russian history between 1676 and 1825, highlighting one of its most anti-modern features: the recurrent crises occasioned by the lack of a fixed law of succession.

Russian history, 1676–1825

Few could have predicted that the dynasty enthroned in 1613 would live to celebrate its 300th anniversary. Yet endurance was to prove one of the Romanovs' greatest assets. Under their cautious stewardship, Muscovy quickly recovered from the Time of Troubles (1598–1613) unleashed by the succession crises that followed the death of Ivan IV (the Terrible) in 1584. Messianic pretensions implicit in the notion of Moscow as the third Rome had made little enough impact on sixteenth-century rulers; under the early Romanovs they were further subjugated to a basic strategy of survival. Risking a policy of selective Westernisation that

---

[22] A. B. Kamenskii, *The Russian Empire in the Eighteenth Century: Searching for a Place in the World*, tr. and ed. D. Griffiths (Armonk, NY, 1997), pp. 35–6, 117–18, 281–6, and *passim*.

[23] A key revisionist work was D. Blackbourn and G. Eley, *The Peculiarities of German History: Bourgeois Society and Politics in Nineteenth-Century Germany* (Oxford, 1984).

helped to reform part of their army, the new dynasty checked the advances of rival neighbours in Poland-Lithuania and the Ottoman empire and strengthened domestic administration. Aleksei Mikhailovich (1645–76) subdued riots in Moscow in June 1648 and put down further revolts in and around Pskov and Novgorod in 1650. Twenty years later, the cossack Stepan Razin was defeated at Simbirsk, though only after Tsaritsyn and Astrakhan' had fallen to his rebellion. The tsar's survival depended not simply on force but also on compromise. By balancing the demands of his wealthiest subjects against those of lesser officers, he was able to turn concessions to his own advantage. Further defining the privileges and responsibilities enjoyed and incurred by various splintered groups, Aleksei Mikhailovich reinforced the development of a loose but increasingly stratified social hierarchy. The key Muscovite principle of service to the state was enshrined in the *Ulozhenie* of 1649, a law code promulgated in response to the riots of the year before.[24] This was the last and most comprehensive of a series of pragmatic Muscovite codes; but it also signalled a novel intention to regulate the activities of society as a whole.

The activist language of the *Ulozhenie* throws into relief the passivity of the achievements I have just outlined: invaders had been repelled, rebels had been quashed, the dynasty had been preserved. Until the middle of the seventeenth century, Muscovy's rulers were more than content with such a strategy; indeed, it approached their ideal. Since the notion of the 'good tsar' was conceived in terms of piety, self-abnega-tion, and humility rather than active interventionism in affairs of state, the monarch's goal was to preserve the status quo, not to reform it. It does not seem to have occurred to Aleksei Mikhailovich's predecessors that they could mobilise the population in search of strategic goals. That he began to think of doing so implies the emergence of unwelcome new pressures, both within and outside his own realm.

At home, the seamless relationship between the Orthodox church and the state was torn apart when the Church Council of 1666–7 pro-nounced anathema on those who rejected a series of liturgical reforms initially proposed by Patriarch Nikon and finally enforced with the support of the tsar. The schism[25] divided adherents of an increasingly 'official' church from so-called Old Believers just when Orthodoxy needed to be at its most supple to face the challenge of Counter-

---

[24] R. Hellie, tr. and ed., *The Muscovite Law Code (Ulozhenie) of 1649. Part I: Text and Translation* (Irvine, CA, 1988). See also Hellie, 'Early Modern Russian Law: The Ulozhenie of 1649', *RH*, 15, 2-4 (1988), pp. 155–80, and commentaries in *RH*, 17 (1990), and *CASS*, 25 (1991).

[25] Like 'the French Revolution', 'the schism' was a more complex series of events and movements than the conventional singular implies.

Reformation Catholicism in Ukraine, incorporated at the treaty of Pereiaslavl' in 1654. Both national unity and royal spiritual authority were damaged to an extent that far outweighed any gain the state may have made by crippling the church as a potential focus of opposition. Neither was Muscovy's international position secure. Condemned by geography to occupy territory with no clearly defined natural borders, Muscovy may have resisted its rivals, but it had not overcome them. Sweden, Poland and the Ottoman empire still rejoiced in what looked, for most of the reign of Louis XIV (r. 1643–1715), like invincible French protection. Moreover, if Muscovy was to compete in Europe, it was bound to incur significant expense. And it was not obvious that its centralised decision-making system, designed to impose order on chaos and to prevent the rise of local power bases, would be able to respond any more flexibly to this new financial imperative than it had to the challenge of the schism.

Latent weaknesses were exposed when Aleksei Mikhailovich died in 1676. Although historians usually pass rapidly over the brief reign of his teenage son, Fedor (1661–82), it is significant from the point of view of modernisation. For the first time in the seventeenth century, Muscovy went on the offensive in a war against the Turks that lasted from 1676 to 1681. The government sought to pay for the campaign by converting in 1679–81 from a system of taxation based on land to one based on households, assessed according to the census conducted in 1678. Ambitious changes to local government were also planned, though their most immediate consequence – the abolition in 1682 of *mestnichestvo*, the outdated precedence system by which boiars had traditionally defended their honour – upset few. Eighteenth-century Russia would become used to a pattern in which international ambition provoked fiscal and administrative reform with important social consequences. But there is still work to do in investigating that pattern's origins in the seventeenth century. Though perhaps not so incapacitated as historians once supposed, the tsar himself was scarcely the moving force behind changes which probably owed most to Prince V. V. Golitsyn (1643–1714). Yet the disturbances which followed Fedor's unexpected death on 27 April 1682 were enough to check the impulse for reform.

The succession crisis temporarily brought into focus the clannish connexions, normally too elastic to be described as factions, which dominated Muscovite élite politics. Two main networks lined up behind the surviving sons of Aleksei Mikhailovich, rival candidates for the throne in the absence of a written law of succession. Peter, aged ten, was promptly 'elected' by his mother's family, the Naryshkins, who hoped to regain influence lost at the death of his father; though weak both in body and in mind, Peter's sixteen-year-old half-brother, Ivan, was backed by *his* mother's family, the Miloslavskiis, on grounds of seniority. However, there was more to the ensuing chaos than this simple rivalry might imply. In particular, it mattered that the 55,000-strong palace guards (*strel'tsy*) not only included a significant number of Old Believers who suspected a plot by 'wicked' Naryshkin advisers to instal a 'false' monarch, but were also the most prominent of those outmoded regiments who resented being sidelined by military reform. Their rebellion on 15–17 May settled scores unconnected with either the Miloslavskiis or Tsar Ivan, in whose name they claimed to act. In the aftermath of the bloodshed, a compromise was reached. While the joint rule of Ivan and Peter was ritually confirmed in the Cathedral of the Dormition on 26 May, *de facto* power passed to Ivan's elder sister, Sophia Alekseevna (1657–1704), in response to a petition from the guards who were to remain guarantors of the Russian throne throughout our period.

Shrewd as she was, Sophia was scarcely in a position to release Muscovy from its political paralysis. She made much of her ambiguous constitutional status, provoking remarkably little opposition as Russia's first female ruler. But she owed the comparative tranquillity of her regency (never formally acknowledged) not to some pre-considered programme of reform but to a tacit compact with boiars who expected no great change. Though markedly receptive to Western culture, this tiny élite had little incentive to modernise government and society as a whole. The limits to their tolerance were revealed when Sophia campaigned for recognition as ruler in her own right in the late 1680s; to contemplate coronation was to overplay her hand. Sophia's reputation had been tarnished by Golitsyn's inglorious Crimean campaigns of 1687 and 1689. In September 1689, having fought to the last for her political life, she herself succumbed to *strel'tsy* pressure, spending her remaining years under arrest in Moscow's Novodevichii convent. Though Tsar Ivan survived until 29 January 1696, Muscovy was now in the hands of Aleksei Mikhailovich's fourteenth child, known to posterity as Peter the Great.

Long fascinated by ships and soldiers, Peter, who had betrayed little interest in government in the early 1680s, soon proved an active interventionist in affairs of state. He had already become the first tsar to visit the central chancelleries in person, descending unannounced overnight in spring 1688. Following the death of his mother, Natal'ia Naryshkina, in January 1694, his domination was unquestioned. A giant of volcanic energy and a scourge of idleness, Peter maintained a lasting preference for impulsive personal supervision in matters both major and minor. He oversaw the compilation of an *Alphabetical Lexicon of New*

Vocabulary, never published, making corrections in his own hand; following his Grand Embassy to the West in 1697–8 and a subsequent visit to Paris in 1717, he was intimately involved with the minutiae of ordering equipment, even specifying the type of birdseed required to feed his new canaries; and he made his own designs for fortifications at newly captured Azov in 1696 and 1706, and at Noteborg (which he rechristened Shlisselburg – 'Key-stronghold') in 1702. More importantly, the tsar made the decisive contribution to key legislation, notably the Maritime Regulation (*Morskoi ustav*) and the General Regulation (*General'nyi reglament*), both promulgated in 1720, and the Table of Ranks issued in 1722. Even in the final five years of his life, when government was nominally in the hands of the administrative system he had created, nearly 60 per cent of the tsar's 3,019 edicts were written by Peter himself, or shaped by his intervention.

Just as there was no question about Peter's capacity for work, so there was no doubting his thirst for novelty. The first tsar to leave Muscovy, he was captivated by scientific instruments, many of which he saw and bought on his travels abroad. Journeys designed to acquaint him with Western advances in military technology stimulated an unprecedentedly large influx into Russia of the sort of foreign craftsmen and technicians who had earlier advised his father and grandfather. Peter's work on maps of the Crimea helped to justify his election to the French Academy of Sciences in 1717, though this honour evidently owed more to his royal status than to his limited scholarly achievements. Had the tsar's fascination for all that was new amounted to no more than caprice, it might have reduced Russia to chaos. As Lord Curzon remarked of the 'childlike passion for novelty' displayed by a later would-be moderniser, Shah Nasir al-Din of Persia (1848–96): 'The lumber rooms of the palace are not more full of broken mechanisms and discarded bric-à-brac than are the pigeon-holes of the government bureaux of abortive reforms and dead fiascos.'[26] By contrast, Peter's carefully catalogued curios were soon displayed in the Kunstkammer, one of the first public buildings in St Petersburg, the city founded in 1703 and made the capital in 1714 to symbolise the dawn of a new era. And this was only the most celebrated of Peter's rejections of Muscovite political culture. Scholars have suggested that his adoption of the title 'Imperator' carried echoes of Byzantine theocracy. But many contemporaries were struck rather by its association with pagan Rome.[27] It was the same with the

---

[26] Quoted in E. Kedourie, *Politics in the Middle East* (Oxford, 1992), pp. 78–9.

[27] See I. de Madariaga, 'Tsar into Emperor: The Title of Peter the Great', in R. Oresko, *et al.*, eds., *Royal and Republican Sovereignty in Early Modern Europe: Essays in Memory of Ragnhild Hatton* (Cambridge, 1997), pp. 351–81.

tsar's campaign against beards and Muscovite dress, his adoption of the classical festive 'entry' as the principal form of public celebration, his abolition of the patriarchate (replaced by an appointed Holy Synod in 1721) and his unprecedented decision to crown his second wife, Catherine, in 1724. Together they amounted to a rhetorical repudiation of almost everything he had inherited. Small wonder that Peter was branded heretical by his opponents.

Beneath the rhetoric, however, much that was redolent of the sixteenth century survived into the eighteenth, when the period of relative security granted by Peter's victory over the Swedes at Poltava in 1709 created the opportunity to translate piecemeal legislation into systematic reform. A crucial stage in the transition from personal to bureaucratic government was heralded in 1720 when the General Regulation set out detailed procedural rules for the colleges Peter had created to run central government in 1718. But these new institutions, like the court and the army, were to be staffed by nobles obliged to climb the Table of Ranks.[28] This was the single most important symbol of the survival of the Muscovite service principle, now openly expressed in terms of merit rather than lineage, though Aleksei Mikhailovich had himself deliberately promoted talented men of modest social background, and lineage, as we shall see in chapter 4, remained a significant determinant of social status throughout our period. The adoption of a military ranking system for civilians showed how little the tsar's outlook had altered: the Military Regulation of 1716, a harsh code of discipline also applied by the civil courts, represented a further application of military principles to the civilian sphere. All these measures bore the imprint of the tsar's technocratic mind; all were designed to create an autonomous state machine; and this in turn was to be a means to Peter's principal end, the mobilisation of Russia's human and natural resources in search of international prestige.

Historians have generally been divided between those who see impulsive personal dynamism as the key to Peter's reign, and those who place the germ of his rational planning no later than April 1702, when a manifesto on the invitation of foreigners to Russia, drafted in German by the Livonian J. R. Patkul, spoke broadly of the need for regulation to secure the common good. Paradoxically, both schools of thought are right. Behind the tsar's modernising rhetoric lay the suspicion that, left

---

[28] The fundamental work remains S. M. Troitskii, *Russkii absoliutizm i dvorianstvo v XVIIIv.: formirovanie biurokratii* (Moscow, 1974), pp. 3–118, one of a handful of outstanding Soviet books on the eighteenth century, but see also the comparative study by A. N. Medushevskii, *Utverzhdenie absoliutizma v Rossii: sravnitel'noe istoricheskoe issledovanie* (Moscow, 1994).

to their own devices, men were too flawed to achieve the rational reform of which in theory they were capable. As a result, the dominant feature of Peter's legislation in the eyes of many contemporaries was not the strategic vision that undoubtedly underpinned it, but the ruthlessness required to implement it. As Lewitter writes, 'so far from enjoying the benefits of a well-regulated state', the majority of Russians by 1725 'were living under a military regime, occupied, laid under contribution and governed by the army and liable to be tried under military law'.[29]

Exemplary was Peter's brutal suppression of the *strel'tsy* revolt that cut short his Grand Embassy in 1698. As in 1682, the guards were motivated not so much by ideology as by resentment of their conditions of service. But their lasting commitment to the Old Belief helped to identify the schism with resistance and subversion in the tsar's mind. He was barely more tolerant of those who supported change. Industrial managers were hampered by inspectors appointed by a tsar who distrusted entrepreneurial ethics; officials in turn were watched over by *fiskaly*, spies placed by Peter as his personal representatives in every college and themselves absolved from the charge of making false accusations. Whilst the tsar's rationally ordered institutions famously provided the framework for Russian government until 1917, the Muscovite culture of denunciation built into his system was to last even longer.

No edict of Peter's was more Janus-faced than the law on the succession enacted after the execution of his son, Aleksei (1690–1718). A disappointment to his father, this sensitive boy became a magnet for Peter's critics. Following a lengthy secret investigation, the tsarevich was publicly convicted of treason by a specially convened assembly of 128 notables. Having renounced all rights to the throne in February 1718, Aleksei died in July in the fortress of St Peter and St Paul. He had certainly been tortured; few doubted that Peter had had him killed. On 11 February 1722, the tsar decreed that the reigning monarch could nominate his own successor. *The Justice of the Monarch's Right to Appoint the Heir to His Throne*, a treatise issued on 28 December, claimed on the authority of the Bible and Roman law that this edict was justified, not only by precedent, but also as a meritocratic way of selecting the monarch: 'not by birthright – a bad rule – but in accordance with moral excellence'.[30] Though in one sense a modernising measure embodying the concept of the ruler as 'servant of the state', the succession edict

---

[29] I. Pososhkov, *The Book of Poverty and Wealth*, ed. and tr. A. P. Vlasto and L. R. Lewitter (London, 1987), p. 106.

[30] A. Lentin, *Peter the Great. His Law on the Imperial Succession: The Official Commentary* (Oxford, 1996), p. 137. The work was attributed to Archbishop Feofan (Prokopovich) (1681–1736), whose authorship is now in doubt.

showed that the tsar still regarded that state as his own property, to dispose of as he thought fit just as he had disposed of Aleksei. There could hardly have been a sharper contrast with the 'fundamental law' that purported to guarantee the succession in many Western states (where Britain's Glorious Revolution of 1688–9 was only one instance of its fallibility). In Russia, as Montesquieu later remarked, the result of Peter's legislation was to render the Russian 'throne as unsteady as the succession is arbitrary'.[31] Ironically, the tsar himself failed to nominate an heir, leaving, at his death in 1725, the first of a series of succession crises that were to punctuate Russian history in the middle of the eighteenth century.

With the connivance of the guards, Peter's principal henchman, Prince A. D. Menshikov, engineered the succession of the tsar's widow. Born Marfa Skavronskaia, a semi-literate Livonian peasant who had caught Peter's roving eye in 1703 and married him in 1712 (Aleksei's mother, Evdokiia, having been incarcerated in a convent on suspicion of involvement in the *strel'tsy* revolt of 1698), Catherine I reigned until her death in May 1727. But she was scarcely able to rule on her own account. Initially a cipher for Menshikov, she was persuaded in February 1726 to sanction a six-member Supreme Privy Council intended by his rivals to rein him in. Menshikov was still powerful enough to ensure that the dying Catherine nominated as her successor the eleven-year-old grandson of Peter the Great, who reigned as Peter II from 1727 until his death from smallpox in January 1730. However, the parvenu prince overreached himself by betrothing his daughter Mariia to the new boy tsar. Stricken by illness, Menshikov was outmanoeuvred by another of Peter the Great's advisers, the Westphalian A. I. (Heinrich) Osterman. Exiled in September 1727, Menshikov died in Siberia in November 1729. Meanwhile the Dolgorukii and Golitsyn families came to dominate the Supreme Privy Council, which itself had eclipsed both the Senate and the colleges.

Unchallenged by any rival body, it was this council that seized the initiative on the night of 18–19 January 1730. In the absence of a direct male descendant to Peter II, the council arbitrarily offered the throne to the 36-year-old Anna, duchess of Courland and niece of Peter the Great, provided that she accept a series of 'conditions' (*konditsii*) drawn up by Prince D. M. Golitsyn (1663–1737). Not only did these conditions bind the widowed Anna not to remarry and not to name an heir, but they also obliged her to consult a revamped eight-member council on all matters of high policy, including the declaration of war and peace.

[31] Montesquieu, *The Spirit of the Laws*, ed. A. Cohler, B. Miller, and H. Stone (Cambridge, 1989), p. 62 (V:11).

Golitsyn, an exceptionally erudite man acquainted with both the Polish and Swedish constitutions, probably intended to place limitations on monarchical power modelled on those imposed on Ulrike Eleonora when she briefly succeeded Charles XII in Stockholm in December 1718. But the rank-and-file Russian nobility, unaware of the council's outline plans to reassess wider social needs, saw only an attempt to strengthen the grip of an already overbearing clique. Gathered in Moscow, where they had expected to witness Peter II's marriage to Princess Ekaterina Dolgorukaia rather than attend his funeral, these nobles proved a surprisingly cohesive political force. They used the interval required to fetch Anna from Mittau to Moscow – where she arrived on 10 February, formally entering the city five days later – to emphasise that absolute monarchy was preferable to rule by the Supreme Privy Council. On 25 February Anna publicly tore up Golitsyn's conditions and embarked on her own unfettered reign.

The potential for constitutional change is evident. But since it remained unrealised, Paul Dukes is probably justified in regarding the significance of these events as an example of relatively sophisticated crisis management within a system that survived unscathed.[32] However, if the Russian élite demonstrated in 1730 a degree of maturity beyond its reach in 1682 and 1698, partly because the reformed guards were now themselves an integral part of it, then the crisis nevertheless confirmed the central rôle of the palace revolution in Russian political culture. The likelihood of another coup was increased when Anna designated as her heir the unborn child of her thirteen-year-old niece who not only had yet to conceive, but was not even engaged at the time. Only in August 1740 did Anna Leopoldovna give birth to the son who became Ivan VI of Russia when the empress herself died childless in October of that year. In turn, Anna Leopoldovna's regency lasted only until the night of 24–5 November 1741, when the baby Ivan was himself ousted by a coup in favour of Peter the Great's daughter, Elizabeth Petrovna, who reigned until her death on 25 December 1761. Ivan was imprisoned until his assassination in 1764.

If Russia came to seem less threatening to its European rivals under the rule of women and children than it had under Peter the Great, then spectacular domestic achievements were no more to be expected of such monarchs than were international triumphs. First collected in 1724, the poll tax that Peter had instituted in 1718 to pay for his army had bequeathed a dangerous legacy in the form of heavy arrears and rampant peasant flight (a Senate commission recorded 327,046 male

---

[32] P. Dukes, *The Making of Russian Absolutism 1613–1801*, 2nd edn (London, 1990), pp. 117–18.

fugitives between 1727 and 1741).[33] Many of the tsar's more ambitious plans, such as those designed to improve local government, remained unfulfilled for lack of funds. Neither did there seem much prospect of central control since the planned codification of the laws, required to supersede the outdated *Ulozhenie*, remained incomplete at Peter's death and was never implemented. Small wonder that such an ambitious initiative as the Academy of Sciences, established in 1725, got off to a slow start without its founder to goad its development. Small wonder, either, that Russian intellectuals, long fascinated by patterns in history, should recently have compared the middle of the eighteenth century with Brezhnev's 'era of stagnation' or, worse, branded it one of Russia's allegedly recurrent phases of reactionary counter-reform.[34]

As several scholars have stressed, such temptations must be resisted: all the most important indices point to continuity and growth. The hostility to contemplative (and thus allegedly useless) monasticism expressed in Peter's Spiritual Regulation of 1721 was maintained under his immediate successors. Between 1724 and 1738, the number of monks, nuns, and novices in Russia was almost halved from 25,207 to 14,282. By contrast, between 1725 and 1763, the number of Russian linen and woollen manufactories grew from thirteen to seventy-nine and from fourteen to sixty-eight respectively. Trade also held up well. Iron exports rose more than 500 per cent in the 1730s alone, reflecting the strength of the industry Peter had established in the Urals to support his reformed armed forces, whilst the value of St Petersburg's trade between 1725 and 1739 increased from 3.4 to 4.1 million rubles. Though inflation ate into these achievements, the overall trend clearly points upwards.

For all that, what is most striking about the years after 1725 is what did not happen: there was no civil war. Following the unexpected death of Peter the Great, a ruler in the mould of Ivan the Terrible, Russia might have been expected to relapse into the sort of chaos that gripped Muscovy from 1584. Yet, *pace* Alexander Yanov, no Time of Troubles recurred.[35] Instead, Russia gained time for consolidation in which, far from being manoeuvred into reaction, even relatively weak rulers presided over the penetration of the Petrine system. Part of the explanation lies in his successors' need to enhance their legitimacy by emphasising

---

[33] N. V. Kozlova, *Pobegi krest'ian v Rossii v pervoi treti XVIIIv.* (Moscow, 1983), p. 145.

[34] The first is among many ambitious parallels ventured by Ia. Gordin, *Mezh rabstvom i svobodoi: 19 ianvaria–25 fevralia 1730 goda* (St Petersburg, 1994); for the second, see, *inter alia*, the historical sociology by V. V. Il'in, *et al.*, *Reformy i kontrreformy v Rossii: tsikly modernizatsionnogo protsessa* (Moscow, 1996), esp. pp. 36–40.

[35] A. Yanov, 'The Drama of the Time of Troubles, 1725–1730', *CASS*, 12, 1 (1978), pp. 1–59, belongs in the tradition mentioned above, n. 34.

continuity with Peter the Great. But this argument was persuasive only because it resonated with a wider acceptance of Peter's reforms. Paradoxically, this in turn depended on the incorporation within those reforms of many Muscovite traditions. But it also signalled that the nobility, at least, had been flexible enough to adapt to a substantial degree of innovation. Though many resented Peter's brutality and some hankered after a return to the patriarchal morals he had flouted, no one seriously supposed that the genie he had released could be forced back into the Muscovite bottle. The need to maintain Russia's new-found international status, enshrined in the treaty of Nystad in 1721, was only the most obvious reason why the reformist impulse had to be sustained.

It remains debatable whether female rule was essential to the survival of the Petrine system because only women 'could claim to defend Peter's heritage without threatening a return of his punitive fury'.[36] Gentleness may have seemed impressive in theory – Montesquieu acknowledged female rule as one of few ways in which Russian despotism might be mitigated – but its impact was less obvious in practice. If it is feminine to be beautiful, frivolous, and fashion-conscious, Elizabeth certainly qualifies. By contrast, the notoriously unattractive Anna was a crack shot at her best with a gun on her shoulder. Since neither empress sustained her initial interest in government, both looked negligent alongside their zealous contemporaries in the rival houses of Habsburg and Hohenzollern. In June 1735, Anna delegated to her ministers the right to sign legislation; advisers and foreign envoys alike struggled to do business with Elizabeth, to whom routine was anathema. Towards the end, suffering from what may have been epilepsy, she withdrew from both work and the public gaze. Mid-century achievements were made not so much by the empresses as in spite of them.

Anna was dominated by Ernst-Johann Bühren (in Russian, Biron) (1690–1772), duke of Courland from 1737, who unwittingly gave his name to the *bironovshchina*, an alleged German conspiracy to denigrate everything the Russians held dear. Biron was certainly corrupt, and the Secret Chancellery (Preobrazhenskii prikaz), revived in 1731 under A. I. Ushakov, who had served in it under Peter the Great, promoted the black arts of denunciation to new levels of sophistication. But there is no evidence of systematic mistreatment of Russians. This was a myth created by Elizabeth's image-makers in the aftermath of her coup when, not for the last time, it suited a new empress to pose as the agent of national salvation. In the 1750s, Elizabeth came to rely on advisers who rescued her from the slavish devotion to her father's legacy that

[36] R. S. Wortman, *Scenarios of Power: Myth and Ceremony in Russian Monarchy*, vol. I, *From Peter the Great to the Death of Nicholas I* (Princeton, 1995), p. 85.

circumscribed her early legislation. In foreign policy, A. P. Bestuzhev-Riumin (1693–1766) was a staunch advocate of the Austrian alliance to which Russia was committed from 1726 to 1762; at home, the most original mind belonged to Petr Shuvalov (1711–62), who conceived the innovative indirect taxation schemes which helped Russia to survive the Seven Years War from 1756 to 1762.

Renewed international conflict gave an irresistible impetus not only to military reform, but also to the loosening of government economic regulation. Like the secularisation of the church lands (1764), another measure motivated primarily by fiscal need, these projects were completed only under Catherine II. But their origins were rooted in the two previous reigns. So were educational reforms. We still understand little about the reformist atmosphere that led to the foundation in 1755 of the University of Moscow, and two years later of the Academy of Fine Arts. And yet recent work has made the links between the 1750s and the 1770s seem increasingly important. Continuities in personnel clearly mattered. For example, D. V. Volkov (1717–85), secretary to Elizabeth's court 'conference' (effectively a council of war), became president of the College of Foreign Affairs under Peter III (when his impact was paradoxically greatest at home), and ended his career, after a brief interval as governor of Orenburg, as president of Catherine's College of Manufactures between 1764 and 1777. But ministerial stability was not enough: monarchical decisiveness was also required and this the cautious Elizabeth lacked. Her successor, born Karl Peter Ulrich of Holstein (1728–62), was if anything too impetuous. Irascible and capricious in his personal dealings, Peter III took more interest in government than historians once thought. It did not help him. He alienated both the army, by making a hasty peace with the Prussians whom it had trounced in the Seven Years War, and the church, by his aggressive attempts to confiscate its lands. Tsars who attempted too much too quickly never lasted long. On 28 June 1762, having reigned for less than a year, Peter was overthrown by guards who thought his wife a more promising champion of their interests.

It is one of the many ironies of the reign of Catherine the Great, born Sophie of Anhalt-Zerbst (1729–96), that, despite having been elevated to the throne by the coup which resulted first in the deposition and soon after in the murder of her husband, she should have done more than any other ruler to supply the stable legal framework that Russia so urgently required. By the 1760s, the institutions created by Peter I were sufficiently well established to allow Catherine to follow Montesquieu's view of the monarch as 'the soul, not the arm' of government: 'it is often better to inspire than to order reforms', she noted.[37] Attracted to ideas as a teenager, she performed the rôle of philosopher-queen with élan. In 1763, she joined the select band of rulers who subscribed to Baron Melchior Grimm's *Correspondance littéraire*, a manuscript digest of the latest Parisian news and thought. Diderot, whose work she subsidised by purchasing his library in 1765, visited her in the winter of 1773–4. She liked him, but could hardly have been expected to share his recent conversion to the doctrine of popular sovereignty. Finding the flattering Voltaire's *thèse royale* more congenial, she made him her principal Western correspondent until his death in 1778. By then Voltaire had been succeeded by Grimm himself, always the least radical of *philosophes*. In part, such contacts were intended to propagate a favourable image of Russia in Europe, an aim in which they were largely successful. But they also reflected the empress's commitment to reason, humanity, and utility.

In 1767 she placed this Enlightened trinity at the heart of her Instruction (*Nakaz*) to the Legislative Commission, a representative body convoked in a further attempt to replace the antiquated *Ulozhenie*, which the empress nevertheless admired as an edict consonant with the demands of its time and place. As Catherine openly acknowledged, her own treatise drew verbatim on Montesquieu and Beccaria.[38] It set out her vision of a tolerant, educated society in which her subjects' liberty and property would be protected by unambiguous laws established by a virtuous absolute sovereign and implemented to the letter by judges who were to assume the accused innocent until proven guilty. Never had such radical ideas been articulated in Russia. Yet, interrupted by war, the commission never completed its work. In 1775, impatient with her subjects' lukewarm response to her exhortations, Catherine resorted to direct intervention in the Petrine manner. Whereas Peter I had concentrated on central government, she now developed her long-standing interest in the local administration that had failed to contain the revolt led by the cossack Emel'ian Pugachev in Russia's south-eastern borderlands in 1773–5. This was to be the last great peasant rebellion of the eighteenth century.

---

[37] 'Istoricheskie i avtobiograficheskie otryvki, zametki, pis'ma', in *Sochineniia Imperatritsy Ekateriny II*, ed. A. N. Pypin, 12 vols., vol. XII (St Petersburg, 1907), p. 627, undated jotting.

[38] See W. F. Reddaway, *Documents of Catherine the Great: The Correspondence with Voltaire and the Instruction of 1767 in the English Text of 1768* (Cambridge, 1931). Subsequent quotations from the *Nakaz* are taken from this edition. Another contemporary translation has been published, with an excellent introduction, by P. Dukes, ed., *Catherine the Great's Instruction (NAKAZ) to the Legislative Commission, 1767* (Newtonville, MA, 1977).

The execution of Pugachev in January 1775 is one of several reasons to regard the mid-1770s as a turning point in Catherine's reign. She had humiliated the Turks in the war of 1768–74, completed the first partition of Poland with Prussia and Austria in 1772, ended her long-standing relationship with the unfaithful Grigorii Orlov in the same year, and, most importantly of all, survived the majority of her son Paul (1754–1801), regarded by some as the legitimate heir to Peter III. In informal partnership with Grigorii Potemkin – her lover between 1774 and 1776, almost certainly her husband, and definitely a key influence until his death in 1791 – Catherine now took advantage of a decade of peace to introduce the provincial reform of 1775, the police ordinance of 1782, and the national system of schools established in 1786. Though these laws owed more to German cameralist regulation than to the unsystematic French *philosophes*, the empress's commitment to their broad conception of reason and humanity remained undimmed until the twin influences of the French Revolution and the radicalisation of Enlightened thought led her to reject the intellectual speculation she had earlier encouraged. A. N. Radishchev, author of the critical *Journey from St Petersburg to Moscow* (1790), was exiled; Voltaire's works were burned. It was in these final years that Catherine's gruesome fascination for her last and least savoury lover, Platon Zubov, thirty-eight years her junior, confirmed the reputation for licentiousness for which posterity would soon condemn her.

By 1796, the upper echelons of Russian society would barely have been recognisable to people who lived a century earlier. Those whom Peter the Great had been obliged to coerce Catherine could afford to coax. Released from compulsory service by Peter III in 1762 – the most important achievement of his brief and turbulent reign – many nobles had continued to serve voluntarily, as the tsar himself expected. Some returned to the countryside to revitalise their provincial estates; others travelled to the West. On her fifty-sixth birthday, 21 April 1785, Catherine rewarded them all by issuing a charter confirming the privileges they had acquired over the course of the century.[39] In conjunction with the didactic Enlightened journalism that Catherine was initially pleased to sponsor, the charter helped to confirm Russian nobles in their corporate sense of identity as a civilised cosmopolitan élite. By 1796, educated society had reached an unprecedented degree of maturity and the most articulate elements within it displayed an unprecedented ambition to participate in government. It was crucial to Russia's devel-

---

[39] See D. M. Griffiths and G. E. Munro, trs. and eds., *Catherine II's Charters of 1785 to the Nobility and the Towns* (Bakersfield, CA, 1991), and below, ch. 4.

opment that Catherine's successor acknowledged none of their aspirations.

Such are the vagaries of the individual mind that, whilst Joseph II of Austria became the ultimate enlightened despot on the basis of an overwhelmingly Catholic education, Tsar Paul developed an obsession with medieval chivalry despite having been systematically schooled in the Enlightenment. To the alarm of one of his former tutors, Metropolitan Platon (Levshin) (1737–1812), the tsar even tried to extend Russian orders of chivalry to the Orthodox episcopate. Paul's personal holy grail was in Malta, where he was elected grand master of the Knights of St John of Jerusalem in 1798. His volatility and mania for Prussian-style parades led generations of scholars to regard him as mad. Doubting this diagnosis, more recent historians have instead looked for a logic behind the flurry of legislation that threw Catherine's work into reverse and his subjects into confusion. Paul's initial rejection of his mother's expansionism might have been expected to please leading Russians resentful of its costs; the tsar's personal frugality complemented his attempts to cut state expenditure; and it was he who resolved the vexed question of the succession by decreeing a fixed male line on 5 April 1797. Yet, ironically for one whose watchword was discipline, Paul's unpredictability rendered his régime unstable. No single measure can be blamed for his overthrow: restrictions on nobles' freedom of expression, legislation that freed their serfs from work on a Sunday, even the odd noble flogging might each have been tolerable in isolation. But together they represented a relapse into the insecurity from which the nobility had struggled for so long to escape. This was too much to bear. On the night of 11 March 1801, a group of disaffected officers – co-ordinated by the governor-general of St Petersburg, General Count Peter von der Pahlen – strangled the tsar in his rooms at the Mikhailovskii palace in St Petersburg. With fitting symmetry, Paul's brief reign ended, like that of Peter III, in cold-blooded assassination.

Alexander I (1777–1825) remains the most elusive of tsars. To Metternich he seemed superficial; some historians have found him hypocritical. His vacillating personality, often explained by the childhood need to please both Catherine and Paul, imperilled many of the friendships in which he placed so much trust. But his troubles owed as much to his political circumstances as to his psychological makeup. Complicity in the coup that culminated in the murder of his father not only left Alexander with a lifelong guilty conscience but also committed him to change. Between his accession and coronation, which portrayed this fundamentally military man as the epitome of angelic gentleness, the tsar made a series of rhetorical obeisances to the 'heart and laws' of his grandmother. In practice, these signified little beyond a disavowal of Paul's arbitrariness. Alexander was his own man with his own aspirations: to confer peace on Europe and a rational legal order on Russia.

Such elevated ideals would have been hard to realise at any time; Napoleon initially made them impossible. Even in the peaceful years 1801–5, achievements were limited. New ministries decreed in 1802 retained features of the old collegiate administration for at least a decade; universities established in the same year were slow to develop; the Free Agriculturalists Law of 1803 merely scratched the surface of serfdom. In 1809, M. M. Speranskii (1772–1839), the tsar's chief minister from 1808 to 1812, tried to coax him into constitutional reform. By proposing a representative state Duma with the power to veto legislation, Speranskii wanted to stimulate the development of a civil society that could ultimately assume a leading rôle in government. But caution led him to mask the most radical ideas from Alexander, who was therefore inclined to believe Speranskii's enemies when they accused him of intrigue and subversion. Tainted by association with Napoleonic rationalism, Speranskii was exiled in March 1812, three months before Napoleon invaded.

Napoleon's defeat in 1814 transformed Alexander's position in both Russia and Europe. Stability became his goal, though few now believe that reaction was the first means he chose to achieve it. Although the inflexible Count A. A. Arakcheev replaced Speranskii as the tsar's principal adviser, Speranskii enjoyed a partial return to favour when charged with the reform of Siberian administration in 1819–22. Moreover, Alexander continued to experiment until 1820 with the abolition of serfdom in the Baltic lands, constitutional reform in Finland and Poland, and multi-denominational religion in Russia itself. Peasant emancipation and a constitution might possibly have followed there, too, had the tsar not been unnerved by recurrent disorder both at home and abroad. As it was, the final years of Alexander's reign served only to depress him and to disillusion those of his subjects who had hoped for swifter progress. When the tsar unexpectedly died in Taganrog on 19 November 1825, the stage was set for one last attempted coup.

This time, however, it was not just the new tsar but the whole system of autocracy that the conspirators sought to overthrow. The crisis developed when it emerged that in 1823 the childless Alexander had flouted Paul's succession law by secretly disinheriting his eldest brother – Constantine, viceroy of Poland – for contracting a morganatic marriage to a Polish Catholic countess. Here was a tsar reverting to the Petrine model and selecting his own heir, in this case his youngest brother Nicholas (1796–1855). Though he almost certainly knew of this arrangement, Nicholas's sense of duty initially prompted him to swear fealty to Constantine on 27 November, unaware that his brother, still in Warsaw, had already determined to refuse the throne. Once this intention became clear, Nicholas urged a public renunciation. The urgency came from intelligence that a cabal of army officers proposed to exploit the crisis to impose lasting constitutional change. Since they were thrust prematurely into action, divided in intent, and lacking broader social support, it proved easy to disarm these Decembrists, so-called because their rebellion failed as the troops assembled to take the oath to Nicholas on 14 December 1825. Yet the consequences of their actions were momentous. Dissent in Russia could never be the same again; the newly enthroned Nicholas determined in vain to suppress it altogether.

Catherine II once described the adolescent Alexander as 'la réunion de quantité de contradictions'.[40] As the events of 1825 revealed, the same could be said of the country over which he ruled. By then, a century of sustained Westernisation had introduced into Russia a hierarchy of rationally ordered government institutions, detailed social regulation and cultural influences ranging from Italian opera to the political economy of Adam Smith. Yet it had also been responsible for freemasonry, fortune-telling, and Swedenborg's mystical Christianity. The theatrical hit of 1816 was Nikolai Il'in's comedy, *The Physiognomer and Chiromancer*; in 1815, the most popular Russian periodical was Labzin's *Messenger of Sion*, a mouthpiece of masonic mysticism suppressed in 1818 because it was offensive to a renaissant Orthodox church which itself was on the brink of an affair with Hegelian theology. Far from promoting modernisation, Westernisation in this guise served chiefly to frustrate it.

The principal restraint was nevertheless indigenous: this was the enserfed peasantry. Behind the glittering façade of St Petersburg and the imperial court, transformed over the course of the eighteenth century into a magnificent icon of secular cosmopolitanism, much of provincial Russia remained rooted in kinship, collective responsibility, and popular religious belief that rarely drew a clear line between animism and Orthodoxy. However, to suppose that rural tradition had remained untouched by modernisation would be to miss the crucial dynamic relationship between the two. Instead, I shall emphasise that the tsars' need to pay for institutional modernisation engendered a degree of social rigidity unknown to Muscovy and eventually helped to sink Russia deeper into economic backwardness. Since the first step in the

---

[40] *SIRIO*, 23 (1878), p. 498, Catherine II to Grimm, 18 September 1790.

argument is to show how far this process flowed from measures taken to secure Russia's imperial expansion, that expansion will be the subject of our next chapter.

BIBLIOGRAPHICAL NOTE

Three general works are outstanding: M. Raeff, *Understanding Imperial Russia: State and Society Under the Old Regime* (Chicago, 1984), distils a lifetime's reflection into a sophisticated short interpretation; R. Pipes, *Russia Under the Old Regime* (London, 1974), remains both provocative and indispensable; G. Hosking, *Russia: People and Empire 1552–1917* (London, 1997), injects the crucial imperial perspective. In a different register, too forceful for some, T. Szamuely, *The Russian Tradition* (London, 1988), insists on Russian authoritarianism. E. Keenan, 'Muscovite Political Folkways', *RR*, 45 (1986), stimulated a debate about continuities in Russian history published in the same issue. Two indispensable collections of essays are M. Raeff, *Political Ideas and Institutions in Imperial Russia* (Boulder, 1994), and I. de Madariaga, *Politics and Culture in Eighteenth-Century Russia* (London, 1998).

P. Longworth, *Alexis: Tsar of All the Russias* (London, 1984), shows how much Peter the Great owed to his father. A. P. Bogdanov's pamphlet, *Tsar' Feodor Alekseevich, 1676–1682* (Moscow, 1994), heralds a much-needed monograph. L. Hughes, *Sophia: Regent of Russia 1657–1704* (New Haven, CT, 1990), at her best on culture, dispels many myths. Although Hughes modestly denies that her *Russia in the Age of Peter the Great* (New Haven, CT, 1998) has superseded R. Wittram, *Peter I: Czar und Kaiser*, 2 vols. (Göttingen, 1964), on international affairs, this new book, which appeared as my own went to press, nevertheless deserves to become the standard modern account of the reign. E. V. Anisimov, *The Reforms of Peter the Great: Progress Through Coercion in Russia*, tr. J. T. Alexander (Armonk, NY, 1993), is a stimulating Russian study. Two contrasting Western interpretations reflect Peter's Manichean dualism: M. S. Anderson, *Peter the Great*, 2nd edn (London, 1995), makes more of the tsar's dynamic personality than L. R. Lewitter, who emphasises strategic vision in his introduction to Ivan Pososhkov, *The Book of Poverty and Wealth* (above, n. 29). The two-volume study by J. Cracraft, *The Petrine Revolution in Architecture* (Chicago, 1988) and *The Petrine Revolution in Russian Imagery* (Chicago, 1997), ranges wider than these titles imply; see also Cracraft's 'Opposition to Peter the Great', in E. Mendelsohn and M. S. Shatz, eds., *Imperial Russia 1700–1917: State, Society, Opposition. Essays in Honor of Marc Raeff* (DeKalb, IL, 1988).

To enter the 'era of palace revolutions' is to stumble into a historiographical black hole. Nevertheless, D. L. Ransel, 'The Government Crisis of 1730', in R. O. Crummey, ed., *Reform in Russia and the USSR* (Urbana, IL, 1989), may be supplemented by the special edition of *CASS*, 12, 1 (1978), and I. de Madariaga, 'Portrait of an Eighteenth-Century Russian Statesman: Prince Dmitry Mikhailovich Golitsyn', *SEER*, 62 (1984), a penetrating study of the key participant. On 1740–1, less well covered, there are J. L. H. Keep, 'The Secret Chancellery, the Guards and the Dynastic Crisis of 1740–1741', *FzOG*, 25 (1973), and I. V. Kurukin, 'Dvortsovyi perevorot 1741 goda: prichiny, "tekhnologiia", uroki', *Otechestvennaia istoriia* (1997, no. 5).

The best general accounts of the post-Petrine era are E. V. Anisimov, *Rossiia bez Petra: 1725–1740* (St Petersburg, 1994), and his *Rossiia v seredine XVIII veka: bor'ba za nasledie Petra* (Leningrad, 1986), translated by J. T. Alexander as *Empress Elizabeth: Her Reign and Her Russia* (Gulf Breeze, FL, 1995). Anisimov's essay on Anna, in a compilation of post-Soviet scholarship edited by D. J. Raleigh, *The Emperors and Empresses of Russia: Rediscovering the Romanovs* (Armonk, NY, 1996), inadvertently demonstrates how well A. Lipski, 'Some Aspects of Russia's Westernization During the Reign of Anna Ioannovna, 1730–1740', *American Slavic and East European Review*, 18 (1959), has stood the test of time. By contrast, J. F. Brennan, *Enlightened Despotism in Russia: The Reign of Elisabeth 1741–1762* (New York, 1987), is best ignored. C. Leonard, *Reform and Regicide: The Reign of Peter III of Russia* (Bloomington, IN, 1993), casts new light on continuity across the decade 1754–64, but, by attributing too much to the tsar himself, fails to refute M. Raeff's critique of 'The Domestic Policies of Peter III and His Overthrow', *AHR*, 75 (1970).

Fundamental on Catherine II is I. de Madariaga, *Russia in the Age of Catherine the Great* (New Haven, CT, 1981), a more accessible introduction being her *Catherine the Great: A Short History* (New Haven, CT, 1990). J. T. Alexander, *Catherine the Great: Life and Legend* (Oxford, 1989), offers a readable scholarly biography. C. Scharf, *Katharina II., Deutschland und die Deutschen* (Mainz, 1996), is at his best on the empress's German background. Ambitious Russian work includes A. B. Kamenskii, *'Pod seniiu Ekateriny': vtoraia polovina XVIII veka* (St Petersburg, 1992), and the more original O. A. Omel'chenko, *'Zakonnaia monarkhiia' Ekateriny II: prosveshchennyi absoliutizm v Rossii* (Moscow, 1993). Important collections are: special editions of *CASS*, 4, 3 (1970), and 23, 1 (1989); A. G. Cross, ed., *Russian Literature in the Age of Catherine the Great* (Oxford, 1976); R. Bartlett and J. M. Hartley, eds., *Russia in the Age of the Enlightenment* (London, 1990); and A. G.

Cross and G. S. Smith, eds., *Literature, Lives and Legality in Catherine's Russia* (Nottingham, 1994).

R. E. McGrew, *Paul I of Russia, 1754–1801* (Oxford, 1992), may be supplemented by a lively collection edited by H. Ragsdale, *Paul I: A Reassessment of His Life and Reign* (Pittsburgh, 1979), and by the special edition of *CASS*, 7, 1 (1973). N. Ia. Eidel'man's *Gran' vekov* (Moscow, 1986) ranks amongst his most stimulating books. In the absence of a full-scale study of Alexander I, good introductions are J. M. Hartley, *Alexander I* (London, 1994), and the first four chapters of D. Saunders, *Russia in the Age of Reaction and Reform, 1801–1881* (London, 1992), almost a book in themselves. On the crisis of 1825, see W. B. Lincoln, *Nicholas I: Emperor and Autocrat of All the Russias* (London, 1978).

2 Imperial great power

Ambitions and achievements

Montesquieu declared that 'toward the middle of the reign of Louis XIV', when France was at the height of its international powers, 'Muscovy was as yet no better known in Europe than was the Crimea.'[1] It was certainly little better respected. Though the temptations of international trade lured a succession of peripatetic European diplomatic missions to Moscow during the seventeenth century, Muscovy's place in the international system was scarcely more secure in the 1670s than it had been in the 1570s. If anything, it had become more precarious as medieval 'Christendom' fragmented under the impact of the Reformation into 'Europe', a secular amalgam of sovereign states.[2] Nor was the question easily resolved: a striking recent survey takes the disputed place of Russia as 'the cardinal problem' in Europe's 500-year history.[3]

There was no more convinced enemy of the Ottoman empire than Muscovy, whose Orthodox rulers always reserved a particular distaste for Islam. It was, indeed, an unfulfilled aim of Peter the Great's Grand Embassy in 1697–8 to bolster the Christian alliance formed against Constantinople in 1686. Yet, to Western writers in search of 'perpetual peace', Muscovites seemed closer to the infidel Turk than to 'civilised' European nations who defined themselves in opposition to a barbarian Oriental 'other'.[4] In 1647, John Milton acknowledged Muscovy as 'the most northerly Region of *Europe* reputed civil'.[5] But the duc de Sully's

[1] Montesquieu, *The Spirit of the Laws*, tr. A. Cohler, B. Miller, and H. Stone (Cambridge, 1989), p. 137 (IX:9).
[2] See P. Burke, 'Did Europe Exist Before 1700?', *HEI*, 1, 1 (1980), pp. 21–9, and J. Hale, *The Civilization of Europe in the Renaissance* (London, 1993), pp. 24–7, 38–42.
[3] N. Davies, *Europe: A History* (Oxford, 1996), p. 10.
[4] F.-D. Liechtanhan, 'Le Russe, ennemi héréditaire de la chrétienté?: La diffusion de l'image de Moscovie en Europe occidentale aux XVIe et XVIIe siècles', *Revue Historique*, 285, 1 (1991), p. 101.
[5] *The Works of John Milton*, 18 vols. (New York, 1931–8), vol. X, p. 327, 'A Brief History of Muscovia', published 1682.

Grand Design (1638) had countenanced the forcible expulsion from Europe of Turk and Muscovite alike, and not until the abbé St-Pierre issued the first version of his 'project' for perpetual peace in 1712 – three years after Peter's victory over the Swedes at Poltava and one year before the Respublica Christiana was last formally acknowledged in the treaty of Utrecht – did Russians find a Western theorist prepared unequivocally to rank them among the European powers.[6] Western liberals, offended by Russian autocracy, long continued to pretend that it was only by courtesy that Russia counted among the civilised states. Palmerston, for example, publicly 'stigmatised' the tsarist repression in Poland in 1863 'as *"barbarous"* a bitter word to Russians, who are peculiarly sensitive upon the point of being so deemed'.[7] By 1825, however, Russia's international prominence was already a stark reality. Gone was the peripheral pariah whose significance seemed so uncertain when Peter I was born. At the congress of Vienna (October 1814–June 1815), no one could afford to underestimate the power that had defied Napoleon. While Turkey had become the 'sick man' of Europe, Alexander I was now its self-proclaimed saviour.

One obvious distinction between tsar and sultan was the eagerness with which Peter I had joined the growing European network of diplomacy. By 1725, there were twelve resident Russian missions in Europe and eleven more or less permanent European representatives in St Petersburg. Since it was only from 1688 that Russia had been continuously represented even in Warsaw, the scale of the change is clear.[8] Although Russian diplomacy had become synonymous with sloth long before 1801, when the foreign ministry employed roughly 300 (over ten times as many as the British Foreign Office in 1822), there was no doubting the civilised credentials of individuals such as Count S. R. Vorontsov, ambassador in London between 1785 and 1806. Indeed, Vorontsov's assimilation into English society sent him so far 'native' as occasionally to defend the British line against his own government.

Still, it was not the charm of its envoys that unnerved Russia's rivals: it was the extent of its territorial ambitions. In 1772, the marquis de Chastellux quoted military reform as evidence of Russia's civilisation: 'The Russians can no longer be regarded as barbarians; they make war with a great artillery train, supplies, ammunition etc.' Yet at that stage

[6] F. H. Hinsley, *Power and the Pursuit of Peace* (Cambridge, 1963), pp. 25–6, 34.

[7] T. A. Jenkins, ed., *The Parliamentary Diaries of Sir John Trelawny, 1858–1865* (London, 1990), p. 227, 27 February 1863; emphasis in original.

[8] Only Warsaw received a Russian 'ambassador' before the late eighteenth century; lesser-ranking 'ministers' were sent elsewhere to save money and avoid precedence disputes: M. S. Anderson, *The Rise of Modern Diplomacy 1450–1919* (London, 1993), pp. 69–73, 83.

the Kalmyks seemed no more likely to take Luxembourg than the Janissaries were Besançon.[9] Forty years on, this certainty had evaporated. Having been extended by 8.6 million square miles between 1750 and 1791 alone, Russia was so huge by 1815 that a British journal described it as 'the most monstrous empire, in extent, that ever spread over the face of the earth'.[10] Even before Napoleon was overthrown, geopolitical anxieties began to congeal in Romantic minds into forebodings of the collapse of civilisation: to the febrile imagination of a Chateaubriand, the Russian apocalypse was nothing less than 'the power that threatens to overwhelm the world'.[11]

In fact, Russian ambitions at Vienna were tempered by Alexander I's aspiration to create a new international order in which *raison d'état* would be subordinated to mutual restraint.[12] Although the tsar's mystical cast of mind conferred an air of unreality on the project, his aim was shared by powers determined never again to collapse under the combined weight of war, revolution, and French hegemonic pretensions. But because this conception of international affairs was novel in 1813–15, contemporaries were still inclined to interpret Russian motives in terms of the ruthless competition for conquest that had hitherto been masked by balance-of-power rhetoric.[13] Looking back on the catalogue of Russian territorial acquisitions – which in the eighteenth century had for the first time been made at the expense of rival great powers – it is not hard to see why Alexander's modified idealism should have been mistaken for insatiable greed.

At Muscovy's western extreme, the Russo-Polish 'Eternal Peace' of 1686 finally ratified the favourable terms agreed after thirteen years of war at the treaty of Andrusovo in 1667. Then the Russians had gained Smolensk, Chernigov, and eastern Ukraine outright; the clause limiting their acquisition of Kiev to a period of two years was never observed. In

---

[9] Chastellux, *De la félicité publique*, 2 vols. (reprinted Farnborough, 1971), vol. II, p. 201. The Janissaries were outmoded infantry who guarded the Sultan.

[10] *Eclectic Review*, quoted in Anderson, *The Rise of Modern Diplomacy*, p. 185. Apart from the medieval Mongol empire, only the nineteenth-century British empire surpassed Russia's in territorial terms.

[11] Quoted in H. G. Schenk, *The Mind of the European Romantics: An Essay in Cultural History* (Oxford, 1979), p. 33.

[12] The tsar, however, did not go so far as V. F. Malinovskii, who had contemplated radical social reform, including peasant emancipation, as the corollary of a reconfigured Europe in which self-governing ethnic units would coexist in just and peaceful equilibrium under the aegis of a General Union governed by an elective General Council. See P. Ferretti, *A Russian Advocate of Peace: Vasilii Malinovskii (1765–1814)* (Dordrecht, 1998).

[13] The transition between the two systems is the subject of the classic book by P. W. Schroeder, *The Transformation of European Politics, 1763–1848* (Oxford, 1994), pp. vi, 5–11, 502–4, 801–2, and *passim*.

the east, the tsars' Siberian conquests, dating from Ivan IV's capture of Kazan' in 1552, were secured against Chinese incursion by the treaty of Nerchinsk in 1689 (though variations in the Latin text and inadequate geographic knowledge led to renewed attempts to define the border in the 1730s). In 1696, Peter the Great conquered the Black Sea fortress port of Azov, which, despite changing hands more than once, remained a lasting symbol of Russian ambitions in the south. The key break-through to the north-west came in September 1721, when the treaty of Nystad guaranteed the Baltic gains of the Great Northern War, in which Peter acquired Ingria, Estonia, Livonia, and the Karelian isthmus (Old Finland), and Russia became guarantor of the constitutions of both Sweden and Poland. This meant seeking to destabilise these rivals by maintaining Poland on the verge of anarchy brought about by the *liberum veto* and by defending the Swedish constitution of 1720 against a revival of royal absolutism. The latter aim was thwarted only by Gustav III's bloodless coup in Stockholm in August 1772; the Polish question, as we shall see, was more complicated.

Though further Finnish territory was taken from the Swedes in 1743, the mid-century marked a lull in Russian aggrandisement. It resumed with a vengeance under Catherine II, whose reign witnessed the second greatest period of Russian expansion after that of Ivan the Terrible. Three partitions (in 1772, 1793, and 1795) removed the name of Poland from the map. It reappeared in 1815 only in the emasculated form of a Congress Kingdom under Russian control. Russia now acquired a swathe of territory in left-bank Ukraine and Belorussia, previously taken by Austria and Prussia in the partitions. Georgia had been absorbed in 1801, Finland as a grand duchy in 1809. Southern conquests from the Turks were incorporated in the treaty of Kutchuk-Kainardzhii in 1774, consolidated by the annexation of the Crimea in 1783, and confirmed by the treaties of Jassy in December 1791, when the Russian frontier reached the Dnestr, and Bucharest in May 1812, which absorbed most of Bessarabia.

Not all these acquisitions were unqualified gains. Verdicts on Siberia fluctuated. Though the region was valued until the 1760s as a mercan-tile colony, populationist qualms (see chapter 8) and the decline of the fur trade subsequently led to its dismissal as a primitive desert. Only the Decembrist generation converted it into a land of opportunity, a second New World. Poland was even more of a mixed blessing. By incorpor-ating lands dominated by Catholic political culture and populated partly by Jews (drawn into Russia in significant numbers only in 1793 and 1795), the partitions made it harder to integrate a multi-confessional empire. Worse, though Russia won the lion's share of partitioned

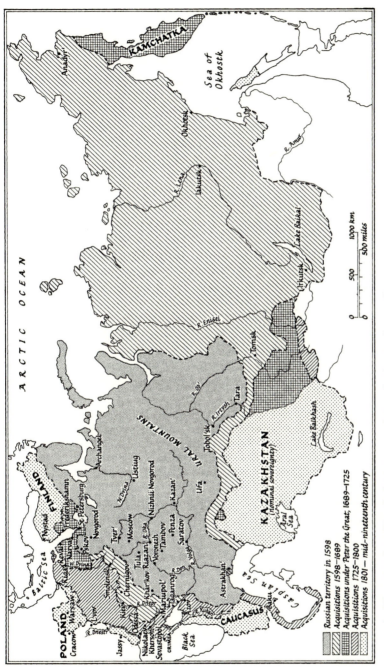

ARCTIC OCEAN

KAMCHATKA

Sea of Okhostk

R. Amor

Okhotsk

R. Lena

Yakutsk

Lake Baikal

Akutsk

R. Enisei

Tomsk

Tara

R. Ob'

R. Irtysh

Tobol'sk

URAL MOUNTAINS

Ustiug

Archangel

N. Dvina

Nizhnii Novgorod

Kazan'

Ufa

KAZAKHSTAN
(nominal sovereignty)

Lake Balkhash

Aral Sea

FINLAND

Frederikshamn

St Petersburg

Novgorod

Tver'

Moscow

R. Oka

Penza

Saratov

Tambov

Voronezh

Ryazan'

Tula

Chernigov

Smolensk

Pskov

Narva

Revel'

W. Dvina

Baltic Sea

Nystad

POLAND

Cracow

Warsaw

L'vov

Kiev

R. Dnepr

Jassy

R. Dnestr

Odessa

Nikolaev

Kherson

Sevastopol'

Crimea

Mariupol

Taganrog

R. Don

Azov

Astrakhan'

R. Kuban'

CAUCASUS

Baku

Black Sea

Caspian Sea

Khar'kov

Russian territory in 1598
Acquisitions 1598–1689
Acquisitions under Peter the Great; 1689–1725
Acquisitions 1725–1800
Acquisitions 1801 — mid-nineteenth century

0   500   1000 km.

0   500 miles

1   The expansion of Russia, late seventeenth to early nineteenth centuries

Poland, it did so only by sacrificing indirect control of the whole kingdom, ceding territory to Austria and Prussia and creating a common border with these rivals by 1795. Another useful buffer state disappeared when Finland was taken. Nor were Russian victories unanimously welcomed at home: a strong current of opposition to war and expansion ran through Russian political culture from the 1760s (see chapter 7). And there was no end in sight, for no matter how much territory the Russians acquired, they still thought their empire vulnerable. Recognised as a strategic linchpin since Byzantine times, the Crimea helped to secure the southern border. But there was no obvious solution to the geopolitical problem posed by the boundless east European plain.

If anxieties about security gave Russian expansion its peculiar hole-in-corner quality, rivals saw only triumphalist aggression. Variously depicted as Jupiter, Mars, Hercules, and Neptune, Peter the Great wanted to excel the glories of ancient Rome; Catherine the Great threatened actually to do so. Sir John Sinclair, who continued to think Russians as brutish as Turks, declared on his return from St Petersburg in 1787 that 'all Europe must unite to check the ambition of a sovereign who makes one conquest only a step to the acquisition of another'.[14] It was in just such an effort in 1791 that Pitt the Younger risked war with Russia, whom many regarded as Britain's natural ally, over its possession of the seemingly insignificant Black Sea fortress of Ochakov, captured from the Turks by Potemkin in 1788. Lord Elgin explained one of the most plausible reasons why:

Who could say where the Court of Petersburg would stop if, after forming a solid footing, not only in the Crimea, but in other parts, of the Black Sea, and striking there at the vitals of the Ottoman Porte, (and Ochakov alone was perhaps sufficient) she should seize some unlucky moment, when the rest of Europe was unable to assist that country, and erect her standard in Constantinople?[15]

Such neuroses helped to generate the russophobia that later inflamed the Eastern Question and prompted Verdi to voice in 1848 a widespread fear of the perils of tsarist expansion: 'If we let the Russians take possession of Constantinople we shall all become cossacks in a few years . . . Christ!!'[16]

---

[14] Quoted in M. S. Anderson, 'Eighteenth-Century Theories of the Balance of Power', in R. Hatton and M. S. Anderson, eds., *Studies in Diplomatic History: Essays in Memory of David Bayne Horne* (London, 1970), p. 195.

[15] Quoted in J. Black, *British Foreign Policy in an Age of Revolutions 1783–1793* (Cambridge, 1994), p. 288.

[16] Quoted in D. R. B. Kimbell, *Verdi in the Age of Italian Romanticism* (Cambridge, 1981), p. 225.

The alarmism is evident. All the same, Russian ambitions to overthrow the Turk were more than a figment of their rivals' imaginations. Muscovite designs on Constantinople had been advertised at the birth of Peter the Great in 1672; the leading figure in Russian foreign policy after his death, A. I. Osterman, drew up plans to partition the Ottoman empire in 1737; and Voltaire repeatedly urged Catherine to topple Sultan Mustafa III during the Russo-Turkish war of 1768–74. It seems odd that Catherine's 'Greek Project' was long dismissed as a myth. Visitors to her palace at Tsarskoe Selo, where the park was laid out from the early 1770s, were presented with a visual allegory: whilst Quarenghi's Turkish pavilion, copied from a building on the Bosphorus, created a Turkish mood, Cameron's church of St Sophia (evoking the image of Hagia Sophia in Constantinople, though not modelled upon it) could be glimpsed across the lake, beyond Rinaldi's column celebrating the naval triumph at Chesme at 1770. Thus 'the symbol of sea victories was combined with the symbol of the re-establishment of an Orthodox Byzantium, while the lake represented the Black Sea, which opened the route to the capital of the Turkish Empire'.[17] In 1780, the year after Catherine had her second grandson christened Constantine, A. A. Bezborodko, the dominant maker of foreign policy in the 1780s, planned to restore him to the Greek throne following 'the complete destruction of Turkey'. Catherine tried to tempt her Austrian ally into the scheme in September 1782. Undeterred by his refusal, she revived the project when the Turks declared war in August 1787. Though ministers remained sceptical, later disowning the idea as Catherine's alone, she might have persevered had her troops performed better and had the Swedes not invaded in July 1788.

Constantinople was not the only exotic location about which Russian rulers harboured ambitions: India also figured in their dreams. Peter I tried to find both a land and a sea route across the Caspian. A. Bekovich's expedition to Khiva and Bukhara in 1716 ended in failure; so did A. P. Volynskii's mission to Isfahan in 1715–17. Having concluded a commercial treaty, Volynskii was forced to leave the Persian capital when his master's ulterior motives were uncovered. As governor of Astrakhan' from 1719, Volynskii prepared for an attack on Persia, launched in 1722, from which Russia gained lands on the Caspian's western and southern shores in 1724. Since these had to be abandoned in 1732 on grounds of expense, it was not until the final year of Catherine II's reign that another Russian army was fielded against Persia. By conquering Baku in July 1796, Valerian Zubov achieved more

[17] D. Shvidkovsky, *The Empress and the Architect: British Architecture and Gardens at the Court of Catherine the Great* (New Haven, CT, 1996), p. 105.

in two months than Peter the Great had managed in two years. Had it succeeded, the empress's 'Oriental Project' would have made Russia ruler of Asia between Turkey and Tibet. As it was, Tsar Paul abandoned the venture. Yet in 1801, at his most anglophobic, Paul ordered the Don cossacks to march on India via Khiva and Bukhara. Like many of the tsar's ideas, this was pure fantasy, though the scheme's collapse did not deter him from contemplating a further campaign, this time jointly with Napoleon, whilst Napoleon himself proposed a Franco-Russian advance on India to Alexander I in February 1808. None of these schemes stood any chance of success. However, by the time of Napoleon's defeat circumstances had changed. Events had shown how rash it was to write the Russians off, whatever the odds against them. And the odds in the subcontinent looked too short for comfort. So insecure did the British route to India seem that the *Edinburgh Review* proclaimed in October 1815 that 'it would have seemed far less extravagant to predict the entry of a Russian army into Delhi or even Calcutta, than its entry into Paris'.[18]

Yet 1814 had seen not only the parade of Russian troops down the Champs Elysées, but the appointment of a Russian governor for the French capital. In terms of both *Realpolitik* and the popular imagination, the Romanovs had reached the zenith of their international prestige. Three questions now arise: how had such gains been achieved, why was no one capable of preventing them, and what were the consequences for Russia of its apparently unstoppable expansion?

Military and naval reform

The most obvious explanation of Russian success lies in military prowess underpinned by institutional modernisation. War dominated every eighteenth-century decade except the 1720s. Russia was successively committed to the Great Northern War (1700–21) in which it combined with Poland, Saxony, and Denmark against the Swedes and also fought the Turks between 1711 and 1713; the War of the Polish Succession (1733–8) in which Russia and Austria fought France and Spain; the Russo-Turkish war of 1735–9; the Russo-Swedish war of 1741–3; the Seven Years War (1756–63) in which Russia allied with Austria, France, Spain, and Sweden against Prussia and Great Britain, before in 1762; the Russo-Turkish war of 1768–74; a further Turkish war in which Russia was joined until 1790 by its unwilling Austrian ally (1787–91); the Russo-Swedish war of 1788–90; and the War of the

---

[18] Quoted in J. H. Gleason, *The Genesis of Russophobia in Great Britain* (Cambridge, MA, 1934), p. 39.

Second Coalition against Revolutionary France (1798–9). Although Russian armies always started hesitantly and ended the last of these wars ignominiously in both Switzerland and the Netherlands, the troops emerged from all these conflicts, as from their battle against Polish insurgents in the 1790s, with their prestige, and above all their reputation for bravery, not only intact but enhanced.

The War of the Third Coalition (1805–7) was less successful. Napoleon followed his triumph over a combined Austro-Russian force at Austerlitz in November 1805 by trouncing the Prussians at Jena in October 1806. The Russians themselves succumbed first at Eylau in February 1807 and then, more decisively, at Friedland on 2/14 June, a defeat which pushed Alexander I into alliance with the dictator at Tilsit on 26 June/7 July only months after the Orthodox church had branded him as Antichrist. At best an uneasy compromise motivated by mutual anglophobia, the Franco-Russian rapprochement lasted for five years only because Napoleon was overcommitted in Spain. Once he had determined not to tolerate the Russians as equal partners, the die was cast. Against advice, Napoleon crossed the Niemen into Russia on 11/23 June 1812. It was the defeat of that invasion which indelibly imprinted on the European mind the image of the indomitable Russian soldier. Let us now take a closer look at the armed forces in which he served.

We begin with the navy, founded in 1696, Peter the Great's most revolutionary innovation. Typically, the tsar began by relying on Muscovite methods. His first serious efforts in shipbuilding, at Lake Pereiaslavl' in 1690–2, resembled those of his father at Dedinovo in 1667–78. Both men ranked the need for close supervision higher than proximity to the sea (which Peter saw for the first time at Archangel in 1693); both relied on inadequate local resources; both initiatives foundered on the difficulty of co-ordinating the various government agencies involved; and, though Peter's motives are unclear, both were almost certainly designed to protect trade with Persia across the Caspian. By contrast, the galleys built under pressure at Voronezh in the winter of 1695–6 were definitely intended to repel the Turkish ships that formed a crucial link in the Ottoman supply line in the Crimea. In the event, the tsar's expensive new ships were less effective than the more primitive cossack boats that entered Azov harbour by stealth and set fire to Turkish galleys, and their construction raised problems that were to hinder subsequent naval development in the Baltic. Voronezh was too far inland, and the use of untreated green timber shortened the ships' lives (twenty-eight of the fifty vessels laid down in 1702–5 had to be broken up).

It was partly in search of solutions to such problems that Peter had travelled to Europe in 1697–8. Like the Swedes and the Danes, who had oscillated between British and Dutch shipbuilders for much of the seventeenth century, he now faced a choice between the different methods adopted by the two maritime powers. As a youth, Peter had admired the Dutch technology demonstrated to him in Moscow's foreign quarter by Franz Timmerman, who encouraged his early fascination with boats. Once in Holland, however, the tsar became frustrated by an apprentice system that transferred its expertise over generations of trial and error when what he required was a science that could be readily, reliably, and repeatedly applied to his own immediate needs. This he discovered in England, where he spent time at Deptford dockyard. No Dutch-built Russian ship was launched after 1703: *Royal Transport*, the yacht given to Peter by William III, returned to Archangel with several British specialists on board. Overcoming understaffing and difficult conditions, they eventually helped to build a Baltic fleet powerful enough to defeat the Swedes off Hangö, on the Finnish coast, in July 1714. Governed from 1720 by a Maritime Regulation based on Western models, Russia's new navy, comprising thirty-four ships of the line, fifteen frigates, and large galley fleet, was by that time numerically superior to both the Swedish and the Danish forces which, only ten years earlier, could have put to sea a combined total of eighty-four battleships to Russia's none.

Catherine II sought to outdo Peter by the creation of a Black Sea fleet numbering twenty-two ships of the line by 1791. Boasting to Potemkin in 1790 that it was only in her reign that Russian naval exploits had 'really begun to be remarkable', she claimed this innovation as 'Our personal achievement, which is why it is so close to Our heart'.[19] One can see why Catherine was inclined to gloat. Twenty years earlier, the appearance of three squadrons of Russian ships in the eastern Mediterranean – plausibly ranked by a modern scholar as 'one of the most spectacular events of the eighteenth century'[20] – heralded the destruction of the Turkish fleet at Chesme on the coast of Asia Minor in July 1770. Promoted following his part in this triumph, Samuel Greig of Inverkeithing, Catherine's Scottish rear-admiral, was still in command in July 1788, when the Baltic fleet engaged with a marginally smaller Swedish squadron under Duke Charles of Sudermania off the island of Hogland. Though by no means a victory on the scale of Chesme – indeed not strictly a victory at all, since the duke merely disengaged –

[19] Quoted in K. Rasmussen, 'Catherine II and the Image of Peter I', *SR*, 37, 1 (1978), p. 65.
[20] M. S. Anderson, 'Great Britain and the Russo-Turkish War of 1768–1774', *EHR*, 69, 1 (1954), p. 44.

Hogland at least dissuaded Gustav III from any thoughts of a descent on St Petersburg.

The subsequent defeat at Svenskund in June 1790, when sixty-four ships and over 7,300 men were lost, warns us not to exaggerate Russian naval power. Though Baltic manoeuvres helped to unnerve successive Swedish Diets, the fleet lay largely dormant in the middle of the eighteenth century. In theory, Peter's Baltic conquests had opened up the prospect of a glorious future for a navy based at Kronshtadt, the island fortress constructed at the mouth of the Neva under the direction of a Welshman, Edward Lane. In practice, the fact that the tsar's men-of-war captured only a single Swedish ship of the line in the Great Northern War was but one reason why his costly innovation was neglected by successors who lacked both the enthusiasm and the resources required to develop it. Chesme apart, the Black Sea fleet's achievements were also modest. Allowed through the Straits by the convention of Ainali Kawak in 1779, Russian ships successfully besieged Corfu in 1799 but were tangential to the result of the Napoleonic wars. Across the century, the fleet performed best in conjunction with land operations. A naval bombardment helped to defeat Bulavin's cossack rebellion at Azov in 1708; amphibious raids between 1719 and 1721 finally forced the Swedes to succumb; and a naval blockade broke Turkish troops' resistance on the Dnestr in 1789 once the fleet had recovered from storm damage inflicted in 1787. For all the empress's pride in her fleet, Russia remained primarily a land power.

The fortified defensive lines by which Muscovy blunted the Tatar threat from the south represented but one symbol of the impact of the 'military revolution' that some claim radiated outwards from the Habsburg lands in the century after 1560.[21] Built under the direction of French Huguenot and Dutch military engineers, the lines were manned by troops who formed part of a rapidly expanding army in which, for the first time, infantry came to dominate cavalry in a ratio of 2:1. New model regiments, allowed to lapse after the Smolensk War (1632–4), were revived after 1650. Officered mostly by foreigners and guided by instructions of 1649 modelled on Maurice of Nassau's, they comprised 80,000 men by 1681. Total troop figures, like battle strengths, are hard to establish with precision. But we can be reasonably sure that the Muscovite army, notionally 200,000 strong but able to muster only

---

[21] C. J. Rogers, *The Military Revolution Debate: Readings on the Military Transformation of Early Modern Europe* (Boulder, 1995), reprints M. Roberts's 1956 lecture with a refinement by G. Parker and a challenge from J. Black, who develops important claims about eighteenth-century dynamism and decisiveness in *European Warfare, 1660–1815* (London, 1994).

rather more than half that number against an enemy, was then the largest in Europe, having roughly doubled in size over the preceding century.

The *strel'tsy* revolt of 1698 reminded Peter the Great that the army he inherited had been only partially reformed. Emphasising his European credentials, the tsar branded his outdated musketeers Janissaries and slaughtered the rebels; the mutiny at Astrakhan' between July 1705 and March 1706 was the last spasm of their discredited rump. By then, Peter was locked into war with the Swedes. His first major levy, launched in November 1699, raised only about 32,000 of the anticipated 80,000 men. Defeated at Narva in November 1700, he developed a new conscription system (*rekrutchina*), decreed in February 1705, by which one 'recruit' – the Western word used for the first time – was to be taken from every twentieth peasant household. Between 1701 and 1709, 130,000 soldiers were drafted. Victorious at Poltava, the tsar turned to the harder task of forming a technically competent officer corps from his native nobility. By the end of his reign, whose fifty-three levies conscripted approximately 300,000 men, Peter had fashioned a standing army which – on paper, at least – could boast uniform conditions of service, a code of discipline (the Military Regulation of 1716), and a degree of technical knowledge fostered by the newly founded educational institutions described in chapter 6. Administered by the College of War, founded in 1718–19, and supported by the textile and iron industries the tsar had established to supply uniforms and weaponry, this was by any standards a formidable fighting force.

Yet although Peter had amalgamated a mixture of Muscovite regiments into a more or less unitary formation, ambition outran achievement. Unlike their predecessors on the Muscovite lines, who carried the latest firearms, soldiers in the century after 1725 acquired their reputation for bravery precisely because they were known to be poorly equipped. Their ranks remained riddled with disease. If the victims of starvation or insanitary conditions are included, then one could probably double the number killed in battle (or who subsequently died of their wounds) – more than 750,000 between 1725 and 1825. Survivors were rarely paid according to the statutory norms, were led by officers of mixed abilities, and remained unhealthily dependent on inspired generalship because the rhythm of military life disrupted training in peacetime. Soldiers spent up to eight months of the winter quartered in peasant homes scattered across the western provinces; only between mid-May and mid-September could regiments regroup for exercises, and even these were disrupted by the rival demands of guard duty and forced labour for state construction projects such as roads and canals.

For all these limitations, however, Russian forces were felicitously adapted to their social and political circumstances: 'the autocracy's "standing army" was actually a quasi-reserve army well suited to the constraints of serfdom and the weak administrative infrastructure'.[22]

Two problems responsible for humiliating V. V. Golitsyn in his Crimean campaigns of 1687 and 1689 continued to trouble Russian strategists. The first, which proved easier to resolve, was the need for forces able not only to fight pitched battles against conventional European enemies, but also to repel lightning raids by the Turk and steppe nomads. Experience of counter-insurgency in the south – again well suited to a pre-industrial economy – helped to fashion something approaching a 'Russian way of warfare' with the emphasis on lightness and speed. But this never cured the problem of distances huge enough to convert every Russian campaign into a test of endurance. Until railways permitted the development of a modern stores system in the aftermath of the Crimean débâcle in 1854–6, imperial expansion only made problems of supply more acute. A recent study suggests that Golitsyn, often judged incompetent, could hardly have done more to provision his army in 1687: allowing for his oversized army, it was the empty steppe that scuppered his plans.[23] Yet even campaigns in the more densely inhabited west proved no easier to supply. Since the responsible department within the College of War – the general-proviantmeister's chancellery – was running at a deficit of 2.3 million rubles by 1749, nearly half the army's annual budget, it is not surprising that Russian commanders planned to take with them only a quarter of their needs at the beginning of the Seven Years War. Cavalry were particularly burdensome – a horse's ration weighed ten times more than a soldier's – and in 1757 S. F. Apraksin's invasion of East Prussia was delayed whilst sufficient grass grew for his 92,000 horses to graze. In the following year, Apraksin's successor as commander-in-chief, V. V. Fermor, was forced to withdraw to revictual despite having built supply depots in advance. Victory merely compounded the problem. In 1759, after his triumph at Kunersdorf, Field Marshal P. S. Saltykov's wagon trains were so overloaded by both casualties and booty that he elected to retreat rather than press on towards Berlin.

In another sense, however, geography was Russia's key defensive asset. Safe in the fastness of the Muscovite heartland, it was all but invulnerable to predators. No invader managed to overcome the effects

[22] E. K. Wirtschafter, *From Serf to Russian Soldier* (Princeton, 1990), p. 95.
[23] C. B. Stevens, 'Why Seventeenth-Century Muscovite Campaigns Against Crimea Fell Short of What Counted', *RH*, 19, 1-4 (1992), pp. 487–504, part of a special issue of twenty-five essays on 'The Frontier in Russian History'.

of route marches long enough to exhaust the hardiest troops in fierce climatic conditions. Even Napoleon failed. Of the 500,000 men who followed him across the Niemen, only 135,000 survived to fight at Borodino on 26 August/7 September 1812, where 40,000 more were lost in a battle of attrition which exhausted both sides. On 2/14 September, when the depleted Grand Army reached nearby Moscow, it found the burning city deserted. What should have been his greatest triumph was actually Napoleon's nemesis. Cut off from their supplies, and devoid of options in the face of an enemy that refused to negotiate and could continue to retreat eastwards if pressed, the French withdrew in late October. Defeat at Maloiaroslavets forced them to retrace their steps through devastated territory, foraging for food in competition with well-coordinated Russian partisans and a peasantry whose resistance became the stuff of national myth. Barely a tenth of the initial invasion force retreated over the Niemen on 1/13 December. Russia had been saved by commanders who, in their anxiety to deny Napoleon the decisive engagement on which he thrived, had reluctantly allowed distances to do their work for them.

Russian generals were rarely so cautious as Barclay de Tolly was in 1812. Stunned by the humiliation at Narva, where a 40,000-strong Russian force was wrongfooted in a blizzard by only 11,000 Swedes, Peter the Great's army had reversed the odds within a year and won a crucial victory at Poltava in Ukraine in June 1709. Peter's reformed troops made the most of their almost twofold numerical advantage partly because they were now under the tsar's personal command, but principally because the Swedes had been exhausted by their punishing drive through Ukraine. Swedish losses totalled approximately 10,000 dead and wounded from their initial force of 24,000, almost all the rest falling captive to the Russians, who lost only a tenth of their 45,000 men. Superior Russian fire power, including 102 mobile light cannon, permitted a switch from defensive tactics to the aggression that culminated in ruthless attacks on the fleeing Swedes. Captain Lars Tiesensten, who himself lost a leg, described the panic among the Upplander infantry, who clambered 'in a heap and as if fallen upon each other or thrown up on the pile, wherein the enemy with pike, sword and bayonet eagerly slaughtered and massacred as much as he was able, despite not recognising what was living and what dead'.[24] Poltava did not end the war, and it could not save an overconfident Peter from a setback in July 1711, when a bigger, more mobile Turkish force overcame his army on the River Pruth. Nevertheless, because it marked the defeat of the

---

[24] P. Englund, *The Battle of Poltava: The Birth of the Russian Empire* (London, 1992), pp. 172–3, is an evocative reconstruction from the Swedish standpoint.

hitherto invincible Charles XII, Poltava proved to be not only the pivotal battle of the Great Northern War but a decisive moment in the rise of Russia's international reputation.

Haunted by Peter's heroic image as commander-in-chief, his successors tried to emulate, or better surpass, his military genius. Alexander I, the first to place himself at the head of his troops, was humiliated at Austerlitz. Prevented by their sex from making the same error, Russia's female rulers relied on generals who did them proud. In the Seven Years War, Apraksin routed the Prussians at Gross-Jägersdorf in the same year (1757) that Frederick the Great himself achieved his historic victory over a French army roughly twice the size of his own at Rossbach. In August 1759, Saltykov, in uneasy collaboration with the Austrian marshal Laudon, inflicted a further humiliation at Kunersdorf. Frederick underestimated the terrain, got his heavy cavalry bogged down on marshy ground – where they became a sitting target for swifter cossacks – and mistakenly attacked the strongest-defended allied position. The Prussians suffered 40 per cent casualties and their king led off the field a mere 4,000 stragglers from the 48,000-strong force with which he had begun.

It was at Kunersdorf that the century's outstanding commander, Field Marshal A. V. Suvorov (1730–1800), was first blooded. Erudite and eccentric, Suvorov personified the paternalist ethos of the Russian army. Though his ruthlessness unnerved the more sensitive officers under his command, his combination of courage with charisma, later praised by Clausewitz, earned both the loyalty and the affection of his men. Suvorov achieved fame by vanquishing the Turks at Fokshani in July 1789 and again on the River Rymnik in September. His attack on Ismail at the mouth of the Danube, where atrocities were committed against the infidel in November 1790, inspired Byron to call him 'A thing to wonder at beyond most wondering':

> Hero, buffoon, half-demon, and half-dirt,
>   Praying, instructing, desolating, plundering –
> Now Mars, now Momus – and when bent to storm
> A fortress, Harlequin in uniform.[25]

True to his reputation, Suvorov smashed the last bastion of Polish resistance in October 1794, when the 16,000 troops under his command assaulted the fortifications at Praga outside Warsaw. Of the 30,000 Poles sheltering there, an estimated 13,000 were butchered within a few hours, a further 14,500 were captured, and 2,000 more drowned in the River Vistula. Based on his belief in training, the

[25] E. H. Coleridge, ed., *The Poetical Works of Lord Byron* (London, 1905), p. 897, *Don Juan*, canto VII, 1822.

philosophy that inspired such victories found expression in Suvorov's *Art of Victory* (1795), and was limpidly summarised in some confidential notes the old man made for Paul I at the onset of his 1799 campaign in Italy and Switzerland. The tsar was advised to:

(1) act only on the offensive;
(2) be speedy on the march and attack furiously with cold steel;
(3) abhor method – see and decide in an instant;
(4) give full authority to the commander-in-chief;
(5) attack and beat the enemy in the open field; and
(6) don't waste time on sieges.[26]

Adherence to these maxims helps to explain why Suvorov became a political liability. Yet it also accounts not only for his rapid conquest of Italy, but for his legendary escape from the Alps when the Swiss campaign turned sour.

Russia's international prestige was inconceivable without a well-led army. But if military prowess underpinned by institutional reform was a necessary condition of Russian success, it was not a sufficient cause. Just as domestic performance was no guarantee of lasting international status in the eighteenth century, so diplomatic manoeuvring could be as decisive as armed combat. And in diplomacy the relative power of Russia's European rivals had as great an impact on its destiny as its own internal strengths.

The primacy of foreign policy

The key question to ask about imperial expansion is not so much how it was propelled from within as why no rival state was capable of preventing it. Since most European powers had something to fear from Russian aggrandisement, and some had everything to lose, why was the Russian steamroller allowed to build up so great a momentum that its advance came to be deemed inexorable? It was not for lack of vigilance, for the foreign envoys in St Petersburg could hardly have been more assiduous in their (usually unsuccessful) efforts to divine the intentions of the Russian court both by official and by covert means. Instead, Russian expansion owed more to the circumstance that at every critical juncture (or, as Lord Elgin put it, 'unlucky moment') its principal international rivals were temporarily either unwilling or unable to oppose it.

Russia was fortunate that its neighbours were distracted by mutual

---

[26] Quoted in C. Duffy, *Russia's Military Way to the West: Origins and Nature of Russian Military Power 1700–1800* (London, 1981), p. 216; translation and punctuation amended.

jealousies of their own. To the north and west, Poland competed with Sweden (in turn locked into rivalry with a third Baltic power, Denmark); to the south, Persia faced the Ottoman empire. The significant rivalry was that between Austria and Prussia. Neither could contemplate action against Russia knowing that failure would grant the other mastery in Germany. On the other hand, Austro-Prussian enmity prevented Russia from joining both: before the threat of Napoleon, the only way that the three Eastern powers could collaborate was by agreeing to carve up Poland. Guarding a frontier which eventually stretched from the Baltic to the Black Sea, Russia needed Prussian co-operation to secure the north and west; Austria was crucial in the south. Ideally, Russia would have kept a free hand between the two German powers, but such was its value as an ally that it was drawn into pacts with each in turn.

Important as these relationships were, international affairs were ultimately contingent upon fluctuating French power. France had traditionally exercised its influence in eastern Europe through intermediaries: the Swedes, the Poles, and the Turks. All three were Russia's neighbours; all three were its sworn enemies – Protestant, Catholic, and Muslim powers against whom Orthodox could legitimately crusade. At the close of the seventeenth century, when there seemed little prospect of any relaxation in Louis XIV's grip on the international system, the omens for Russian advance looked poor. With hindsight, however, we can see that the Sun King's dazzle was already a mirage and his successors inherited intractable domestic problems which, exacerbated by the expensive and ultimately humiliating attempt to dominate America as well as continental Europe, sent France into decline. The consequences for its satellites were severe. French impotence allowed Russia successively to eclipse Sweden's great power status, to dominate and partition Poland, and to annexe the Crimea in 1783. Western powers who expected revolution to cripple France's international ambitions were surprised when instead it inflamed them. Russia could not restrain revolutionary France, with which it was the last great power to go to war. But, within eastern Europe – the emergent sphere of influence over which France lost control after 1763 – Catherine the Great took advantage of the revolutionary wars to redraw the map to her own advantage. Napoleon once again placed Russia's international status in doubt. But its crucial part in his defeat in 1812–14 permitted a fitting end to a century of Russian expansion based on French weakness when Alexander I insisted on rehabilitating France as part of the new community of great powers that emerged from the congress of Aix-la-Chapelle in 1818. How had the tables been turned?

Sweden's dependence on French diplomatic protection was demonstrated in 1679, when the treaty of St Germain effectively nullified the Prussian victory at Fehrbellin four years earlier. In 1721, however, the French were no longer in a position to intervene on behalf of clients vanquished in the field. In the War of the Spanish Succession (1701–14), they had themselves been routed by the duke of Marlborough at Blenheim in 1704, a humiliation unprecedented in Louis XIV's reign, only to suffer further indignities at Ramillies in 1706 and Oudenarde in 1708. When the king died in 1715, leaving the throne to his young great-grandson, Louis XV, and France in the hands of a regent, French international power was already severely weakened. Since even the Swedes' new British allies were temporarily distracted by the South Sea Bubble crisis of 1720, Russia could dictate its terms at Nystad with relative impunity.

As if to signal impending French impotence in eastern Europe, Russia was now drawn into the international system by France's fiercest rival, Austria. Despite Charles VI's earlier presentiment that an alliance with Russia would bring Austria 'more evil than good',[27] Prince Eugene of Savoy persuaded him in 1726 of the virtues of a defensive pact which, renewed in 1746 and converted into an offensive alliance in 1757, remained the cornerstone of Russian foreign policy until 1762. The Austro-Russian alliance assuaged recurrent Habsburg fears that Russia might seek to destabilise their empire by stirring up the Orthodox subjects of Transylvania, Moldavia, and Transcarpathia, a notion sufficiently widely touted that Peter the Great, who never openly espoused it, had nevertheless felt obliged to deny it in 1711. More urgently, Austria gained a measure of insurance against the rival alliance of Herrenhausen, concluded by Britain, France, and Prussia in response to Charles's alliance with Spain in 1725. Since it was only in 1699 that the Austrians had withdrawn from the Christian pact against the Turks to conclude a separate peace at Karlowitz, the Russians were doubtless conscious that Vienna might prove a fickle partner (as indeed it did). But they nevertheless welcomed the alliance as a way of gaining time for internal consolidation after the exhausting Petrine wars and as protection against Britain and the Ottoman empire, the two powers most feared by Osterman.

The French, however, had yet to shoot their final bolt. Resurgent under Cardinal Fleury in the 1730s, they regained sufficient diplomatic influence to undo Russia's hard-fought victories in the Russo-Turkish war of 1735–9. The sight of 10,000 Russian soldiers on the Rhine,

---

[27] Quoted in K. A. Roider, Jr, *Austria's Eastern Question 1700–1790* (Princeton, 1982), p. 47.

when Russia came to Austria's aid during the War of the Polish Succession, had haunted Fleury with the spectre that Vienna might 'inundate Germany with barbarian troops'.[28] Once the Turks had been defeated – at the cost of more than 100,000 Russian lives – France intervened to protect them against aggrandisement by Russians who had again been abandoned by their Austrian allies. French mediation at the peace of Belgrade in September 1739 not only denied Russia access to the Black Sea, but also deprived it of all captured territory except Azov (where the fortress had been razed and was not to be rebuilt) and the cossack lands between Azov and the Dnestr. All the military might the Russians could muster had proved powerless in the face of a reassertion of French diplomatic pressure.

One can see why Frederick the Great should still have dismissed Russia, with Turkey, in 1746 as mere 'machines in European politics, which are made use of by France and England in case of necessity'.[29] Other powers were also reluctant to accept Russian pretensions. Not until 1742 did Britain and Austria formally agree to recognise the tsar's imperial title; France and Spain delayed a further three years. Versailles remained supercilious even then, excluding Russia from the negotiations at Aix-la-Chapelle in 1748 specifically on the grounds that it was but a mercenary power. Doubts lingered even after Kunersdorf. Sir George Macartney, appointed British resident in St Petersburg in 1765, argued in his *Account of the Russian Empire* in 1768 that, though 'no longer to be gazed at as a distant glimmering star', Russia remained no more than 'a great planet that had obtruded itself into our system, whose place was yet undetermined, but whose motions most powerfully affect those of every other orb'.[30] The most closely affected 'orbs' knew what he meant. Facing the prospect of Russian advances into the Danubian delta, Joseph II described Russia in 1768 as 'undoubtedly the most formidable Power in Europe', admitting a year later that 'we especially shall always have much to fear, and little to hope except that, pushed back behind her old frontiers, she will revert to us and again seek our alliance'.[31]

Russia formally abandoned ties with Austria in April 1764 when Frederick the Great, who had contemplated suicide after Kunersdorf, recovered sufficiently to inveigle the inexperienced Catherine II into a

---

[28] Quoted in Roider, *The Reluctant Ally: Austria's Policy in the Austro-Turkish War, 1737–1739* (Baton Rouge, LA, 1972), p. 120.

[29] Quoted in F. Meinecke, *Machiavellism: The Doctrine of Raison d'Etat and Its Place in Modern History*, tr. D. Scott (London, 1957), p. 332.

[30] Quoted in M. Roberts, 'Macartney in Russia', *EHR*, Supplement 7 (1974), p. 80.

[31] 'General picture of the affairs of the Monarchy', quoted in D. Beales, *Joseph II*, vol. I, *In the Shadow of Maria Theresa 1741–1780* (Cambridge, 1987), pp. 275, 281.

Russo-Prussian alliance by threatening an improbable deal with the Turk.[32] In the same year, Frederick helped Catherine to instal her former lover, Stanislas Poniatowski, as king of the Poles, a move which confirmed French impotence in eastern Europe in the aftermath of its defeat at Rossbach. But Stanislas proved less pliant than Catherine anticipated, and Russian attempts to intimidate the reforming Polish Diet of 1767–8 in turn provoked resistance from the confederation of Bar. When Russian troops in pursuit of confederate insurgents crossed the Ottoman border, the Porte declared war. This was an eventuality not covered by the incomplete defensive 'Northern System' of alliances planned by Count N. I. Panin, Russian foreign minister in all but name from 1763 to 1781. Against southern incursion, the Danish alliance of 1765 was useless; the British, traditionally indifferent to Poland and now entering a period of isolation, had deliberately remained aloof. Panin's authority was never the same again.

Russian progress against the Turk raised the spectre of a war involving all three Eastern powers. With the aim of defusing that danger and limiting Russian gains, Frederick proposed a tripartite partition of Poland, effected in August 1772. Knowing that France was powerless to object, Austria was reluctantly drawn in. Catherine, however, showed no signs of being sated and continued to push southwards. French intervention was deterred by British threats motivated more by hostility to France than any partiality for Russia, with whom negotiations for an alliance had once again recently broken down. At the treaty of Kutchuk-Kainardzhii in July 1774 the Russians not only gained land in the Caucasus and between the Bug and Dnepr, but were confirmed in their possession of Azov where they were at last allowed to rebuild the fort. The logic of Russian foreign policy, swivelled towards the south, now led back to co-operation with the Austrians, who, anxious for support against Prussia, concluded a secret alliance in 1781. When, two years later, this pact was used to underwrite the annexation of the Crimea, its revelation stunned French ministers who, distracted by their commitment to the War of American Independence (1775–83), had legitimately expected their Austrian allies to support their own opposition to further Russian gains at Turkish expense.

Debilitated by financial crisis, the French – who had already had to accept Catherine as joint arbiter of the German lands at the peace of Teschen in 1779 – now sought to join those they could not beat by developing trading links with Russia. The Franco-Russian commercial

---

[32] A good story well told by H. M. Scott, 'Frederick II, the Ottoman Empire and the Origins of the Russo-Prussian Alliance of April 1764', *European Studies Review*, 7 (1977), pp. 153–75.

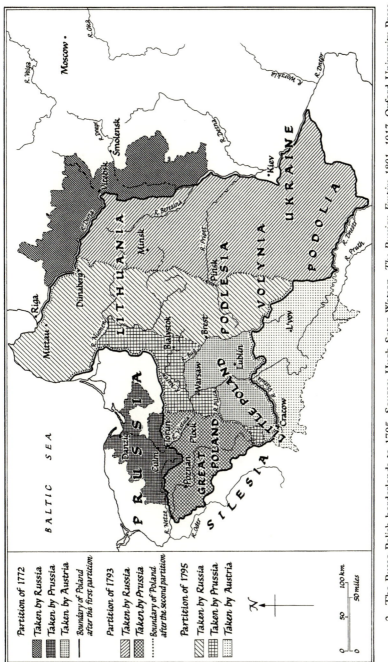

2 The Russo-Polish borderlands to 1795. Source: Hugh Seton-Watson, *The Russian Empire 1801–1917*, Oxford University Press, 1967, p. 772.

treaty of 1787 hit Britain harder than it hit Turkey. Having missed opportunities to ally with Russia in the 1760s and early 1770s, the British had been irritated by Catherine's armed neutrality of 1780, an anglophobic bid by the neutral states to defend their freedom of the seas in the American war. In the light of the Franco-Russian rapprochement and Russian conquests against the Turk in 1788–9, Britain became increasingly hostile. Its ultimate attempt to restrain Russian expansion came in March 1791, when, buoyed by his success in facing down the Spanish at Nootka Sound in 1790, Pitt once again tried to extract concessions by threatening war over Ochakov. The prime minister wanted Russia to return to the *status quo ante bellum*, as Britain had been responsible for forcing Austria to do at the convention of Reichenbach in July 1790.[33] This time, lacking domestic and international support, he had to back down. The British, it transpired, were no more powerful in eastern Europe than the French.

The settlement of the Turkish war on Catherine's terms at Jassy allowed her to turn her attentions to Poland, where Russian control had been challenged by the reforming four-year Diet summoned in 1788. Had it ever been implemented, the constitution of 3 May 1791 would have established a hereditary monarchy owing something to English-style checks and balances.[34] It was not so much these as the prospect of a rejuvenated neighbour that Catherine found intolerable. Whereas in the 1760s Russia had ostensibly intervened to defend Polish religious 'Dissidents', it now acted on the pretext of protecting the confederation of Targowica, a noble front for Russian interests which, much to the Poles' chagrin, promptly received papal blessing. Since France had declared war on Austria at the end of April 1792, Russian troops had a free path into Poland in May. But Targowica proved a weak reed and in April 1793, Catherine pushed through the second partition, this time shared with Prussia alone. Humiliated at Ochakov, Britain could hardly object. In any case it, like Austria, was now anxious to keep Prussia in a coalition to restrain French aggression. By contrast, it was the vain hope of persuading Prussia to abandon the coalition which 'tempted France to acquiesce in that unholy transaction'.[35] Provoked by Kosciuszko's Polish rising, which was mercilessly suppressed by Suvorov, all three

---

[33] The latest study of Reichenbach, reappraising a neglected work by Pavel Mitrofanov (1873–1917), is T. C. W. Blanning, 'An Old But New Biography of Leopold II', in Blanning and D. Cannadine, eds., *History and Biography: Essays in Honour of Derek Beales* (Cambridge, 1996), pp. 61–70.

[34] See R. Butterwick, *Poland's Last King and English Culture: Stanisław August Poniatowski 1732–1798* (Oxford, 1998), pp. 275–309.

[35] R. H. Lord, *The Second Partition of Poland: A Study in Diplomatic History* (Cambridge, MA, 1915), p. 447.

Eastern powers embarked on the complex negotiations that led to the third and final partition in 1795.

Catherine II had made Russia dominant in eastern Europe only by acknowledging its limitations in the West. Russia took no active part in the first anti-revolutionary coalition formed in 1793. When Tsar Paul withdrew the troops finally committed by his mother in 1796, it was unclear what international rôle Russia might play. In one sense peace offered a free hand; in another it threatened isolation. Like the 1730s, the late 1790s showed that Russia's great power status did not develop in linear fashion. Even when Paul did join the second coalition against France in 1798, his attempts to cut a figure in Europe were disastrous. Prompted not by the tsar's aversion to republicanism but by the menace of unchecked French expansion to Russian interests in Poland and the Mediterranean, intervention itself was rational enough. Yet Paul's subsequent conduct left much to be desired. Confusing the other powers' utility to Russia with their attitude to his own ambitions as grand master of the Knights of Malta, Paul not only concluded an improbable alliance with the Turk but alienated first Austria and then Britain, a move which automatically pushed him towards rapprochement with the French, never a natural position for states that shared so few common interests. Anyone who doubts the power of the monarch as late as 1800 might recall Schroeder's assessment of the tsar's personally directed foreign policy:

By the time Paul was assassinated, he had pushed Russia into open war with Britain, caused Denmark, Sweden and North Germany to be menaced by the British fleet, brought about the paralysis of Prussian and Russian maritime trade, threatened Russia's own fleet, compromised Russia's moral and political position in Europe, helped Napoleon expand at will in the West and South, and sent Russian troops on a mad expedition into Central Asia – all for no concrete Russian interest.[36]

In view of the mess he inherited, Alexander I's desire to withdraw from the war was not so much an option as a necessity. He duly made peace with Napoleon in late September 1801. Russia's restricted position made a mockery of the tsar's wider ambitions to confer peace on Europe. In 1803, his young friend Czartoryski, appointed deputy foreign minister in the following year, spoke grandly of the need for 'a union of Slav peoples' to offset French expansion and restore his native Poland. Other powers looked up to Russia, he claimed: let it play its part.[37] In reality Russia was confined to a secondary rôle in Europe.

---

[36] Schroeder, *Transformation of European Politics*, p. 220.

[37] P. K. Grimsted, 'Czartoryski's System for Russian Foreign Policy, 1803: A Memorandum', *California Slavic Studies*, 5 (1970), pp. 19–91, glossed by W. H. Zawadzki, *A*

Before Tilsit all it could do was tinker in the Ionian islands and the Balkans in an attempt to restrict French expansion; after Tilsit it played second fiddle to Napoleon. Only his defeat restored Russia's moral and political authority. Both, indeed, were transformed. As Clausewitz concluded: 1812 'was a vast success; and it cost the Russians a price in blood and perils that for any other country would have been higher still, and which most could not have paid at all'.[38] It remained to be seen whether it was a price that Russia could afford.

The consequences of imperial expansion

Rulers faced two ways of governing multi-ethnic territories: they could either follow a policy of ruthless integration in pursuit of unitary state power, or instead seek to conciliate minorities by tolerating a degree of cultural and religious diversity and by incorporating local élites into a power structure which respected their privileges in return for loyalty to the imperial dynasty. The ultimate early-modern *étatiste* was Joseph II, whose passion for homogeneity foundered on the inherent complexity of his empire. It simply proved impossible to bind territories ranging from Belgium to Bohemia and from Tuscany to Transylvania into a single, uniform whole. Although faced with fewer constitutional tangles and hereditary privileges than the Habsburgs, the tsars were more patient. Persuaded by cameralist ideas, they made no secret of the fact that regularity and uniformity were their ultimate goal; the privileges they granted to the non-Russians were always intended to be temporary. But, recognising that the passive quiescence (and preferably active collaboration) of these ethnic minorities was a precondition of state security in the borderlands, they persevered with the cautious policies that had served their Muscovite predecessors so well. Military conquest was followed by gradual economic absorption and administrative incorporation; only fitfully were religious and cultural penetration attempted.

Peter the Great's reign signalled a major departure from tradition. Muslim Volga Tatars, Buddhist Kalmyk nomads, and a variety of Siberian natives were threatened with loss of land and even death if they refused to embrace Orthodoxy. Not until Catherine II, impressed by the fertility of the Islamic population, reverted to collaboration with the Tatar élite were the Muslims allowed to rebuild mosques closed during conversion campaigns begun in 1735. As governor of Astrakhan', the rapacious Volynskii abandoned the Muscovite policy of collaboration

Man of Honour: Adam Czartoryski as a Statesman of Russia and Poland 1795–1831 (Oxford, 1993), pp. 61–91.
[38] Clausewitz, *On War*, tr. and ed. M. Howard and P. Paret (Princeton, 1976), p. 616.

with central Kalmyk authority and instead sought to divide and rule – 'to restrain the ungrateful Kalmyk people', as he later explained to Catherine I.[39] Alarmed by the revolt of the Don cossack *ataman* (headman), Kondratii Bulavin, in 1707–8, Peter also began the long process of integration that was completed only in 1836. In 1721 the Don cossack host was subordinated to the college of war and from 1723 its chiefs were to be appointed by the tsar. Further west, Aleksei Mikhailovich had started to lean on Ukrainian institutions soon after *hetman* Bogdan Khmel'nitskii swore fealty to him at the treaty of Pereiaslavl' in 1654: the Kievan metropolitanate was subordinated to the Moscow patriarchate in 1686, and the *hetman*'s autonomy in foreign policy was severely restricted. *Hetman* Ivan Mazepa's defection to Charles XII (see chapter 7) prompted a concerted attempt by Peter I to emasculate the hetmanate. After Poltava, a resident Russian minister was appointed with powers to scrutinise the *hetman*'s correspondence; then the establishment of the Little Russian College (Malorossiiskaia kollegiia) in 1722 signalled a move towards institutional integration.

However, even as he attacked Ukrainian autonomy, Peter guaranteed between 1710 and 1712 the privileges of the Lutheran church and the urban corporations in the Baltic lands, and gave the élite *Ritter* greater autonomy under Russian rule than they had enjoyed under Sweden. German was retained as the language of administration and justice. The Russians' position here was weaker than in Ukraine (where they could claim, however controversially, to inherit the legacy of Kievan Rus'), and among Germans the tsars encountered the kind of corporate privilege that did not exist among Slavs and heathen. But it was not merely the strength of opposing forces that prompted Peter to handle the Baltic knights with kid gloves. Their institutions seemed worth preserving as an example to be imitated; their superior administrative and technical expertise gave them an entrée into government circles in St Petersburg; and their presence in the capital generated a lobby powerful out of all proportion to its relatively small size. Estonia and Livonia retained separate administrations until 1775, when Baltic models helped to shape Catherine the Great's provincial reform. Governed jointly until 1801, when Alexander I created the office of governor-general for all three Baltic provinces following the formal incorporation of Courland at the third partition of Poland, the Baltic lands had their autonomy reduced in 1783 when Catherine introduced the poll tax and restricted corporate privileges. Yet most of these were restored by her son in 1796

---

[39] Quoted in M. Khodarkovsky, *Where Two Worlds Met: The Russian State and the Kalmyk Nomads, 1600–1771* (Ithaca, NY, 1992), p. 183.

and the Baltic Germans remained throughout our period the most privileged non-Russians in the empire.

Elsewhere, Peter's successors had reverted to his predecessors' caution, without losing sight of their ultimate centralising goal. Sedentarisation impoverished the steppe nomads in the Russians' favour; cultural differences continued to ensure that non-Russian leaders misunderstood Russian intentions. Abulkhair, khan of the Kazakh little horde, took the oath of allegiance to Anna in 1731 in order to strengthen his authority over his own people, extend it over the middle horde, and gain trading and grazing privileges on the Russian frontier. But he soon discovered that his own conception of personal vassalage (which might be abandoned if the tsar failed to protect him) was not shared by Russians who interpreted his oath as submission to their state authority. Ukrainian *hetmen* had earlier made the same mistake. Their own position reached crisis point when an ill-judged attempt to exploit the position of *hetman* Kyril Razumovskii, a supporter of Catherine II's coup, in the cause of greater Ukrainian autonomy was answered by the abolition of the hetmanate in October 1764. After a period of cautious reform, the Ukraine was fully integrated into the Russian system of local government by Governor-General P. A. Rumiantsev in 1782. There was little resistance. The gentry willingly joined St Petersburg's imperial élite, co-opted by a patronage network dominated by A. A. Bezborodko and P. V. Zavadovskii, both appointed as Catherine's secretaries on Rumiantsev's recommendation in 1775. Across the empire, a combination of stealth and flexibility had culminated in successful élite integration personified by Osip (Otto Heinrich) Igelström, proconsul of Orenburg from 1784 to 1791: 'A Baltic baron with a Swedish name bringing order and Russian civilisation to restless nomads at the gates of Asia and assisted in his task by the senior commandant of Orenburg with the Tatar name of Iakov Zembulatov, major-general in the Russian army'.[40]

The same philosophy persisted in the nineteenth century, exemplified by Alexander I's generous treatment of the Finns, who were allowed to rejoin Old Finland to the remainder of the grand duchy in 1811, and the Poles, who were granted a constitution in 1815. But there was ultimately a price to pay. The Russian people, who comprised just under half the imperial population by 1834, became increasingly disenchanted with the only empire where the interests of the dominant nationality appeared to have been subordinated to those of foreign minority élites. When forced to choose between native peasants and the cosmopolitan nobility

---

[40] J. P. LeDonne, *Ruling Russia: Politics and Administration in the Age of Absolutism, 1762–1796* (Princeton, 1984), p. 285.

or between the Russian church and its heterodox rivals, the tsars always opted for imperial security. Now that the empire has fallen apart, the ultimate consequences of the tension between territorial (*rossiiskii*) and ethnic (*russkii*) forms of Russian national identity are obvious. The full implications of that tension emerged only when most of Russia's rivals had become what it has never been – a modern nation-state. But they were implicit in everything the eighteenth-century empire did.

How, then, should we understand imperial expansion in relation to two key features of Russian historical development, autocracy and backwardness? The standard explanation is russophobic. According to a prominent champion of the Poles, internal inadequacy was the root *cause* of pathological Russian expansion: 'Here, if ever, was an extreme case of *bulimia politica*, of the so-called "canine-hunger", of gross territorial obesity in an organism which could only survive by consuming more and more of its neighbours' flesh and blood.' Standing this argument on its head, the russophile Geoffrey Hosking has recently insisted that autocracy and backwardness must be seen as *symptoms* of imperial expansion: 'The effort required to mobilise revenues and raise armies for the needs of the empire entailed the subjection of virtually the whole population, but especially the Russians, to the demands of state service, and thus enfeebled the creation of the community associations which commonly provided the basis for the civic sense of nationhood', whilst 'the economic policies deemed necessary to sustain the empire systematically held back the entrepreneurial and productive potentialities of the mass of the people'.[41] Guided by this latter interpretation, let us begin by examining Russia's response to the requirements of spiralling military expenditure.

BIBLIOGRAPHICAL NOTE

The important synthesis by J. P. LeDonne, *The Russian Empire and the World 1700–1917: The Geopolitics of Expansion and Containment* (Oxford, 1997), overplays a strong geopolitical hand. H. M. Scott, 'Russia as a European Great Power', in R. P. Bartlett and J. M. Hartley, eds., *Russia in the Age of the Enlightenment* (London, 1990), concentrates on Catherine II, as does H. Ragsdale, 'Evaluating the Traditions of Russian Aggression: Catherine II and the Greek Project', *SEER*, 66 (1988). J. D. Klier, *Russia Gathers Her Jews: The Origins of the 'Jewish Question' in Russia, 1772–1825* (DeKalb, IL, 1986), examines a consequence of Polish partition. Starting points on Siberia include W. B. Lincoln, *The*

---

[41] Davies, *Europe: A History*, p. 655; G. Hosking, *Russia: People and Empire 1552–1917* (London, 1997), pp. xxiv, xxvii.

Conquest of a Continent: Siberia and the Russians (London, 1994), and J. Forsyth, *A History of the Peoples of Siberia: Russia's North Asian Colony 1581–1990* (Cambridge, 1992), the latter overtly sympathetic to the non-Russians. More original is M. Bassin: 'Expansionism and Colonialism on the Eastern Frontier: Views of Siberia and the Far East in Pre-Petrine Russia', *Journal of Historical Geography*, 14 (1988), and 'Inventing Siberia: Visions of the Russian East in the Early Nineteenth Century', *AHR*, 96 (1991).

Wider military contexts are sketched by M. S. Anderson, *War and Society in Europe of the Old Regime, 1618–1789* (London, 1988), and H. Strachan, *European Armies in Conflict* (London, 1983). Three major books are J. L. H. Keep, *Soldiers of the Tsar: Army and Society in Russia, 1462–1874* (Oxford, 1985); D. Beyrau, *Militär und Gesellschaft* (Cologne, 1984); and W. C. Fuller, Jr, *Strategy and Power in Russia 1600–1914* (New York, 1992), a particularly stimulating work. See also W. M. Pintner, 'Russia's Military Style, Russian Society and Russian Power in the Eighteenth Century', in A. G. Cross, ed., *Russia and the West in the Eighteenth Century* (Newtonville, MA, 1983), and Pintner, 'The Burden of Defense in Imperial Russia, 1725–1914', *RR*, 43 (1984). Among more specialised studies, R. Hellie, *Enserfment and Military Change in Muscovy* (Chicago, 1971), may be supplemented by C. B. Stevens, *Soldiers on the Steppe: Army Reform and Social Change in Early Modern Russia* (DeKalb, IL, 1995). R. Hellie, 'The Petrine Army: Continuity, Change, and Impact', *CASS*, 8 (1974), retains its value. J. L. H. Keep, 'Feeding the Troops: Russian Army Supply Policies During the Seven Years War', *CSP*, 29 (1987), is of general significance. J. P. LeDonne, 'Outlines of Military Administration 1762–1796', *JfGO*, 31 (1983), 33 (1985), and 34 (1986), inspired by a study of Roman strategy, is invaluable for its imperial perspective. Also useful are B. Menning, 'Russian Military Innovation in the Second Half of the Eighteenth Century', *War and Society*, 2 (1984); Menning, 'A. I. Chernyshev: A Russian Lycurgus', *CSP*, 30 (1988); and V. Aksan, 'The One-Eyed Fighting the Blind: Mobilization, Supply and Command in the Russo-Turkish War of 1768–1774', *International History Review*, 15 (1993). P. Longworth, *The Art of Victory: The Life and Achievements of Generalissimo Suvorov* (London, 1965), is excellent. On the impact of Napoleon, see L. G. Beskrovnyi, *Russkaia armiia i flot v XIX veke: voenno-ekonomicheskii potentsial Rossii* (Moscow, 1973), and the two-part article by J. M. Hartley, 'Russia in 1812', *JfGO*, 38 (1990).

On the fleet, see E. J. Phillips, *The Founding of Russia's Navy: Peter the Great and the Azov Fleet, 1688–1714* (Westport, CT, 1995); M. S. Anderson, 'Great Britain and the Russian Fleet, 1769–1770', *SEER*, 31

(1952); and A. Bode, *Die Flottenpolitik Katharinas II. und die Konflikte mit Schweden und der Türkei (1768–1792)* (Munich, 1979). A. Cross, *By the Banks of the Neva: Chapters from the Lives and Careers of the British in Eighteenth-Century Russia* (Cambridge, 1997), traces the British contribution. For clarity of detailed factual exposition, R. C. Anderson, *Naval Wars in the Levant 1559–1853*, 2nd edn (Liverpool, 1952), and his *Naval Wars in the Baltic 1522–1850*, 2nd edn (London, 1969), are hard to beat.

The outstanding survey of international relations is D. McKay and H. M. Scott, *The Rise of the Great Powers 1648–1815* (London, 1983). On the relationship between the rise of Russia and the decline of France, see T. C. W. Blanning, *The Origins of the French Revolutionary Wars* (London, 1986). P. P. Cherkasov, *Dvuglavyi orel i korolevskie lilii: stanovlenie russko-frantsuzskikh otnoshenii v XVIII veke 1700–1775* (Moscow, 1995), is a workmanlike chronicle, unfortunately unaware of Western scholarship since 1955. L. J. Oliva, *Misalliance: A Study of French Policy in Russia During the Seven Years War* (New York, 1964), shows why the Franco-Russian rapprochement lapsed; H. M. Scott, 'France and the Polish Throne, 1763–1764', *SEER*, 53 (1975), helps to explain the two powers' customary hostility. Scott's *British Foreign Policy in the Age of the American Revolution* (Oxford, 1990) is authoritative on 1763–83. I. de Madariaga, *Britain, Russia and the Armed Neutrality of 1780: Sir James Harris's Mission to St Petersburg During the American Revolution* (London, 1962), is of general significance. W. Mediger, *Moskaus Weg nach Europa: der Aufstieg Russlands zum europäischen Machtstaat im Zeitalter Friedrichs des Grossen* (Braunschweig, 1952), is unmatched on the middle of the eighteenth century. M. S. Anderson, *The Eastern Question* (London, 1966), seems unlikely soon to be superseded. On Austria, see A. V. Florovsky, 'Russo-Austrian Conflicts in the Early Eighteenth Century', *SEER*, 47 (1969); H. L. Dyck, 'Pondering the Russian Fact: Kaunitz and the Catherinian Empire in the 1770s', *CSP*, 22 (1980); and I. de Madariaga, 'The Secret Austro-Russian Treaty of 1781', *SEER*, 38 (1959–60). S. P. Oakley, *War and Peace in the Baltic, 1560–1790* (London, 1992), tells a complex story clearly. Synoptic articles include H. A. Barton, 'Russia and the Problem of Sweden–Finland, 1721–1809', *East European Quarterly*, 5 (1971); and H. Bagger, 'The Role of the Baltic in Russian Foreign Policy, 1721–1773', in H. Ragsdale, ed., *Imperial Russian Foreign Policy* (Cambridge, 1993), an important collection. In the absence of a study of Russo-Polish relations, see J. Lukowski, *Liberty's Folly: The Polish-Lithuanian Commonwealth in the Eighteenth Century, 1697–1795* (London, 1991); on the early period, see L. R. Lewitter, 'Russia, Poland

and the Baltic, 1697–1721', *HJ*, 11 (1968). A. Zamoyski, *The Last King of Poland* (London, 1992), is appropriately elegant and elegiac. B. H. Sumner, *Peter the Great and the Ottoman Empire* (Oxford, 1949), is unsurpassed. Aspects of Catherine II's relations with the Turk are covered by R. Davison, ' "Russian Skill and Turkish Imbecility": The Treaty of Kutchuk Kainardji Reconsidered', *SR*, 35 (1976), and A. W. Fisher, *The Russian Annexation of the Crimea* (Cambridge, 1970). N. E. Saul, *Russia and the Mediterranean 1797–1807* (Chicago, 1970), and M. Atkin, *Russia and Iran 1780–1828* (Minneapolis, 1980), remain standard.

With Hosking (above, n. 41), A. Kappeler's study of the non-Russians' rôle in the empire, *Russland als Vielvölkerreich: Entstehung, Geschichte, Zerfall* (Munich, 1992), ranks among the best recent books on Russian history. On Ukraine, see O. Subtelny, 'Russia and the Ukraine: The Difference that Peter I Made', *RR*, 39 (1980); and Z. E. Kohut, *Russian Centralism and Ukrainian Autonomy: Imperial Absorption of the Hetmanate 1760s–1830s* (Cambridge, MA, 1988), summarised in Kohut's chapter in M. Greengrass, ed., *Conquest and Coalescence: The Shaping of the State in Early Modern Europe* (London, 1991). A crucial topic is outlined by B. W. Menning, 'The Emergence of a Military-Administrative Elite in the Don Cossack Land, 1708–1836', in W. M. Pintner and D. K. Rowney, eds., *Russian Officialdom: The Bureaucratization of Russian Society from the Seventeenth to the Twentieth Century* (London, 1980). E. C. Thaden, *Russia's Western Borderlands, 1710–1870* (Princeton, 1984), is a fine synthesis. W. H. McNeill, *Europe's Steppe Frontier, 1500–1800* (Chicago, 1962), A. S. Donnelly, *The Russian Conquest of Bashkiria, 1552–1740* (New Haven, CT, 1968), and A. Bodger, 'Abulkhair, Khan of the Kazakh Little Horde and His Oath of Allegiance to Russia of October 1731', *SEER*, 58 (1980), explore the southern frontier. M. Rywkin, ed., *Russian Colonial Expansion to 1917* (London, 1988), and the more stimulating D. Brower and E. J. Lazzerini, eds., *Russia's Orient: Imperial Borderlands and Peoples 1700–1917* (Bloomington, IN, 1997), concentrate on Islam. M. Khodarkovsky, ' "Not by Word Alone": Missionary Policies and Religious Conversion in Early Modern Russia', *CSSH*, 38 (1996), covers a subject also broached by Y. Slezkine, *Arctic Mirrors: Russia and the Small Peoples of the North* (Ithaca, NY, 1994), who takes their story into the twentieth century.

3   Finance and taxation

'If there is one thing about kings', remarked Sir John Hicks in a masterly essay on the finances of the sovereign, 'it is that more often than not they were hard up.'[1] As we shall see, the Russian crown's fiscal embarrassment owed most to the rising costs of international rivalry, which, as elsewhere in Europe, surpassed the resources provided by impoverished agrarian economies and by populations resentful of the imposition of regular taxation. It was long commonplace to rank the former obstacle as the more daunting. 'No king can be rich, nor glorious, nor secure', warned Hobbes in *Leviathan* (1651), 'whose Subjects are either poore, or contemptible, or too weak through want, or dissention, to maintain a war against their enemies.'[2] A century or so later, Quesnay emphatically concurred: '*POOR PEASANTS, A POOR KINGDOM*'.[3] Historians once echoed this sentiment. But their observation that economic progress offered no guarantee of increased revenue has recently persuaded them to focus instead on attempts to establish flexible ways of tapping existing wealth. This chapter follows their example.

Muscovite taxation

What little we know about Muscovite finances can be thrown into relief by comparisons with Britain and France, where, in different ways, money became a crucial political and constitutional issue. For the Tudors and Stuarts, who operated a relatively cheap and reliable, centralised collection mechanism from the time of Henry VIII, the difficulty lay in securing Parliamentary consent to direct taxation which they wanted to convert from extraordinary wartime subsidies to a permanent tool of peacetime policy. On the one hand, debates over the monarch's right to tax without consent stimulated treatises on the limits

[1] J. Hicks, *A Theory of Economic History* (Oxford, 1969), p. 81.
[2] Hobbes, *Leviathan*, ed. C. B. Macpherson (Harmondsworth, 1968), p. 242 (ch. XIX).
[3] Quoted in C. B. A. Behrens, *Society, Government and the Enlightenment: The Experiences of Eighteenth-Century France and Prussia* (London, 1985), p. 134.

of their subjects' political obligations (not least *Leviathan* itself). On the other hand, consent, once granted, helped to disarm public opposition. By contrast, the French crown never persuaded its subjects that regular peacetime taxation was not an infringement of their liberties. As James Collins has shown, without the collaboration of tax-farmers who had purchased their offices, the kings of France would scarcely have been able to collect taxes at all. Yet by promoting venality in the seventeenth century, the crown unwittingly impeded its own attempts to modernise the system in the eighteenth, for, whilst the revenue collection of rival powers became increasingly bureaucratic, French finances remained a business in private hands.[4] Since neither the Bourbons nor the Tudors and Stuarts could meet their expenditure from regular income, each sought to borrow. But because only the most sophisticated governments (the Netherlands was in the vanguard) managed to carry forward a long-term debt without risking bankruptcy, others relied instead on unpopular short-term forced loans. Many a profligate monarch, teetering on the brink of financial collapse, might, like James VI and I of Scotland and England, have regarded money as his Achilles' heel.

By contrast, we can be fairly sure that the tsars, while never sanguine about money, came under severe fiscal pressure only in the middle of the seventeenth century. Until then, provided that the purposes of government remained limited and that Muscovy avoided expensive competition with the West, they could usually supply their needs from their own private domains, and from a relatively primitive taxation system that relied on two components: direct taxation on land farmed by the peasantry, and indirect taxation on consumption (principally of salt and alcohol) collected by townsmen. Like the kings of France, the tsars found that tax assessment and collection required a degree of collaboration with their wealthiest subjects – ritually expressed (some would say actually negotiated) in the periodic deliberations of the Assembly of the Land (Zemskii sobor) which spent much of its time on financial affairs. Unlike the Bourbons, however, the tsars succeeded in retaining a crucial measure of control.

Although they continued to grant concessions in periods of turbulence, ceding specific immunities and a greater measure of control over collection – possibly to laymen and definitely to landowning monasteries which had survived a sixteenth-century assault by ecclesiastical 'non-possessors' – these concessions remained a flexible political tool, fluctuating according to the relative strength of the ruler. They never became

---

[4] See J. B. Collins, *The Fiscal Limits of Absolutism: Direct Taxation in Early Seventeenth-Century France* (Berkeley, CA, 1988), and W. Doyle, *Venality: The Sale of Offices in Eighteenth-Century France* (Oxford, 1996).

enshrined in rigid corporate or regional privilege and they could always be withdrawn if necessary. In the end, most monasteries did indeed surrender their immunities to Patriarch Filaret, when Tsar Michael, in 1625, granted him financial control of a large swathe of church properties (the so-called patriarchal domains) along with the right to review existing concessions.

Not even the introduction of tax-farming (*otkup*) for customs and highway tolls in 1556 dented the crown's authority. Farming remained an option until September 1682, widely used, except in the north, for the collection of urban tavern monies which became an important feature of indirect taxation from the reign of Boris Godunov (1598–1605). However, for reasons which remain obscure, farming oscillated with an alternative – the system of collection 'on trust' (*na veru*) by sworn elected officials (*tseloval'niki*, renamed *burmistry* after Peter I's Ratusha reform of 1699). Fragmentary evidence makes it hard to generalise. But it is striking that, though the operation was not well monitored, tax-farmers failed to exploit it in their own interests. From the middle of the seventeenth century, French farmers-general not only built up fortunes large enough to make them money-lenders to the crown, but also gained sufficient influence to make them effectively a state within a state by the 1780s. By contrast, most Muscovite tax farmers, far from ranking among the tsar's most powerful subjects, were middling merchants content with a relatively modest degree of financial security.

One reason for their political passivity lay in the crown's lasting ability to resort to force. It was partly by virtue of their position as tribute collectors to the Mongol khans that the Muscovite grand princes had been able to dominate seemingly more powerful rivals in the fourteenth century. Once the Golden Horde had been repelled, Muscovy maintained or adapted for its own benefit methods of collection learned from its conqueror. That is why so much modern Russian financial vocabulary – including the words for money, treasury, and customs – derives from Mongol terminology. So long as crude but effective Asiatic techniques could satisfy their needs, tsars convinced by the calculus of minimum effort saw no reason to pay the increased overheads that would have been required by attempts to improve their revenue collection. *In extremis*, as Hellie has pointed out, they simply refused to pay their debts.[5]

By 1645, however, such methods no longer met the needs of a government obliged to support a newly reformed army and contemplating the

[5] Everything Richard Hellie has written is sensitive to fiscal issues: see, especially, his *Enserfment and Military Change in Muscovy* (Chicago, 1971).

extension of its public responsibilities. New fiscal techniques were now required, and they could not be introduced without controversy. B. I. Morozov's levy on salt, decreed in February 1646, had such an adverse effect on consumption that it had to be withdrawn in December 1647. Direct taxation was increased in compensation. But Aleksei Mikhailovich found that by purchasing political stability in return for grants of land, his predecessors had inadvertently contributed to a growing division between, on the one hand, the urban settlements (*posady*) and free communities of tax-paying peasants (known as black people, *chernye liudi*) to the north of Moscow, and, on the other hand, a growing body of private estates to the south, whose owners evaded tax by falsely claiming that their peasants were too poor to pay.

Though the dimensions of this division remain uncertain – Miliukov's claim that the north eventually paid forty times more tax than the centre may well be an exaggeration – its impact is not in doubt. Once urban taxpayers signalled their resentment at their increasing burden in the Moscow rebellion of 1648, the tsars became as frustrated as other early-modern rulers by their inability to draw effectively upon resources to which in theory they had unrestricted access. They, too, discovered the limitations of a land tax which not only underassessed the rich but endangered agriculture by tempting peasants to cultivate a smaller acreage. Worse still, they found that the household tax, which replaced the land tax as the basis of direct taxation in September 1679, merely stimulated more elaborate evasion as peasants merged their households in order to reduce their burden. Though the government responded by taxing in terms of the highest number of households ever recorded, often that of 1678, even this subterfuge was not enough. In all probability, Muscovy relied on indirect taxation throughout the seventeenth century. Hellie calculates that it supplied about 45 per cent of income in the 1680s by comparison with 34 per cent from direct taxation. LeDonne's analysis of the estimated revenue budget suggests that, by 1701, the balance had slipped further, allowing for only 20 per cent of revenue from direct taxation, half the contribution of indirect taxation.

As LeDonne has pointed out, our own distinction between direct taxes (taxes on wealth or income paid straight to the treasury) and indirect taxes (taxes on consumption transmitted to the treasury by an intermediary) is in some ways anachronistic when applied to early-modern Russia. It made more sense to contemporaries to distinguish instead between taxes that could be expected to yield a fixed amount (*okladnye*) and those that could not (*neokladnye*). In the case of indeterminate indirect taxes, the problem lay not so much in taxing the consumer as in regulating the agent. But if the tsar always received less than his subjects paid, corruption probably did no more to deplete his income than the contradictions inherent in a system which had developed so haphazardly that each new tax risked reducing the revenue from a welter of existing imposts. Neither corruption nor confusion was easy to detect, still less to remedy, whilst so many central chancelleries retained some financial function. Miliukov counted thirty-five chancelleries authorised to collect funds in the 1680s. Since none showed its accounts to the others, incipient attempts at state budgeting foundered on administrative fragmentation. Small wonder that Kliuchevskii concluded that finance had become 'probably the sorest spot in the Muscovite state order'.[6]

War and financial modernisation, 1700–1762

Whereas his predecessors had campaigned only intermittently, Peter I was almost continuously committed to war between 1695 and 1723, and it was this semi-permanent state of conflict, much of it against advanced Western rivals, that did most to expose Muscovite financial inadequacy. Because states calculated their revenue and expenditure in different ways, precise comparisons are impossible. Even figures for a single country are open to interpretation. Clearly, however, war was the greatest drain on the resources of every European state in 1700, including those usually regarded as 'unmilitarised'. According to Brewer, current military expenditure between 1689 and 1713 accounted for around 70 per cent of Britain's total annual outlay. LeDonne calculates that Russia spent 51.5 per cent of its total on the military in 1701 and 70.4 per cent in 1724. Between these years, the military budget was not only larger – regularly between 80 and 85 per cent, and over 96 per cent of total expenditure in 1705 according to Miliukov's rather different estimates – but the proportion this represented of gross national income must have been markedly greater than that supported by Britain's more advanced economy.[7] Since armies were costly by virtue of their size, and navies by virtue of the many specialised skills required to construct men-of-war (technologically the most advanced eighteenth-century military hardware), expenditure on a grand scale was unavoidable once Russia competed to join the great powers.

Where was the money to come from? Rivals, more experienced in

---

[6] V. O. Kliuchevsky, *A Course in Russian History: The Seventeenth Century*, tr. N. Duddington, intro. A. J. Rieber (Armonk, NY, 1994), p. 229.

[7] J. Brewer, *The Sinews of Power: War, Money and the English State, 1688–1783* (London, 1989), pp. 37–42, esp. p. 40, table 2.2; J. P. LeDonne, *Absolutism and Ruling Class: The Formation of the Russian Political Order, 1700–1825* (Oxford, 1991), pp. 276–7, table 15.1. I owe much to these two important books.

efficient revenue collection, supplemented their income by loans from the capital markets of London and Amsterdam, which had largely replaced declining Italian cities at the heart of international finance. In theory, Western governments could choose whether to borrow or whether to tax. But since only credit-worthy states could raise loans at affordable rates, and a sound regular income was the sole means of servicing the debt in peacetime, the two were in practice complementary rather than alternative methods of raising revenue. As Brewer points out, the more they borrowed, the more important it became for rulers to maximise their domestic income.

The balance between direct and indirect taxation was less a matter of choice than of necessity. Western governments faced stringent limitations on what they could do. The French crown was inhibited by direct taxation's association with despotism, and further restricted after 1720 by the collapse of the credit scheme devised by the Scot, John Law – a famously unsuccessful attempt to make a virtue of despotic royal currency manipulation.[8] What is more, by reducing the per capita output of land, demographic growth diminished the revenue which could be gained from the existing land tax (*taille*). So there were both political and economic reasons why the proportion of French revenues supplied by direct taxation declined from about 44 per cent in 1726 to 35 per cent in 1788. In Britain, the land tax introduced in 1693 proved a useful expedient in wartime, but much less effective than the bureaucratically managed excise in time of peace. As a result, the proportion of British revenue derived from direct taxation declined from around 47 per cent in the 1690s to 21 per cent a hundred years later, and rose again to 33 per cent in 1810 only under the impact of the Napoleonic wars. Though the British were more successful than the French in taxing the rich, it was not until 1799 that the needs of war against revolutionary France gave Pitt the political courage to introduce a graduated income tax. Until then, both governments shied away from root-and-branch tax reform – the only way in which they might have gained the knowledge about incomes necessary to eliminate the tax evasion which so heavily depleted their revenues – by resorting instead to domestic and foreign loans.

These sophisticated options were not open to Peter the Great. He was prevented from borrowing abroad by lenders' doubts about Russian financial stability (the first Muscovite application had been rejected during the Thirty Years War). Both his undermonetised economy and the primitive state of domestic finances made it impossible for him to

---

[8] See T. E. Kaiser, 'Money, Despotism, and Public Opinion in Early Eighteenth-Century France: John Law and the Debate on Royal Credit', *JMH*, 63, 1 (1991), esp. pp. 20–3.

conjure a Russian 'financial revolution'.[9] Unlike his contemporaries in the West, however, there was nothing to prevent Peter from indulging in arbitrary fiscal management. As if to symbolise his commitment to despotic methods, the tsar tried in vain to persuade the discredited John Law to move to Russia in 1721, offering him the title of prince, 2,000 peasant households, and the right to build and populate with foreigners a new town of his own. Since Law was not to be tempted, Peter continued to trust coercion rather than risk sophistry in matters of finance as Lewitter has pointed out.

The state monopolies that had satisfied his predecessors had exhausted their fiscal potential, and the major new one Peter introduced on salt in 1705 proved so expensive to operate that it was temporarily withdrawn in 1727 after Peter's death. Since indirect taxation was vulnerable when trade was disrupted in time of war, Peter concentrated on raising existing direct taxes and imposing a myriad of new ones including the significantly named 'dragoon money', 'ship money', and 'recruit money'. An exhaustive list is impossible here: by 1714–16, the population of Kiev province alone was subject to more than forty different taxes. Many were supposedly temporary or extraordinary. But 'temporary' taxes soon became such a key part of Peter's revenue that, by one estimate, they accounted for nearly 60 per cent of the state's total income by 1720–3.[10]

To mobilise idle ecclesiastical resources, Peter rescinded surviving monastic immunities, placed new limits on the amount of property that monasteries could acquire, and in 1701 revived the Monastery Chancellery (Monastyrskii prikaz) founded by his father to regulate the revenues from those ecclesiastical estates which had so far remained outside the patriarchal domains. Peter now strengthened the chancellery's fiscal powers: churchmen, who had already been obliged to form 'companies' to finance the construction of the Azov fleet at Voronezh in 1696–7, were made not only to subsidise charity and medical treatment for wounded soldiers but also to pay for a regiment of dragoons founded in 1706.

Though he may have known that Aleksei Mikhailovich had helped to provoke the Moscow 'copper riots' of 1662 by paying his troops in worthless coin, Peter was even more ruthless than his father in his manipulation of the currency. From 1698 to 1723 the tsar reduced the silver content of the ruble while simultaneously increasing the iron content of an ever lighter bronze coinage. In this way, Peter gained some

---

[9] Cf. P. G. M. Dickson, *The Financial Revolution in England* (London, 1967).
[10] E. V. Anisimov, 'Remarks on the Fiscal Policy of Russian Absolutism During the First Quarter of the Eighteenth Century', *Soviet Studies in History*, 28, 1 (1989), p. 18.

4,400,000 rubles from debasement between 1701 and 1709. At just over a quarter of his income, the minting of new coin constituted not only the largest single contribution to the estimated revenue budget of 1701 but probably Peter's most effective means of taxing stockpilers of currency.

However, the significance of all these measures was dwarfed by the decree of 1718 which introduced what the West regarded as the ultimate in despotic direct taxation: the poll tax, or 'soul tax' (*podushnaia podat'*). The tsar had been searching since at least 1714 for a means of consolidating the direct taxation paid by the peasantry. He found it in a measure of stark simplicity: a single tax, calculated to match the needs of his troops, to be collected by the College of War from landlords held responsible for organising their peasants' payment. The total sum required was divided among the taxable male population so that each man should in theory contribute a uniform sum. In the sense that the individual male became the nominal unit of taxation, the poll tax was in principle novel. But in its flagrant disregard of the capacity of these individuals to pay, it was firmly in the Muscovite tradition. In the event, the tax-paying townsmen and peasants simply maintained the Muscovite pattern of communal collective responsibility in which wealthier households subsidised poorer neighbours in time of need.

So vital was its immediate contribution that when revisions of the census begun in 1719 finally allowed the poll tax to be collected in 1724, it alone accounted for 54 per cent of the revenue budget. In the short term its simplicity was attractive. In the long term, however, it had serious limitations. Unless the rate were raised, revenue would remain stagnant until a growing population could be registered by a new census. Since a census was both cumbersome and expensive there were only five between 1719 and 1795. Yet so unpopular was the poll tax among the peasantry – as the incidence of peasant flight testified – that successive governments kept the rate at 70 kopeks for peasants and 80 kopeks for townsmen until 1794, when it was raised to 1 ruble and 1 ruble 80 kopeks respectively. In 1825, the peasants' poll tax stood at 3 rubles 30 kopeks, but by then the tax's contribution to the total revenue had dropped sharply and its initial correlation with military needs had long since lapsed.

In part, the loss could be compensated by increasing the quitrent (*obrok*) – the tax exacted from the state peasantry in addition to the poll tax in a notional attempt to match in monetary terms the obligations which privately owned serfs paid to their lords. The 1723 *obrok* rate of 40 kopeks was raised to 1 ruble in 1760 and further increased in 1764, 1769, 1783, and 1794. Tsar Paul again raised *obrok* in 1797, differen-

tiating between peasants occupying land of different quality: the highest
rate was set at 5 rubles. Further rises followed under Alexander I so that
obrok levied at roughly half the poll-tax rate in the 1720s was up to three
times as expensive a century later. Indeed, the poll tax, though it
continued to be collected into the 1890s, had become no more than a
supplement to the quitrent, as Speranskii remarked in his financial plan
of 1810.

Before resorting to manipulation of the quitrent, governments in the
middle of the eighteenth century sought to balance their books by
increasing indirect taxation. Between 1724 and 1769, the share of direct
taxes in the state's total revenue dropped by 11.6 per cent whilst the
share of indirect taxes rose by 10.6 per cent. The key period was the late
1740s and 1750s, when Petr Shuvalov used tax reform as part of a
broader strategy designed to liberate the Russian economy.

Conscious of the success of indirect taxation in the West, Shuvalov
argued that rises in the price of salt and alcohol would be not only more
equitable than a rise in the poll tax, but also a more effective way of
increasing revenue. He overestimated the popularity of his reforms:
2,489 people were convicted of crimes against the salt-tax regulations
between 1750 and 1762. But he was right in the short term about the
fiscal benefit the measure would confer on the state. By raising the price
of a pood of salt (1 pood = 36 lbs/16.4 kg) from 21 to 35 kopeks in
January 1750, and again to 50 kopeks at the beginning of the Seven
Years War, Shuvalov nearly tripled the government's income from the
salt monopoly between 1749 and 1761. In 1754, he also transformed
the operation of the alcohol excise by introducing a noble monopoly
which lasted until 1817. Nobles signed four-year contracts to deliver
distilled alcohol at a uniform price to state-owned warehouses, where
duty was collected before the product was sold on to the consumer. By
this means, and by sharply increasing wholesale prices, the monopoly's
contribution to the revenue budget increased in the decade after 1749
from 12.8 per cent to 21.1 per cent. Largely as a result of Shuvalov's
reforms, the alcohol monopoly provided approximately 25 per cent of
Russian revenue in the mid-1760s and the salt monopoly a further 7–10
per cent. The contribution made by the poll tax had meanwhile dropped
to only 30 per cent.

Unfortunately for Shuvalov, improvements in revenue collection were
overshadowed by the inexorable rise of expenditure after 1725. While
cuts in local government sliced its budget from 0.6 million rubles in
1725 to 0.1 million in 1744, economies elsewhere proved elusive. The
demands of a growing bureaucracy in St Petersburg kept the central
institutions' budget at or above the 1725 level of 0.2 million rubles.

Peacetime international relations were also expensive. To maintain its new-found prestige, Russia had not only to fund embassies in Western capitals but also to invest in its own court. Whilst spending on public construction was halved between 1725 and 1744, the savings were used to double expenditure on the court, which devoured almost 12 per cent of annual state expenditure under Catherine the Great (a priority which alone justifies the extended discussion of the court's place in government in chapter 5).

Most importantly, military spending remained exorbitant even in peacetime, the majority consumed not by new equipment but by basic subsistence for the troops. Approximately 1.3 per cent of the Russian population were in uniform in the middle of the eighteenth century (compared with 1.5 per cent in France and an unsurpassed 4.2 per cent in Prussia). Pay, uniforms, and food accounted for 89 per cent of an infantry regiment's budget in 1731. Taking into account peacetime obligations and the requirements of war, it is not surprising that the proportion of total annual expenditure consumed by the military stood at approximately 80 per cent in 1744 and 74 per cent in 1762.

Rising expenditure pushed up the annual Russian deficit from approximately 8 per cent of the budget in 1733 to some 40–5 per cent in 1760. Contemporaries were only imperfectly aware of the details, but they could sense the trend since their audit and budgetary procedures were less feeble than scholars once supposed. Here Russia conformed to a European pattern. From Colbert's time, French bureaucrats drafted estimates and accounts (so-called *arrangements* and *états de prévoyance*) which were budgets in all but name. So they were accustomed to compiling the sort of documents that became public only with Necker's notoriously duplicitous *Compte rendu* of 1781. The Universal-Bancalität in Vienna kept Austrian revenue accounts and estimated expenditure in conjunction with the Hofkammer from 1714, a system refined by Haugwitz in the late 1740s. Muscovy, too, had an elementary auditing mechanism, capable of producing estimated accounts of revenue and expenditure, though not a single state budget. An Accounting Chancellery (Schetnyi prikaz) had existed as early as the 1650s, though it no longer operated in the 1690s. Peter the Great's attempts to force each chancellery to submit accounts were only partially successful. But he signalled his determination to bring order to his finances in the contract issued to Heinrich Fick, one of his principal German advisers, in 1717. Among his new administrative creations in the following year, Peter included a Kamer-kollegiia (College of Revenue), where Fick was appointed councillor, a Shtats-kontor-kollegiia (College of State Expenditure), and a Revizion-kollegiia (Audit College), the last being abolished in 1722 but revived in 1733 after an interval in which accounts were supposedly kept by the Senate.

Impressive as they seemed on paper, all these systems collapsed in time of war and were unreliable even in peacetime. Moreover, since no state developed a uniform system of controls – mid-century Austrian accounts, for example, might be estimated or actual, net or gross, and inclusive or exclusive of loans and transfer items – growing sophistication in bookkeeping methods was more often a barrier than an aid to understanding. Russia could not escape these difficulties. Pososhkov criticised unnecessarily complex accounts as early as 1724. Things were little better by 1762, when both Peter III and Catherine II demanded in vain to see clear statements of their financial position.

Financial administration in 1762 therefore resembled the confusion bequeathed to Peter the Great in the 1680s. Though he had attempted a measure of modernisation by reducing the amount of taxes paid in kind, Russia's economy was incapable of supporting a completely cash-based system and retained many features of the medieval arrangement of 'feeding off the land' (*kormlenie*). Even Peter's administrative rationalisation had left three major colleges with responsibility for finance, and the poll tax was collected by none of them: it remained in the hands of the College of War. Far from diminishing, the number of agencies authorised to collect revenues had actually increased by the 1760s to approximately fifty. Hypothecation (the allocation of specific revenues to specific resources) remained common: so, for example, the salt tax supported the court for a time. The lack of a single treasury thus continued to prevent the compilation of an accurate state budget.

War and financial modernisation, 1762–1825

Although, in the wake of the Seven Years War, Russia emulated its rivals by embarking on a period of internal consolidation, it would be illusory to suppose that consolidation came cheap. Military spending may have been reduced, but it rarely fell below half the net budget even in peacetime, and Catherine the Great's plans to revitalise local administration soon led her to contemplate fiscal innovation of her own. Still, her initial response to financial difficulty was a traditional one: the secularisation of the church lands in 1764.

Catherine's confiscation of ecclesiastical property was greeted by anticlerical French *philosophes* as one of the first fruits of the new empress's Enlightened policy. In this sense, it might seem to have anticipated Joseph II's reforms of the 1780s, which suppressed 55 per cent of all religious houses in the Habsburg monarchy's hereditary lands and 75 per cent in Hungary, ejecting in the process some 14,000 regular clergy. In 1764, only 161 of Russia's 572 monasteries and 67 of her 217 convents survived. There are, however, distinctions to be made between the two measures. Although Joseph and Catherine both disliked contemplative monasticism (and especially 'useless' nuns, whose 'unnatural' confinement to the convent retarded demographic growth), Joseph's reduction of monastic numbers formed part of a programme of ecclesiastical rationalisation designed to improve parochial provision.[11] Since Catherine was worried rather by an alleged superfluity of parish clergy, her secularisation had no such motive. Also important was the difference between the political status of the two churches: the Roman Catholic church in the Habsburg empire was a far more influential institution than was the Russian Orthodox church, which could rely neither on a strong native episcopate nor, crucially, on external papal power. Virulent Russian anticlericalism remained an impossibility whilst clericalism was itself stillborn.[12]

In fact, the Enlightenment's influence on Russian secularisation owed more to economics than to anticlericalism, and the most revealing comparison is not with Joseph's dissolution but with the disentail (*desamortización*) of Spanish ecclesiastical property begun in 1798.[13] Like this later Spanish legislation, Catherine's secularisation was undertaken primarily in response to a financial crisis induced by war. The essential steps towards it had been taken long before she came to the throne. Exploitation of ecclesiastical property was first proposed in moderate but vague terms to Elizabeth's War Commission in 1757 by Ia. P. Shakhovskoi (1705–77), a former over-procurator of the Holy Synod, as an alternative to Shuvalov's currency reform. But if war created the need for secularisation, it could not provide the conditions in which it could be accomplished. Not until 1762 did Peter III make the decisive move, surpassing anything that Shakhovskoi had contemplated. Alarmed by evidence from a Senate investigation that arbitrary ecclesiastical taxation had generated revolts on monastic estates, Peter simply confiscated the church's peasants on 21 March. In view of the circumstances of her accession, Catherine was understandably cautious before confirming her late husband's edict. Indeed, in July 1762, when the Senate, having deliberated for less than a fortnight, recommended that sequestered ecclesiastical estates be returned, it seemed that the

---

[11] See D. Beales, 'Joseph II and the Monasteries of Austria and Hungary', in N. Aston, ed., *Religious Change in Europe 1650–1914* (Oxford, 1997), pp. 161–84.

[12] See G. L. Freeze, 'A Case of Stunted Anticlericalism: Clergy and Society in Imperial Russia', *European Studies Review*, 13, 2 (1983), pp. 177–200.

[13] See R. Herr, *Rural Change and Royal Finances in Spain at the End of the Old Regime* (Berkeley, CA, 1989), especially ch. 19, on which the following comparison draws.

tide had turned in the church's favour. Instead, Catherine subsequently exploited disunity among the bishops to force through her own definitive legislation, finalised on 6 February 1764.

Drawing on the Scottish school of political economy, the Spanish officials who devised Charles IV's disentail in the 1790s were convinced (wrongly, as it turned out) that both state and society would profit from the agricultural improvement which they believed would result from allowing the small landowner freer access to the land market. How far was such a wider economic logic found in Russia? G. N. Teplov (1717–79), the moving influence behind the Commission on Church Lands set up on 29 November 1762, was among the most flexible Russian economic thinkers of his time. He drew eclectically on a range of Western authorities to stress the need for widespread participation in the economy. In particular, he wanted to allow peasants to join merchants in trade because commerce became 'much more useful when capital is divided among many hands'.[14] However, since he intended the state to regulate the economic mechanism he envisaged, even Teplov could not yet conceive of a free market in land on a par with the mass of small-scale Spanish landowners – churchmen and old régime officials, rather than bourgeois – who paid for their purchases from cash savings, thereby matching the supply of ecclesiastical lands sold off by the government with a thriving level of demand.

Perhaps this was a missed opportunity. Since some Russian landowners *did* try illegally to acquire secularised church property, demand apparently existed. The question is as elusive as it is important. Yet it seems clear that instead of looking forward to a free market in land, as would the Spanish disentail, Catherine's legislation looked back over more than a century of expropriation of ecclesiastical wealth by a state driven by military needs. Already in 1649, chapter XIII of the *Ulozhenie* had decreed the creation of a Monastery Chancellery to regulate the finances of those ecclesiastical lands not subject to the patriarch. Though the new institution fell victim to ecclesiastical pressure in 1677, Peter I, as we have seen, revived it in 1701. He, however, stopped short of outright confiscation, limiting his intervention to the temporary appropriation of surplus revenue. Between 1711 and 1721, the tsar restored almost all that he had taken in the previous decade, keeping only the yield from a tenth of the former patriarchal domains (placed

---

[14] W. Daniel, 'The Merchantry and the Problem of Social Order in the Russian State: Catherine II's Commission on Commerce', *SEER*, 55, 2 (1977), p. 200. The fullest study of Teplov is Daniel's *Grigorii Teplov: A Statesman at the Court of Catherine the Great* (Newtonville, MA, 1991).

under the management of the new Holy Synod in 1721) which gave the state an annual income of around 50,000 rubles.

How far, then, was Catherine's secularisation the logical extension of Peter's policy? She herself was conscious of the link since she explicitly praised his approach to the problem as wise and just and announced in one of her earliest legislative acts in 1762 that she intended to follow his precedent.[15] Just as there was nothing inevitable about the slide from Leninism to Stalinism, so there was nothing inevitable about the development from the temporary nature of Peter's attempts to tap the church's wealth to the permanence of Catherine's secularisation. But, as in the twentieth-century example, neither was there anything other than self-restraint to prevent it from happening. These were phenomena which differed not in nature, but in degree.

Secularisation gave the state control over the wealth of monasteries whose riches were out of all proportion to their numbers. In 1762 they owned roughly two-thirds of Russian ploughed land, approximately twice as much as in the 1560s. Only 13 per cent of the nobility possessed more than a hundred peasants; 70 per cent of landed ecclesiastical institutions did so. The greatest, the Trinity–St Sergius Monastery near Moscow, owned more than 106,000 male peasants on estates dispersed over six provinces, eclipsing even the wealthiest magnates. Approaching a million peasants in total, the church's 'human capital' constituted approximately a seventh of the rural population in 1762, and a larger proportion of the population of the northern and central lands where most ecclesiastical estates were concentrated. Though much of this land was of poor quality, when transferred to state control it yielded an annual income of almost 1,370,000 rubles, of which less than 463,000 was returned to the church each year between 1764 and 1768. By 1784, the state's income from former ecclesiastical properties had reached 3,648,000 rubles, whilst its grant to the church had risen to only 540,000 rubles in 1782.

Though Catherine's munificent new resource combined with the relative parsimony of her early years to build up a reserve of 8.5 million rubles by the time of the Turkish attack in 1768, this was insufficient to fund a major war. In response to the new emergency, Catherine relapsed into the standard pattern of fiscal intensification: the quitrent was raised to 2 rubles a year in 1769, a levy of 115,000 thalers was imposed on the Baltic provinces, and half a million rubles were gained from war taxes imposed on factories and merchants. Russia's ally, Frederick the Great,

[15] K. Rasmussen, 'Catherine II and the Image of Peter I', *SR*, 37, 1 (1978), pp. 57–8, notes that this early example of deference to the Petrine model was later supplanted by a more critical attitude on a wide range of issues.

reluctantly provided a 1,200,000-ruble subsidy. But spending was so heavy that Russia was now forced to embark for the first time on alternative means of revenue raising: foreign borrowing and paper money. Together they covered 95 per cent of the deficit under Catherine II.

By the end of the Seven Years War, a crucial turning point in every participant's finances, all except Prussia and Russia had already had recourse to foreign capital. Subsequently, only Prussia managed to avoid a long-term state debt, cushioned by the income from extensive crown lands which supplied almost half its revenue at Frederick the Great's accession in 1740 and still accounted for around 30 per cent at his death in 1786. By contrast, the Russian imperial domains generated less than a quarter of what the state gained from former church properties in 1762–5. After Paul's reorganisation of 1797, crown monies were used only to support lesser members of the imperial family; the tsar drew his income from state revenues. Clearly the financial security of the Russian crown could not compare with that of its Prussian rival. But now that its credit had been bolstered by military success, Russia could partly compensate by at last entering the international finance market on favourable terms.

Between 1769 and 1773, Prince A. A. Viazemskii, the procurator-general, negotiated with R. and Th. de Smeth, one of Amsterdam's most prestigious firms, loans equivalent to about 5 million rubles after costs to finance the current Russo-Turkish war. Rather less than half was subsequently repaid by the indemnity exacted from the defeated Turks in 1774, the remainder being rescheduled for a further ten years in 1779 when the interest rate came down from 5 per cent to 4 per cent as victory enhanced Russia's financial credibility. New loans, totalling more than 39 million rubles, were negotiated between 1787 and 1792 to pay for expansion in the 1780s. Dependence on foreign borrowing forced up expenditure on debt servicing from 0.6 million rubles in 1782 to 4.2 million in 1796, when foreign loans totalled over 33 million rubles. But these loans were negotiated at such an advantageous interest rate that Russia was obliged to devote a far smaller proportion of its expenditure to the national debt than France, by then paying rates of up to 12 per cent and so profoundly obliged to its bankers that it required half its annual revenue simply to service its debts.

Recognising that institutional change was required to support their borrowing, Catherine and Viazemskii embarked on a series of reforms which, according to LeDonne, provided Russia not only with its first state budget in 1781 but also with co-ordinated regulation. Operated by specialists under the direction of Aleksei Vasil'ev, the Office of State

Revenues created in 1773 was the prototype of a single treasury; the procurator-general, to whom this office reported, became a forerunner of the first minister of finance, appointed in 1802. Temporarily dismantled by Paul, the centralised management of state revenues was restored by Dmitrii Gur'ev, whose career – as deputy minister of finance from 1802 to 1810, and minister from 1810 to 1823 – spanned almost the whole of Alexander I's reign.

We can agree that Viazemskii did much to transform the congeries of collegial responsibilities Catherine inherited into what looked like a streamlined system. In practice, however, crucial anomalies survived. The tsars not only retained but frequently exercised the right to intervene in budgetary matters and their meddling was enough to subvert unitary controls at least until 1862, when the Ministry of Finance was belatedly given responsibility for expenditure as a whole. Even then, Russian financial planning, if such it can be called, remained a hand-to-mouth operation dependent largely on ministerial competition for resources. In our period, Russian embassies abroad give a hint of the difficulty. Beyond bureaucratic control, these fell under the aegis of the court banker, an office to which Catherine II appointed Richard Sutherland (1739–91), son of a Scottish master-shipbuilder contracted into Russian service in 1736. All was serene until spring 1791, when the Russian minister at Florence, having lost 120,000 rubles owing to Sutherland's negligence, helped to expose a scam which, it transpired during a two-year investigation after the banker's death in October, had defrauded the court of almost 2 million rubles in order to finance Sutherland's nefarious money-lending.

More significant in quantitative terms were problems plaguing revenue from indirect taxation. The cost of carrying salt from the Urals to centres of consumption in European Russia undermined the fiscal logic of Shuvalov's tax reforms, restated in the Salt Code of 1781. By the 1780s, transport costs consumed up to 94 per cent of the sale price of Perm' salt, inadvertently transposing what was intended to be an excise tax into a consumer subsidy. Had the government been able to increase prices, some of its losses could have been recouped. But it knew that demand for salt was just as elastic in the 1780s as it had been in the 1640s, when Morozov's tax was scuppered by falling sales. Contrary to Shuvalov's expectations, price rises in the 1750s had provoked both a reduction in consumption and a rise in smuggling. So Catherine was reluctant to sacrifice the popularity she had sought by lowering prices in 1762 (from 50 to 40 kopeks per pood) and again in 1775 (to 35 kopeks). By contrast, the government raised alcohol prices because its anxiety to profit from increased sales was tempered by the conviction that drunkenness was a social liability. Although Grand Duke Paul, in his instruction of 1788, expressed an explicit preference for the promotion of mining and manufacturing, his mother persisted with the alcohol monopoly. Price rises help to explain the comparative buoyancy of the excise in the second half of her reign: revenue reached an estimated 15 million rubles in 1796. But profits were depleted by inflation, the rising price of grain, and the costs incurred by granting the nobility a monopoly. If the salt and alcohol monopolies are taken together, the difference between gross receipts and net revenue (a crude but revealing index of the cost of overheads as Kahan observes) had risen from around 27 per cent in 1763–5 to 58.5 per cent in 1791–3.

The greatest strain on Russian finances came from the issuance of paper money. The government had first been tempted to print assignat rubles during the Seven Years War, but it was only in December 1768 that assignat banks were set up in Moscow and St Petersburg. Each was initially authorised to circulate half a million rubles, backed by an equivalent reserve in copper coinage. Although the government managed a measure of self-restraint during the first Turkish war – issuing only 20 million assignats, and keeping their level at about 5 per cent of annual revenue – it had already abandoned the security of full metal reserves by 1769, a failure which boded ill for monetary discipline once assignats were reissued, after a lull in the mid-1770s, in 1781, and again, more rashly, in 1787. Viazemskii recommended higher taxes as a safer alternative. But A. A. Bezborodko, stressing the potentially explosive consequences of overt increases in the burden of taxation, prevailed in the secret commissions set up in 1783 and 1786 to find ways of maximising revenue.

Within fifteen years of the first issue, assignats, initially conceived as a temporary expedient, had become a conventional tool of Russian fiscal policy. Whilst foreign bankers put a brake on the debts Russia could incur abroad, only their own self-discipline could limit officials' licence to print money at home. And self-discipline consistently proved beyond them. Although a manifesto of 28 June 1786 limited the number of assignats in circulation to 100 million, that threshold was passed within three years. Tsar Paul, recognising the need for a stable currency, signalled his intention to curtail the circulation of paper money by burning more than a million rubles' worth in front of the Winter Palace. As this gesture demonstrates, the tsar's intentions were not matched by his fiscal grasp. Despite his determination to balance the budget by cutting Catherine's provincial administration, he failed to restrain expenditure, which rose from around 76 million rubles to 81 million between 1797 and 1800, exceeding income by some 23 to 26 million rubles.

In the circumstances, Paul's attempt to reduce the number of assignats to just over 53 million was but a pious hope. By 1800 there were four times as many in circulation, and by 1814 the number had been forced up to almost 800 million by Russia's commitment to the Napoleonic wars, during which military expenditure never fell below 40 per cent of the current annual total and on occasion reached two-thirds. The silver value of the one-ruble assignat dropped by 1814 to a fifth of its price forty years earlier. Looking back in 1810–11, Karamzin limpidly summarised 'the inevitable result' of printing virtually unlimited money: 'the price of things went up, while the value of the currency went down'.[16] Karamzin wrote to undermine Speranskii's constitutional plans. But on finance the two concurred: assignats were nothing but hidden debts. Too late, a commission to liquidate the national debt was set up in May 1810.

Like its European rivals, eighteenth-century Russia presents the image of a financial administration constantly chasing its own tail. No sooner had the government devised new ways of increasing revenue than fresh military demands took expenditure beyond the level that its income could hope to support. More damaging still, peacetime expenses were kept high by an expanding bureaucracy and a huge standing army. *Plus ça change, plus c'est la même chose.* But not, perhaps, for the tsar's subjects? Whilst the *relative* relationship of income to expenditure remained much the same, the *absolute* amounts of money at stake rose dramatically between the 1680s and the 1820s. Contemporaries were persuaded – and some historians have agreed – that the burden of taxation became intolerable. Yet, as we shall now see, to try to quantify that burden with any precision is a hazardous exercise.

The burden of taxation

Since Russian reformers drew explicitly on Western models, the widespread Western concern for distributive justice was reflected in their legislation. In 1718, the College of Revenue's Regulation stressed cameralist principles of equity (*pravda*) and uniformity (*ravenstvo*). But the cameralists wanted equitable treatment of social estates, not progressive taxation of individuals. And, unlike those Frenchmen who later strove to distribute the burden more evenly, Peter's officials were more interested in increasing state revenues than ensuring an equitable burden of taxation.[17] Nobles had a vested interest in keeping state taxes

---

[16] R. Pipes, *Karamzin's Memoir on Ancient and Modern Russia: A Translation and Analysis* (New York, 1972), p. 167.

[17] For comparisons, see J.-P. Gross, 'Progressive Taxation and Social Justice in Eighteenth-Century France', *P&P*, 140 (1993), pp. 79–126.

low so that their serfs would be able to make a greater contribution to their owners' income. Newly enthroned tsars who temporarily reduced the poll tax were as interested in bolstering their own nascent régimes as in improving the lot of individual subjects. So were those who granted amnesties in the payment of arrears. Elizabeth abolished the Arrears Chancellery straightaway in December 1741, thereby writing off some seventeen years' of arrears worth 5 million rubles – roughly equivalent to the current annual revenue from the tax. But by so doing, and by 'forgiving' in 1752 a further 2.5 million rubles' worth of arrears up to 1746 inclusive, she probably helped to make current collection more efficient.

Arrears are sometimes said to offer a way of measuring the burden of taxation. When the poll tax was introduced, they were massive: up to 1 million rubles from an expected total of 4.5 million remained uncollected. The proportion of urban arrears was greater still: 64.3 per cent in the first four years of collection, 1724–7. However, between 1724 and 1742, the overall level dropped sharply to an average 6.5 per cent, ranging between 7 and 14 per cent in the 1750s. Comparisons are complex, but since Austrian accounts for 1774–7 show that between 13 and 15 per cent of revenue was collected from previous years – a figure which in itself compared favourably to the much larger proportion of arrears in the collection of the Contribution (Austria's principal direct tax) in the earlier part of Maria Theresa's reign – it may be that Russian arrears roughly approximated to those of a principal competitor. Whether or not this is true, it is arguable that, since the highest levels of arrears (including the initial years of the poll tax) coincided with war and natural disaster, arrears tell us more about the temporary incidence of famine and other calamities than about the burden of taxation. According to Kahan, in years unaffected by natural disaster, arrears annually amounted to no more than 4 or 5 per cent of the total collected revenue.

Contemporary opinion may be no more reliable an indicator of the fiscal burden. Radishchev, who studied taxation in St Petersburg province, was among the most eloquent critics who testified that the peasantry was intolerably burdened by the 1780s. However, the burden then borne with relative equanimity by the British was actually heavier than the one to which the French reacted so violently in 1789.[18]

Three further problems complicate any assessment of the impact of taxation: inflation, regional variations, and corruption. Inflation is thought to have reduced the value of the ruble by as much as 50 per cent

[18] P. Mathias and P. K. O'Brien, 'Taxation in England and France 1715–1810', *JEurEcH*, 5 (1976), pp. 601–50.

during the first decade of the century, by a further 20 per cent in the second decade, and again by perhaps 13 per cent between 1725 and 1767. Paper money stimulated a further bout of inflation from the late 1780s which kept the real level of taxation lower than it sometimes seems. There were also sharp regional differences in the burden of taxation. Regional and local taxes survived, partly to serve local needs and partly because piecemeal imperial expansion made it difficult to impose uniformity. Since the Russian government was anxious to prove its own administration more bearable than that which it replaced, it was not until 1783 that the poll tax was introduced into Livonia, Little Russia, and Belorussia; and the Baltic provinces, Little Russia, and the territory acquired in the first partition of Poland remained exempt from the alcohol excise. Some frontier regions were offered a reduction in taxation to offset the burden of feeding troops quartered there. On the other hand, corruption was everywhere endemic. Collectors continued to risk execution in their attempts to exceed their entitlement. In the 1730s it was estimated that, on average, poll-tax collectors were demanding an extra 10 kopeks per soul in excess of the 70 kopeks peasants were supposed to pay. Since Tsar Paul justified his grants of state peasants into private ownership on the grounds that they would be less likely to suffer from fraudulent tax collectors in their new status, there is no reason to suppose that matters subsequently improved.

Finally, it is worth repeating the fact that even such an apparently straightforward impost as the poll tax – set at a uniform national rate that took no account of either age or infirmity – tells us nothing about what was actually paid by the individual male peasant who remained locked into a system of collective responsibility in which his contribution would vary over time and form only a small part of the complex amalgam of labour and cash obligations he owed to his lord.

Taking into account all these difficulties, it is no surprise to find disagreement between historians on even such a basic issue as the initial impact of the poll tax. Miliukov's contention that it increased direct taxes by 61 per cent has been challenged by Anisimov, who counters that the burden may actually have been reduced by the inclusion in the registry of peasants who were formerly exempt. In the present state of research, though the balance of probabilities lies with an increasing burden, it is hard to regard the issue as anything other than 'not proven'.

The political and social impact of taxation

Peter the Great swelled the chorus of authorities who christened money 'the artery of war'. For the cameralist Johan von Justi (1720–71), it was more even than this: money was the state's blood, pumped through the system by the government at its heart. Justi's master, Frederick the Great, compared finance to 'the nerves in the human body that set all its limbs in motion'. However questionable the clinical accuracy of these metaphors, they show that rulers understood that in tackling taxation they were approaching the crux of their régimes. As well they might. Finance was crucial not only to a great power's international status but to its very survival as a state. Just as a crippled financial administration precipitated the breakdown of the *ancien régime* in France, so a more supple one made a crucial contribution to social and political stability in Britain (though even the British fell foul of the American colonies).

Russia fell between these two extremes. Despite institutional reform, the tsars were spared from bankruptcy only by recourse to a coercive power which must have made them the envy of many a Western monarch trapped in a constitutional quandary. The most sophisticated fiscal technique at the Russians' disposal – paper currency – was the one which led them closest to disaster. Under Alexander I, modern institutions still depended on traditional methods to keep them solvent. Far from becoming obsolete, taxation in kind was formally institutionalised in 1802 as 'contributions from the land' (*zemskie povinnosti*) administered by the Ministry of Internal Affairs, which only partially succeeded in converting them into cash payments. The alcohol code of April 1817, which came into effect in January 1819, abolished the tax farms but replaced them with an institutionalised version of the seventeenth-century 'sworn collectors', only now it was tavern keepers who were formally agents of the provincial vice-governors, acting for the Ministry of Finance. Above all, the language of Alexander's tax edicts remained as rich in threats as any Muscovite legislation. No matter what refinements they made to their bureaucratic machinery, the tsars never succeeded in establishing a system capable of coping with abrupt transitions from peace to war. Collection continued to rely less on a modernised revenue system than on a crude alternation between brute force and amnesties on arrears. Peasants can be forgiven for thinking that they felt the stick more often than they tasted the carrot.

Michael Mann offers a helpful conceptualisation. Whereas the tsars were increasingly unrivalled in their *despotic power* – the 'range of actions' they were 'empowered to undertake without routine, institutionalised negotiation with civil society groups' – their *infrastructural power* – 'the capacity of the state actually to penetrate civil society and to implement logistically political decisions throughout the realm' – still left much to be desired.[19] It was not, of course, for want of trying. One of the most important consequences of fiscal innovation in terms of state-building was the impetus it gave to bureaucratic restructuring and the specialisation of domestic administration in general. We shall come to this in chapter 5. First, however, we must consider the social impact of fiscal policy.

BIBLIOGRAPHICAL NOTE

Though I have tried to offer an accessible account of a technical subject, a glance at the specialist literature will show that almost everything in this chapter is less straightforward in detail than in outline I have allowed it to seem. A good contextual starting point is R. Bonney, ed., *Economic Systems and State Finance* (Oxford, 1995). Fiscal weakness also plays a pivotal rôle in the ambitious synthesis by J. A. Goldstone, *Revolution and Rebellion in the Early Modern World* (Berkeley, CA, 1991). However, the most daunting example of what can (and cannot) be done is P. G. M. Dickson, *Finance and Government Under Maria Theresia 1740–1780*, 2 vols. (Oxford, 1987).

A small but impressive corpus of modern work on Russia has developed in dialogue with the pre-revolutionary scholarship of N. D. Chechulin, P. N. Miliukov, and V. O. Kliuchevskii. Much the best survey in English is J. P. LeDonne, *Absolutism and Ruling Class* (above, n. 7), to be read with the penetrating chapter on finance in A. Kahan, *The Plow, the Hammer and the Knout: An Economic History of Eighteenth-Century Russia* (Chicago, 1985). I have drawn extensively on both. W. Pintner, 'The Burden of Defense in Imperial Russia, 1725–1914', *RR*, 43 (1984), and J. M. Hittle, *The Service City: State and Townsmen in Russia, 1600–1800* (Cambridge, MA, 1979), are sensitive to fiscal change. A. I. Iukht, *Russkie den'gi ot Petra Velikogo do Aleksandra I* (Moscow, 1994), provides a point of entry into the complex history of the coinage.

Among specialist studies, S. M. Kashtanov summarises the conclusions of a career devoted to Muscovite finance in *Finansy srednevekovoi rusi* (Moscow, 1988); his article, 'The Centralised State and Feudal Immunities in Russia', *SEER*, 39 (1971), is available in translation. Also important is P. Bushkovitch, 'Taxation, Tax Farming and Merchants in Sixteenth-Century Russia', *SR*, 37 (1978). I. Pososhkov, *The Book of Poverty and Wealth*, ed. and tr. A. P. Vlasto and L. R. Lewitter (London, 1987), complements E. V. Anisimov's fundamental study of the poll tax,

---

[19] M. Mann, 'The Autonomous Power of the State: Its Origins, Mechanisms and Results', in John A. Hall, ed., *States in History* (Oxford, 1986), p. 113.

Podatnaia reforma Petra I: vvedenie podushnoi podati v Rossii 1719–1728gg. (Leningrad, 1982). S. M. Troitskii, *Finansovaia politika russkogo absoliutizma v XVIIIv.* (Moscow, 1966), informs the work of all Western scholars on the post-Petrine period. J. Cracraft, *The Church Reform of Peter the Great* (London, 1971), and C. S. Leonard, *Reform and Regicide: The Reign of Peter III of Russia* (Bloomington, IN, 1993), examine the background to secularisation. The policies of Catherine II have been studied in depth by J. P. LeDonne: see *Ruling Russia: Politics and Administration in the Age of Absolutism 1762–1796* (Princeton, 1984); 'Indirect Taxes in Catherine's Russia I: The Salt Code of 1781', *JfGO*, 23 (1975); and 'II: The Liquor Monopoly', *JfGO*, 24 (1976). See also J. A. Duran, Jr, 'Catherine the Great and the Origin of the Russian State Debt', in R. P. Bartlett, *et al.*, eds., *Russia and the World of the Eighteenth Century* (Columbus, OH, 1988), and A. G. Cross, 'The Sutherland Affair and Its Aftermath', *SEER*, 40 (1972). K. Heller, *Die Geld- und Kreditpolitik des russischen Reiches in der Zeit der Assignaten, 1768–1839/40* (Wiesbaden, 1983), discusses the paper currency. V. I. Neupokoev, *Gosudarstvennye povinnosti krest'ian Evropeiskoi Rossii v kontse XVIII–nachale XIX veka* (Moscow, 1987), makes a cautious attempt to assess the peasant burden before emancipation.

4   Society

Social policy

Russian rulers' ambitions to regulate society grew in inverse proportion
to their knowledge of it. Setting aside the Commerce Commission's
investigation of the merchantry in the 1760s, it was not until the 1840s,
when positivist-inspired officials undertook detailed empirical studies,
that the government began to understand how rural society worked.
Even then, there were only glimmers of comprehension. Local government was still less well informed. Only after the revolution of 1905–7
did ministers begin to respond to what they discovered when designing
social reform. By then it was probably too late.

   Undaunted, Russia's eighteenth-century rulers assumed that social
policy should derive not from experience but from first principles. They
therefore strove to regulate every aspect of people's lives, not so much
for their own individual benefit as for the greater good of the state as a
whole. This regulation they called 'police' (*Polizey*). Since they also
needed to extract revenue from the population, we must consider the
dual impact on Russian society of fiscal change (representing the
government's immediate requirements) and social engineering (the
expression of longer-term aims). Neither should blind us to the fact that
social change remained in many ways haphazard, often occurring as the
partially or wholly unintended consequence of measures designed to
achieve quite different results.

   A clear example of the contingency of social change is provided by the
history of serfdom, the defining characteristic of Russian society in this
period. Serfs were rarely mentioned in legislation which adversely
affected them. Not until c. 1800 did legislators begin to think of them as
human beings. Repelled by serfdom's inhumanity, Alexander I issued
the Free Agriculturalists Law of February 1803, allowing serfs whose
lords consented to buy not only their freedom, but also land. Full of
good intentions, the tsar commissioned further reform projects in
1815–19. But by then serfdom had become so integral to the Russian

80

régime that, however distasteful it might seem to maintain it, fears of civil unrest led to its retention except in the Baltic provinces where serfs were emancipated without land in Estonia (1816), Courland (1817), and Livonia (1819).

Serfdom had not always been central to Russian society: it took nearly 200 years to enshrine it in law. Although the high cost of free labour in sparsely populated Muscovy offered a powerful economic incentive to enserf the peasantry during a period of territorial expansion, and although it was broadly in the government's interest to cede control over the peasantry to its élites in order that they in turn could serve the tsar, it is striking that the relevant legislation was enacted at times of crisis. Three measures were crucial. First Vasilii II (reigned 1425–62) limited monastery peasants' movement to two weeks around St George's Day (*Iur'ev den'*, 26 November) in the hope of gaining monastic allegiance in a turbulent period. Then Boris Godunov curtailed peasant movement altogether in 1592 or 1593 in order to satisfy the demands of middle-ranking military men for a guaranteed workforce. At the same time, he mollified aristocrats who profited from a measure of peasant mobility by imposing a five-year limit, usually too short, on the time allowed to lesser landowners to reclaim runaway peasants. If the aristocrats who dominated the government had had their way, the five-year limit might never have been rescinded. But riots in 1648 prompted concessions to lesser-ranking frontiersmen who had seen their labour supply depleted by peasant flight. Enserfment was finally decreed in chapter XI of the *Ulozhenie*: from 1649 on, serfs were tied to the land they worked.

In the seventeenth century, the state's interest in serfdom was essentially military; serfs who worked noble lands freed their masters to officer the cavalry. The need for revenue therefore played an insignificant rôle in the process of enserfment. However, once the state became more interventionist, and once military reform rendered the cavalry increasingly obsolete, the enserfed peasantry provided not only a pool of recruits for the infantry, but also a more reliable basis for taxation than their mobile predecessors. By taking advantage of this new resource, the tsars helped to reinforce serfdom. Poll-tax legislation of 1722–4 not only strengthened landlords' powers over their serfs, but also tended to consolidate and simplify Muscovy's splintered social structure. For whilst the privileged exempt minority (the nobility and the clergy) were detached from the mass of the population who were liable (townsmen and peasants, though not soldiers), distinctions within the latter group were overridden by their common obligation to pay the tax.

Slaves (*kholopy*), who accounted for perhaps 10 per cent of the Muscovite population, were the most significant group to disappear. For them, the poll tax marked the culmination of a process reflecting changes in both supply and demand. Former slaveowners could now satisfy their need for labour and prestige from the expanding serf population; the government had found a more efficient source of revenue; the reformed army removed military demand. More importantly, the supply of slaves from the peasantry had dried up, as those who had previously been driven into slavery increasingly sheltered in the multiple-family serf household, to which we shall return. Slavery was therefore not so much abolished as allowed to wither away, though native Siberian slaves continued to be traded through the eighteenth century.

So far we have stressed the incidental social consequences of fiscal reform. However, since human resources were just as important as material ones in Peter I's drive to increase Russia's productive capacity, it would be wrong to imagine that he had no positive social policy. On the contrary, the tsar aimed to determine each group's obligations and privileges according to the contribution it made to the state. Though the zenith of cameralism lay in the future – not until 1727 did Frederick William I of Prussia endow the first chair of *Oeconomie, Policey und Kammer-Sachen* at Halle – Peter's functionalism owed much to the early German cameralists. So novel was their vocabulary that Russian equivalents could rarely be found: the foreign loan-words littered through Petrine legislation symbolised the tsar's commitment to innovation. Yet cameralism nevertheless served to intensify rather than to interrupt Muscovite traditions. Indeed, in reinforcing service to the state as the prime function of society, Peter's reign marked not so much a rejection as the apogee of Muscovite policy.

Since Peter developed principles that were already familiar in Russia, his social engineering cannot be thought revolutionary in conception, even if it sometimes proved radical in effect. Occasionally he formed new groups, an example being the creation in 1719 of 'soldiers' children' (*soldatskie deti*) – a utilitarian attempt to supply a body of technical specialists in response to military need. On the whole, however, the tsar was content to reshape existing social strata. Edicts adjusting the status of townsmen (*posadskie liudi*) may have altered tax-collection procedures, but they did little to change the tax-collecting function of the towns. Most significant of all, the rôle of the nobility in government was regularised and made compulsory by the Table of Ranks, which stimulated the formation of a cohesive noble élite, uniting both military and civil servitors, to supersede the highly differentiated conglomeration of service ranks (*sluzhilye liudi*) who had served Aleksei Mikhailovich.

Social legislation continued to develop haphazardly under Peter I's successors, who never managed to convert the detailed edicts generated by the ethos of 'police' into a stable regulatory system. Even the qualifications for noble status remained uncertain as late as 1767. Catherine the Great set out to eradicate such anomalies, making the impulse to regularise the dominant characteristic of her social policy. Its legislative monuments are the Charters to the Nobility and to the Towns of 1785. Though there were few novelties in the Charter to the Nobility, it fulfilled one of the nobles' prime ambitions by recognising them as what they had effectively become as a result of Peter I's reforms: a permanent, hereditary, corporate estate. Dividing the nobility into six groups, the charter specified the proofs which had to be furnished in order to qualify for noble status. Ignoring the question of a noble's relationship with his serfs, which it left unaltered, the charter confirmed his exemption from compulsory service and corporal punishment (a privilege which Tsar Paul later ignored) and conferred on him the exclusive right to buy villages and establish industrial enterprises. Following this example, the Charter to the Towns defined the individual and collective rights of the urban estate, drew on foreign models to establish craft guilds (*tsekhi*) new to Russia, and, still more innovative, set up three tiers of urban self-government. Both charters should be considered alongside the draft of a third to the state peasantry which, although never promulgated, was probably drawn up no later than 1787, owes much to the Charter to the Towns, and constituted an incipient attempt to codify peasant rights. Though all three charters drew on a variety of sources, collectively they exemplify Catherine's ambition to introduce what Russia had hitherto lacked – a formally constituted hierarchy of carefully delineated estates.

It was not, however, to be a hierarchy based on any single Western model. Both the serfs and the clergy were excluded. Furthermore, Catherine abandoned her support for I. I. Betskoi (1704–95) who attempted to create a third estate of unskilled labourers, craftsmen, and men distinguished in sciences and the arts – a rudimentary version of Russia's missing bourgeoisie – from illegitimate and abandoned children brought up in foundling homes. Neither were Catherine's charters the last word in estate formation. The coalescence of a heterogeneous group of 'people of various ranks' (*raznochintsy*), a category never fully defined in law, epitomises the difficulty the régime experienced in imposing a formal social hierarchy. Not until the nineteenth century did the Russian word *soslovie* come to signify 'estate' in the sense that historians now use it, and even then it was applied not only to such major estates as the nobility, the peasantry, the clergy, and the merchantry, but also to groups such as doctors which we would think of as professions. Thus the period 1800–50 'represented not only a terminological break-through but also a peculiar modernisation of *sosloviia* into more special-ised occupational status groups'.[1] This meant that Russia's estate consciousness was still developing when estates in the West had already begun to dissolve into social classes.

Alexander I's 'military colonies' show that Russia's rulers remained no less confident in the power of rational social engineering at the end of our period than they had been at the beginning. Drawing on the example of southern frontier settlements, established since the seven-teenth century, this ill-fated attempt to convert soldiers into farmers whilst maintaining military discipline was designed partly to absorb troops demobilised after the Napoleonic campaigns. But it also sought to fulfil the tsar's idealistic ambitions to confer order and educated happiness on the countryside. The first colony, founded in Mogilev province in 1810, fell victim to Napoleon's invasion. But the project was revived under Arakcheev who in 1816 established a model colony near his estate at Gruzino in Novgorod province. By 1825, the settlements comprised about a third of the peacetime army and housed some 750,000 including women and children. Yet the whole experiment failed. Though the colonies offered security and sanitation at levels beyond the reach of most peasants, settlers hated the road-building to which they were condemned and sufficiently resented the imposition of forcible improvement to rise in open revolt. Here was a lesson that successive governments were reluctant to learn. Whilst they continued to assume that they could reshape society at will, society had internal dynamics of its own.

Social identities: the peasantry

Peasant heterogeneity

Peasants, in particular, lived in a world of their own, separated, though not severed, from the other estates in ways which we have barely begun to understand. Though peasants constituted over 90 per cent of the population, this monolithic proportion conceals a kaleidoscope of jur-idical status which fluctuated over time. After Peter the Great's reforms, the most important legal division lay between free peasants administered by the state, who lived mostly on the empire's periphery – in the north, in Siberia, and in the south-east – and unfree serfs (*krepostnye*) concen-trated in the longest-settled Muscovite lands. All peasants in permanent

[1] G. L. Freeze, 'The *Soslovie* (Estate) Paradigm and Russian Social History', *AHR*, 91, 1 (1986), p. 24.

bondage to an individual lord were classified as serfs, except for the imperial family's 'court peasants', of whom there were 506,000 in 1719 – 9 per cent of the total peasant population. From 1762 the monarch's own peasants also fell into this category. Rechristened 'appanage peasants' by Tsar Paul in 1797, they numbered 666,000 (6.3 per cent) by 1815.

In 1719, serfs constituted the most numerous category of the peasantry at 55.8 per cent of the total. By 1795 the proportion had dropped to 54.2 per cent in the central lands; elsewhere numbers had increased, not because Catherine II enserfed free peasants to lavish on her favourites (she did not) but because partitioned Poland already contained a disproportionate number of serfs from which many of her grants were made, the remainder being drawn from a pool of serfs confiscated from disgraced nobles. Because serfs accounted for only 48 per cent of the peasantry by 1858, emancipationists claimed that deprivation had stunted their rate of growth. In fact, transfers to the free peasantry probably did more than natural wastage to reduce the proportion of serfs, for perhaps as many as 1.7 million entered the non-servile population between the eighth census in 1836 and 1858, the date of the tenth and last census before the emancipation of 1861.

Though Peter I permitted industrial entrepreneurs to purchase a labour force of 'possessionary peasants' (*possessionnye krest'iane*), the great majority of serfs worked on rural estates. They were divided between those who worked the land and 'household' serfs (*dvorovye liudi*), who included labourers as well as domestic servants. These last, a growing minority, were particularly vulnerable to mistreatment: the Jansenist abbé Jacques Jubé (1674–1745), visiting Russia in the cause of ecclesiastical reunion in the early 1730s, reported an old lackey being forced to grovel before being kicked in the face and stomach for the most minor offence.[2] Yet all serfs languished at the bottom of the social pile as their terms of bondage became harsher. Excluded from the Table of Ranks and banned after 1727 from government employ of any kind (a measure which, like many others, was honoured in the breach), serfs were forbidden to hold land in their own name from 1730. Two years later their lords were permitted to transfer them without warning, and they could also be traded like cattle (which were often more expensive). Laws of 1771 and 1798 forbade the public barter of human beings and the sale of members of the same family to different owners, a practice more frequent among American slaves than Russian serfs. Nevertheless,

---

[2] J. Jubé, *La religion, les moeurs et les usages des Moscovites*, ed. M. Mervaud, *SVEC*, 294 (Oxford, 1992), p. 155, a volume whose remarkable ink drawings make it interesting even to those with no French.

serfs still needed permission to leave their village, to join the army, or to enter a monastery. One of the few powers denied to a lord by 1800 was the right to kill his serf, though some nevertheless perished under the lash. In legal terms, it is hard to imagine a more circumscribed existence.

It was Peter I, in poll-tax legislation of 1724, who first referred to the free successors to Muscovy's tax-paying 'black people' (*chernye liudi*) as state peasants (*gosudarstvennye krest'iane*). Many continued to call them treasury peasants (*kazennye krest'iane*). Of the thirty-three subcategories listed in 1838, three deserve mention. By 1782, there were nearly 264,000 'assigned peasants' (*pripisnye krest'iane*) – created by Peter to man his state factories – many of whom chopped timber for the furnaces of the Ural foundries. The church peasants transferred to state control in 1764 became known as 'economic peasants', not because they offered value for money but because they were administered by the College of Economy. The increasingly impoverished *odnodvortsy*, whose 1.3 million males constituted about 12 per cent of the state peasantry by the 1830s, were 'single-homesteaders' concentrated in the southern provinces of Orel, Kursk, Tambov, and Voronezh, where their ancestors had been lesser-ranking servitors on the Muscovite defensive lines.

The obvious question to ask about these complex juridical categories is whether they made any difference to a peasant's existence. Some are sure that they did not: according to LeDonne, 'legal distinctions counted for little in a system marked by the constant resort to arbitrary power'.[3] Alternatively, we might argue that juridical status did less than market forces to shape peasant life, and folklore suggests that the law merely rippled the surface of a deep reservoir of popular custom. Against this, we know that many serfs saw graduation to the state peasantry as the route to a better life, and the *odnodvortsy* remained the only non-noble Russians permitted to *own* serfs (though few did so).

It might be easier to agree that all peasants were essentially serfs if our understanding of the peasantry were broader based. As things stand, we know little about the majority of small estates where lord and serf coexisted in barely distinguishable circumstances. Instead, our principal evidence comes from accounts, punishment books, and household censuses sent by bailiffs to estate offices in Moscow and St Petersburg belonging to absentee aristocrats such as the Gagarins, the Sheremet'evs and the Iusupovs, who by 1806 controlled land in fifteen provinces and owned more than 17,000 serfs. Such magnates were, of course, excep-

[3] J. P. LeDonne, 'The Eighteenth-Century Russian Nobility: Bureaucracy or Ruling Class?', *CMRS*, 34, 1-2 (1993), p. 144, summarises the most controversial recent thesis about the period.

tional: in 1719, only 0.3 per cent of serfowners possessed as many as 1,000 serfs. Nevertheless, these few owned 17 per cent of the serf population. By 1833, 26 per cent of serfs were divided among the 3 per cent of serfowners with more than 1,000 serfs to their name. It is this lasting concentration of 'human capital' in the hands of a few absentee lords – another distinction between the experience of Russian serfs and American slaves, most of whom lived in small groups on the plantations of resident slaveowners – that justifies the emphasis on the larger estates. But it would be hazardous to generalise about the 'typical' Russian peasant. As recent research has shown, local particularism and regional variation deserve greater emphasis in Russian social history than they have hitherto received.[4]

The peasant household

With this warning in mind, we turn to the household, the primary characteristic of a peasant society.[5] The predominant Western pattern comprised small, nuclear-family units, late and far from universal marriage, and a relatively large age difference between partners. By contrast, Russian evidence indicates the prevalence of multiple-family households, early and virtually universal marriage, and a relatively small age difference between spouses. A further distinction contrasts the strictly patrilineal kinship relationship of Russian households, which rarely contained anyone unrelated to the family, with the customary presence of unrelated servants in the West. Whilst we still rely on a handful of studies of the period 1800–61, caution is advisable. We already know that Russia's urban households seem not to have emulated peasant households' tendency to expand. Until we are sure that differences between East and West were indeed as profound as they now seem, it may be unwise to advance too firm an explanation for them. Yet, despite its narrow base, the available evidence is highly suggestive.

Though the prevalence of multiple-family households in Russia was once explained by age-old behavioural patterns, this cultural argument has been undermined by research suggesting that the nuclear family was the Muscovite norm. The years c. 1675–1725 mark the crucial period of change to the larger unit. Whereas in 1678, 58.5 per cent of all

---

[4] The latest survey is E. Melton, 'The Russian Peasantries, 1450–1860', in T. Scott, ed., *The European Peasantries from the Fourteenth to the Eighteenth Centuries* (London, 1998), pp. 227–66, a volume which emphasises diversity and heterogeneity.

[5] For comparative discussion, see D. W. Sabean, *Property, Production and Family in Neckarhausen, 1700–1870* (Cambridge, 1990), pp. 88–123, and N. Tadmor, 'The Concept of the Household-Family in Eighteenth-Century England', *P&P*, 151 (1996), pp. 111–40.

households in Vologda province were simple-family units, by 1716 the proportion had plunged to 39.2 per cent. To put it another way, among serfs as a whole there were 2.4 males per household before 1645, 3.3 between 1649 and 1679, and 4.6 by 1680–1725. These averages conceal sharp regional differences: where arable land was scarce, work could be done by smaller households than in areas where it was plentiful; here, scarcity of labour prompted the formation of larger, multi-generational households. Averages also fail to show that household size was larger on lay than on church estates and smallest of all amongst the poorest, landless peasants, just as it was amongst indigent townsmen. It is hard, therefore, to speak of an average or even an optimum household size. Yet we can nonetheless point to a rise towards what, on many large estates in the central black-soil region, seems to have become a *common* size of eight or nine.[6]

If we have correctly identified the critical period of expansion, then the main explanation of large household size in Russia lies in the need to preserve economically viable units in order to meet collective tax obligations. As we saw in chapter 3, it was from c. 1650 that the state began to tighten its grip on the tax-paying population. The transfer in 1679 from assessment based on land to assessment based on households was crucial. Officials, lords, and household heads now shared an interest in maintaining large households because these best guaranteed stable productivity and regular tax-paying capability. By contrast, small, break-away households risked lapsing into indigence and becoming a burden on others. Historians of France have suggested that officialdom served to consolidate tradition rather than to modernise it.[7] In Russia, it is worth stressing, peasant society's response to the fiscal pressures of absolutism allowed *less* room for individualism after the 1680s than it had before.

Anxious to prevent incest, the church conformed to a European pattern by increasing its vigilance in sexual matters from the late 1750s (a period when, as we shall see in chapter 8, unfounded fears about a shrinking population were at their most intense). The Holy Synod prosecuted those who married below the age limit, twelve for girls and fourteen for boys, raised to thirteen and fifteen in 1774, and finally to sixteen and eighteen in 1830. Russians nevertheless continued to marry earlier than the Western norm of the mid-twenties: on the Gagarin

[6] For a synthesis of regional studies, warning against oversimplification, see the chapters by V. A. Aleksandrov and I. V. Vlasova in G. A. Nosov, ed., *Russkie: istoriko-etnograficheskie ocherki* (Moscow, 1997), tables at pp. 88 and 101.
[7] See, for example, H. L. Root, 'State Power and the Persistence of Communal Institutions in Old Regime France', *Politics and Society*, 15 (1986–7), p. 241.

estate at Petrovskoe, for example, the average age at marriage between 1813 and 1827 was 18.4 for females and 18.8 for males. Few weddings resulted from individual choice, and some peasants were forced into wedlock by lords whose conception of 'police' extended to govern the most intimate details of their serfs' lives. In 1758, Prince M. M. Shcherbatov (1733–90) ordered that all girls on his estates in Iaroslavl' province must be married at age eighteen and men by their twentieth year; in December 1817, girls at Mishino were threatened with transfer to another Gagarin estate if they refused to marry.

At first sight, these look like classic instances of the lordly interference condemned by Lomonosov in 1761 and by Radishchev's *Journey from St Petersburg to Moscow* (1790). But how widespread was such meddling? Recent work suggests that it was priestless Old Believers, for whom marriage was a controversial sacrament, who were most likely to resist early marriage.[8] Among other peasant women, enforcement was rarer because high mortality rates invested high rates of procreation (and hence early marriage) with a powerful demographic logic. Household patriarchs also saw economic sense in early marriage for sons in a society in which land was redistributed according to the number of co-residing couples in the household. Some, though, preferred to pay fines rather than marry off adolescent daughters who had just begun to contribute to the household's income.

The peasant commune

Vital as the household is in any peasant society, the Russian peasantry was distinguished by the institution through which most business was done – the commune (*mir* or *obshchina*), in which several households came together. On lesser landholdings, the estate itself was generally the unit of communal organisation; on greater estates, village communes operated under the aegis of a larger, central commune. Governed by elders (*starosty*), elected from among their own number by the commune's adult males gathered in assembly (*skhod*), the commune was responsible for organising the work of its members. It set dates for sowing and harvesting grain, and times for cleaning out wells; it allocated use of whatever primitive machinery it might possess, distributed communal lands, collected taxes, and administered basic discipline. Though its origins are uncertain, the commune may have been a self-governing body when it first appeared in the late fifteenth century. By our period, however, whilst it remained a means of defending

---

[8] J. Bushnell, 'Did Serf Owners Control Serf Marriage?: Orlov Serfs and Their Neighbors, 1773–1861', *SR*, 52, 3 (1993), pp. 419–45.

peasant interests, the commune had been emasculated, in ways which remain uncertain, into an instrument of estate management. State and economic peasants seem to have fared little better than serfs in this respect. Immediately after secularisation, some former church peasants enjoyed a brief period of autonomy, but to a government obsessed with regulation their new-found freedom looked more like chaos. As Governor Sievers reported from Novgorod in December 1764, 'the peasants govern themselves in republican fashion, and that government is usually stormy and incompatible with the welfare of each individual'.[9] District organisations (*volosty*) set up for the state peasantry in 1797, comprising around 3,000 male peasants headed by an administrator elected by the *volost'* assembly, were therefore more a 'downward' channel of official direction than an 'upward' channel of local initiative.

The exceptions to this rule were communes on estates whose lords deemed it profitable, c. 1750–1800, either to replace peasant labour services (*barshchina*) with payment in cash or in kind (*obrok*) or more commonly to require some combination of the two. Provided that taxes were promptly paid, communes on *obrok* estates were given considerable latitude in decision-making. Yet the extent to which even they operated on a participatory basis remains uncertain. Communal functions were often taken for granted, rendering assemblies infrequent and debate rare. Resolutions were often made by alleged consensus, so that the commune might be dominated by a few overbearing household heads known as 'yellers and screamers' (*gorlany i krikuny*). Indeed, patriarchal power on *obrok* estates was sufficient to frustrate attempts by members of twenty or so prominent noble families to govern according to rational instruction in order to protect poorer peasants from abuse. 'Enlightened seigniorialism', to adopt Edgar Melton's term, failed because 'its written laws based on more or less abstract norms of conduct' were 'no match for village oligarchies whose control over economic resources, employment, and recruit selection offered concrete advantages to villagers linked to them through patronage and kinship'.[10]

Amongst the most sadistic serfowners was the Moscow heiress Dar'ia Saltykova, imprisoned in a convent in 1768 following the deaths of as many as 100 serfs, most at her own hand. Yet contemporaries concurred that a servile existence was generally more bearable under the direct control of a resident noble, whose serfs were his principal asset, than of a bailiff anxious to impress an absentee master. N. I. Novikov added an

---

[9] Quoted in R. E. Jones, *Provincial Development in Russia: Catherine II and Jakob Sievers* (New Brunswick, NJ, 1984), p. 69.
[10] E. Melton, 'Enlightened Seigniorialism and Its Dilemmas in Serf Russia, 1750–1830', *JMH*, 62 (1990), p. 705.

explicit moral imperative to this tacit economic logic: according to the image promoted in his journal *The Drone* (*Truten'*, 1769–70), it was ignoble to mistreat one's peasants. Untroubled by such niceties, bailiffs depended on the birch. Yet the sources testify to a diversity of punishment practice. Though statistics are rarely an eloquent index of human misery, it is revealing that, whilst thirty-one individuals were flogged more than ten times on Count N. P. Sheremet'ev's estate at Ivanovskoe between 1790 and 1809, only 5 per cent of the 6,624 peasants were formally punished. By contrast, on the Gagarin estate at Petrovskoe punishment was both frequent and widespread: a smaller population of 1,305 serfs suffered 714 floggings between September 1826 and August 1828. Though women were rarely flogged, at least 79 per cent of the adult men were punished, 24 per cent more than once. Considering this range of experience, references to life under 'the servile system' may conceal as much as they expose.

Recent scholars have rightly emphasised the tensions within peasant society. Yet it would be misleading to overlook the collaborative mentality that did so much to form a sense of peasant identity. The prevailing system of collective responsibility (*krugovaia poruka*), whose origins date from Kievan times, naturally obliged the peasantry to undertake much on a collective basis. But not all such co-operation was enforced. Indeed, mutual aid (*pomoch'*), whereby peasant families collaborated to perform tasks beyond the resources of any one of them, was an important feature of peasant life. Though most of our sources date from the late nineteenth century, there are grounds to assume a long tradition. Far from contradicting noble interests, *pomoch'* was usually encouraged by the lord. The instruction sent to the Iusupov estates in Tula and Riazan' provinces in 1825 provides a case in point: bailiffs were to exhort peasants to assist each other whenever possible, since *pomoch'* served to underwrite not only their own well-being, but also the fortunes of the estate as a whole.

Peasant soldiers

Since ninety recruit levies wrenched some 4,500,000 men from their villages between 1705 and 1825 (2 million from twenty-eight levies in the reign of Alexander I alone), it is worth considering their fate separately. Conditions in the army were brutal. Punishments were frequent, severe, and sometimes fatal; few survived running the gauntlet. Crowded garrisons were vulnerable to disease; within four months in 1690, plague destroyed two-thirds of the 762-man fort at Novobogoroditsk. War inflicted still greater havoc. Early nineteenth-century estimates by C. Th. Hermann suggest that the military mortality rate of males between the ages of twenty and forty-five was almost three times higher than that of all Orthodox males. If the precision of these figures is doubtful, the general point seems indisputable. Nor were things any better a century earlier: of the 25,000 men called up in a single draft in 1711, 16,000 were required simply to compensate for losses. Survivors found that inflation damaged their purchasing power. An infantryman's earnings, which in 1711 could have bought him eleven quarters of grain, would have bought less than four in 1796. But a soldier could supplement his income by working privately for his officers, an arrangement which, though plainly open to abuse, may sometimes have been mutually convenient.

Behind the hierarchy of life in uniform, recruits discovered much that was familiar. Just as much in the village depended on the lord, bailiff, and household patriarch, so much in the regiment depended on the company commander, especially whilst unreliable central supplies left soldiers dependent on inadequate local resources. Once peasants had settled in (a transition intended, in a typically paternalist way, to be eased by the advice of an old hand – *diad'ka* – who was supposed to teach the raw recruit the ropes but sometimes bullied and abused him), they found that that communal life flourished as much in the army as in the village. Formerly subordinated to the *mir*, they now joined the *artel'* (co-operative), of which there were four in each division. As in the commune, only a minimum of popular participation was tolerated, the *artel'* being used both as a way of distributing supplies and of monitoring recruits prone to desertion, a phenomenon reduced after the reign of Peter I.

Although in these ways the army constituted peasant society in disguise rather than a modernising instrument of social change, the experience of the soldier, recruited for life (twenty-five years after 1793) or until debility, nevertheless diverged from that of peasants who stayed in the village. If soldiers had remained true to their agricultural origins, they might have found more to admire in Alexander I's military colonies. Instead, soldiers formed a culture apart. Discipline held not only when they were used to suppress localised disturbances, but also against Pugachev. Despite the fragility of regimental identities fractured by the quartering system, it may be that the army became 'the principal social base for an imperial Russian consciousness which was weak or absent in the village'.[11]

---

[11] G. Hosking, *Russia: People and Empire 1552–1917* (London, 1997), p. 190.

Social identities: the nobility

The vanguard of that imperial consciousness was nevertheless the nobility (*dvorianstvo*). Although a dynamic estate – it grew twice as fast as the population between 1782 and 1858 – the nobility remained tiny in proportion to the whole, rising from 0.5 per cent in 1744–5 to 1.4 per cent in 1833. Since this increase owed much to expansion into Polish and Baltic lands, it is debatable whether it marked a strengthening or a dilution of native noble power. In absolute terms, the estate grew from perhaps 19,000 adult males in c. 1700 to over 90,000 by 1816. Small by comparison with the French *noblesse*, the *dvorianstvo* encompassed not only those aristocrats who bear a degree of comparison with the English peerage, which grew from 173 in 1700 to only 267 in 1800, but also a legion of lesser nobles comparable to all armigerous gentry. There is no way round the awkwardness which has led many to remark on the inadequacy of 'aristocracy', 'nobility', and 'gentry' as translations of 'dvorianstvo'. I have preferred 'nobility' when discussing the estate as a whole, 'aristocracy' when discussing the élite within the élite.

Despite the inflation of noble numbers in the seventeenth century (which saw a fivefold increase in the Boiarskaia duma), and the challenge from new men climbing the Table of Ranks, the great boiar families of Muscovy clung tenaciously to the circles of power. Whereas not a single provincial noble figured among the 179 members of the *generalitet* in 1730, there were representatives of no fewer than thirteen of the twenty-two families who had sat on the Boiarskaia duma over the course of the sixteenth century. Men of pedigree continued to prosper under Catherine II, who acknowledged that, 'though free of prejudice and of a philosophical turn of mind', she had 'a great inclination to respect families of ancient descent'.[12] In fact, the Muscovite élite dominated the whole imperial period. A glance at Nicholas II's State Council confirms that, among others, the Dolgorukiis, the Sheremet'evs, and the Golitsyns – all still there at the end of the old régime – must be counted among Europe's most stubborn survivors.

They owed their longevity to a capacity, shared with most European counterparts, to adapt to circumstances: far from the rigid stereotype manufactured by the cruder Marxists, the nobility was one of the empire's most flexible social estates. Indeed, a comparison of Russian nobles with their English and German contemporaries in the nineteenth century suggests that 'it was the Russian [nobility] which offered fewest

---

[12] Quoted in D. L. Ransel, *The Politics of Catherinian Russia: The Panin Party* (New Haven, CT, and London, 1975), p. 51.

challenges to modernity and was the most likely to survive'.[13] Of course, nobles obstructed particular tsarist reforms. Peter I's law of single inheritance of 1714 – designed to protect the state's income, to preserve noble dynasties, and to drive younger sons into state service – ran so far counter to the nobles' traditional reliance on clannish connexions that it was repealed by Anna in 1731.[14] Alexander I's attempt in 1809 to demand rigorous qualifications from noble entrants to the bureaucracy was abandoned in 1834 in the face of noble non-cooperation. Crucially, however, nobles did not seek to subvert the Petrine system as a whole. Most swam with the tide and the few adamant critics are not easily categorised. It is hard, for instance, to distinguish 'new men' supporting Peter from older families harking back to a Muscovite golden age: Shcherbatov, an advocate of pre-Petrine morals who could trace his ancestors back to the fifteenth century and belonged to a princely family claiming descent from Riurik, was the son of one of Peter's most ardent admirers. Even Shcherbatov's own views of Peter were ambivalent. Though contemptuous of their consequences, he praised the tsar's achievements and acknowledged their historical significance.

Whilst tightening their grip on high office, the same few aristocratic families simultaneously consolidated their wealth. Though wealth was assessed in terms of serf-ownership rather than landholding, this alternative measure calibrates no less sharply the chasm between an opulent few and the relatively impoverished majority who, released from obligatory service by Peter III, farmed their own land and enjoyed a standard of living barely higher than that of their peasants. In 1700, all twenty-five of the greatest serfowners, each controlling over 1,000 peasant households, were drawn from fifteen families on the Boiarskaia duma, eleven of which had members on it both in the middle of the seventeenth century and at the end. The same broad pattern persisted: in 1730, two-thirds of the *generalitet*'s serfowners still came from such aristocratic families. Yet they were not representative of the nobility as a whole. In 1762, 51 per cent of the nobility owned fewer than twenty serfs; by 1777 this proportion had grown to 59 per cent, over half of whom owned fewer than ten. In 1800, when a handful of aristocrats could afford to fit out whole regiments, Kursk's governor-general reported that ninety-one nobles in his province had never served in the army because they were too poor to buy the necessary equipment: each owned an average of 4.6 serfs.

Different economic circumstances were reflected in the economic attitudes of the landowners (*pomeshchiki*). For the poorest, the challenge

[13] D. Lieven, *The Aristocracy in Europe, 1815–1914* (London, 1992), p. 248.
[14] See L. A. Farrow, 'Peter the Great's Law of Single Inheritance: State Imperatives and Noble Resistance', *RR*, 55, 3 (1996), pp. 430–47.

was simply to make ends meet; even the rich were less interested in economic development than in regulating peasants' lives. Parallels between the absolute power of a noble over his serfs and the power of the monarch over his state proved impossible to resist. Irrespective of their wealth, few Russian nobles understood investment: their accounts scarcely registered profit and loss. Although relatively few nobles were involved in factory production, the proportion of manufacturing in noble ownership grew thanks to monopolies granted by the tsars. Nobles had always been at the forefront of industry – the Stroganovs, for example, made their fortune in the seventeenth century from salt production at Solikamsk. Yet whereas only 5 per cent of private manu-factories belonged to nobles between 1700 and 1725, by 1813 nobles owned more than half the plants employing more than fifteen workers; 64 per cent of mining enterprises, 78 per cent of woollen cloth factories, 60 per cent of paper mills, 66 per cent of crystal and glass works, and 80 per cent of potash works were also in noble hands.

Swift to see the gains to be made from urban property, nobles owned more than a quarter of the buildings in Moscow by 1775. In time, however, they paid the price of persuading the tsar to deprive the merchantry of the right to own serfs, seeing their grip on the urban property market loosened by rivals whose resources could no longer be invested elsewhere. By the early 1830s, more than a fifth of St Peters-burg's 8,000 buildings were in the hands of merchants. Most nobles remained property-owners rather than developers, though the Belo-sel'skii-Belozerskii family did well out of Krestovskii Island in St Peters-burg. By 1815 they had already built and let some villas there; later in the century they profited from attractions ranging from a prestigious yacht club to pigeon-shooting.

Since there was little comparison between bumbling provincial gentry and the patrician metropolitan magnates who treated their country cousins with open condescension, it is hard to regard the nobility as a class sharing common social and economic interests. Still less, as the crisis of 1730 showed, were they consciously united by these interests in pursuit of agreed political goals. Despite tensions over wars that dis-rupted the estate economy, the relationship between tsar and nobility, like that between the grand prince of Muscovy and his boiars, relied on co-operation rather than conflict. Yet if the language of class seems inappropriate, it is plausible to see the *dvorianstvo* as a Weberian 'status group' with a developing identity – a sense of superiority to which even the poorest could aspire, shaped partly by their commitment to state service and partly by the civilising image of the *honnête homme* propa-gated by journalists from the late 1760s.

A crucial facet of this élite image depended on conspicuous consumption. Although competitive hedonism led many Russian nobles into debt, importunate aristocrats knew that the state would bail them out: financial support was part of its strategy to develop a corporate noble identity. Tsar Paul tried in vain to limit expenditure through the Noble Land Bank, founded in 1754 and merged with the new Government Loan Bank in 1786. But under Alexander I's last finance minister, Kankrin, the bank's activities were expanded. Borrowing rose sharply from 700,000 rubles in 1823 to 13 million in 1825. Since foreclosure was rare, noble indebtedness rose in parallel. Individual loans, some raised against inadequate security (generally in the form of mortgaged serfs), reached huge proportions: in 1828 Count Stroganov alone was granted a loan of 3.2 million rubles.

Contemporaries' preoccupation with status shows that social and economic distinctions between and within estates were not so clear in practice as in theory they should have been. Carefully defined obligations and privileges concealed differences in wealth and power within each estate. Not unnaturally, such differences were accompanied by growing social aspirations. How did the government react?

Social mobility

Since the dominant social ideal remained static and hierarchical, the régime sought to reinforce stability and a distinct sense of degree. However, attempts to restrict mobility conflicted with a dawning recognition that the way to increase efficiency was to reward merit rather than lineage. The government resolved this paradox by discouraging open expressions of *desire* for mobility whilst maintaining an accommodating attitude to mobility itself. Since Catherine II's charters of 1785 explicitly allowed for a degree of controlled progression, it was already a forlorn hope for Shcherbatov to conclude his unpublished tract *On the Corruption of Morals in Russia* (1786–7) with a plea for a return to a world in which 'nobles will serve in various offices with a zeal proper to their calling; merchants will cease to aspire to be officers and noblemen; [and] each will keep to his own station'.[15]

Of the three most promising channels of upward mobility – the church, the army, and state employment – the church offered the slimmest prospects of advancement. So feeble was Orthodoxy's prestige that, in contrast to the pattern among scions of the Western aristocracy,

---

[15] Prince M. M. Shcherbatov, *On the Corruption of Morals in Russia*, tr. and ed. A. Lentin (Cambridge, 1969), p. 259. This was precisely the kind of inflexible Utopia that Shcherbatov depicted in his *Journey to the Land of Ophir*.

almost no Muscovite 'younger sons' entered the episcopate. Apart from those retired boiars who retreated to a monastery to die, the church continued to tempt only 'the pious, the insolvent, and the unambitious'.[16] Since Orthodox bishops are drawn solely from the monastic clergy, incumbency as a parish priest rarely offered a way up the social ladder. But the Muscovite clergy was nevertheless more accessible than it became in the eighteenth century, when it resembled an hereditary caste sufficiently rigid to resist successive attempts at reform after 1825.

From 1700, the number of outside entrants dropped as incumbents' efforts to reserve livings for kinsmen combined first with the clergy's exemption from the poll tax and then with stricter educational qualifications, attainable only by graduates of church schools, to prevent members of other estates from taking up a vocation. Few needed to be discouraged since the miserable status of priests dependent on the material support of their parishioners deterred all but the lowliest from aspiring to join them. Symbolic of the clergy's declining social standing was its exclusion from the Legislative Commission in 1767, a departure from its prominent representation in the Muscovite Zemskii sobor. Just as outsiders were discouraged from entering the clerical estate, so insiders were prevented from leaving it. The Synod resented the brain-drain to the bureaucracy and strove to stem the flow until growing demand from the 1760s made resistance impossible. It was from this generation that Speranskii, son of a priest in Vladimir province, emerged to become Alexander I's principal minister. Until then, the only mobility most clergy experienced was involuntary and unwelcome. Peter I temporarily drafted clerics into the poll-tax population; Anna conscripted them into the army. Catherine II allowed superfluous clergy revealed by the census of 1781-3 to choose their own alternative status. In Moscow province, 49 per cent became townsmen, a further 28 per cent joined the bureaucracy, 18 per cent became merchants, and 5 per cent state peasants. None was enserfed and none was conscripted, though this policy was reversed when the Turks declared war in 1787.

Except in wartime, when increased demand and heavy casualties allowed unusually rapid promotion, the army also proved unreliable as a channel of social mobility. Although Peter I stressed technical competence as the principal criterion for promotion, 'merit' subsequently proved an ambiguous concept. Officers' promotions became more commonly determined by seniority. Buggins's turn favoured time-servers, but there was also a subjective element in which family standing counted for more than ability. Whilst promotions of NCOs could be

[16] G. Alef, 'The Origins of Muscovite Autocracy: The Age of Ivan III', *FzOG*, 39 (1986), p. 67.

sanctioned by the regimental colonel, advancement to the rank of first officer required the divisional commander's decision to be confirmed by the College of War. That college reserved to itself all promotions to the higher ranks, though the tsar might also personally intervene. Adjutants to a field marshal or a court favourite were best placed to benefit: nepotism under Tsar Paul brought two sons of Field Marshal M. F. Kamenskii (1738–1809) to the rank of major-general at the ages of twenty-six and twenty-two when humbler men were taking fifteen years to be promoted captain. Even without such corruption, there would still have been too few senior vacancies in peacetime to satisfy the growing number of qualified applicants, a problem made more acute by the noble preference for military rather than civil service.

Discounting a few upstarts promoted by favourites, military patronage operated overwhelmingly in favour of the nobility. Of a sample of roughly half the officer corps in 1720–1, some 2,245 (61.9 per cent) were nobly born whilst only 13.9 per cent came from non-privileged groups. In 1755, 83.4 per cent of officers were sons of hereditary nobles, and most of the 16.6 per cent who had been promoted from the ranks were 'soldiers' children' whose education had given them the transferable skills which became a necessary passport to promotion. If anything, noble domination was strengthened by legislation of 1796 forcing non-nobles to serve twelve years as NCOs before they could be promoted to officer rank whereas nobles were to serve only three. Two years later, Tsar Paul tried to prevent entirely the promotion of non-nobles (an attempt subsequently wrecked by the revolutionary wars). Even by 1863, only 5.9 per cent of the Russian army's 12,652 officers had been born into the poll-tax population, a figure which scarcely speaks of social mobility on a grand scale.

The most promising peacetime opportunities for advancement were therefore offered by the government employment into which many retired military men moved. Here we must distinguish between the landed nobility, linked only tenuously with state service, and the noble-born career bureaucracy, most of whom were landless. These last, in the ascendant by 1800–50, included a substantial number of 'new men' who rose up Peter I's Table of Ranks. But it would be misleading to ante-date their influence.

In the 1680s and 1690s, Peter's inner circle was proportionately more aristocratic than the Boiarskaia duma as a whole and included none of the 'specialists' the tsar is reputed to have encouraged. Lineage remained especially advantageous in diplomacy, seen as an extension of the dynastic relationship between monarchs. Of the twenty-three Russian permanent diplomatic representatives appointed between 1700 and 1725, eighteen were members of families granted their title before 1600. The best index of the importance of a social pedigree is a parvenu's pretensions to one. And no sooner had a princedom been granted to A. D. Menshikov, the most successful (and most corrupt) 'new man' in Peter's entourage, than he invented a family tree claiming descent from Riurik, though what little is known about Menshikov's social origin suggests that his father, described as a pie-man in one well-known anecdote, was probably a non-commissioned officer in the army.

Peter certainly elevated men of undistinguished origin to high office. P. I. Iaguzhinskii (1683–1736), son of the organist at the Lutheran church in Moscow, became the Senate's first procurator-general in 1722. But this was a promotion brought about by the tsar's personal intervention rather than by a concerted campaign to reward talent. Indeed, in an attempt to preserve the social composition of the higher echelons of officialdom, Peter disqualified the appointment of non-nobles as secretaries in 1724. Though his ban lasted until 1762, a shortage of suitable candidates left the government with little option but to co-opt commoners through the Table of Ranks. By 1755, however, only a quarter of officials at the ennobling eighth rank and above were not of noble origin. While access became easier lower down the table, the social composition of senior positions grew more select. By 1850, 77 per cent of officials at ranks 1–5 were nobly born by comparison with 65 per cent at ranks 6–8. The pinnacle of Russian government was increasingly the preserve of an expanding corps of career service nobles.

In an effort to buttress the nobility, the tsars barred a growing proportion of the non-noble population from taking a place on the Table of Ranks. Household servants and peasants were excluded in 1727, followed in 1766 by soldiers' children and in 1771–2 by the whole poll-tax population. This left only the clergy, whose sons were therefore prominent among the early nineteenth-century *raznochintsy*. Neither the Table of Ranks nor any subsequent legislation defined methods of promotion. The careers of civil officials were therefore dependent on some of the same ambiguities as those of their contemporaries in the military. After 1802, when new universities were founded to streamline entrance to the bureaucracy, a vain attempt was made to define objective standards of performance. Yet even when the government later generated more functional specialisation, it managed to limit social change. Ransel's judgement on the reign of Catherine II remained valid until 1825:

The terms merit and service, while certainly implying a minimum level of competence, were most prominently associated with such ideas as the status and quality of one's family over several generations, the proved merit of one's forbears through long service to the crown, and a level of culture and refinement that reflected not merely technical expertise but, more important, an aristocratic and courtly manner.[17]

This is not to say that there was no social mobility in Russia: it simply suggests that it operated more easily *within* estates than *between* them. The debate on peasant differentiation is one of the most fundamental in Russian historiography. Seizing on a remark in Lenin's *The Development of Capitalism in Russia* (1899), Soviet scholars used to argue that nascent capitalism encouraged peasant stratification within the village from the late seventeenth century. Too many, however, relied on evidence from a single year, which naturally revealed some peasant families to be richer than others at any one time. Dynamic analyses of household mobility – a better index of lasting differentiation – are still rare, but from what we know about communal repartition of land it seems improbable that permanent differentiation predominated on *barshchina* estates where it was in no one's interest to allow a permanently impoverished stratum to develop. Here, as Steven Hoch has shown, cyclical mobility is more plausible. We ought, however, to distinguish between the mobility of peasants on estates in the fertile black-soil region and those elsewhere. By the 1780s, 63 per cent of peasants in the non-blacksoil provinces were on *obrok*, by comparison with fewer than 20 per cent in the 1700s. Even Shcherbatov, convinced that labour services were the serf's proper obligation and that the peasantry's abandonment of agriculture was 'the fundamental evil in Russia', nevertheless encouraged his serfs in Vladimir province to seek the profits he knew they could make as far afield as Kostroma, Moscow, and Kazan'. 'Encouraged' may be the wrong word: paragraph 33 of Shcherbatov's instruction to his bailiffs was entitled 'On forcing peasants to trade in grain'.

Released from the fields, peasants engaged in industrial and proto-industrial activities. In a few spectacular cases, whole villages were transformed into businesses run by serf entrepreneurs. Contrary to the implications of modernisation theory, serfs were proportionately more numerous among wealthy peasants than either state or crown peasants. The most famous was the Sheremet'ev estate at Ivanovo in Vladimir province, which could boast forty-nine cotton printing plants by 1803. Profiting from the havoc wreaked on their Muscovite competitors by the Napoleonic invasion, the men of Ivanovo (mostly Old Believers) achieved an output valued at 1.75 million gold rubles by 1817. Of course, only a tiny proportion of serfs achieved such success. On the Sheremet'evs' metal-working estate at Pavlovo, bailiffs found in 1811

[17] Ransel, *The Politics of Catherinian Russia*, p. 279.

that, whilst there was a 5 per cent stratum of 'capitalist' peasants commanding a capital of at least 1,000 rubles each, 93 per cent of households were unable to pay their taxes. It was only in the 1850s that a significant number of serf entrepreneurs were granted (or allowed to purchase) their freedom. Until then, they worked in the name of their lord, since it was only in 1848 that they were allowed to own immovable property in their own right.

Extravagant operations like Ivanovo and Pavlovo were exceptional. More common was the practice of *otkhodnichestvo*, which allowed peasants temporarily to 'move away' to trade in the towns. Mobility was supposedly restricted by the internal passport system introduced with the poll tax between 1719 and 1726. The scheme was presumably designed to standardise the handwritten passports granted by landlords since at least the 1680s. If so, it failed. Further attempts in the same vein, such as Elizabeth's in 1743, were also only partially successful. It is therefore hard to quantify internal migration. By repeatedly renewing their passports, some peasants managed to absent themselves almost permanently from their villages by the 1760s. To the chagrin of urban residents with whom they came into competition, they took up a trade in the towns. By 1798, some 20 per cent of the male population of Iaroslavl' province had been issued with such passports. Even those irregular traders who legally remained peasants shared many characteristics of the urban population, being socially indistinguishable from them. The Moscow suburbs, for example, sheltered numerous small textile enterprises operated by peasants who escaped regulation and taxation by failing to renew, or never taking up, the necessary licences.

Nevertheless, thousands of peasants did improve their legal status by joining the *posad* community, though to do so they must in theory have acquired immovable urban property and been able to pay taxes in both the town and their native village until the poll-tax register was revised at the next census, which might be a lifetime away. In Moscow province, the majority of the new influx became petty merchants and craftsmen, presumably better off than immigrants who remained in the peasant estate, but not easily distinguishable by occupation. A list compiled in 1803 of 346 'trading peasants' from a Sheremet'ev estate in Tver' province, midway between the two capitals, shows around half of them living in either St Petersburg or Moscow and another two in Riga. We cannot, however, assume that peasant migration grew over time. According to Mironov, it shrank in the second half of the eighteenth century and in some years, for example 1779–83, went into reverse so that the proportion of the population living in towns dropped dramatically from 12 per cent in 1742 to 8 per cent in 1801 (still a larger proportion than many other scholars would allow).

Even so, geographical mobility was a more promising route to permanent change of status than that taken by serfs who stayed put and enjoyed the dubious fruits of a specialised education. The proliferation of serf talent is not in doubt. At least 1,100 former serfs worked in the capital's ministries between 1797 and 1826; we know more than 100 serf architects and interior decorators by name (including Andrei Voronykhin, a Stroganov serf freed in 1786, who designed the Kazan' cathedral in St Petersburg); and there were countless actors and singers. Yet for most the prospects were slim. Parasha Zemchugova, who in 1800 crowned a dramatic career at Kuskovo by marrying a Sheremet'ev, was the exception who proved the rule. Many were employed in a cultural rôle for only part of the year; some, once trained, scarcely used their talents. Though the successful were well paid, their education merely accentuated their degraded status. Some found this intolerable (Field Marshal Kamenskii was murdered by his musicians); others reconciled themselves to a life of shame. Count Shakhovskoi's troupe at Nizhnii Novgorod (1798–1827) was segregated by gender and subjected to corporal punishment. Following the sale of the company for 100,000 rubles on Shakhovskoi's death, the actors were freed on condition that they remain in their jobs for at least ten years. Few were so fortunate. On inheriting Arkhangel'skoe in 1831, B. N. Iusupov was so appalled at the annual expenditure of more than 60,000 rubles on household serfs that he disbanded the school for artists founded by his father in 1818. Of the thirty-two artists then working on the estate, only one family was freed, as decreed in N. B. Iusupov's will: twelve more were sent on *obrok* to St Petersburg and five went back to work in the fields.

As their fate demonstrates, social mobility was just as likely to operate downwards as upwards. No one knew this better than the merchantry who spent most of our period on a social and economic seesaw. Only three families achieved continuous representation among the merchant élite (*gosti*) between 1623 and 1710. By 1725 the *gosti* as a whole were practically extinct, a victim of Peter I's state monopolies. Freer trade in later years offered no greater security. An analysis of sixty merchant families in Moscow between 1780 and 1840 found that 35 per cent originated in the peasantry, 48 per cent were merchants from other towns, and 17 per cent former townsmen (the category into which most failed merchants fell). Only a quarter of the Russian merchants engaged in foreign trade in 1772 remained active in 1804, and only a fifth managed to sustain regular trade between 1796 and 1804. Under the impact of the Napoleonic invasion, the number of merchants registered in all three guilds fell by around half between 1812 and 1824. It is some indication of the uncertainty experienced by the merchantry in Alexander I's time that petitions solicited by the minister of finance in 1823 looked back on Peter the Great's reign as a golden age of prosperity.

We need finally to consider the position of women, on which much work remains to be done. Frustrated by sources so thin for the early part of our period that even élite individuals remain anonymous, one scholar has been reduced to inventing some evidence of her own.[18] Yet more conventional methods are nevertheless revealing. Russian noblewomen's property rights were superior to those of their European counterparts. Curiously, the *Ulozhenie* gave them greater rights over land granted in return for military service than it did over hereditary estates. When Peter I abolished the distinction between the two types of land in 1714, a woman earned the right to inherit all her husband's lands. As widows, therefore, noblewomen were generously treated both in Muscovy and under the empire. But their youth and married lives were often more restricted. Confined to separate quarters (*terem*), whose origins remain unclear, Muscovite women of royal and noble birth became pawns in the power struggle for marriage alliances between rival boiar clans. So severe was the pressure to accept arranged marriages that for some the only escape was to the convent. From the time of Peter I there may have been some improvement, though surely not everyone rejoiced in her obligation to attend the 'assemblies' he initiated – social gatherings of both sexes which were praised abroad (by men) for marking the beginnings of women's acceptance in society. Later in the century, Western literature introduced a new image of the woman as lover, and noblewomen themselves, profiting from Catherine II's interest in education for girls, formed a growing readership for sentimental novels. Foreigners in the 1780s and 1790s continued to note the comparatively restricted part played by women on the Russian social scene. But by the mid-1830s it was no mere whimsy for Pushkin to claim that Russian women were 'in general more educated, better read, and more up-to-date with European ways of doing things than us proud [men], God knows why'.[19]

There was, however, an uglier side to the coin. Peasant women were punished for holding up the example of a female ruler to husbands who

[18] R. Bisha, 'Reconstructing the Voice of a Noblewoman of the Time of Peter the Great: Daria Mikhailovna Menshikova. An Exercise in (Pseudo) Autobiographical Writing', *Rethinking History*, 2, 1 (1998), pp. 51–63.
[19] A. S. Pushkin, *Dnevniki, zapiski*, ed. Ia. L. Levkovich (St Petersburg, 1995), p. 111, 'Table-talk'.

put them in their place. Abandoned soldiers' wives (*soldatki*), despised as women of easy virtue, were the only peasant widows to head their households. Many, however, slid into vagrancy. If caught, they risked being set to work in state manufactories, though repeated decrees in 1736, 1744, 1753, and 1762 imply that prosecution was inefficient. Household serfs were vulnerable to noble sexual predators and a few *pomeshchiki* maintained serf harems (paradoxically represented as a Europeanised way of life requiring literate girls to read to their master). But women could just as commonly expect loathsome treatment from their husbands as from their lords. If the rigid patriarchal mores of the Domestic regulation (*Domostroi*)[20] of 1550 had been relaxed for noble-women, peasant girls were still raised in fear of their fathers and husbands. Not until in 1906 were the head of household's disciplinary powers tempered by law. Meanwhile, women could be beaten and abused with little chance of redress until the reforms of the 1860s allowed them to appeal to peasant courts.

The origins of the saying 'a crab is not a fish and a woman is not a person' – one of many misogynist peasant proverbs – are therefore not far to seek. But it would be wrong to underestimate the significance of women in the village. As domestic industry developed, women were valued not only as wives and mothers but also as workers in a variety of specialised rôles assigned according to sex, including reaping, milking, spinning, and weaving. It may even be that attitudes towards female children changed for the better, at least in the most modernised city in the empire. Girls were probably more often victims of infanticide than boys in Muscovy and there was certainly a marked preponderance of females among the first abandoned children admitted to Betskoi's foundling homes in the 1760s. In St Petersburg, however, this discrepancy between the sexes disappeared between 1780 and 1820, some fifty years before it did so in Moscow, a change which has been attributed to the higher degree of urbanisation in St Petersburg province (where, in 1832, 75 per cent of the population lived in towns, compared with 26 per cent in Moscow province), to the high demand for female servants in the capital, and to the relatively high degree of mechanisation in the textile industry, which required unskilled female labour. Whether St Petersburg's women noticed any improvement as a result of these changes is a moot point. Social mobility was beyond the majority in 1825. Like their menfolk, they had their place and were expected to keep it. But what of those who did not like it?

---

[20] *The Domostroi: Rules for Russian Households in the Time of Ivan the Terrible*, ed. and tr. C. J. Pouncy (Ithaca, NY, 1994).

Social conflict

If exploitation and brutality had been not only necessary but sufficient causes of rebellion, then the natural state of Russian society would have been civil war. No régime could have survived that. What had to be found – between lord and peasant, no less than between ruler and ruled – was a workable compromise. Sometimes that compromise was actively negotiated; sometimes it was merely resentful and sullen.

Peasant resentment was bound occasionally to flare into rebellion. Revolt was most common after the accession of a new tsar, when popular trust in the monarchy as the fount of natural justice raised expectations of reform to their highest pitch and the despondency of disillusion was correspondingly severe. A new landowner could cause trouble by reimposing control on estates where serfs had grown accustomed to a modicum of independence; thus the reintroduction of labour services on *obrok* estates contributed to a noticeable increase in unrest in the years around 1800. Troops were called to suppress serf revolt 150 times in the reign of Alexander I alone, when the aftermath of the Napoleonic wars proved a particularly troubled time. Most resented of all were attempts to move peasants to another village or to break up family units. Peasant society was far from inflexible. But change of any kind, when imposed from outside, was enough to unsettle it, and a bailiff who tactlessly transgressed the unwritten code of peasant justice could unwittingly spark off a disturbance.

The greatest revolts – those of Razin (1670–1), Bulavin (1707–8), and Pugachev (1773–5) – were directed less against noble exploitation than against the extension of state power to the south-eastern borderlands, the undergoverned frontier that had traditionally provided a refuge for society's outcasts. As such, the lands between the Volga and the Don came to shelter, alongside native Bashkirs and Kalmyks, a heterogeneous combination of freebooting Cossacks, Old Believers, and peasants in flight from the burden of taxation. In 1773 they combined for one last time in protest against the intrusion of rational colonial authority. Pugachev, a Don Cossack who pretended to be the murdered Peter III (see chapter 7), attracted support by attacking the secularised imperial élite and promising to protect the people (*narod*) by restoring a just personal monarchy, rooted in Russian Christian tradition. He briefly captured both Kazan' and Saratov, but ultimately proved no match for the regular troops.

Conflict on this scale was exceptional. In general, violent resistance remained geographically scattered and politically uncoordinated. It was also remarkably rare. As David Moon observes, 'The main conclusion to be drawn from the enormous efforts Soviet historians made to find evidence of a "peasant movement" in servile Russia is not how much peasant resistance there was to serfdom, but how little.'[21] For most peasants, most of the time, the chance of a successful revolt must have seemed negligible. When they saw authority collapsing around them during Pugachev's revolt, the few recently enserfed peasants in the south-east took advantage of mayhem begun by others to burn down their lords' manors; when serfs elsewhere heard that the rebellion had been suppressed, resistance collapsed. Opportunities such as the one Pugachev provided were infrequent. Elsewhere, the chances of organised rebellion were slim and further weakened by conflicts of interest within the peasantry. Was, then, the serf's natural response to exploitation simply apathy and random violence? Folklore suggesting that the lords who were most vulnerable in 1773–4 were those considered 'bad', 'unjust', or 'cruel' casts doubt on the idea that peasants were predisposed to passivity. Indeed, considering the manipulative ways in which they dealt both with each other and with higher authority, it is more likely that deliberate lying, cheating, and backsliding were among the most effective forms of 'everyday' peasant resistance.[22]

If the low level of peasant violence can be interpreted partly in these negative terms, many would agree that there is also a positive explanation for it. For all the degradation it imposed upon him, serfdom was not without advantage to the serf. On the southern frontier, serfs were protected by the army from raids by dispossessed nomads. Most significant of all, serfdom offered a haven from the ravages of the market: starvation and unemployment. To the risk-averse Russian peasant, Moon suggests, these were no mean temptations. He is surely right to argue that serfdom did more to reinforce than it did to undermine the stability of Russian society.

This is not to say that Russian society was not shot through with violence. It is simply to recognise that, like mobility, tensions were more prominent within estates than between them. Whilst communal society compelled collaboration, peasant life was far from the fraternal nirvana later fantasised by Slavophile publicists (who themselves ranked among the wealthiest serfowners). Indeed, though it has so far been convenient for us to separate collaboration and conflict, to do so is artificial: it was

---

[21] D. Moon, 'Reassessing Russian Serfdom', *European History Quarterly*, 26, 4 (1996), p. 495, an excellent synthesis.

[22] The key conceptual work is J. C. Scott, *Weapons of the Weak: Everyday Forms of Peasant Resistance* (New Haven, CT, 1985), a study of a Malaysian village in the late 1970s. On Russia, see R. D. Bohac, 'Everyday Forms of Resistance: Serf Opposition to Gentry Exactions, 1800–1861', in E. Kingston-Mann and T. Mixter, eds., *Peasant Economy, Culture and Politics of European Russia* (Princeton, 1991), pp. 236–60.

the need for constant co-operation that created so many occasions for dispute. And disputes between peasants were integral to the taxonomy of serfdom. 'In the end', as Hoch concludes, 'far outweighing the economic exploitation of the landlord was the social oppression of serf over serf.'[23]

Conflict began in the household. Whereas 80 per cent of men in their thirties could expect to be heads of household in pre-industrial England, only 10 per cent were likely to have reached that enviable pinnacle on the Russian estates we know best. Thus the median age for heads of household at Mishino in 1814–34 was between fifty and fifty-four years. In a rigidly patriarchal society, where peasant families lived in the cramped intimacy of a one-room hut (izba), both intergenerational conflict and sibling rivalry were naturally prime causes of dissent. Six of the nine household partitions at Mishino between 1812–16 were caused by 'constant fighting' among brothers. At Petrovskoe, serfs could expect to head their households earlier, at about the time they became a grandfather, between the ages of thirty-five and forty-five. Here it was more distant relatives who separated as households divided. There was little room for sentimentality whilst the family remained principally an economic unit of production and whilst patriarchs dominated at their relatives' expense. And yet the emotional aspect of kinship cannot be ignored. What is interesting, as anthropologically inspired studies of early-modern Germany have shown, is the interaction of emotional and economic needs.[24] In the Russian context, we have scarcely begun to understand its complexity.

From the household, conflict radiated out into the commune. Conscription was a prime cause of tension between household heads. Peasants went to extraordinary lengths to avoid being called up. Few can have emulated Tolstoy's fictional peasant, Platon Karataev, who rejoiced in the suffering of conscription, to which he was condemned in *War and Peace* for stealing, because by sinning he had spared his brother who had a family to support. Despite dire penalties, most peasants preferred to mutilate themselves, run away, or feign disability rather than be recruited. Those who could afford it bought themselves out after the ban on paying for substitutes, imposed on the poll-tax population in 1737, was lifted by Peter III in 1762. Substitutes were often chosen from among household serfs, or from poorer peasant families. Exemption

[23] S. L. Hoch, *Serfdom and Social Control in Russia: Petrovskoe, a Village in Tambov* (Chicago, 1986), p. 160. This is the most powerfully argued recent study of the peasantry.

[24] See, e.g., H. Medick and D. W. Sabean, eds., *Interest and Emotion: Essays on the Study of Family and Kinship* (Cambridge, 1984).

certificates provided a profitable trade for middlemen. In 1816 alone, a commune on the Lieven estate in Kostroma province paid 64,000 rubles for thirty-two exemption certificates, a sum sufficient to cover the commune's *obrok* bill for three and a half years.

Conscripts still had to be found, their departure being mourned in ceremonial dirges (*plachi*) in the manner of a funeral. Though many estates kept household registers to give successive drafts the appearance of equity, abuses were common. Most communes took the opportunity to get rid of drunks, debtors, and criminals. Other choices were more controversial, prompting complaints that dishonest commune officials conspired to conscript peasants who had complained about them. Landowners were anxious to ensure that older men were drafted since they contributed least to the estate economy. Household heads shared their concern: to lose a young recruit was to lose a vital worker. Yet some were bound to lose because fairness was impossible. Though no system was codified until 1831, drafts generally relied on a rota of families defined by the number and ages of male workers and dependants. Alternatively, recruits might be chosen by lot from households with the largest number of males. A universal lottery system for males over twenty was adopted in 1854 as the least unsatisfactory system from the state's point of view. Not until the introduction of universal conscription in 1870 was the commune relieved of its duty to select recruits, but by then demographic pressure on the land had probably converted 'surplus' males into a communal liability rather than an asset.

Since land lay at the core of peasant society, disputes about its distribution were uniquely vituperative and rarely rational. Believing that peasants on his newly acquired estate in Penza province had insufficient land, M. A. Obreskov reallocated it in 1813 on a more egalitarian basis, only to find that he had inadvertently stirred up long-standing antagonisms which erupted in violence. Similar frustrations had long deterred reformers. Sievers realised that, 'without oppressing the peasant, far more income could be drawn from them than at present, if they were handled differently'.[25] But when he tried to lease land to peasants on the court estate at Korostina in the mid-1770s, they first petitioned for a return to the former arrangements and then refused to work. When the administration of the estate at Tsarskoe Selo began a new land survey in 1772, it met with resistance quelled only by troops and the temporary exile of the ringleaders to Siberia.

A third level of conflict was between villages. Although *otkhodnichestvo* offered some the chance to travel (and state peasants, like soldiers,

[25] Quoted in R. P. Bartlett, 'J. J. Sievers and the Russian Peasantry Under Catherine II', *JfGO*, 32, 1 (1984), p. 17.

could be moved at will), many serfs never left their native village which formed as much a cultural as a geographical horizon. Peasants probably became most conscious of their wider social class – 'the peasantry' – only when separated from it. Thus, peasants 'ascribed' to Ural factories joined Pugachev not out of some radical belief in Western notions of 'freedom' but out of a desire to abandon the industrial labour to which they had unwillingly been assigned and return to the fields where they felt they belonged.

More powerful than any class affiliations were peasants' loyalties to their own commune or village, defined in contradistinction to 'outsiders'. Outsiders defy simple definition. The priest, for example, might be either an insider or an outsider, depending on circumstances: clergy were suspected by both peasants and officials of being greedy self-seekers, capable of switching to either side. Some did indeed inspire or participate in peasant rebellions, though they were legally forbidden to draft petitions for serfs. In the aftermath of Pugachev, the Kazan' and Orenburg commissions punished forty-five of the seventy-three clergy they investigated, a high proportion which has plausibly been ascribed to the authorities' unrealistic expectations of instinctive clerical obedience. *Pomeshchiki* and officials counted as outsiders, but so did peasants from other villages with whom rivalries developed. *Pomeshchiki* commonly felt the need to instruct bailiffs to ensure that serfs lived peacefully with neighbouring villages, especially when the neighbours belonged to the same lord.

All outsiders were suspect to peasants whose sole recognised authorities were the tsar and the village. But the greatest suspicion was reserved for the rootless men and women who slipped between the estate system's juridical boundaries into the social margin. The biggest menace came from gangs who sheltered in the forest between nocturnal raids. Brigandage had been sufficiently prevalent in Muscovy to require a chancellery (Razboinyi prikaz) to suppress it. Towns, including Moscow, remained as vulnerable as villages until the middle of the eighteenth century. Banditry was subsequently confined to Russia's major roads and waterways, on which valuable salt caravans were a sitting target. Only the undergoverned south-east – along the Volga around Saratov, in the steppe around Orenburg, and on the borders of the Caspian Sea – remained a permanent danger zone. Elsewhere, trouble recurred sporadically during times of dearth such as the mid-1780s. Retired or escaped soldiers often acted as ringleaders. The legendary idleness of supernumerary clergy encouraged the belief that they too were prone to disorder. Some probably were, especially after secularisation thrust many into unanticipated need. Crowds of clerical beggars who appeared in Moscow in the autumn of 1764 were returned to their dioceses, a move which soon prompted complaints to the Synod of gangs of clerical youths ransacking the countryside.

Though we can understand brigandage in part as a form of social protest – the reaction of deserters and serfs in flight from injustice – the class-conflict approach has clear limitations. Like nobles elsewhere in early-modern Europe, landowners themselves participated in banditry, leading their own peasants against local rivals. Referring to Britain, Vic Gatrell observes that 'the word "crime", when used at all before the 1780s, usually referred to a personal depravity. It lacked the problematic and aggressive resonance it was soon to acquire.'[26] In eighteenth-century Russia, where the virtues of regulation and 'police' were so heavily stressed by the authorities and notions of the individual conscience so poorly developed, law-breaking could not escape social connotations. Yet no modern conception emerged in our period of either crime or 'the criminal' as pathologically subversive. Though they terrorised their victims, Russia's vagabond gangs were as innocuous to the régime as the bands of youths roaming western Europe at the time, appropriately characterised by Olwen Hufton as an escape valve for a hierarchical society.[27]

Conflict was not confined to the lower orders. So intense was rivalry between Muscovite boiar clans that a sophisticated system of precedence (*mestnichestvo*) had to be devised to resolve disputes. Following the system's uncontentious abolition in 1682, nobles found new ways to defend their integrity. Duelling was one that persisted in the face of legislation threatening death under Peter I and dishonour under Catherine II, who issued a manifesto condemning duels as 'alien' to Russia on 21 April 1787. Only after 1800 did the duel acquire a firm place in the culture of nobles inspired partly by Western notions of chivalry and partly by a lasting psychological need for an autonomous and consistent code of behaviour, beyond the vagaries of state control.

A different sort of noble conflict loomed large in the Legislative Commission of 1767. Petitions preoccupied by provincial parochialism rather than by national politics suggest a widespread feeling that the repeal of Peter I's law of single inheritance had produced estates so small as to be worthless. Had it not been for the supply of new land to the south, the situation would have been worse still. Parcellisation posed

[26] V. A. C. Gatrell, 'Crime, Authority and the Policeman-State', in F. M. L. Thompson, ed., *The Cambridge Social History of Britain, 1750–1950*, 3 vols. (Cambridge, 1990), vol. III, p. 248.

[27] O. Hufton, 'Attitudes Towards Authority in Eighteenth-Century Languedoc', *Social History*, 3, 3 (1978), p. 292.

two problems: it encouraged the longstanding temptation for wealthier lords to prey on vulnerable neighbours and it generated a plethora of inheritance disputes.

The lack of standardised measures and instruments, combined with the need to rely on the word of rivals, made the recorded Muscovite boundaries dubious; recent acquisitions, many surreptitious, were seldom registered at all. Here were circumstances ripe for dissent and there is abundant evidence of litigation over title to land. Struggles were intensified by complex patterns of tenure which divided villages among as many as a dozen landowners, often in unequal proportions. In 1778–81, for example, the general survey of Voronezh province showed the villages of Utkino and Verkhnee Kazache, comprising a total male population of 289 and 4,061 *desiatiny* of land, divided among more than eleven landholders, some of whom also shared other villages. In some areas, single ownership of a village had become the exception rather than the rule by 1800.

Fearful of taxation or confiscation, Russian nobles conformed to a European pattern in their reluctance to submit to surveys which might have eased the difficulty. Even the intransigent Joseph II failed to complete his 1784 survey of Hungary, though he defied opposition until nine days before his death in 1790. Some sense of the welcome accorded to surveyors sent out by Sophia in a vain attempt to complete the Muscovite survey begun in 1676 is given by an edict of 1686 stipulating that landowners who stole their measuring rods must be publicly flogged. Pososhkov devoted a chapter of his *Book of Poverty and Wealth* (1724) to a scheme recording permanent, unambiguous boundaries. However, as he tacitly acknowledged, this was a Utopian ambition: 'people of consequence will do their best to hinder it because they are accustomed to do just as they please and are not so fond of giving as of receiving'.[28] In the long term, this pessimism was vindicated. As Yaney puts it, 'the better traditional society worked on the basis of bogus measures, the more capable it became of resisting the imposition of accurate measurement'.[29] Catherine II's surveyors had to agree to recognise *de facto* possession, after an attempt begun under Elizabeth in 1754 had foundered on noble arguments over the extent of title. Officials thus left both title and multi-ownership as unresolved problems, providing plenty of work for the upper land court (*verkhnyi zemskii*

---

[28] I. Pososhkov, *The Book of Poverty and Wealth*, ed. and tr. A. P. Vlasto and L. R. Lewitter (London, 1987), p. 331.

[29] G. L. Yaney, *The Systematization of Russian Government: Social Evolution in the Domestic Administration of Imperial Russia 1711–1905* (Urbana, IL, 1973), p. 117.

sud) created by the provincial reform of 1775 specifically to settle such recurring complaints.

Russian society in 1825 was still dominated by many of the attributes which modernisation theory associates with 'traditionalism'. Juridically, Russian subjects were beginning to be classified by estate in ways which already seemed too rigid in the West. Stability was imposed and reinforced by a potent combination of government policy and an ethos identifying the desire for promotion with dissent. Peasant family size remained large, household structure complex. Both formed part of a communal network of collective responsibility which placed greater restrictions on individual choice and social mobility than Muscovy had ever known.

Eighteenth-century Russia therefore manifested almost all the characteristics of Frederick Tönnies's 'community' (*Gemeinschaft*) – based on spontaneous association, kinship-ties, household co-operation, and custom. It showed only incipient traces of a more modern 'society' (*Gesellschaft*) based instead on contractual and commercial relationships between autonomous individuals. However, since Tönnies intended neither *Gemeinschaft* nor *Gesellschaft* to serve as an all-embracing description of any one society, and sensibly allowed instead for combinations of both, it would be artificial to ossify his insight. In the same way, modernisation theory is useful only if we reject its more restrictive implications. Emphasis on the stability and homogeneity of traditional society should not be taken to imply stasis and stagnation. On the one hand, stability partly derived from the informal negotiations between individuals that were a crucial feature of such an underinstitutionalised society. On the other hand, society was alive with tensions and rivalries, many deriving precisely from the fact that social reality was too complex to be confined within the state's juridical straitjacket. Undeterred, the régime persisted in its efforts to categorise. As a historian of medieval England remarks, in estate-minded societies 'the reaction to overt signs of changing conditions is not to conclude that the framework needs loosening, but almost the opposite, to seek to define more narrowly and relate more carefully functions and "degrees" within the social whole'.[30] That was what happened in imperial Russia. But with what consequences? In the long term, the state can be pictured striving to contain social forces which it had created out of need, but could not afford to allow to develop independently. But it would be wrong to underestimate the 'plasticity and complexity in the *soslovie* system', a flexible structure

---

[30] M. Keen, *English Society in the Later Middle Ages 1348–1500* (London, 1990), p. 8.

permitting 'specialisation and occupational professionalisation' within 'a formal system of hereditary estates'.[31]

The 'traditional' and the 'modern' were not successive stages in Russia's social development: they overlapped and interacted.[32] Indeed, the very attempt to modernise paradoxically reinforced the archaic elements in Russian society. Mobility *was* possible, and more wide-spread than scholars once supposed. But for every one who took his chance, there were thousands for whom the mirage of opportunity – on those rare occasions when it shimmered into view – swiftly dissolved into the despair of thwarted ambition. Only a tiny minority of Russians could afford to indulge in 'getting and spending'. What mattered was self-preservation. For aristocrats, self-preservation was a matter of status, and status was demonstrated by display. But for others, including many lesser nobles, it was a matter of survival: the spectre of economic ruin hung over every village. Once disaster struck, the first line of defence lay in the family and the household. But in their collective attempts to prevent the worst, each social group looked for state intervention to defend its own privileges against encroachment by others. The next chapter therefore seeks to explain why an avowedly paternalist Russian state failed in its ambition to overcome arbitrariness and was unable to provide the predictable government and justice that its subjects so clearly desired.

BIBLIOGRAPHICAL NOTE

M. L. Bush, ed., *Social Orders and Social Classes in Europe Since 1500* (London, 1992), discusses strategies of stratification. Freeze's pene-trating synthesis (above, n. 1) underestimates the importance of estates to Catherine II. For a corrective, see the special issue of *CASS*, 23, 1 (1989), on the charters of 1785. M. Raeff, 'The Well-Ordered Police State and the Development of Modernity in Seventeenth- and Eight-eenth-Century Europe: An Attempt at a Comparative Approach', *AHR*, 80 (1975), introduces the *Polizeistaat* model. D. M. Griffiths is more incisive on 'Eighteenth-Century Perceptions of Backwardness: Projects for the Creation of a Third Estate in Catherinian Russia', *CASS*, 13 (1979), than H. D. Hudson on 'Urban Estate Engineering in Eight-eenth-Century Russia: Catherine the Great and the Elusive Meshchan-stvo', *CASS*, 18 (1984). D. L. Ransel, *Mothers of Misery: Child*

---

[31] Freeze, 'The Soslovie (Estate) Paradigm', pp. 23–4.
[32] For a trenchant warning against the developmentalist assumptions implicit in modernisation theory, see S. Reynolds, *Kingdoms and Communities in Western Europe, 900–1300*, 2nd edn (Oxford, 1997), pp. 333–9.

Abandonment in Russia (Princeton, 1989), focuses on Betskoi. Two case studies by E. K. Wirtschafter, 'Soldiers' Children, 1719–1856: A Study in Social Engineering in Imperial Russia', *FzOG* (1982), and *Structures of Society: Imperial Russia's 'People of Various Ranks'* (DeKalb, IL, 1994), carry broad implications for the complexity and vitality of society. R. Hellie, *Enserfment and Military Change in Muscovy* (Chicago, 1971), analyses the institutionalisation of serfdom. V. Semevskii, *Krest'ianskii vopros v Rossii v XVIII i pervoi polovine XIX veka*, 2 vols. (St Petersburg, 1888), is the populist classic on the peasant question, complemented (and criticised) by: I. de Madariaga, 'Catherine II and the Serfs: A Reconsideration of Some Problems', *SEER*, 52 (1974); P. Dukes, 'Catherine II's Enlightened Absolutism and the Problem of Serfdom', in W. E. Butler, ed., *Russian Law: Historical and Political Perspectives* (Leiden, 1977); R. P. Bartlett, 'J. J. Sievers and the Russian Peasantry Under Catherine II' (above, n. 25); and Bartlett, 'Catherine II's Draft Charter to the State Peasantry', *CASS*, 23 (1989). R. Pipes, 'The Russian Military Colonies, 1810–1831', *JMH*, 22 (1950), is still a good starting point.

The striking synthesis by E. K. Wirtschafter, *Social Identity in Imperial Russia* (DeKalb, IL, 1997), stresses that mobility fostered integration rather than instability. J. Blum, *Lord and Peasant in Russia: From the Ninth to the Nineteenth Century* (Princeton, 1961), is a readable classic, but its methods are made to seem pedestrian by M. Confino, *Domaines et seigneurs en Russie vers la fin du XVIIIe siècle* (Paris, 1963).

T. Shanin, ed., *Peasants and Peasant Societies*, 2nd edn (Harmondsworth, 1987), introduces the conceptual debate. R. P. Bartlett, 'The Russian Peasantry on the Eve of the French Revolution', *HEI*, 12 (1990), complements Melton's survey (above, n. 4). In addition to Hoch (above, n. 23), see R. D. Bohac, 'Peasant Inheritance Strategies in Russia', *JIH*, 16 (1985); P. Czap, 'The Perennial Multiple-Family Household, Mishino, Russia 1782–1858', *Journal of Family History*, 7 (1982); Czap, 'A Large Family: The Peasant's Greatest Wealth: Serf Households in Mishino, Russia 1814–1858', in R. Wall, ed., *Family Forms in Historic Europe* (Cambridge, 1983); and Czap, 'Marriage and the Peasant Joint Family in the Era of Serfdom', in D. L. Ransel, ed., *The Family in Imperial Russia: New Lines of Historical Research* (Urbana, IL, 1978). G. L. Freeze, 'Bringing Order to the Russian Family: Marriage and Divorce in Imperial Russia, 1760–1860', *JMH*, 62 (1990), goes beyond the peasantry. Russian scholars explore anthropological perspectives in M. M. Balzer, ed., *Russian Traditional Culture: Religion, Gender and Customary Law* (Armonk, NY, 1992). Valuable Soviet work includes Iu. A. Tikhonov, *Pomeshchich'i krest'iane v Rossii:*

feodal'naia renta v XVII–nachale XVIIIv. (Moscow, 1974), and V. A. Aleksandrov, *Sel'skaia obshchina v Rossii* (Moscow, 1976).

Apart from N. M. Druzhinin's mammoth *Gosudarstvennye krest'iane Rossii i reforma P. D. Kiseleva*, 2 vols. (Moscow, 1946), the state peasantry are relatively poorly served. To the quantitative study by V. M. Kabuzan, 'Gosudarstvennye krest'iane Rossii v XVIII–50kh godakh XIX veka: chislennost', sostav i razmeshchenie', *Istoriia SSSR* (1988), add W. Sunderland, 'Peasants on the Move: State Peasant Resettlement in Imperial Russia 1805–1830s', *RR*, 52 (1993). On the *odnodvortsy*, see J. Pallot and D. J. B. Shaw, *Landscape and Settlement in Romanov Russia 1613–1917* (Oxford, 1990). R. Hellie, *Slavery in Russia, 1450–1725* (Chicago, 1982), is as learned as it is long. P. Kolchin, *Unfree Labour: American Slavery and Russian Serfdom* (Cambridge, MA, 1987), offers sustained comparisons and contrasts. For a still wider range, see M. L. Bush, ed., *Serfdom and Slavery: Studies in Legal Bondage* (London, 1996). On the army, see chapter 2, above.

On nobles, see first I. de Madariaga, 'The Russian Nobility', in H. M. Scott, ed., *The European Nobilities in the Seventeenth and Eighteenth Centuries*, vol. II (London, 1994). Lines of recent research appear in *Noblesse, état et société en Russie, XVIe–début du XIXe siècle*, a special edition of *CMRS*, 34, 1-2 (1993), which includes several essays in English. N. S. Kollman, *Kinship and Politics: The Making of the Muscovite Political System, 1345–1547* (Stanford, CA, 1987), R. O. Crummey, *Aristocrats and Servitors: The Boyar Elite in Russia* (Princeton, 1983), and B. Meehan-Waters, *Autocracy and Aristocracy: The Russian Service Elite of 1730* (New Brunswick, NJ, 1982), make the case for continuity. M. Raeff's portrait of an alienated class in *The Origins of the Russian Intelligentsia: The Eighteenth-Century Nobility* (New York, 1966), is undermined by M. Confino, 'A propos de la noblesse russe au XVIIIe siècle', *Annales: Economies, Sociétés, Civilisations* (1967). W. R. Augustine, 'Notes Toward a Portrait of the Eighteenth-Century Nobility', *Canadian Slavic Studies*, 4 (1970), and R. D. Givens, 'Supplication and Reform in the Instructions of the Nobility', *CASS*, 11 (1977), analyse noble petitions to the Legislative Commission, the focus of P. Dukes, *Catherine the Great and the Russian Nobility* (Cambridge, 1967). R. E. Jones, *The Emancipation of the Russian Nobility 1762–1785* (Princeton, 1973), is first-rate. R. D. Givens, 'To Measure and Encroach: The Nobility and the Land Survey', in R. P. Bartlett, *et al.*, eds., *Russia and the World of the Eighteenth Century* (Columbus, OH, 1988), complements P. G. M. Dickson's more detailed 'Joseph II's Hungarian Land Survey', *EHR*, 106 (1991). On noble entrepreneurship, see A. Fenster, *Adel und Ökonomie in vorindustrielle Russland: die unternehmerische*

Betätigung der Gutzbesitzer in der grossgewerblichen Wirtschaft in 17. und 18. Jahrhundert (Wiesbaden, 1983). I. Reyfman, 'The Emergence of the Duel in Russia: Corporal Punishment and the Honor Code', *RR*, 55 (1995), complements V. G. Kiernan, *The Duel in European History* (Oxford, 1989), whose Russian evidence is mostly literary.

The best account of social mobility is B. N. Mironov, *Russkii gorod v 1740–1860e gody* (Leningrad, 1990), which moves beyond the urban. On the early merchantry, see J. Kaufmann-Rochard, *Origines d'une bourgeoisie russe (XVI et XVII siècles)* (Paris, 1969), and S. H. Baron, *Muscovite Russia* (London, 1980). W. Daniel, 'Grigorii Teplov and the Conception of Order: The Commission on Commerce and the Role of the Merchants in Russia', *CASS*, 16 (1982), contrasts ideal and reality. If a full-blown study of the merchants is lacking before the nineteenth century, covered by A. J. Rieber, *Merchants and Entrepreneurs in Imperial Russia* (Chapel Hill, 1982), the detail in G. L. Freeze, *The Russian Levites: Parish Clergy in the Eighteenth Century* (Cambridge, MA, 1977), is rivalled only by its exhaustive sequel, Freeze, *The Parish Clergy in Nineteenth-Century Russia: Crisis, Reform, Counter-Reform* (Princeton, 1983). For the bureaucracy, see chapter 5, below.

D. Morrison, *'Trading Peasants' and Urbanization in Eighteenth-Century Russia: The Central Industrial Region* (New York, 1987), offers a case study of *otkhodnichestvo*. For Manuilovskoe, see R. Bohac, 'Agricultural Structure and the Origins of Migration in Central Russia, 1810–1850', in G. Grantham and C. S. Leonard, eds., *Agrarian Organisation in the Century of Industrialisation: Europe, Russia and North America, Research in Economic History*, Supplement 5, Part B (1989). M. D. Kurmacheva, *Krepostnaia intelligentsiia Rossii: vtoraia polovina XVIII–nachalo XIX veka* (Moscow, 1983), is informative if overblown on the 'serf intelligentsia'. For limited studies of noblewomen, see Iu. M. Lotman, *Besedy o russkoi kul'ture: byt i traditsii russkogo dvorianstva (XVIII–nachala XIXv.)* (St Petersburg, 1994), and G. G. Weickhardt, 'Legal Rights of Women in Russia, 1100–1750', *SR*, 55 (1996). Like most good work on the subject, B. E. Clements, B. A. Engel, and C. D. Worobec, eds., *Russia's Women: Accommodation, Resistance, Transformation* (Berkeley, CA, 1991), skirts our period but offers a good bibliography. More on this important subject is expected soon from a younger generation of scholars.

For approaches to the relationship between crown, nobility, and peasantry, see T. Robisheaux, *Rural Society and the Search for Order in Early Modern Germany* (Cambridge, 1989), W. Beik, *Absolutism and Society in Seventeenth-Century France* (Cambridge, 1985), and H. L. Root, *King and Peasant in Burgundy* (Berkeley, CA, 1987). There is nothing quite like them on Russia, though E. Melton discusses the 'peasant state' in 'Household Economies and Communal Conflicts on a Russian Serf Estate, 1800–1817', *Journal of Social History*, 26 (1993), emphasising the divisiveness of conscription, on which see R. D. Bohac, 'The Mir and the Military Draft', *SR*, 47 (1988). Good studies of Pugachev include M. Raeff, 'Pugachev's Rebellion', in R. Forster and J. P. Greene, eds., *Preconditions of Early Modern Europe* (Baltimore, 1970), and P. Longworth, 'The Pugachev Revolt: The Last Great Cossack–Peasant Rising', in H. A. Landsberger, ed., *Rural Protest: Peasant Movements and Social Change* (London, 1974). There is no book on crime, though J. L. H. Keep, 'Banditry and the Law in Muscovy', *SEER*, 35 (1956), and D. Eeckaute, 'Les brigands en Russie du XVIIe au XIXe siècle: mythe et réalité', *Revue d'Histoire Contemporaine*, 12 (1965), cover aspects of law-breaking. Compare them with R. J. Evans, ed., *The German Underworld: Deviants and Outcasts in German History* (London, 1988).

5   Government and justice

The court

So dazzling was the court's display that its political significance is in danger of eclipse. Not even its composition has been properly studied. Yet the court lay at the heart of Russian government. Its ceremonial offered a magnificent representation of tsarist rule and constituted a distinctive form of power in itself; as the tsar's residence, the court exerted a magnetic attraction on all who hoped to influence him, thus becoming the forum of Russian politics and the fount of imperial patronage; and, under rulers who chose to exercise their prerogative as the ultimate decision-maker, the court became the crucible of personal monarchy.

The ambivalence of the word 'court' makes it hard to define. Yet whilst one must distinguish between the court as a government institution, as a society of the tsar's acolytes, and as the setting for both, to divorce any one of these meanings from the others is to lose sight of the distinctive whole. I shall therefore take a synthetic approach demonstrating that each tsar played a vital part in forming his own court ethos: in this sense, at least, Sir James Harris was right to declare in 1778 that, 'in an absolute monarchy, everything depends on the disposition and character of the Sovereign'.[1]

Though it is often said that early-modern monarchs modelled their courts on Versailles, many similarities owed more to these institutions' common origin in the medieval household than to deliberate imitation.[2] The Muscovite household was distinguished by the design of its palaces and by its unique practice of confining women to separate quarters (*terem*). But Muscovy shared, from c. 1500, in a wider European transition from a relatively unselfconscious princely household – serving

[1] *Diaries and Correspondence of James Harris, First Earl of Malmesbury*, 4 vols. (London, 1844), vol. I, p. 204.
[2] H. M. Baillie, 'Etiquette and the Planning of the State Apartments in Baroque Palaces', *Archaeologia*, 101 (1967), p. 170.

both the military and civil needs of the government – to the calculated
formality of a court acting as the political centre of a régime whose
administrative business was now transacted elsewhere.

The scale of the transformation must not be overstated. Whilst
Muscovite ceremonial developed precociously, one of the later court's
greatest attractions was its combination of the formal with the informal:
foreigners often noted the relaxed atmosphere at St Petersburg, especially under Catherine II. Furthermore, the chronology of the transition
is blurred, not least because Russian uses the same word (*dvor*) for both
household and court. Yet transformation there surely was, as expanding
noble numbers in the seventeenth century helped not only to subordinate the political significance of the Boiarskaia duma and the Zemskii
sobor (nineteenth-century names for assemblies in which the tsar
respectively consulted all his boiars and representatives of his other
subjects) but simultaneously to elevate that of the court (where he could
deal more effectively with a select few – the *blizhniaia* or *komnatnaia
duma*, so called because it met in the tsar's private apartments – holding
informal gatherings of larger groups as and when necessary). Muscovite
court protocol reached a new peak of self-consciousness under Aleksei
Mikhailovich, a man of remarkable devotion and habit, who imposed on
his entourage a rigid routine based at one level on a round of banquets
and secular ceremonies and at another on the Orthodox liturgical
calendar.

Ritual allowed the tsar to demonstrate the divine origin of his power,
to legitimate what was still a parvenu dynasty enthroned only in 1613,
and to cement his relationship with prominent boiars by ceremonially
acknowledging the value of their service. Public appearances reached a
still wider audience. In the most important of these – the Blessing of the
Waters at Epiphany (dating from around 1520 and last celebrated on 6
January 1905), and Palm Sunday (when the tsar led into the Kremlin a
donkey ridden by the patriarch in a re-enactment of Christ's triumphal
entry into Jerusalem) – the tsar and his boiars expressed their common
respect for the church, and symbolised the notional consensus between
the ruling trinity of monarch, patriarch, and boiars.

It was partly because it fostered a régime of unspeakable tedium that
the structure erected by Aleksei Mikhailovich could be dismantled
without demur by his son. Muscovite ceremonial, symbolising a mutually supportive relationship between the tsar and his boiars, may have
been a psychological necessity for both. But that did not make it
popular. Though admission to the court's ritual was in itself a valued
sign of favour, the pleasure of accompanying pious tsars to monasteries
near Moscow soon palled among their more vigorous henchmen.

Neither was it long before warriors wearied of the lugubrious baroque dramas for which their sovereigns, and some of their more learned fellows, showed such unaccountable enthusiasm in the late seventeenth century. Aleksei Mikhailovich punished boiars who arrived late for services by ducking them in the river. It was still more humiliating to be demoted by Sophia for lax observance of one's duties. So it was unlikely that courtiers would clamour to reinstate the rarefied rituals which Peter I allowed to lapse.

The last time Peter took part in an established court ritual was his appearance with Tsar Ivan in the Easter procession in 1694. Following his half-brother's death two years later, Peter was away from Moscow at Easter between 1697 and 1700. It was in that year that the Palm Sunday ceremony lapsed forever with the patriarchate (though whether it was then *deliberately* discontinued in the way that the patriarchate was subsequently abolished in 1721 remains debatable).[3] It was not that Peter was insensitive to the power of ceremonial: on the contrary, he strove to represent his rule with an impressive array of both religious and secular celebrations. Nevertheless, the tsar's lasting preference for debauchery and drink in the company of his notorious All-Mad, All-Jesting, All-Drunken Assembly stood in contrast to the mannered cultivation of Louis XIV's etiquette at Versailles. Brutal methods prevailed even when Peter attempted to inculcate courtly behaviour on the European model at St Petersburg during the latter part of his reign, notably among the entourage of his second wife: he and Catherine regularly danced on and on until his nobles collapsed with exhaustion.

The prospect of being force-fed with alcohol for failing to match Peter's new standards of conduct must have been as offensive to his leading subjects as it was to the foreign envoys who dreaded what seemed to them his incurably boorish behaviour. It is all the more striking, therefore, that his ruthless efforts to establish a Western-style court should subsequently have borne fruit under Anna and Elizabeth, whose indolence in government did not prevent them from presiding over the consolidation and expansion of ceremonial and display. It is hard to be sure of the court's exact dimensions since the few available figures are difficult to compare. Still, a list of 1730 named 625 people who accounted for an annual salary bill of 83,571 rubles, and eleven years later the court establishment stood at 559, costing 87,426 rubles. Servants, tradesmen, casual employees, and hangers-on made the court as a whole much larger. One estimate of the total number of satellites in its orbit has been derived from the fact that the court's move back to

[3] See L. Hughes, 'Did Peter I Abolish the Palm Sunday Ceremony?', *SGECRN*, 24 (1996), pp. 62–5.

Moscow in 1725 reduced the population of St Petersburg by about 5,000. Such a figure is not improbable. In 1550 the *dvor* numbered around 3,000, about two-thirds of them servants; during the Time of Troubles, the figure dropped to around 1,000; by the 1690s it had recovered to 3,500 or so. A document from 1701 speaks in terms of more than 6,000. An early eighteenth-century Russian court of between 5,000 and 7,000 would fit plausibly into a European scale rising from around 1,500 in George I's Royal Household to 10,000 at Versailles. Whatever its size, the court was transformed in style and substance between 1730 and 1761. Elizabeth's reign in particular saw the building of new palaces to furnish a suitably refined setting for the court's lengthy calendar of processions and ceremonies, most by this time secular and all governed by arcane rules of precedence.

Scholars have found it hard to decide whether European ceremonial was intended to reflect the centralisation of power (as, for example, in France), to compensate for its absence (as in the case of the papacy), or to buttress belief in the supernatural powers of the monarch. In Russia, the crucial stimulus was surely the desire for international recognition. Muscovite tsars had always been sticklers for diplomatic protocol, and as part of his plan to reassert Russia's rightful place among its European rivals, even Peter the Great, so many of whose habits were inimical to the development of a court culture, understood the value of ceremonial celebration of his foreign conquests. These began with the parade to mark the capture of Azov in 1696 and culminated in the celebrations following the treaty of Nystad in 1721. Triumph in the Great Northern War offered an irresistible opportunity to create new festivals and firework displays in St Petersburg, the ultimate *Residenzstadt*. The palace at Peterhof, built by the German architect J. F. Braunstein and the Frenchman J. B. LeBlond between 1714 and 1721, was begun from elementary sketches by the tsar himself. Even Peter's most apathetic successors saw the need to compete with their European rivals, and Russia's powerful performance in the Seven Years War generated still more elaborate ritual. Catherine II's adviser on foreign affairs, Count N. I. Panin, could hardly have been more explicit in his justification of the new formalities: 'etiquette strictly regulates forms of correspondence between states precisely because it serves as a measure of the mutual respect for each other's strength'.[4]

Since nobles knew that intimacy with the tsar might enhance both their fortunes and their political influence, commitment to court life from above was matched by interest from below. Seven of Peter I's

[4] Quoted by H. M. Scott, 'Russia as a European Great Power', in R. Bartlett and J. M. Hartley, eds., *Russia in the Age of the Enlightenment* (London, 1990), p. 28.

twenty-three favourites had served in his entourage, and the others had all been in contact with the court before 1689. Only those with regular access to the tsar were likely to catch his eye. The principal secretary, in particular, might wield an influence greater than that of a college president. The Table of Ranks granted those ranked four and above a special 'right to court'. But others were also admitted by mechanisms which remain uncertain: the closed Muscovite court had now opened its doors to a wider range of people, including women released from the *terem* by Peter the Great.

There were undoubtedly dangers for a monarch who kept too large a court. La Harpe echoed centuries of advice to princes by warning the future Alexander I that a tsar could maintain his mystique only by staying aloof. As if to exemplify the point, one of the century's most powerful rulers, Frederick the Great, effectively dispensed with a court altogether. On the other hand, a large entourage could multiply the numbers of those indebted to the monarch: the fate of the reclusive Louis XVI offers a pertinent counter-example of the perils of isolation.

If, for the ruler, the attraction of a court lay in the opportunity to consolidate the loyalty of powerful acolytes, then, for the courtier, it lay in the chance to progress from the penumbra of its outer fringes to the limelight of its inner sanctum, there to bask in the ultimate glory (not to say personal advantage) of familiarity with the monarch. Just as the benefits to be gained by 'making' one's court could hardly have been greater, so the hurt caused by exclusion was bitter: it carried implications for the reject's status far beyond the palace's narrow confines. 'People are well or ill received in society, in proportion as they are well received at Court', noted a perceptive British visitor, who christened it 'the thermometer of the town'.[5] This was in 1790, the same year that Radishchev's motive for writing his critical *Journey from St Petersburg to Moscow* was ascribed by Catherine II to the fact that '*he does not have entrée to the palace*'.[6] Exclusion was the sovereign's ultimate sanction. Peter III's manifesto of 1762, freeing the nobility from obligatory service, warned that those who failed to pursue it voluntarily would be despised, scorned, and banned from court. Though the *Ulozhenie* of 1649 specified disgrace (*opala*) as the penalty for a range of offences, its use as a political weapon declined sharply during the seventeenth century from its zenith under Ivan the Terrible. No longer were troublesome nobles dressed in tattered, black clothing, with their heads shaved

[5] A. G. Cross, 'British Sources for Catherine's Russia: (1) Lionel Colmore's Letters from St Petersburg, 1790–1791', *SGECRN*, 17 (1989), p. 23.
[6] A. N. Radishchev, *A Journey from St Petersburg to Moscow*, tr. L. Wiener, ed. R. P. Thaler (Cambridge, MA, 1958), p. 240; emphasis in original.

as a sign of disfavour. They could still be deprived of their property. But this, too, was a penalty used sparingly after 1740. Most outcasts were simply ostracised. Though they continued to regard ritual as burdensome, courtiers were thus ineluctably drawn into what Elias, referring to Versailles, has called 'a ghostly *perpetuum mobile*' of etiquette and ceremony, 'impelled ... by the competition for status and power of the people enmeshed in it – a competition both between themselves and with the mass of those excluded – and by their need for a clearly graded scale of prestige'.[7]

The 44-grade court hierarchy decreed in the Table of Ranks attempted to provide such a scale. Though a list of Louis XIV's court establishment dating from 1721 was found in the archive of Peter the Great's closet (*Kabinet*), the titles he eventually adopted were not French but German. Moreover, the transition to the new terminology was gradual rather than abrupt: just as most of the 'new' titles dated from the late seventeenth century, so some of the 'old' Muscovite nomenclature survived into the 1730s. Other idiosyncrasies also outlived the imposition of a rational structure. In particular, tsars showed a marked tendency to promote their courtiers to inflated military ranks since these were more prestigious. In 1737, for example, Anna advanced her chamberlains from the seventh to the fourth rank, equating them with major-generals.

As such irregularities imply, the Russian court long bore a closer resemblance to the courts of petty German princes than to Versailles. If life was unpredictable under Elizabeth, it was often arbitrary under Anna, herself the widow of a petty German prince. Though it is tempting to associate female rule with femininity, Anna's vindictiveness could be categorised as feminine only by a misogynist. In the 1730s, the Muscovite image of the courtier as the tsar's 'slave' (*rab*, generally best translated as humble servant) survived in more than symbolic terms. Anna's minister A. P. Volynskii (1689–1740) had the writer V. K. Trediakovskii (1703–69) beaten for insolence; subsequently he was himself executed. Anna condemned Prince M. A. Golitsyn to become her jester for converting to Catholicism, sentencing him not only to marry a Kalmyk but to consummate the union in a huge ice-palace in which the wretched couple nearly froze to death. Later, under Catherine II, Princess Dashkova amused her friends with stories of how Golitsyn had been made to sit cackling like a hen in a basket of straw. By then, court circles had developed a new sense of corporate and even individual dignity that was lacking in earlier years when violence among élites was

---

[7] N. Elias, *The Court Society*, tr. E. Jephcott (Oxford, 1983), pp. 86–7.

still common. Except during the succession crises of the late seventeenth century, not many nobles elected to play a purely ceremonial rôle: 31 per cent did so in the unsettled period between 1676 and 1689, three times as many as between 1600 and 1675. After 1700, the court overlapped as before with military and civil officialdom, suggesting that, whilst personal contact with the monarch offered access to high office, secure careers required a broader base. Yet not even the risk of rough treatment could dissuade 'all those who had the honour to serve' the court from ruining 'themselves past redemption in the effort to make a figure', as the Austrian envoy under Anna observed.[8]

Although Catherine II believed a degree of self-restraint to be incumbent upon a monarch ruling in the interests of the general good, she also stressed the utility of display. Even her expedition to the Crimea in 1787, accompanied by only three foreign envoys and the leading courtiers, required 14 carriages, 124 sledges, and 40 supplementary vehicles to service it. Like her contemporaries, however, she faced a dilemma: whilst Joseph II caused resentment by cutting back court expenditure to 2 per cent of the state budget, a quarter of what his mother had spent, Catherine's allocation of up to 12 per cent to her court offended those who equated luxury and extravagance with degeneracy and corruption (see chapter 7).

Though a penchant for uniform is usually taken as an index of militarism, in Catherine's case it signalled a relaxation of etiquette. About the militarism of her son, however, there is no room for doubt. Shortly after Paul's accession, the British minister was among many who reported that 'with respect to the Character and outward appearance of the Court, it is absolutely necessary to see in order to believe it. The ease and tranquillity of the late Reign are lost with Her from whom they derived. Everything is now military, and that most minutely.'[9] Whilst aristocrats loath to suffer Paul's cane fled to Moscow or abroad, soldiers rejoiced in the expectation that Peter III's barrack-room culture might now be restored. Yet far from implying an ascetic rejection of ceremonial, the new militarism provided an opportunity to indulge in it to excess. In his 'Instructions' to his second wife in 1776, Paul had suggested that an exacting daily régime offered 'protection from our own fantasies, which frequently become caprices' (an acute self-diagnosis, if nothing else). A monarch's observance of etiquette thus set an example to those 'obliged to subject themselves to the same rules'. In keeping with these senti-

[8] C. H. von Manstein, *Contemporary Memoirs of Russia from the Year 1727 to 1744* (reprinted London, 1968), p. 255.
[9] Quoted by R. E. McGrew, 'A Political Portrait of Paul I from the Austrian and English Diplomatic Archives', *JfGO*, 18 (1970), p. 513.

ments, it was Paul who set the court on a new administrative footing in 1797, forming a hierarchy of separate households for members of the Imperial family and reshuffling the orders of chivalry created piecemeal over the course of the eighteenth century into a formal ladder of prestige headed by Peter the Great's Order of St Andrew.

If the Austrian ambassador found Paul's obsession with etiquette 'incredible', the endless parades and ceremonies at Gatchina fascinated Grand Duke Alexander, not least because they offered relief from the clutches of his grandmother. Following his unexpectedly early accession, Alexander preserved a military manner at court and revived parade-ground pageantry after 1815. Many who remembered the old days under Catherine thought him miserly, being struck by the comparative pomp of the French court when they arrived triumphant in Paris. Alexander's palace interiors were indeed severe by comparison with those of his predecessors. But their calculated simplicity was deceptive. Between 1808 and 1812, the tsar received a full monthly account of the work of architects at the court of his ally, Napoleon; entering the Tuileries in 1814, he anticipated the opening gambit of a subsequent conqueror, Adolf Hitler, on arrival at the Paris Opera, by declaring himself so familiar with the building that he had no need to be shown round.

In the early nineteenth century, however, the dowager empress Mariia Fedorovna, who presided over a comparatively intimate domestic régime at Pavlovsk, inspired a change of tone. Here were the origins of a new vision of monarchy shared elsewhere in Europe, not least in Britain, where George III bequeathed to his successors a potent combination of apparent domesticity, ritual splendour, and a willingness to travel. The final element in this successful formula was adopted in Russia by Catherine the Great, and belatedly revived by Alexander II, who toured the provinces in the late 1850s and early 1860s in an effort to expunge the image of Nicholas I as fearful despot and to portray himself instead as a benevolent tsar, raised above politics and sensitive to popular needs.

Superficially, the domestication of the Russian court signalled its isolation and a recognition that power had passed to the ministerial bureaucracy. That was what Nicholas I's secret police implied in their 'Brief survey of public opinion' for 1827:

In Catherine's time, people with court positions had great weight in the eyes of society at large and, each being a fixed star at court, stood in the city as a small sun with its own planetary system receiving movements and impulses from that sun. Now the matter stands quite differently. Courtiers form a sect apart ... The opinion of the court plays no role in society.[10]

[10] Quoted by S. Monas, *The Third Section: Police and Society in Russia Under Nicholas I* (Cambridge, MA, 1961), p. 67.

Whereas the court had previously given politics a certain focus, its secret machinations now served more often to subvert than to support ministers. In fact, the court's withdrawal from the public gaze ranks among the most significant destabilising influences in Russian politics after 1800. So long as the court remained at the centre of government, it was usually possible to neutralise favouritism's potentially disruptive effects. By contrast, nineteenth-century ministers might be undermined by a court camarilla whose influence they were powerless to combat. One of the most prominent groups plotting the fall of Speranskii in 1811 was a clique orchestrated by Mariia Fedorovna in concert with an improbable array of foreign residents, including the Sardinian ambassador, Joseph de Maistre. Of course, it remained possible for court contacts to promote rather than stifle ministerial policy: the grand duchess Elena Pavlovna played a pivotal rôle in gaining reformist bureaucrats a hearing from Alexander II in the 1850s. For the most part, however, the court's growing isolation served only to intensify the later tsars' mistrust of even their most loyal servants.

Central and local government

If the court was the arena in which eighteenth-century nobles competed for the attention of monarchs who themselves inspired and sometimes formulated legislation, then the degree to which it was integrated into the machinery of government is less certain. How supple was the linkage between politics and administration?

A succession of institutions which might have become the linchpin of Russian government bore scant resemblance to the Western bodies whose titles they echo. Created mostly to disguise or to exploit monarchical weakness, they owed their origins to national emergencies and operated best in time of war, when they played a key part in co-ordinating strategy. Under Peter the Great, the closet (*Kabinet*), founded in 1704 and run by A. V. Makarov (1675–1750), allowed the tsar to monitor his central administration. After Peter's death, co-ordinating power passed to the Supreme Privy Council, a front for nobles who saw off Menshikov. Anna's closet was intended to bypass Biron, though it succumbed to him in the end. A Special Conference at the Imperial Court was created in 1757 to co-ordinate the Russian attack on Prussia during a period of lax imperial control. None of these bodies carved out a stable, supervisory rôle for the court. Peter III simply abolished the conference and replaced it with his own personal council, never given a name. In practice, the Russian administration was co-ordinated by a fluctuating series of *ad hoc* groups with varying degrees of influence over the monarch and of control over officials. Most modern bureaucracies stand for continuity in government: this was an ambition that Russian officialdom struggled to achieve.

Posing as the hammer of favourites whilst inwardly bidding to augment his own influence, Panin proposed in 1762 the creation of a regular, permanent Imperial Council. Catherine the Great, having toyed with the idea, rejected its implicit restriction on her absolute power. Ironically, the subsequent creation in January 1769 of a 'council attached to the court' at the onset of the war against Turkey marked a defeat for Panin, architect of the Northern System that had so palpably failed to secure Russia's southern borders. Initially established only for the duration of the war, Catherine's council remained until 1796 a forum for discussion amongst senior officialdom. The dominant influence under Catherine, however, was Prince A. A. Viazemskii, procurator-general of the reformed Senate between 1764 and 1792. The Senate had been created in 1711 to co-ordinate central government whilst Peter the Great campaigned against the Turk; the procuracy-general had been established in 1722 to keep a characteristically distrustful 'tsar's eye' on his administration.

Contemporaries sensed the fragility of a system that relied so heavily on one individual. But they took insufficient account of the inherent difficulties facing officials. Logistics were prominent among them. Since it could take up to three years for a reply to be received from an order sent to Kamchatka, Siberia was a law unto itself for much of the eighteenth century, and only partially integrated by Speranskii's reforms in 1822. The distances involved compelled St Petersburg first to delegate a wider range of powers to Siberia's governor than to any of his counterparts and then to set up a series of *ad hoc* investigative commissions, very much in the Muscovite tradition, to expose officials' black-market fur-trading and corrupt collection of the tribute (*iasak*). The shortest such commission lasted six months; the longest, conducted by Vul'f between 1745 and 1765, cost more than 71,000 rubles. Yet problems of communication were not confined to the Far East. Even in the middle of the nineteenth century, it could still take fourteen months to receive a reply from so relatively accessible a province as Tambov. The sheer size of the empire would therefore have taxed the best bureaucratic machine. Since not even Frederick the Great could perfect a system in which his own decisions were transmitted down a rational hierarchy of trained specialist bureaucrats, it is not surprising that the Russian system also failed. Instead, Russian administrative history may be characterised as a vain series of attempts to reach a workable balance between central direction and local implementation.

By the 1680s, Muscovite administration had become heavily over-centralised. Local affairs – by which seventeenth-century governments understood little more than the maintenance of order and the collection of taxes – were entrusted to about 150 unpaid and unpopular military governors (*voevody*), sent to suppress the countryside after the Time of Troubles. *Voevody* roved more or less at will out of provincial towns, 'feeding off the land'. Mostly middle-aged service nobles, they were appointed by the tsar (generally for a two-year term, in an attempt to forestall corruption and to prevent them from 'going native') on the advice of a network of central chancelleries (*prikazy*) dating from the late fifteenth century. A core of forty or so permanent institutions – dominated by the Chancellery of Foreign Affairs (Posol'skii prikaz), the Service Estates Chancellery (Pomestnyi prikaz), and especially in time of war by the principal Military Chancellery (Razriad) – was complemented by a fluctuating range of transitory bodies, created, merged, closed, or revived as the need arose. Between 1613 and 1699 their total annual number fluctuated between sixty and seventy. By 1700, this system had outgrown the point at which it could readily be controlled. Haphazard development had generated irreconcilable conflicts of jurisdiction between chancelleries with functional responsibilities and those detailed to administer particular regions. Riddled with quirks, the system looked clumsy alongside its Western counterparts: for example, there were eighteen chancelleries dealing with military affairs in the 1680s, when V. V. Golitsyn, who headed the Chancellery of Foreign Affairs, found himself dealing with religious schismatics occupying Siberian territory which had fallen under his chancellery's control. No longer capable of supplying the state's growing financial needs, the *prikazy* had become the selfish preserve of the families who dominated them. Thus, although Peter I initially founded further *prikazy* to service his military requirements (sixteen new chancelleries, by comparison with his father's thirty), he later determined on the need for systematic change.

Quite why, how, and when he arrived at his chosen alternative, the collegiate model used in Sweden, remains a matter for debate. Collective decision-making clearly held attractions for a ruler seeking to undermine the arbitrary 'judges' (*sud'ia*) who dominated the *prikazy*. The strengths it appeared to confer upon Peter's Swedish rival, Charles XII, were a further powerful allure. Yet although the collegiate model had been recommended to the tsar as early as 1688, it was not until January 1712 that he first recorded his intention to establish a college. Three years later, he was boasting of more concrete plans to Leibniz, who shared and encouraged his ambition to create an administration capable of running like clockwork. Intelligence was gathered by Peter's newly appointed adviser, the Holsteiner Heinrich Fick, who spent most of 1716 *incognito* in Stockholm. On his return to St Petersburg, Fick worked with Ia. V. Bruce (born in Moscow, the grandson of a Scots officer in the Muscovite army) on the establishment of the nine colleges listed in a decree of December 1717. With a few later additions, these formed the core of Russian central government for the remainder of the century.

After 1720, each college had ten members: a president appointed by the tsar, a vice-president from among three candidates nominated by the Senate, and the remaining eight chosen by the Senate from a short list recommended by the college. The most important institutions were the College of War (initially under the presidency of A. D. Menshikov), the College of Foreign Affairs (G. I. Golovkin), and the Admiralty College (F. M. Apraksin). In numerical terms, however, the list was dominated by colleges concerned with finance and the economy. Only in the case of the admiralty regulation of 1722 were Russians clearly creative in their use of foreign models: other officials sent to consult the Swedish legislation that Fick had brought back from Stockholm were simply told to ignore anything that did not apply to Russia.

Preoccupied by the needs of the centre, Peter paid less attention to local affairs. On paper, his division of the country into eight provinces (*gubernii*) in 1708 marked a radical decentralisation. By eclipsing the chancelleries, it effectively subjected Russia to martial law administered by governors (*gubernatory*) who were initially all related to the tsar. But this was an emergency measure prompted by the dual threat of Swedish troops from the north-west and Bulavin's revolt in the south-east. The reform of 1708 was succeeded in 1719 by a better-planned scheme designed to integrate provincial administration with the newly established colleges. Twelve provinces, administered by governors directly subordinate to the central administration, were to be divided, on the Swedish model set out by Fick, into sub-provinces (*provintsii*) and districts (*uezdy*). Civilian officials were to dominate. In the event, however, the tsar could not afford a reform motivated, at least in part, by the need to increase his revenue. Although the new provinces and their governors survived until 1775, provincial administration fell once again under the control of restored *voevody* as early as 1727: 'the institutions borrowed by Tsar Peter from the Swedish monarchy were defeated by the Muscovite administrative tradition almost as decisively as the Swedes had been beaten by the Russians at Poltava'.[11]

---

[11] I. Pososhkov, *The Book of Poverty and Wealth*, ed. and tr. A. P. Vlasto and L. R. Lewitter (London, 1987), 'Introduction', p. 131.

Despite periodic attempts to improve it, the same Muscovite tradition subjected the Russian provinces to arbitrary government until the reign of Catherine the Great. Though local affairs were never far from her mind, the empress initially intended to postpone major reform until the Legislative Commission of 1767 had completed its work. Some work was done in the lands acquired in the first Polish partition. But it was Pugachev in 1773 who forced the provinces to the top of her priorities. The result was the Statute for the Administration of the Provinces of the Russian Empire of 5 November 1775. Many of its provisions had been drafted by Catherine herself in a bout of self-diagnosed 'legislomania', though her mentors in provincial affairs included both Landrat von Ulrich, whom she summoned from Estonia at the Ritterschaft's expense to help her in the work, and J. J. Sievers, whose appointment as governor-general of Tver', Novgorod, Olonets, and Pskov placed him in overall charge of the main experimental region.

The reform's first aim – to bring local government closer to the people by reducing the size of its units and increasing their number – was accomplished in a characteristically rational way. In the decade after 1775, the boundaries of the twenty-five existing provinces, far from uniform in size, were redrawn to form forty-one new ones, each with a population of between 300,000 and 400,000. These, in turn, were further subdivided into *uezdy* each with a population of between 20,000 and 30,000. The former sub-provinces (sixty-eight of them) disappeared, not least because it would have been difficult to staff them. By 1796, the empire comprised fifty provinces and 493 *uezdy*, roughly triple the number of 1775. Governors-general (vice-gerents, *namestniki*) were appointed to head two or more provinces. Those with no resident *namestnik* were placed under a governor, now removed from the jurisdiction of the colleges and placed directly under the authority of the Senate and the empress.

So far, the reform accomplished little that had not previously been mooted: its second aim, however, was innovative. In a radical departure from Catherine's earlier measures, the legislation of 1775 entailed a devolution of authority unparalleled since 1708, this time to civilian rather than to military authority. Whilst the major source of power in each province was still to be an appointed governor, many of the functions of the *voevody*, now abolished, were to be transferred to a newly constituted hierarchy of courts, police offices, and boards of welfare and education, partly staffed by elected members of the local nobility and the urban population.

It was this participative element which did most to anger Grand Duke Paul; it offended his authoritarian instincts, and he condemned it as wasteful both of resources and of the monarch's authority. Contemptuous of his mother's local government policy during her lifetime, Paul determined to reverse what she had done. In one respect only did the militarist mode of government he adopted, consciously modelled on the achievements of his Prussian hero, Frederick the Great, mark a development of Catherine's policy rather than a rejection of it: this was the decision, whilst increasing the rôle of the army in provincial administration, firmly to separate its sphere of competence from that of civil officialdom. Otherwise, the pendulum swung swiftly back from the localities to the centre. The number of provinces was cut (from fifty to forty-one) along with the number of provincial officials; the office of governor-general was abolished. In St Petersburg, Paul revived the Colleges of Commerce, Manufacture, Mines, and State Revenue, abolished as redundant by Catherine between 1779 and 1796. This time there was no pretence to collective administration. Each college was placed under the jurisdiction of a single director, and in 1797 Russia acquired its first 'minister', appointed to manage the imperial family's reorganised 'appanage' estates.

Committed to repudiating his father's tyranny, Alexander faced a choice in 1801 between restoring his grandmother's mode of government or capitalising on Paul's centralising reforms in less arbitrary fashion. Recalling the days of Viazemskii, high-ranking survivors from Catherine's time, led by her former favourite P. V. Zavadovskii and the anglophile brothers Counts A. R. and S. R. Vorontsov, argued that increased Senatorial power could best guarantee monarchical efficiency. The new tsar's accession manifesto encouraged them to think that he agreed. But Alexander's 'Unofficial Committee' of friends (Czartoryski, Stroganov, Kochubei, and Novosil'tsev) recommended instead the ministerial model of Napoleonic France, and it was the Unofficial Committee that prevailed. Since it, too, wanted to see imperial initiatives emerge intact from the bureaucracy – 'There are few monarchical states where the will of the Sovereign is as badly carried out as in Russia', complained Czartoryski in February 1802[12] – there was no chance that the tsar's authority would be sacrificed. Although the decree establishing eight ministries on 8 September 1802 subordinated their ministers to the Senate, this clause remained ineffectual. The tsar's formal reaffirmation of his autocratic power on 21 March 1803 was therefore less dramatic than it seemed. As Yaney puts it, 'The Senate did not lose its institutional position in 1803, because it had never had one.'[13] At first,

[12] Quoted by W. H. Zawadzki, *A Man of Honour: Adam Czartoryski as a Statesman of Russia and Poland 1795–1831* (Oxford, 1993), p. 46.
[13] G. L. Yaney, *The Systematization of Russian Government: Social Evolution in the Domestic*

the committee of ministers, which emerged more or less accidentally, was an important co-ordinating body which met forty-three times in 1803. But after the failure of Speranskii's constitutional plans its significance receded. Though it took time for the transition to become fully effective, nineteenth-century Russian government would be characterised not by collective discussion and collegiate co-operation but by competition among rival ministers, each entitled to direct access to the tsar.

By encouraging ministerial despotism at the same time as they themselves withdrew into the privacy of an increasingly isolated court, the tsars further destabilised the Russian government. But this paradox would become clear only with hindsight. To contemporaries, the novelty of Alexander's ministries seemed less significant than continuities of personnel. Of the eight new institutions, four simply replaced surviving colleges: these were the Ministries of War, Commerce, Foreign Affairs, and the Admiralty. A fifth, the Ministry of Education, grew out of the Schools Commission created in 1782. Zavadovskii, its ageing president, became the first minister, assuming additional responsibility for the universities. The remaining ministries – Finance, Justice, and Internal Affairs, the three key institutions for the remainder of the imperial period – emerged from the old Senate. Institutional reform can thus tell us only part of the story of Russian government: to understand more about how it operated we must turn to the men who gave it life.

Patrons, clients, and bureaucrats

It is often said that the greatest beneficiaries of administrative reforms are those charged with putting them into effect. On the face of it, the Russian numbers tell their own story. In the 1690s, the Military and Service Estates Chancelleries were among the country's largest employers: the Razriad alone employed more than 2,000. By 1755, the total number of officials at both central and local levels had nearly doubled since 1725 to reach about 10,500. Of these, only 20 per cent occupied rank fourteen or higher on Peter's Table. In 1763 Catherine allowed for 16,500 civil servants and imperial expansion, and provincial reform during the course of her reign demanded more. Even accounting for Paul's economies, there were probably some 38,000 officials by 1800 and their number kept on growing: a government source listed 113,990 in 1856, of whom 72 per cent now held rank fourteen and above. Since the ratio of officials per head of population changed from around

Administration of Imperial Russia 1711–1905 (Urbana, IL, 1973), p. 99. This idiosyncratic book emphasises well the weaknesses of constitutionalism under Alexander I.

1:2,000 in the mid-1750s to about 1:500 a century later, it is no wonder that the arbitrary 'government inspector' and the downtrodden clerk were so prominent in nineteenth-century literature.

Yet although it seemed in the reign of Nicholas I (1825–55) that Gogol's nightmare vision had come true, the prevailing image of a huge, paper-pushing bureaucracy motivated more by selfishness than by a concern for the common good was only a caricature. The numbers are misleading, artificially inflated by the inclusion of many low-level military men in the provinces. Behind its monolithic exterior, the Russian bureaucracy of the middle of the nineteenth century concealed not only a talented élite, paternalist guardians of their own distinctive vision of the public welfare, but also a variety of educational backgrounds which produced a multiplicity of career patterns.[14] Yet a high degree of damaging formalism was nevertheless undeniable, and its descent can be traced directly from the Muscovite chancelleries.

By the 1680s, the legal record testifies to the existence of a finely graded hierarchy of officials (prikaznye liudi) performing specialised tasks according to regular procedures. This élite, precociously modern in its bureaucratic techniques, communicated in an orthographically and syntactically distinctive 'officialese' (the prikaznyi iazyk, written but never spoken) and was already statutorily entitled to regular salaries. By the 1680s, the best-paid dumnyi d'iak at the top of the pyramid could in theory draw up to 500 rubles a year (calculated quarterly and paid either annually or every six months) to supplement the grants of land which rewarded his service. In all these ways, Muscovite officialdom approached the classic Weberian model of a modern bureaucracy.

But the legal record hides significant discrepancies which cast a different light on the prikaznye liudi. In practice, their procedure was probably dictated more by custom than by system. Particularly at the lower levels, grain or Siberian furs often substituted wholly or partly for cash payments. In more distant areas, officials were simply left to fend for themselves. Neither was irregular payment a passing phenomenon. Despite Peter I's efforts to rationalise the salary structure, his successors could not afford to fulfil his plans. The salaries of local officials were always the first casualty in straitened times: most were cut or abolished in 1727, not to be restored until after the Seven Years War. Later still, levels of payment stipulated by the provincial reform of 1775 were eaten away by inflation because they were paid in worthless assignats (see chapter 3). Army officers who experienced similar difficulties commonly

[14] D. Lieven, *Russia's Rulers Under the Old Régime* (New Haven, CT, 1989), the best book in any language on the ethos of the late nineteenth-century bureaucracy's upper ranks, begins with a synoptic review 'from the Tatars to the twentieth century'.

withheld their men's pay in compensation. Even foreigners lured by the prospect of generous reward fell victim to cuts once it emerged that their contribution failed to justify the expense. As early as 1716, the English naval engineer John Perry devoted the first part of his vivid description of *The State of Russia* to a bitter account of his struggle to persuade a procrastinating Admiral Apraksin to pay his promised £300 per annum.[15]

Although regular salaries should have obviated the need for corruption, their persistent non-payment merely encouraged it. Fierce disciplinary measures were impotent because the worst culprits could often bribe their way out of punishment. Peter the Great prosecuted the misappropriation of state funds. Yet his efforts to stamp out corruption foundered when the accused, who included some of his most influential backers, managed to implicate their judges in crime. Subsequent rulers intent on purging the administration encountered a similar obstacle: to weed out the worst culprits was to undermine their own support. The same held true in the provinces, where a governor determined to expose embezzlers could easily cause more trouble than he was worth. The irascible poet, G. R. Derzhavin, fell into this trap in Olonets and Tambov in the 1780s, allegedly provoking Catherine II to retort: 'Let him write verse!' Since a degree of peculation served to keep the system going rather than to bring it to a halt, a compromise was clearly called for. Bribery had to be publicly denounced but tacitly tolerated. The only tsars unwilling to accept this – Peter III and Paul I – were rapidly overthrown.

Peter the Great hoped to sever corrupt links between Muscovite bureaucrats by dismantling patronage networks within the chancelleries and transferring staff to new institutions. The Senate, assuming responsibility for personnel from the Razriad, acted as an employment exchange, reallocating specialists to the appropriate colleges. In this way, the College of Revenue alone drew men from the former Admiralty, Estates, and Monastery Chancelleries, from the Ratusha and the customs, and from Moscow, Archangel, and Nizhnii Novgorod among other places. In December 1717, Peter specifically ordered the presidents of the new colleges not to appoint their own relatives and protégés, but the repetition of this edict six years later implies that it had been ignored.

In the long term, the tsars realised that only by inspiring service

---

[15] J. Perry, *The State of Russia Under the Present Czar* (London, 1716, reprinted 1967), esp. pp. 30–9, 'An Humble REPRESENTATION of the hard Fortune and Discouragement that the underwritten *John Perry* hath met with, from the time of his being entertained in *England* to the Present Year, 1710'.

motivated by an official's own honour and integrity could they achieve the standards of honesty and efficiency to which they aspired. Otherwise, it would be impossible to convert a body of officials capable (at best) of a mechanical response to coercion into one supple enough to generate public-minded policy from within. In the event, a complete conversion proved beyond them. So successfully had Muscovite centralisation prevented boiars from uniting in opposition to the monarchy that the *dvorianstvo* never achieved the social and political cohesion that might have allowed it to become a mature instrument of government policy. Diversity within the noble estate ensured not only that it was generally weak as a pressure group from below but also that it was unreliable as an instrument of change directed from above. So whilst European absolute monarchs consolidated their power by restricting provincial noble affinities and dismantling traditional corporate privileges, eighteenth-century tsars were ironically forced first to establish and later to consolidate such privileges as they strove initially to oblige and then to coax the nobility to accept its responsibilities as Russia's ruling class.

Where Peter I's unpopular Table of Ranks enforced noble service, Peter III's manifesto of 1762, which freed them from this obligation, hoped that zealous and loyal nobles would volunteer to serve with pride. The immediate response was encouraging: young, active men willingly returned to the provinces, creating a boom in provincial towns by the 1780s. By 1795, more than half the empire's nobles were resident on their estates. Yet it still proved easier to fill prestigious offices in Petersburg than lowly provincial positions. Since even governorships had long been regarded (and used) as a means of exile from influential court circles, we can understand why junior office seemed less than enticing and why many provincial posts remained unfilled.

Catherine and her image-makers did everything they could to encourage 'high-minded sons of the fatherland' to respond to their new opportunities to serve in elected office after 1775. Echoing the article 'Patriote' in the *Encyclopédie*, N. I. Novikov (1744–1818) made keenness to serve a crucial attribute of the noble paragon whose profile he defined in his 1774 journal *The Bag* (*Koshelek*). Initially, these efforts met with success: the quality of both electors and elected was high enough at the first provincial assemblies in 1776 to satisfy both Catherine and Sievers. Yet despite the ceremony that surrounded them, virtually all these assemblies witnessed a decline in attendance at subsequent triennial sessions. By the early nineteenth century, elective service had fallen into disrepute and the state had been obliged to turn instead to non-noble groups, primarily by recruiting surplus seminarians from the clergy.

It might have been easier to recruit nobles had there been an established system of preparation for entry to state service to match the one provided for Prussia by the German universities. But Russian officialdom had no such regular supply line. Peter I began the practice of sending promising youths abroad, notably to Göttingen, but three-quarters of the Russian civil service in 1755, the year in which the first Russian university was founded at Moscow, had no formal education whatsoever. The remainder were mostly products of the St Petersburg Cadet Corps. This weakness did not go unnoticed. A law of 1740 complained of 'base and mediocre' cadets who showed no inclination to study civil procedures, and Catherine II, in her preliminary notes to the Commission on Commerce, lamented that improperly trained and poorly motivated officials encouraged arbitrariness and disorder.

Not until the reign of Alexander I was a concerted solution attempted. Five new universities were decreed in 1802, to be modelled on Göttingen and to supply graduates to the state service. The results were mixed. The curator at St Petersburg so disliked the Göttingen model that his refusal to follow it delayed the foundation of the university there until 1819; at Khar'kov, German professors became embroiled with their Russian colleagues in disputes over poor student standards; Vilna, the most successful university, remained Polish in ethos. Only the University of Moscow, where a tradition of contact with German academics was long established, recruited professors from Göttingen.

In a notorious edict of 6 August 1809, Speranskii set out rigorous educational requirements for promotion to the ennobling eighth rank. The new curriculum stipulated that candidates must qualify in Russian and one foreign language, natural law, Roman law and civil law, economics, geography, and statistics, Russian and general history, mathematics, and physics. Opposition was instant and vociferous. Karamzin denounced the scheme as sophistical; the nobility simply refused to comply. The worst failure was at Kazan', where student numbers remained below fifty, whilst even at relatively successful Dorpat, which had five times as many by 1812, few stayed more than a year. Faced with such disdain, the government diluted the 1809 legislation in 1825 and abandoned it in 1834. Even so, the increasing functional separation of the Russian ministries encouraged new levels of specialisation among Russian officialdom between 1800 and 1850. The proportion of military men sharply declined, the average age of entrants rose from under sixteen to nearly twenty-two, and progress up the bureaucratic ladder came increasingly to depend on prior professional training.

Eighteenth-century professionalisation was limited by the lack of such preparation. During periods of high demand – notably the creation of the colleges in 1718–22 and the reformation of government by Catherine the Great in the 1770s and 1780s – stop-gap appointments were often necessary. In the circumstances, the tsars relied on loyalty rather than specialist talent. Thus I. I. Nepliuev (1693–1773) became Peter the Great's last representative in Constantinople although his education at the Novgorod 'cipher' school, where arithmetic was the principal subject, qualified him primarily in naval affairs. An incipient sense of professionalisation was particularly slow to reach the provinces. The overwhelming majority of governors appointed between 1727 and 1764 were retired military officers who had reached at least the rank of colonel. Though most had received no training prior to their civilian appointment, some went on to senior office in the colleges. Indeed, of the 134 members of the *generalitet* in 1730, 68 per cent performed both military and civil duties during the course of their careers and many switched back and forth between the two.

Some have argued that, without proper legal training and professional specialisation, Russia could never create a productive bureaucracy. Yet once one looks behind the rhetoric which persistently stressed order and rationality in Russian officialdom, its bureaucratic features seem increasingly insignificant. In practice, as LeDonne has stressed, placement probably depended more on patronage than on any regulatory system. This is most easily demonstrated with reference to high office. Nearly half the empire's senior provincial positions – governorships, vice-governorships, and chairs of civil and criminal chambers – changed hands between the onset of Viazemskii's fatal illness in 1791 and his death in 1793. Though details are scarce at lower levels, it seems likely that noble patronage networks spread out their tentacles to the localities. So whilst successive tsars strove to increase the efficiency of their executive through administrative reform, they continued to rely in practice on the politics of patronage, as our discussion of corruption has already implied.

From the 1780s, the novice could consult model 'letter-writers' – published guides to the intricate world of flattery and *politesse* necessary to secure an influential patron. So far, scholars have agreed that such a patron was almost certain to be a relative. Nearly two-thirds of the 1730 *generalitet* were related by blood or marriage to another of its members, and the proportion of its Russian members so linked was still higher (76 per cent). LeDonne has gone further, tracing virtually all significant appointments between 1689 and 1796 to two kinship networks linked ultimately to the Naryshkins and the Saltykovs. Remarkably, every procurator-general of the Senate between 1722 and 1796 had links to the Naryshkin group, whilst the Saltykov group seems to have had a more or less continuous hold on financial offices.[16]

If it is true that kinship dominated to the extent that LeDonne suggests, then Russian patronage networks stand in marked contrast to others we know about. In France, for example, kinship was only one of several potential linkages between patrons and their clients: friendship mattered too. Perhaps it came to matter more in Russia than we have so far realised. Initially, the cult of friendship was a reaction *against* the establishment. Promoted by freemasonry, friendship became a dominant motif in the culture of younger nobles anxious to break free from the habits and mores of an older generation. Some of the stress on friendship must be put down to literary rhetoric. The Ciceronian 'friendly letters' by which the Arzamas group of writers communicated in 1815–18 were an explicitly rhetorical device. Still – as one of the group's best-known members, Karamzin, could legitimately claim – by then the nobility had outgrown its primitive clannishness and begun to form relationships more consonant with polite sociability. Alexander I himself was famously surrounded by a group of 'young friends', and the Ukrainian clientage network at the courts of Catherine the Great and Paul I hints at reality behind the rhetoric. Whilst Bezborodko shamelessly placed even distant relatives in plum positions, others looked beyond the family. In 1780, D. P. Troshchinskii strove explicitly to place a client 'both because he is my fellow-countryman and because his brother is a dear friend of mine'.[17]

These are no more than straws in the wind. Thanks to the paucity of the sources, the full story may never be known. Lacking private correspondence and other personal papers, we owe our understanding of officialdom primarily to statistics computed from impersonal service records (*formuliarnye spiski*). Even the foremost eighteenth-century statesmen remain shadowy figures. Still, the suspicion must remain that it was not only relatives but friends in high places who formed the essential links in Russian patronage networks by 1800.

The awkwardness facing those who try to categorise Russian officialdom either as a modern bureaucracy or as a traditional web of patronage networks is that even after the ministries began to exert control over the provinces in the 1830s, it surely combined features of both. Patronage networks still cut across institutional boundaries and defied the prevailing rhetoric of systematic order even in the contem-

---

[16] J. P. LeDonne, 'Ruling Families in the Russian Political Order, 1689–1825', *CMRS*, 28, 3-4 (1987), pp. 233–322.
[17] D. Saunders, *The Ukrainian Impact on Russian Culture 1750–1850* (Edmonton, 1985), pp. 94–5.

porary Russian Federation. Significantly, however, the 1830s saw not only the beginnings of bureaucratic triumph, but also of major growth. The number of local representatives of the three principal ministries (internal affairs, finance, and justice) more than doubled in two decades after 1829. Yet even then, there were probably four times as many civil servants per thousand head of population in Britain and France as there were in imperial Russia.

In view of the shortage of officials and their poor preparation, governmental business was transacted slowly even at the centre. In 1796, Catherine II was still working personally on a procedural manual to replace the outdated General Regulation. Despite her efforts, the backlog of Senate business she bequeathed to her son (14,231 unresolved cases by one account) was greater than the one she had inherited. By doubling the number of senators and tripling the staff, Paul managed not only to reduce the arrears but regularly to transact three times as much business as before. Whether he thereby improved government is a moot point. In the 1840s, it has been calculated that a provincial governor had to sign some 270 papers daily, a task which alone would have consumed four and a half hours at a rate of one paper per minute. The governor's mind can have absorbed little of these papers' purpose, if, indeed, they had one. In this sense, the Russian old régime's problem was not that it governed harshly but that it scarcely governed at all.

The church in government

Although undergovernment left a yawning gap which other agencies might have been co-opted to fill, the prevailing tendency was to limit the administrative competence of any agency not directly under state control. This restriction applied above all to the diocesan and parochial networks of the Orthodox church. In almost every other European state, the episcopate was either involved in or close to government: not so in Russia. Peter the Great strove to distinguish the civil responsibilities of the state from the spiritual concerns of the church; his successors preferred to siphon surplus clerics to swell the ranks of an expanding bureaucracy, crying out for educated officials, rather than restore the church's administrative powers.

When they were not seeking to subvert the schism, most bishops confined their administrative efforts to attempts to subdue unruly clergy. They rarely got on well with secular officials. Speranskii, as governor of Penza (1816–19), was exceptional: a product of the church's own schools, he enjoyed discussing theology with the local bishop. When subsequent diocesan expansion, inadequately matched by resources, forced bishops to live not only in unwelcome exile but, worse, in what many regarded as insultingly inferior accommodation, the result was often unseemly rivalry between temporal and spiritual leaders, famously mocked by Leskov in *The Little Things in a Bishop's Life*.

At local level, ecclesiastical impotence owed much to the changing nature of the parish. Whereas the Muscovite parish and commune had shared a function as self-governing units of local administration, in the eighteenth century the two diverged. Whilst the commune was exploited as the most convenient mechanism for apportioning social and fiscal obligations, the parish's secular powers were stripped. The change was far from sudden since the overwhelmingly centralist emphasis of Peter the Great's reforms left him in need of parish priests as local administrators. They remained responsible until 1917 for collecting and compiling statistical information on births, marriages, and deaths, and for reading out newly promulgated legislation to parishioners in church (a task the Lutheran clergy performed in Scandinavia and Protestant Germany). Such duties, onerous enough in themselves, carried the additional disadvantage of identifying the clergy as agents of the state, even after Catherine the Great's provincial reform, which laid a greater degree of responsibility for local government on the shoulders of the nobility, had effectively allowed most parochial functions to wither away. As a combined result of these changes with the piecemeal rationalisation of parish distribution, the parish and its church, formerly an important administrative and economic centre of each community, were left by 1800 with a strictly religious function.

In one sense only did the church continue to play a major administrative rôle. It exerted a wide social influence by retaining jurisdiction not only over disciplinary offences committed by the clergy but also over a much broader range of moral issues, notably marriage, divorce, and family law. Though the canon law incorporated in the medieval *kormchaia kniga* was modified by secular officials, especially in the reign of Alexander I, the church remained empowered to sentence culprits not only to public penance (*epitim'ia*) but also to imprisonment in monasteries whose facilities, restricted after the secularisation of church lands in 1764, were increasingly regarded in government circles merely as a repository for criminals and lunatics.

The symmetrical classical building Carlo Rossi designed for the Senate and Synod in 1829–34, overlooking the square in St Petersburg where the Decembrists had hoped to effect their coup, accurately symbolises their intended relationship in the administrative hierarchy established by Peter the Great: on the southern side of its arch stood the Synod, at the apex of the ecclesiastical court system, whilst on the northern side stood the Senate, the ultimate court of appeal in the parallel secular jurisdiction. It is to that jurisdiction that we now turn.

Justice

The Muscovite tradition of justice, inherited from Orthodox Byzantium, differed sharply from the Roman civil law and German common law traditions dominant in the West. It would be difficult to exaggerate the impact of the study of jurisprudence in continental Europe from late medieval times. Quite apart from stimulating humanist scholarship, it generated a force which has yet to relinquish its grip on the modern world: lawyers. Early-modern England had its inns of court; legal training formed the backbone of bureaucracy in the German states; in France, a legal profession tracing its origins to 1274 became a major political power based in the *parlements*. In Muscovy, by contrast, lawyers were neither professionally nor politically significant.

In the absence of secular education, legal training was unknown and, while Western notions of legality remained alien, no native academic tradition developed. The first published history of Russian legislation was the *Discours sur l'origine et les changements des lois russiennes*, a lecture read to the Academy of Sciences in 1756 by F. H. Strube de Piermont, a Halle graduate who had become a naturalised Russian subject in 1750. His innovatory manual of Russian laws (*Compendium juris ruthenici*) remained unpublished. Not until 1767 did a Russian professor give lectures in Russian positive law at a Russian university. This was S. E. Desnitskii, a former pupil of Adam Smith in Glasgow, who, whilst drawing on comparative European insights, determined to rescue his subject from foreigners. Still, even Speranskii's capacious curriculum for intending bureaucrats found no place for Russian law in 1809. In 1825 there were only eighteen law students at the University of St Petersburg, where no course in Russian law was offered. Some studied jurisprudence abroad, but Derzhavin, the first minister of justice appointed in 1802, had no legal training and his panegyric poetry naturally found more room for the language of autocratic mercy and wrath than for discussion of legal norms. The heyday of Russian legal education – provided by the law faculty of the University of Moscow in the 1840s and in a more utilitarian way by the Imperial School of Law (f. 1835) – still lay in the future.

The theoretical content of the Muscovite law codes (*Sudebniki*) issued in 1497 and 1550 was therefore minimal. Though individual articles drew on both Byzantine and Lithuanian sources, the final form of the *Sudebniki*, like that of their successor, the *Ulozhenie* of 1649, owed more to political circumstance than to academic tradition. Their primary purpose was practical: to stabilise a turbulent régime. Thus the *Ulozhenie* followed the central questions of religious and political obligation with chapters covering property, inheritance, and a seemingly random catalogue of crimes and punishments. In Muscovy, where 'law and order' were inseparable and 'justice' was arbitrarily dispensed by the agents of central government, 'the law' remained an edict requiring unquestioning submission rather than a source of moral authority open to interpretation by professionally trained minds.

It seemed at first that Peter the Great might break with this tradition. Much of his legislation borrowed directly from Western models and Russia's new international status obliged his officials to learn something of the law of nations. Grotius' *De jure belli ac pacis* and Pufendorf's *Juris naturae et gentium* were translated in manuscript form for their use, and in 1717 P. P. Shafirov, a converted Jew who was vice-president of the College of Foreign Affairs, published the first unofficial treatise on the subject.[18] This, however, was as much a work of political propaganda as it was of legal scholarship, and it long remained unique.

The new College of Justice, set up under A. A. Matveev in April 1718, was to be modelled on the Svea court of appeals in Sweden, where the judicial system was separate from state officialdom. Yet so foreign did this concept prove in the Russian context that, although Matveev turned repeatedly to the tsar for guidance, no formal instruction for the college was ever issued. Practice proved no more straightforward than theory. A decree of December 1718 provided for a five-tier hierarchy of courts, ascending from those in provincial towns through the college itself to the Senate, the ultimate court of appeal. But the scheme predictably foundered on a shortage of qualified personnel: by 1720, only 199 of the 371 vacancies it created had been filled. Many judicial positions had to be taken by army officers and *voevody*, a move which vitiated the proposed separation between judicial and administrative functions. In 1727, the Supreme Privy Council returned the whole judicial system to government officials, thereby effectively restoring the Muscovite status quo.

To a monarch so committed to unquestioning obedience as Tsar Peter, lawyers were a liability. The Military Regulation (1716) banned them from criminal trials on the grounds that their 'worthless, pro-

---

[18] P. P. Shafirov, *A Discourse Concerning the Just Causes of the War Between Sweden and Russia: 1700–1721*, intro. W. E. Butler (Dobbs Ferry, NY, 1973). See also W. E. Butler, 'Grotius' Influence in Russia', in H. Bull, B. Kingsbury, and A. Roberts, eds., *Hugo Grotius and International Relations* (Oxford, 1990), pp. 257–66.

longed arguments' would be 'a burden to the judge'.[19] But that did not mean that judicial opinion was valued. On the contrary, successive tsars remained resolutely opposed to the common law notion of interpretation on the basis of precedent: interpretation was to be the sole preserve of the legislator, and the sole legislator was the sovereign, as Catherine II, paraphrasing Beccaria's *On Crimes and Punishments* (1764), insisted in her *Nakaz* (art. 151).

When Desnitskii argued in his *Representations on the Establishment of Legislative, Judicial and Punitive Powers in the Russian Empire* (completed in 1768 but not published until 1905) that 'to make laws, to judge according to the laws, and to put that judgement into effect' were three separate functions, he was not saying anything of which Catherine would have disapproved. Although Desnitskii's treatise was more radical than the *Nakaz* – it proposed trial by jury and the appointment of judges for life, something not introduced in Russia until 1864 – he did not recommend the formal separation of powers. Instead, he advocated a more restricted distinction between the various state institutions charged with fulfilling the three functions he described. Whether Desnitskii directly influenced drafts of the 1775 provincial reform remains unproven. In the event, Catherine showed that she was prepared to contemplate a marked degree of separation by creating courts in which members of each social estate, including the state peasantry, were to be judged by their peers. In practice, such separation was limited by incomprehension on the part of many judges, which fatally undermined Desnitskii's conception of them as enlighteners and educators.

The difficulty of reconciling the absolute sovereignty of the monarch with the objective rule of law proved a stumbling block to legal codification in many parts of Europe. The Austrian *Codex Theresianus* begun in 1753 achieved its final form as the *Allgemeine Bürgerliche Gesetzbuch* only in 1811; the Prussian *Codex Fridericianus*, drawn up for Frederick the Great by Samuel Cocceji in 1748, was reworked as the *Allgemeines Landrecht* in 1794 only after both had died. In some ways the tsars faced less formidable obstacles, since they were confronted by neither the tangled web of the Holy Roman Empire's jurisdiction nor long-standing provincial liberties, except in the case of the Baltic lands. Yet they found it no easier than their rivals to codify their legislation.

Peter the Great's first attempt was the *Palata ob Ulozhenii* commissioned in 1700 to integrate the laws issued since 1649 with the outdated code. The conclusions it reached in 1703 were shelved, possibly because Western norms and Muscovite custom were still incompatible. Peter

---

[19] Quoted by R. S. Wortman, *The Development of a Russian Legal Consciousness* (Chicago, 1976), p. 12.

tried again in 1714 and once more in 1720, this time charging a Senate commission to adapt the Swedish code to Russian circumstances. A comprehensive code was indeed completed, but only after Peter's death, which helps to explain why it was never put into effect. In his lifetime, Peter promulgated only the partial codification of his own Westernised measures represented by the Military Regulation and the General Regulation.

Two further fruitless commissions existed between 1728 and 1730 and between 1730 and 1744, as did a fifth, inspired by Petr Shuvalov in 1754, on which Strube de Piermont initially served. Promising to synthesise the work of thirty-five subcommissions and reports from provincial chancelleries, it collapsed during the Seven Years War, though it remained formally in existence until 1766 when its papers were sent to Catherine II's new Legislative Commission, summoned in 1767. This, too, was disrupted by war. Following the Turkish attack in 1768, plenary sessions were depleted from early in 1769 by the departure of delegates to the army. Yet although the work of its subcommissions was officially discontinued in October 1771, progress towards codification continued behind the scenes until 1796, when fifty-six officials and fifty clerks were listed as still working on the project. They, however, were probably engaged in digesting the materials which had already been generated before 1771 (or at the latest 1774) rather than initiating new proposals.

The novelty of Catherine's commission is debatable. Previous attempts at codification had been designed primarily to systematise a mass of unregulated legislation, the purpose of the unproductive Commission for the Drafting of Laws established after Catherine's death in December 1796. Omel'chenko has argued that Catherine strove, in addition, to found her system on 'eternal and fundamental' laws.[20] Catherine's advocacy in the *Nakaz* of concepts drawn from the latest continental jurisprudence was certainly innovative. However, here, as in her other writings on positive law, her emphasis was distinctly practical: the 700 pages of notes she took on Sir William Blackstone's *Commentaries on the Laws of England* ignored all his references to natural law. In a sense, the question is academic, for although Catherine examined the first drafts of a civil law code in January 1774 and a criminal code was almost complete by the second half of the decade (much of which appeared in the cameralist police ordinance of 1782 and the manifesto on duels of 1787), work on a unitary code, begun after 1787, was never finished. Yet one may doubt whether the tension between *raison d'état*

---

[20] O. A. Omel'chenko, *'Zakonnaia monarkhiia' Ekateriny II: prosveshchennyi absoliutizm v Rossii* (Moscow, 1993).

and the subject's civil rights could ever have been resolved. Catherine's notes on Blackstone suggest that she could never have brought herself to subordinate the former to the latter. Tsar Paul sensed even more acutely that legality would weaken autocracy. And it was not a concession that he was prepared to make.

Recurrent attempts to impose 'the rule of law' (*pravosudie*) reflected a desire to subordinate all Russian subjects to a uniform system of justice based on statute. As the preamble to the *Ulozhenie* put it, 'justice' was to be 'equal for all ... ranks of people from the greatest to the least'; 'However extensive a state may be, *every part* of it must depend upon the laws', confirmed Catherine's *Nakaz* (art. 224); 'Law is the guarantee of each and all', declared Alexander I's coronation medal.[21] Since regularity and predictability were key aims, it was a handicap to the judiciary that the precise content of Russian statutes remained hard to determine. Judges' fear of being punished for mistakes was one reason why so many unresolved cases continued to be referred to higher courts. As M. S. Anderson has stressed, there existed a myriad of legislation, often ambiguously drafted and sometimes mutually contradictory even when it could be found: not all laws were published, especially if they were politically sensitive or of merely local relevance. Numbers hint at the scale of the problem. Between 1650 and 1700, an average of thirty-six decrees was issued annually. Under Peter I, the figure rose to 160. By one estimate, Tsar Paul issued 48,000 orders in the first calendar year of his reign alone. His son was barely exaggerating when he complained, on setting up the tenth abortive codificatory commission in 1801, that the laws issued since the *Ulozhenie*, still being reprinted in 1820, lacked all unity and connection. Speranskii simply thought Russia lawless and dependent on personal power.

In the circumstances, it is not surprising that delays were common despite recurrent attempts, beginning with Sophia's government in the mid-1680s, to speed up judicial procedure. Petitions to the Legislative Commission of 1767 were permeated with complaints on this score. 'Justice', however, was certainly terrible even when it was not swift. Evidence is slim – there is no full-scale study of any eighteenth-century court – but we know that punishment commonly took the form of a flogging of various degrees of severity with a chilling variety of implements. Until 1817, the worst offenders had their nostrils slit. Even after that, exiles could still be branded. Millions of serfs never came within the jurisdiction of any court, remaining subject to their landowners'

---

[21] P. Longworth, *Alexis: Tsar of All the Russias* (London, 1984), pp. 49–50; R. S. Wortman, *Scenarios of Power: Myth and Ceremony in Russian Monarchy*, vol. I, *From Peter the Great to the Death of Nicholas I* (Princeton, 1995), p. 197.

arbitrary discipline. In practice, landowners relied on peasant justice, whose workings remain largely unknown though it seems that a good deal of reliance was placed on the reputation of an accused peasant and his family within the village. The Sheremet'evs granted their communal courts relatively generous room for manoeuvre: on smaller estates, others may have been more dictatorial.

A few glimmers of light suggest that the overall picture was not wholly negative. Elizabeth opposed torture and spared certain groups from capital punishment in 1741, extending the measure to all in 1744, twenty years before Beccaria published *On Crimes and Punishments*. Mysteriously, the legislation was repeated several times as though it had never been promulgated. Elizabeth's motivation remains obscure. If it was not, as the cynical Shcherbatov later suggested, mere squeamishness, it may have owed something to the combined humanitarian influence of court preachers and French novels. The simultaneous progress of similar legislation elsewhere in Europe is also significant; Frederick the Great effectively abolished torture in 1740 and again without qualification in 1755. Catherine's conscience court (*sovestnyi sud*), whereby she introduced the principle of habeas corpus in 1775, operated in both the civil and criminal spheres, unlike the English equity court from which it may have been partly adapted. Significantly, the attraction of the conscience courts seems principally to have lain in the prospect of a speedier resolution than other courts could provide.

Although most judges entered the nineteenth century with unreconstructed views of the law as administrative edict, there was at least some hope that a judicial system which had undergone marked institutional change since the 1680s might soon be infused with new attitudes as well as new procedures. In 1769–70, Novikov mocked corrupt judges in both *The Drone* (*Truten'*) and *The Tattler* (*Pustomelia*), and by 1800 at least a few were imbued with a dawning legal consciousness (*pravosoznanie*). The freemason I. V. Lopukhin resigned as a judge rather than violate beliefs derived from Fénelon and Beccaria; K. F. Ryleev, a leading Decembrist who served as an assessor at the St Petersburg criminal court between 1821 and 1824, complained of 'tortuous chicanery' and was offended by several gross breaches of justice. Speranskii even finally managed to codify the law in 1832, though not, as he had originally intended in 1809–12, according to rational legal principles modelled on the French *code civil*. Instead he followed a less ambitious, historical method, better suited to Nicholas I's Russia. Full-scale change awaited the judicial reform of 1864. Even then, it remained doubtful whether legality could be reconciled with absolute monarchy.

Eighteenth-century Russia was governed by monarchs who, if they so chose, could exercise a powerful personal influence either by drafting legislation themselves or by delegating the task to a small group of trusted officials whose work they revised and co-ordinated. In political terms, the tsar was limited only by the need to balance the interests of fluctuating noble factions and individual favourites at court, an institution whose history in this period can hardly be understood in terms of linear progress as it lurched from fashion to fashion and from ruler to ruler. Whilst no noble connection could undermine an industrious tsar who recognised the power of patronage (rash or negligent rulers were more vulnerable), the existence of such connections served to complicate the government's administrative channels because they cut across the boundaries of the formal administrative hierarchy. Institutional modernisation – justified by a rhetoric which not only argued the need for a high degree of order, but claimed actually to have imposed it on Russian government – therefore concealed a reality in which, until the 1830s, the 'power of persons' continued to dominate the 'authority of state institutions', as N. I. Panin put it with reference to the reign of Elizabeth.

Imperfect co-ordination between politics and administration evidently impeded the uniform implementation of legislation. But, setting aside problems of finance which have already been examined, the most pressing difficulty facing a reforming tsar lay in the uncomprehending response to his legislation among his subjects. The ignorance of officialdom was a minor problem by comparison with the profound cultural challenge posed by the mass of the population. Since this was a problem of which the tsars were conscious, it is natural to turn next to their attempts to address it by reforming Russia's education system.

BIBLIOGRAPHICAL NOTE

A masterly interpretation of royal ritual is R. S. Wortman, *Scenarios of Power*, vol. I, *From Peter the Great to the Death of Nicholas I* (above, n. 21), which draws on the excellent S. L. Baehr, *The Paradise Myth in Eighteenth-Century Russia* (Stanford, CA, 1991). Studies of the court remain fragmentary. A neglected field is explored by C. R. Jensen, 'Music for the Tsar: A Preliminary Study of the Music of the Muscovite Court Theater', *Musical Quarterly*, 79 (1995). See also N. S. Kollman, 'Ritual and Social Drama at the Muscovite Court', *SR*, 45 (1986); R. O. Crummey, 'Court Spectacles in Seventeenth-Century Russia: Illusion and Reality', in D. C. Waugh, ed., *Essays in Honor of A. A. Zimin* (Columbus, OH, 1985); P. A. Bushkovitch, 'The Epiphany Ceremony of the Russian Court in the Sixteenth and Seventeenth Centuries', *RR*,

49 (1990); and L. Hughes, 'Sophia, "Autocrat of All the Russias": Titles, Ritual and Eulogy in the Regency of Sophia Alekseevna', *CSP*, 28 (1986). M. S. Anderson may overemphasise discontinuity in 'Peter the Great: Imperial Revolutionary?', in A. G. Dickens, ed., *The Courts of Europe: Politics, Patronage and Royalty* (London, 1977). R. G. Asch and A. M. Birke, eds., *Princes, Patronage and the Nobility: The Court at the Beginning of the Modern Age c. 1450–1650* (Oxford, 1991), offer further comparative insights relevant to our period. Though lightweight, C. Marsden, *Palmyra of the North: The First Days of St Petersburg* (London, 1942), is not negligible. On *opala*, see A. Kleimola, 'The Muscovite Autocracy at Work: The Use of Disgrace as an Instrument of Control', in W. E. Butler, ed., *Russian Law: Historical and Political Perspectives* (Leiden, 1977).

On central government, P. B. Brown, 'Muscovite Government Bureaus', *RH*, 10 (1983), serves as a guide to the maze. On the replacement of the *prikazy* by colleges, E. V. Anisimov, *Gosudarstvennye preobrazovaniia i samoderzhavie Petra Velikago* (St Petersburg, 1997), critically reassesses a huge historiography, from which C. Peterson, *Peter the Great's Administrative and Judicial Reforms* (Stockholm, 1979), is outstanding. The contentious thesis advanced by J. P. LeDonne, *Ruling Russia in the Age of Absolutism, 1762–1796* (Princeton, 1984), is extended in his *Absolutism and Ruling Class: The Formation of the Russian Political Order 1700–1825* (Oxford, 1991), an encyclopaedic and readable interpretation. At a different level, M. M. Safonov, *Problema reform v pravitel'stvennoi politike Rossii na rubezhe XVIII i XIXvv.* (Leningrad, 1988), dissects the events of 1801–2. M. Raeff, *M. M. Speransky: Statesman of Imperial Russia*, 2nd edn (The Hague, 1969), remains the best account of his administration, if not of his ideas. On the latter part of Alexander I's reign, see S. V. Mironenko, *Samoderzhavie i reformy: politicheskaia bor'ba v Rossii v nachale XIXv.* (Moscow, 1989).

On local government after Peter I, J. P. LeDonne, 'The Evolution of the Governor's Office (1727–1764)', *CASS*, 12 (1978), supplements the classic Iu. V. Got'e, *Istoriia oblastnogo upravleniia v Rossii ot Petra I do Ekateriny II*, 2 vols. (St Petersburg–Leningrad, 1913–41). For a sequel, see J. P. LeDonne, 'The *Guberniia* Procuracy in the Reign of Catherine II, 1764–1796', *CMRS*, 36 (1995). Siberia is covered by L. S. Rafienko, 'Kompetentsiia sibirskogo gubernatora v XVIIIv.', in A. P. Okladnikov, *et al.*, eds., *Russkoe naselenie pomor'ia i Sibiri (period feodalizma): sbornik statei* (Moscow, 1973). J. M. Hittle, *The Service City: State and Townsmen in Russia, 1600–1800* (Cambridge, MA, 1979), summarises the published sources on urban government; J. M. Hartley, 'Saint Petersburg *Guberniya* After the Charter to the Towns of

1785', *SEER*, 62 (1984), shows that more remains buried in the archives.

LeDonne's *Absolutism and Ruling Class* challenges the dominant view of Russian bureaucracy by stressing the enduring significance of patronage networks. D. L. Ransel, *The Politics of Catherinian Russia: The Panin Party* (New Haven, CT, 1975), remains the only monograph on the politics of faction. See also Ransel's 'Bureaucracy and Patronage: The View from an Eighteenth-Century Russian Letter-Writer', in F. C. Jaher, ed., *The Rich, the Well-Born and the Powerful* (Urbana, IL, 1973); and his 'Character and Style of Patron–Client Relations in Russia', in A. Maczak, ed., *Klientelsysteme im Europa der Frühen Neuzeit* (Munich, 1988). Like this useful collection, W. Reinhard, ed., *Power Elites and State Building* (Oxford, 1996), puts the issue into European context.

N. F. Demidova, *Sluzhilaia biurokratiia v Rossii XVIIv. i ee rol' v formirovaniia absoliutizma* (Moscow, 1987), is impressive on the Muscovite bureaucracy. H. J. Torke, 'Crime and Punishment in the Pre-Petrine Civil Service', in E. Mendelsohn and M. S. Shatz, eds., *Imperial Russia, 1700–1917: State, Society, Opposition* (DeKalb, IL, 1988), helps to balance the overlaudatory B. Plavsic, 'Seventeenth-Century Chanceries and Their Staffs', in W. M. Pintner and D. K. Rowney, eds., *The Bureaucratization of Russian Society from the Seventeenth to the Twentieth Century* (London, 1980), an important collection. Pintner was the pioneering author of 'The Social Characteristics of the Early Nineteenth-Century Russian Bureaucracy', *SR*, 29 (1970). B. Meehan-Waters, *Autocracy and Aristocracy: The Russian Service Elite of 1730* (New Brunswick, NJ, 1982), is narrow in focus but broad in implication. J. Hassell's article on 'The Implementation of the Russian Table of Ranks During the Eighteenth Century', *SR*, 29 (1970), must be supplemented by S. M. Troitskii, *Russkii absoliutizm i dvorianstvo v XVIIIv.: formirovanie biurokratii* (Moscow, 1974). W. B. Lincoln, *In the Vanguard of Reform: Russia's Enlightened Bureaucrats, 1825–1861* (DeKalb, IL, 1981), shows how far professionalism and specialisation had developed. The doyen of Soviet scholarship on the nineteenth-century bureaucracy was P. A. Zaionchkovskii, *Pravitel'stvennyi apparat samoderzhavnoi Rossii v XIXv.* (Moscow, 1978).

On the foreign service, see D. Altbauer, 'The Diplomats of Peter the Great', *JfGO*, 28 (1980); S. M. Troitskii, 'Russkie diplomaty v seredine XVIIIv.', in V. T. Pashuto, *et al.*, eds., *Feodal'naia Rossiia vo vsemirno-istoricheskom protsesse* (Moscow, 1972); and P. K. Grimsted, *The Foreign Ministers of Alexander I: Political Attitudes and the Conduct of Russian Diplomacy, 1801–1825* (Berkeley, CA, 1969).

A. V. Kartashev, *Ocherki po istorii russkoi tserkvi*, 2 vols. (Paris, 1959), remains the only general account of the church. G. L. Freeze, 'Handmaiden of the State?: The Church in Imperial Russia Reconsidered', *Journal of Ecclesiastical History*, 36 (1985), shows how much we have to learn. I. Smolitsch, *Geschichte der Russischen Kirche*, vol. I (Leiden, 1964), and vol. II, *FzOG*, 45 (1991), is essentially a work of reference. J. Cracraft, *The Church Reform of Peter the Great* (London, 1971), is thorough and informative. B. V. Titlinov, *Pravitel'stvo Anny Ioannovny v ego otnoshenii k delam tserkvi* (St Petersburg, 1905), is good on Anna's reign; his *Gavriil Petrov, mitropolit novgorodskii i sanktpeterburgskii* (Petrograd, 1916), incorporating a wealth of primary material, easily surpasses K. Papmehl, *Metropolitan Platon of Moscow (Petr Levshin, 1737–1812): The Enlightened Prelate, Scholar and Educator* (Newtonville, MA, 1983), as the best study of an eighteenth-century bishop. S. K. Batalden, *Catherine II's Greek Prelate: Eugenios Voulgaris in Russia, 1771–1806* (Boulder, 1982), concentrates on scholarship; G. L. Bruess, *Religion, Identity and Empire: A Greek Archbishop in the Russia of Catherine the Great* (Boulder, 1997), is a somewhat wider-ranging study of Nikiforos Theotokis. On Catherine II's policy, see O. A. Omel'chenko, 'Tserkov' v pravovoi politike "prosveshchennogo absoliutizma" v Rossii', in *Istoriko-pravovye voprosy vzaimootnoshenii gosudarstva i tserkvi v istorii Rossii: sbornik nauchnykh trudov* (Moscow, 1988).

On justice, R. S. Wortman, *The Development of a Russian Legal Consciousness* (above, n. 19), is a sophisticated chronological successor to Peterson, *Administrative and Judicial Reforms* and LeDonne, *Ruling Russia*, infusing ideas into their primarily institutional concerns. A. N. Medushevskii, *Utverzhdenie absoliutizma v Rossii* (Moscow, 1994), attempts an ambitious comparative framework for Peter I's reforms. M. Raeff, 'Codification et droit en Russie impériale', *CMRS*, 20 (1979), characteristically offers *multum in parvo*. For Habsburg comparisons, see H. E. Strakosch, *State Absolutism and the Rule of Law* (Sydney, 1967). O. A. Omel'chenko, *Kodifikatsiia prava v Rossii v period absoliutnoi monarkhii: vtoraia polovina XVIIIv. Uchebnoe posobie* (Moscow, 1989), should be set against M. Raeff, 'The Empress and the Vinerian Professor: Catherine II's Projects of Government Reforms and Blackstone's Commentaries', and A. H. Brown, 'S. E. Desnitsky, Adam Smith and the *Nakaz* of Catherine II', both in *OSP*, NS, 7 (1974). Desnitskii is the subject of a biography by P. S. Gratsianskii, whose *Politicheskaia i pravovaia mysl' Rossii vtoroi poloviny XVIIIv* (Moscow, 1984), is wider-ranging. J. M. Hartley, 'Catherine's Conscience Court – An English Equity Court?', in A. G. Cross, ed., *Russia and the West in the Eighteenth Century* (Newtonville, MA, 1983), probes practice as well as theory. I. de Madariaga surveys 'Penal Policy in the Age of Catherine

II', *La Leopoldina*, 11 (Milan, 1990). The death penalty is discussed by C. Bryner, 'The Issue of Capital Punishment in the Reign of Elizabeth Petrovna', *RR*, 49 (1990), and A. Lentin, 'Beccaria, Shcherbatov and the Question of Capital Punishment in Eighteenth-Century Russia', *CSP*, 24 (1982).

There is little in English on peasant justice, covered by N. A. Minenko, 'Traditsionnye formy rassledovaniia i suda u russkikh krest'ian zapadnoi Sibiri v XVIII–pervoi polovine XIXv.', *Sovetskaia etnografiia* (1980, no. 5), and L. S. Prokof'eva, *Krest'ianskaia obshchina v Rossii vo vtoroi polovine XVIII–pervoi polovine XIXv. (na materialakh votchin Sheremet'evykh)* (Leningrad, 1981). On customary law, V. A. Aleksandrov, *Obychnoe pravo krepostnoi derevni Rossii, XVIII–nachalo XIXv.* (Moscow, 1984), promises more than it delivers. On the army, see E. K. Wirtschafter, 'Military Justice and Social Relations in the Prereform Army, 1796–1855', *SR*, 44 (1985), and J. Keep, 'No Gauntlet for Gentlemen: Officers' Privileges in Russian Military Law, 1716–1855', *CMRS*, 34 (1993).

6   Culture

Education and literacy

Absolute monarchs never escaped the dilemma that, by expanding educational provision to foster a society capable of comprehending their laws, they risked undermining the social stability that they strove to secure. So intimately was schooling linked to politics that Helvétius doubted whether education could be reformed without constitutional change. The tsars tried in vain to prove him wrong.

Because Muscovites ranked obedience to authority higher than intellectual speculation, education, like the sole pre-Petrine printing press (*pechatnyi dvor*), was kept in the hands of the church. However, Peter I lifted the ecclesiastical monopoly and by the 1760s it seemed not only desirable to set up a nationwide system of secular schools but possible to use it to reshape society. Catherine II set out to create a body of rational, active subjects for whom organised religion would remain an essential discipline. Yet the response was lukewarm and her successors rejected the experiment. A. S. Shishkov, minister from 1824 to 1828 (who himself translated Italian literature and appointed a French tutor for his nephews), so distrusted the subversive potential of a general education that he sought to free Russia from the 'swollen pride and sinful self-conceit' instilled by earlier 'schools of vice'. Whilst religious nationalism prevailed in government, reason would once again be subordinated to revelation.

Only in administrative terms was educational modernisation a linear process, and few would now write the history of education as a catalogue of institutional change. Nevertheless, since the subject can scarcely be understood without reference to institutions, it is with them that we begin. Peter the Great laid the foundations of secular education with the Moscow School of Mathematics and Navigation in 1701 (modelled on the Royal Mathematical School at Christ's Hospital in London), whose advanced classes, transferred to St Petersburg in 1715, were redesignated as the Naval Academy there in 1716. In addition to vocational establishments teaching engineering and mining, Peter also founded 'cipher' schools to teach arithmetic, diocesan schools modelled on the Western classical grammar schools, and finally the Academy of Sciences in 1725. These institutions looked back as well as forward. The navigational school's syllabus, though new to Russia, was unexceptional in European terms. Henry Farquharson, its Aberdonian teacher, was conscientious but no innovator; the Slavonic *Arifmetika* (1703) assembled by his Russian pupil, L. F. Magnitskii, was a translated compilation of foreign texts; the school itself extended rather than transformed the Muscovite practice of using foreign specialists to train native officials.[1] Beyond military ranks, the impact of vocational education was limited, even in the long term: Russian nobles were always more interested in Western culture than in Western technology. Only 11 per cent of the 2,000 graduates from the Artillery and Engineering Corps became engineers between 1762 and 1819, when professional training was inaugurated on French models at the new Main Engineering School. Peter I may have been a passionate advocate of literacy and numeracy, but he did not create a nationwide network of secular education and he did not conceive of education as an instrument of social change.

Neither did his immediate successors. By 1764, though 6,000 were enrolled in the twenty-six church 'grammar' schools, most came from the clerical estate and these schools were being transformed into specialist theological seminaries. Nobles were either educated at home by foreign tutors (in 1825, more than four-fifths of Alexander I's State Council had no formal education) or given a superficial schooling in preparation for state service. Neither the boarding school attached to the Academy of Sciences nor the two which prepared students for the University of Moscow found it easy to recruit pupils. Promising military prestige, the St Petersburg Cadet Corps (Shliakhetnyi kadetskii korpus) was more successful: opened in 1731 for 200 boys, it could take 600 by 1762, though only 985 of the 2,186 eighteenth-century entrants graduated. Here a relatively civilised régime prevailed under Count Anhalt from 1786 to 1794. Even so, until the foundation of the Alexander lycée at Tsarskoe Selo in 1811, Russia's élite tended to remember their schooldays as a nasty, brutish period that they would rather had been shorter.

In this, of course, they echoed their European contemporaries. Yet Catherine II determined not only to improve standards but to change

---

[1] See W. F. Ryan, 'Navigation and the Modernisation of Petrine Russia: Teachers, Textbooks, Terminology', in R. Bartlett and J. M. Hartley, eds., *Russia in the Age of the Enlightenment* (London, 1990), pp. 75–105.

the nature of education, a subject much in vogue in Europe in the early 1760s. At first, as projectors ranging from the Anglican cleric Daniel Dumaresq (1713–1805) to Academician G. F. Müller showered her with schemes for reform, the schools she inherited continued to develop unsystematically. I. I. Betskoi set up the Moscow foundling hospital in April 1764 and in May opened Russia's first girls' school – the Smol'nyi Institute for Noble Girls at St Petersburg – based on the French Maison royale de Saint Louis (f. 1686). In March 1764, Betskoi's *General Plan for the Education of People of Both Sexes* set out his dream of a new generation of civilised, virtuous subjects, brought up away from the corrupting influence of their parents. But the dream was shattered by mortality rates reaching almost 100 per cent at the foundling homes. In the end, it was not Betskoi but Johann Ignaz Felbiger (1724–88) who shaped the uniform system of education inaugurated in 1786.

Felbiger, a disenchanted product of Jesuit schools, made his name as a pedagogue in Sagan, a Protestant area of Silesia where he became abbot of the Augustinian monastery in 1758. Impressed by Felbiger's reform of local parish schools, based on the Pietist model he had studied *incognito* in Berlin, Frederick the Great entrusted to him the reform of all Silesian Catholic schools in 1764. A decade later, Maria Theresa delegated to him the Austrian school reform necessitated by the suppression of the Jesuits. When Catherine met Joseph II in 1780, Felbiger's achievements were still highly regarded. Since his subsequent dismissal in Vienna failed to deter F. U. T. Aepinas, the driving force behind the national schools commission set up in St Petersburg in 1782, Russia became the third major power to adopt Felbiger's methods, introduced by his protégé, F. I. Jankovic de Mirjevo (1741–1814), an Orthodox Serb with experience of school administration in the Banat of Temesvár.

The statute of 5 August 1786 set up free, co-educational high schools (modelled on Felbiger's *Realschulen*) and primary schools (*Trivialschulen*) in provincial towns. District towns were to have primary schools only; rural schools, contemplated in drafts, were missing from the final legislation. A tertiary level of teacher training (*Normalschulen*) had already been created in 1783. Over 75 per cent of teachers trained before 1801 came from the clerical estate. Jankovic stuck rigidly to Felbiger's stress on memory, supposedly facilitated by tables designed to act as a visual guide. Pupils were to be taught according to age and ability; corporal punishment was banned. Yet if Felbiger's methods were modern, then his curriculum was not. *On the Duties of Man and Citizen* (1783), buttressed by biblical quotations, stressed that members of each estate must rest content with their prescribed social rôle.[2] Even this text, reprinted eleven times, was banned in 1819 at the instigation of Archbishop Filaret (Drozdov) (1782–1867) for being excessively rationalist and insufficiently critical of republican government.

Alexander I's statute of 1804 added a fourth tier to Catherine's system – village parish schools, where priests, whom she had prevented from teaching, were to take classes open to children of all ranks, regardless of age or sex. Administration was divided among six 'circles' (*okrugi*), each under the supervision, until 1834, of one of the new self-governing universities discussed in chapter 5. Again Russia had adopted a foreign model, this time from revolutionary France. It survived until superseded by the statute of 8 December 1828, which restricted access to schools and deleted the most modern elements from their curriculum.

How far were the state's plans implemented? In view of flogging's central place in society, it is hard to believe that many Russian schools escaped it; certainly, there was frequent recourse to the birch in the clerical seminaries. As for institutional development, even potentially inflated official claims point to limited results. The provincial reform of 1775 charged boards of social welfare with the creation of schools at both provincial and district level. Outside the capital and Tver' province, where Sievers had opened schools in all eleven towns by 1779, the response was patchy. Provision remained irregular, even after 1786. Most school boards either failed to report or submitted vacuous generalisations. Only Vyborg in Old Finland, an exceptional area in many ways, is known in any detail. By 1795–6, this board was working hard. It supplemented its initial capital not only from donations (the most reliable form of support if a school were to survive), but also from customs and municipal revenues, though not on a scale capable of realising Catherine's ambitious aims. Nor did matters subsequently improve. Although Alexander I rewarded benefactors – a noble who donated 40,000 rubles had his bastard son declared legitimate – local initiatives resulted in the foundation of only about 600 parish schools by 1825, half of them in towns, and there was no school in at least 131 district towns in European Russia. Not all schools were moribund. At Nezhin in Ukraine, the school orchestra performed Mozart in the 1820s, when the young Gogol and his fellow boarders contributed to their own literary magazines. Still, few scaled such heights. Perhaps 176,000 children passed through Russian public schools between 1786

[2] J. L. Black, *Citizens for the Fatherland: Education, Educators and Pedagogical Ideals in Eighteenth-Century Russia* (Boulder, 1979), pp. 209–66, translates a text shorn of its notes from the Scriptures.

and 1796, 8 per cent of them girls, and it is estimated that less than 0.5 per cent of the Russian school-age population were enrolled in 1807.

Nowhere in Europe was it easy to establish elementary education; finance and personnel were everywhere lacking. Russia was no exception. Catherine's commission accepted only dementia or fatal illness as grounds for teachers to retire. Yet shortages of money and staff were only part of the problem. Crucial was the lack of popular demand. Most peasants saw no point in schooling. Most children who enrolled dropped out: of the 1,432 pupils who entered secondary schools in Archangel province between 1786 and 1803, only fifty-two completed the course. It was not that peasant literacy lacked advocates. Pososhkov urged it in his *Book of Poverty and Wealth* (1724) on the radical grounds that illiteracy exposed peasants to exploitation by unscrupulous lords and tax-collectors; A. Ia. Polenov ranked literacy first among ways to improve peasant morals in his entry to the Free Economic Society's essay competition in 1766 (see chapter 8). More prosaically, a few youths on large estates were taught to read and write for the purposes of administration. For the church, however, reading remained not a utilitarian but an edificatory process (2 Tim: iii, 14–15) by which to assimilate the spiritual guidance incorporated in the 'ladder of literacy' – a hierarchy of texts rising from daily prayers through the creed to the psalter – often purchased collectively and kept at the local church or monastery where they could be read aloud and copied under supervision.

It was this far-from-modern view of literacy that struck the most sympathetic chord among the peasantry. As yet, only those engaged in proto-industrial occupations in the north saw benefit in acquiring functional skills; their level of achievement was higher than that of peasants on *barshchina* estates in the central provinces. Only after 1861 did demand for functional literacy spread among the peasantry as a whole. Even then, many preferred to teach themselves rather than allow outsiders to disturb village life. De Maistre, whose conservatism permeated the 1828 statute, was probably justified in thinking that only time, rather than government initiatives, would create demand for popular education.

Literacy in early-modern Russia was therefore as geographically and socially stratified as it was elsewhere in Europe. Occupations requiring technical ability naturally scored highest. Burgeoning chancellery paperwork generated a body of literate Muscovite clerks. Accounts for the Belgorod defensive 'line' in 1669–70, where officers (including some foreigners) had to sign for their salaries and check the calculations, show literacy levels of between 17 and 55 per cent. Among the eighteenth-century lower ranks, the best performers were 'soldiers' children' and sons of clergy, who together accounted for two-thirds of the 2,000-odd intake of Peter I's cipher schools by 1727. Reluctant to send their sons to the seminary, many priests and their wives inculcated high standards at home. A late 1730s survey of clerical sons aged seven to fifteen recorded literacy rates of up to 94 per cent. Provincial élites were apparently less consistent: *voevody* in the 1720s were not even asked whether they could read or write. Only 84 per cent of male nobles could do both in 1760. Among nobles signing petitions to the 1767 Legislative Commission, 17.9 per cent were identified as illiterate in Moscow province, but none in Kiev and the Baltic provinces, where Catholic and especially Protestant influences fostered higher standards. By 1800, overwhelmingly Protestant Estonia was 70 per cent literate (including both sexes over age nine), Livonia, a mixture of Protestants and Catholics, was 50 per cent literate, and in predominantly Catholic Courland the level of literacy was 27 per cent.

Nationwide figures can only be estimated. Scholars tentatively place adult male literacy in Muscovy at between 3 and 5 per cent in c. 1680, when the urban rate may have reached 13 per cent. Projecting back from the first national data of 1897, Mironov suggests an overall level of between 3 and 7 per cent in 1797 and between 7 and 11 per cent in 1827 (with urban males touching maxima of 29 and 40 per cent respectively). These figures are probably too high, but are revealing in relative terms. First, the eighteenth century made little difference to literacy rates (though population growth ensured that the *absolute* numbers of those who could read and write rose). Secondly, whilst the overall level of Russian literacy in 1800 was around 6 per cent for males and 4 per cent for females, in France the comparable figures were 47 and 27 per cent, in Britain 68 and 43 per cent, and in Prussia 80 and 50 per cent. If few historical facts speak for themselves, then these are surely among the more eloquent.

Hierarchies of culture

The chasm between the literate and illiterate is but one temptation to accept a model contrasting traditional 'popular' culture with the 'high' sophistication of a privileged few. It is easy enough to make a case for polarity after Peter the Great. The illiterate remained wedded to a world of visual imagery and religiosity, deriving their acquaintance with literature from stories read aloud from manuscript miscellanies or from texts appended to the engravings (*lubki*) which reached a wider audience as printing brought prices down. Meanwhile, a small élite rejected the past in favour of eclectic borrowings from Western styles and secular printed culture, turning to manuscripts only as antiquarian collectors towards 1800. Even when private publishers strove to broaden the reading public by selling cheap editions, nobles still constituted 95 per cent of subscribers to the literary journals which proliferated in the 1780s.

In dress and diet, no less than in aesthetic taste, élite and people were poles apart. Some boiars resented Peter's imposition of Western costume. Its coincidental resemblance to Muslim dress gave extra ammunition to those who impugned the tsar's religious orthodoxy. But by mid-century, bewigged, smooth-shaven metropolitan grandees had begun to compete in Westernised foppery and even the provincial nobility had adopted 'German' costume. Nobles cultivated a palate for fine wines; sugar replaced honey as their principal sweetener, permitting new delicacies and a new meal with a ritual borrowed from the English – afternoon tea. Peasant diets apparently changed little, though variations in regional productivity prevented them from being either uniform or monotonous and peasants in some areas probably ate more meat (or, at any rate, meat products) than has often been assumed. Not until the middle of the nineteenth century did a modern culture of drinking – regular, moderate, and driven by individual choice – begin to rival traditional Russian binges in which peasant groups of both sexes indulged with the express intention of passing out. Even then, contemporaries described the latter as the more 'calculating' drinkers, since only they had a purpose: 'Despite Max Weber, when it came to drinking vodka, modernity was not always the partner of rationality.'[3]

Seductive as the symmetry of opposites may be, the distinction between high and low culture ignores the spectrum of opinion *within* an élite divided in its evaluation of Peter's reforms. Like later lampoons in the moral weeklies (which, in imitation of Addison and Steele's daily *Spectator*, became a feature of mid-century Russian journalism), the satires of A. D. Kantemir (1709–44) mocked obscurantists who stuck to the old Muscovite ways. Since such jibes were addressed to their authors' fellow nobles, their persistence half a century after Peter's death testifies to a lasting suspicion of change. Secondly, by distinguishing too sharply between the two cultures we risk obscuring the extent to which élite concerns overlapped with popular ones. A preference for oral examinations in education, the flourishing 'circles' which formed the social context for intellectual debate after 1800, and the passion for poetry recitals that long allowed Russian literature to

---

[3] D. Christian, *Living Water: Vodka and Russian Society on the Eve of Emancipation* (Oxford, 1990), p. 89.

triumph over censorship all testify to the lasting prestige of the spoken word among the élite. Urban fortune-tellers (mostly old women) served both well- and lowly born clients. And, as contemporary engravings show, one did not have to be a peasant to enjoy sliding down the massive ice-hills that dominated Russian fairgrounds at Shrovetide. As Lady Cathcart reported in 1768, 'some of the Russian Nobility were very dextrous in going down alone' on the little wooden trays provided. 'But most of them took the help of a peasant. Only two ladies of our company ventured, though all the rest had done it often upon former occasions.'[4]

Was popular culture prescribed by the élite, was it parasitic, or was it essentially self-contained? In practice the relationship between the two levels was often mutually reinforcing. Successive rulers strove to communicate moral and political messages 'downwards'. The national holiday commemorating Peter's triumph at Poltava was the first popular tradition 'invented' in an attempt to fashion a patriotic consensus: by 1850 political celebrations constituted half the church's formal holidays. Allegorical firework displays adopted from the West were transposed from their original religious setting to mark coronations and military victories. Peter's successors also appreciated the didactic uses of drama. Elizabeth encouraged well-dressed traders to attend the court theatre and Catherine II, always conscious of the need to educate and impress 'the public', opened her theatre to all on the Table of Ranks and non-commissioned officers in the guards in the 1760s.

Meanwhile, the infusion of popular pastimes 'up' the social ladder reached the apex of Russian society, for beneath its highly polished veneer the court never lost touch with the rich obscenity of popular life. Peter the Great's All-Mad, All-Jesting, All-Drunken Assembly has already been mentioned in chapter 5 as a crucial counterpart to his more formal ceremonials. His daughter, Elizabeth, similarly combined apparently popular tastes – she maintained a practice supposedly banned by Aleksei Mikhailovich by keeping bears trained by a servant at the Alexander Nevskii monastery – with a taste for splendour and ritual complexity at court. Catherine II's bear was baited in front of courtiers during the week and again on Sunday morning 'for the amusement of the populace'. Society was equally fascinated by grotesque humans: pickled corpses were displayed in the Kunstkammer and Peter I offered a reward for live human monsters. The giant Bernardo Gigli performed for Catherine in 1765, and the aristocratic fashion for dwarves survived

---

[4] Letter to Mrs Walkinshaw of Barrowfield, 8 February 1768, in E. Maxtone Graham, *The Beautiful Mrs Graham and the Cathcart Circle* (London, 1927), p. 9.

beyond 1800 as a reflection of popular interest in freaks paraded at fairgrounds.

Peter I's well-advertised preference for simplicity of uniform and behaviour was an affectation whose motivations remain to be fully explored.[5] Clearly the learned never fully shared the culture of the unlearned. Though their recreations may have had shared roots in a common popular heritage, Russia's noble élite, urged on by their rulers, consciously refined their own Europeanised manners and morals. Just as sentimental literary portraits of the peasantry were designed to bring tears to noble eyes, so pastiche rustics gambolling across idyllic pastoral stage-sets brought an indulgent smile to their faces. But the wart-encrusted, louse-infested, and infinitely various reality that lurked behind the powdered mask was neither affecting nor amusing. Only late in the nineteenth century did 'society' abandon its paternalist view of the peasantry for a pathological demonology. Yet even before 1825, nobles recognised that the superficially childlike externals of peasant life concealed an impenetrable counter-culture that they found hard to control.

Whilst it is possible to exaggerate the distance between peasants and those nobles who were brought up on rural estates in the hands of a peasant nanny, no shared national culture could be formed so long as the peasantry as a whole remained insulated from the élite in so many ways. Instead, two rival national identities diverged: the one ethnic and popular (*russkii*), the other imperial and élitist (*rossiiskii*). As we shall see, the latter was defined not only by a lasting conviction among nobles that 'they themselves *were* the nation',[6] but also by an unprecedented influx of Western ideas.

Cosmopolitanism and national consciousness

From its place in the Byzantine 'Commonwealth' – culturally increasingly central if eternally condemned to the geographical periphery – medieval Rus' turned in on itself after the Mongol invasion to the point where xenophobia is sometimes held to have isolated it from the European mainstream. In fact, sporadic links were maintained and the seventeenth century witnessed an intensification of Western contacts. Religious rivalry stimulated Orthodox divines to tap the regular current

[5] L. Hughes, 'Biographies of Peter', in A. Cross, ed., *Russia in the Reign of Peter the Great: Old and New Perspectives*, 2 vols. (Cambridge, SGECRN, 1998), vol. I, pp. 18–19, a useful guide to current issues in Petrine studies.
[6] I. Serman, 'Russian National Consciousness and Its Development in the Eighteenth Century', in Bartlett and Hartley, *Russia in the Age of the Enlightenment*, p. 43.

of Counter-Reformation Catholicism which passed with remarkably little resistance through the Petr Mogila Academy once Kiev had been taken from the Poles. Sympathetic understanding nevertheless remained patchy. Erudite courtiers may have immersed themselves in baroque literary theory, but one need only read the diary of Petr Tolstoi – a chamberlain in his fifties who travelled to Venetia to study shipbuilding in 1697–9 – to see how much of what an educated Westerner took for granted amazed his Muscovite contemporaries.[7] Moreover, foreigners resident in Moscow had to live in the ghetto-like 'German suburb' (*nemetskaia sloboda*), set up in 1652; not until the foundation of St Petersburg were they encouraged to mingle with Russians. Only after 1700 was the scale of Western involvement in Russia, and Russian acquaintance with the West, transformed.

We remain unsure how some foreign influences took hold. Italian architects had worked in the Kremlin before 1500 but left no lasting tradition. 'Moscow baroque',[8] which originated in the 1680s and flourished in the 1690s, bore signs of foreign influence. But since no Russian architect is then known to have visited the West, and no Moscow baroque building can confidently be ascribed to a foreigner, the style is better characterised as a hybrid incorporating Renaissance characteristics into the Russian vernacular than as an imitation of any one foreign example. Its buildings were designed and built by Russians inspired by Western books. Peter I's own library contained at least 164 European works on architecture, some of which he had translated into Russian.

Translation remained a vital means of cultural transmission accounting for over 70 per cent of all eighteenth-century published literature excluding odes.[9] Peter set up a print-shop in Amsterdam in 1698 to issue Russian versions of foreign textbooks. Seventy years later, Catherine II subsidised a society of translators in an effort to disseminate Enlightenment. One in four books published in Russian between the 1760s and 1800 was translated from the French. By then, many educated Russians could read French and German in the original. Few knew English before 1800, but English works were often available in French and German versions which also acted as intermediaries for

---

[7] *The Travel Diary of Peter Tolstoi: A Muscovite in Early Modern Europe*, tr. M. J. Okenfuss (DeKalb, IL, 1987).

[8] The term is here discussed with reference to architecture, but has also been applied to music: see O. Dolskaya-Ackerley, 'Vasilii Titov and the "Moscow Baroque"', *Journal of the Royal Musical Association*, 118, 2 (1993), pp. 203–22.

[9] Ju. D. Levin, ed., *Schöne Literatur in russischer Übersetzung: von den Anfängen bis zum 18. Jahrhundert*, 2 vols. (Cologne, 1995–6), text in Russian, is more encyclopaedic than analytical.

most of the 245 English books translated into Russian between 1741 and 1800. More than 3,500 foreign-language books were published in eighteenth-century Russia, most in German or Latin. Between 9,000 and 15,000 French books (3,000 titles at between three and five copies each) found their way to the two capitals between 1730 and 1760, initially from Dutch dealers but increasingly from Germany. Distribution remained uncertain. By 1781, when the *Encyclopédie*'s publishers managed to supply five perfect folio editions to Christian Rüdiger in Russia, four years had passed since the bookseller first requested them and two of his customers had given up in disgust. Still, by the 1770s contact with Europe was almost as likely to be made in person as through books, since successive tsars had assiduously recruited foreign talent and Russian nobles, released from compulsory state service by Peter III in 1762, had begun to visit the West.

Italians dominated the musical life of St Petersburg. *Opera seria* reigned from the 1730s until the 1750s and 1760s, when Italian and French comic opera made their débuts. Because it replaced heroic classical scenes with contemporary plots, *opéra comique* has sometimes been seen as a modernising influence. But its adoption at court suggests that Russia's rulers were titillated rather than unnerved by any subversive social implications they may have detected. Neither was *opera seria* supplanted: the success of E. I. Fomin's *Orpheus and Eurydice* in 1792 shows its lasting attraction. The rarity here was not the genre but the nationality of the composer, for in no field were foreigners so prominent as in secular music. Francesco Araia, in Russia between 1735 and 1759, composed the first opera written there, *Cephalus and Procris* in 1755, and was succeeded by musicians who now extended to St Petersburg a continental itinerary begun in Vienna, Prague, Dresden, and Leipzig. Galuppi was followed by Catherine II's favourite, Paisiello (whose *Barber of Seville* was premiered in St Petersburg in 1782), and later by Cimarosa. During concert seasons inaugurated in the 1770s, the violinist and composer Ivan Khandoshkin, who appeared in 1780, was the only Russian to grace programmes otherwise performed entirely by foreigners.

More surprisingly, foreigners penetrated popular entertainments with native traditions. Il'ia Iakubovskii, whose puppet theatre performed in Moscow in 1753–5, is the only known Russian entrepreneur among puppeteers at fairs and carnivals, formerly the preserve of *skomorokhi* (wandering minstrels banned at the instigation of the church in 1648 but active in Siberia until the 1760s). Between 1810 and 1840, Western marionette shows, concentrating either on biblical subjects or on classic Western plots such as *Don Juan* or *Doctor Faustus*, were joined by Italian street theatre and especially the Pulcinella glove puppetry (a sort of Italian Punch and Judy) which became popular in their Russian variant, Petrushka, only gradually accumulating local Russian features.

Whilst the tsars remained loath to 'postpone events until our nationals become masters of every function that they have to perform', as Alexander I told Admiral Chichagov in 1806, foreign talent remained indispensable.[10] And so long as demand was sanctioned at the highest level, Westerners could always be persuaded to brave the journey, the climate, and the occasional hostility of Russians unaccustomed to working with foreigners and resentful of the fees they could command: 'I have been of greater service to Russia's theatre than French actors and Italian dancers, and yet I am paid less', complained the dramatist A. P. Sumarokov (1718–77) in 1759.[11] Money was indeed the principal temptation to Western artistes; the tsars promised, even if they did not always pay, rewards greater than could readily be earned elsewhere. Some found their new wealth elusive. After a brilliant début in St Petersburg, where he arrived as Clementi's pupil in 1802, the Irish virtuoso pianist and composer John Field (1782–1837) frittered away the fortune he earned from teaching alone before subsiding into alcoholism. Not even this dismal prospect could deter those who had yet to win glittering prizes. Some, such as the architect Charles Cameron (1746–1812), whose only known commission in London was the reconstruction of 15 Hanover Square between 1770 and 1775, never achieved recognition in their native lands. Yet within four years of reaching Russia in 1779, Cameron had built the neo-classical gallery that bears his name at Catherine's summer palace at Tsarskoe Selo, where he was also responsible for the Roman baths, on which he had published a treatise in 1772. Cameron's masterpiece, the Palladian palace at Pavlovsk, followed in 1782–6. Mocked by purists, his work symbolises the ebullience of an artist working within the bounds of tradition yet unrestricted by convention.[12]

No isolated shooting stars, such individuals were only the most brilliant among whole constellations of foreigners in Russia, for they brought with them not only colleagues and acquaintances but also craftsmen and labourers. By the mid-1720s, foreigners accounted for about a fifth of the registered tradesmen in the capital and a quarter of the craftsmen employed by its Chancellery of Construction. Later, it

---

[10] Quoted in N. V. Riasanovsky, *The Image of Peter the Great in Russian History and Thought* (Oxford, 1985), p. 65.

[11] *F. G. Volkov i russkii teatr ego vremeni: sbornik materialov* (Moscow, 1953), p. 136, A. P. Sumarokov to I. I. Shuvalov, 15 November 1759.

[12] See the magnificently illustrated D. Shvidkovsky, *The Empress and the Architect: British Architecture and Gardens at the Court of Catherine the Great* (New Haven, CT, 1996).

was thanks to Cameron that a group of Scottish workmen arrived, helping to build N. A. L'vov's neo-classical cathedral at Mogilev to celebrate Catherine's meeting with Joseph II in 1780.

Although increasingly overshadowed, permanently settled foreign communities still had an impact. The British, from their base on St Petersburg's 'English embankment', made their mark by brewing beer, which found a ready market. They also helped to establish Russian freemasonry: from 1771 the British had their own lodge, Perfect Union, and it was the duke of Beaufort in London who authorised I. P. Elagin as provincial grand master of the first openly acknowledged network of fourteen Russian lodges in 1772. Rosicrucianism was introduced to Moscow by I. G. Schwarz, a German professor born in Transylvania. Significantly, it was the foreign element in Russian masonry that attracted most suspicion: Catherine II was less worried by the ideological menace of the masonic lodges than by their potential as a network for subversives among the Prussians who courted her son.

During a period of international rivalry, state scientific secrets became contentious, especially in applied military technology. Russians complained that Western master-craftsmen refused, once in Russia, to transmit their trade secrets to native apprentices. The engineer N. I. Korsakov (1749–88) found the British ironworks he visited in 1776 'very jealous'; at the Carron foundry in Scotland he was permitted neither to make drawings nor to see a secret cannon-boring machine. The director of the Carron works, Charles Gascoigne (1738?–1806), was ostracised by the British community in St Petersburg when he took with him to Russia in 1786 both skilled workers and machine tools which he subsequently used to restructure Russian cannon production.

Theoretical science proved less divisive. Newton's critique of the Cartesian system was introduced into Russia by Ia. V. Bruce, who collected a library of Newtonian works after Peter I became fascinated with the subject during his Grand Embassy. Lacking a native scientific establishment with a vested interest in Cartesianism, Russia might seem to have offered a receptive base for new thinking. But it was some time before Newtonian principles were widely accepted. Perhaps this was because Leonhard Euler (1707–83), the most distinguished mathematician to make his career in Russia, was a staunch opponent; more probably it was because 'Cartesianism seemed to conflict less with traditional Christian dogma and its cosmology.'[13]

Like Euler, scientists came to Russia permanently, in the service of the Academy of Sciences, temporarily in pursuit of particular research,

[13] M. Raeff, 'The Enlightenment in Russia and Russian Thought in the Enlightenment', in J. G. Garrard, ed., *The Eighteenth Century in Russia* (Oxford, 1973), p. 30.

or, as in the case of some early German Pietists, intending to combine scholarship with proselytism. By mid-century, a smaller number of Russians had travelled westwards. Russians as far apart as Oxford and Irkutsk collaborated with their European colleagues in measuring the solar parallax – a major gap in the Newtonian system – since, had it not been for the clouds, the transits of Venus across the sun in 1761 and 1769 should have been visible from Siberia. Scholarly diplomats were well placed to monitor the latest Western developments. At The Hague in the 1770s, Prince D. A. Golitsyn worked for a time in van Marum's laboratory. When he published (in Russia) studies of electricity inspired by the work of Benjamin Franklin, only the advertisement was printed in his native language. Golitsyn's works appeared initially in French and then in German when they were reprinted by the Academy of Sciences, where the German influence had dominated since its foundation. Not until 1747 was the first Russian, M. V. Lomonosov (1711–65), granted full membership, having probably impressed the electors as much by his training at Freiburg and Marburg as by his innate ability. Of the 107 eighteenth-century academicians, barely a quarter were native Russians, though the proportion regularly increased to reach eight out of sixteen in 1800. German domination of Russian science continued when the empiricist tradition of the Enlightenment gave way to the metaphysical *Naturphilosophie* of the Romantic Schelling, whose Russian disciples, D. M. Vellanskii and A. S. Pavlov, both educated in church schools, initiated a lasting fascination with organic ideas extending far beyond the natural sciences.

Whilst science offered obvious opportunities for cultural transfer, one might expect the Russian Orthodox church to have been a bastion of xenophobia. Amvrosii, bishop of Novgorod, did indeed help Elizabeth to vilify Anna's 'devilish' German advisers and other clerics contributed to the posthumous image of Peter the Great as national hero. However, as the presence of its men among the scientists implies, cosmopolitan influences penetrated even the church's portals. In the West, modernity is often measured by the *decline* of Latin: already in 1651, in a passage mocking the papacy, Hobbes dismissed Latin as a language 'not commonly used by any Nation now in the world'.[14] Yet this was just as the Orthodox church was about to *encounter* Latin humanism in its Ukrainian Catholic form. A trenchant recent book insists that this particular

[14] Hobbes, *Leviathan*, ed. C. B. Macpherson (Harmondsworth, 1968), p. 712. See P. Burke, '*Heu dominae, adsunt Turcae*: A Sketch for a Social History of Post-Medieval Latin', in P. Burke and R. Porter, eds., *Language, Self and Society: A Social History of Language* (Cambridge, 1991), pp. 23–50.

Western import never took root in Russia.[15] But Latin remained the dominant medium of instruction in ecclesiastical schools until 1808, partly, as Metropolitan Platon himself acknowledged, to preserve the clergy's vestigial scholarly reputation in the West.

Ascetics looked down on learning, but not all provincial prelates were like Ioasaf (Gorlenko) (1705–54), bishop of Belgorod, who possessed only sixteen books. Doubtless his decade of study in Halle helped the erudite Semen (Todorskii) (1700–54) to convert the future Catherine the Great to Orthodoxy when she arrived in Russia in 1744. From the late 1740s, successive bishops of Kostroma developed the seminary library into a repository not only of Orthodox theology, but also of Western literature; in 1791 the bishop founded one of Russia's first accessible public libraries, stored in the cathedral cupola. Court preachers maintained a scholarly tradition in the church during the eighteenth century and the reformed theological academies nurtured a network of learned monks in the nineteenth. Prominent was the antiquary Evgenii (Bolkhovitinov) (1767–1837), Metropolitan of Kiev and compiler of the first comprehensive guide to Russian secular writers, published 1805–45. Until c. 1820, the dominant influence in the church was a universalist, mystical Christianity in which national and denominational distinctions were blurred. Symbolised by the Russian Bible Society, founded in 1813 on the model of the Protestant British and Foreign Bible Society, this was a supranational religion well suited to a time when the tsar himself envisaged a Holy Alliance (1815) of the great powers under the ultimate sovereignty of the one true Christ.

Naturally, Russians were not wholly overshadowed in their own church. The early nineteenth century saw the start of a quest for the patristic roots of Orthodox theology and art. Specialists from the Synodal typography had already begun to revise Orthodox liturgical music: the *Irmolog*, *Oktoikh*, *Obikhod*, and *Prazdnik* (1772) were later praised as a national treasure by the savant prince V. F. Odoevskii (1804–69). But though Russia retained its distinctive tradition of unaccompanied choral sacred music, foreign stylistic influences were dominant even here. They were exemplified in the work of D. S. Bortnianskii (1751–1825), the Ukrainian-born composer whose decade of study in Italy (1769–79) was the formative influence in his subsequent career as director of the imperial chapel choir.[16]

---

[15] M. J. Okenfuss, *The Rise and Fall of Latin Humanism in Early-Modern Russia: Pagan Authors, Ukrainians and the Resilience of Muscovy* (Leiden, 1995).

[16] See M. Kuzma, 'Bortniansky à la Bortniansky: An Examination of the Sources of Dmitry Bortniansky's Choral Concertos', *Journal of Musicology*, 14, 2 (1996), pp. 183–212.

Even in the eighteenth century, an excessive attachment to foreign culture was perceived as unbalanced. Around 1800, in a transition which hints at changing foreign influences, 'anglomania' succeeded 'gallomania' as the disease afflicting those who went too far. Ironically, it was admirers of foreign culture who were most resentful of sneers from abroad and most anxious to assert Russian achievements. Catherine II's *Antidote* (1770), a denunciation of the unflattering portrait of Russia painted by the abbé Chappe d'Autéroche in his *Voyage en Sibérie* (1769), exemplifies the Russian defensive reaction. However, few Russians supposed that they could define their own national identity simply by rejecting the West. Instead, the eighteenth century witnessed the first attempt to draw on foreign models in an effort to reinvent Russianness.

Translation allowed Russian writers to experiment with a new native literary language in a variety of genres. From the 1730s, classical forms offered continuity and depth to a culture cut off from its roots by Peter the Great. Russians who mastered them hoped to rival the glories of antiquity. But the attempt to formulate an authentic Russian identity from Western concepts and vocabulary foundered on a paralysing belief in normative aesthetics. No sooner did one writer claim to have established a model for a new Russian literature than his efforts were dismissed by another as a breach of neo-classical rules. By 1779, when M. M. Kheraskov (1733–1807) completed his *Rossiada*, imperial Russia's first major epic, efforts to recover a native Russian culture had begun both to rehabilitate Muscovy – Novikov's *Essay at a Historical Dictionary of Russian Writers* (1774) included no fewer than fifty-four pre-Petrine authors – and to return to its popular roots among the *narod*.

Profiting from interest in the peasant question in the aftermath of Pugachev, A. O. Ablesimov's comic opera *The Miller-Sorcerer, Cheat and Matchmaker* became the most popular Russian piece in the repertoire after its première in Moscow in 1779. Derived from Rousseau's *Le devin du village*, its plot featured both an *odnodvorets* and Russian folk music. Adventure stories with Russian plots sold well, Matvei Komarov's *The Factual and True History of a Russian Swindler* appearing seven times between 1779 and 1794. Folk culture became an object of study in its own right. And the Russian Academy, founded under the presidency of Princess Dashkova in 1783, crowned two decades of national revival by sponsoring an etymological dictionary of the Russian language (1789–94).

Prompted in part by a reaction against foreigners, this Russian revival was no self-denying retreat into insularity. Yet neither was it a self-aggrandising assertion of Russian superiority. Integral to nationalist thought, struggle and the urge to dominate found incipient expression

in Trediakovskii's dissertation 'On the Primacy of the Slovenian Language over the Teutonic' (1757), a dubious attempt to prove that it was
from the proto-Slavic language of the Scythians that all other tongues
were descended. In 1792, P. A. Plavil'shchikov (1760–1812) ascribed
the success of Ablesimov's technically imperfect *Miller* at the expense of
Molière's classically proportioned *Misanthrope* to the fact that 'the *Miller*
is one of us, whereas the *Misanthrope* is alien'. Such neuroses provided a
basis for the aggressive nationalist particularism which, fuelled by the
events of 1812, began to replace tolerant cosmopolitanism as the
dominant tone of Russian culture after the Napoleonic invasion. Until
then, however, they were relatively subdued. Still at the building-block
stage – in which it seemed possible to create a distinctively Russian
landscape garden by 'reconciling' the best of the English and French
traditions – Russian nationalism in 1800 had only partially regained the
messianic note which invigorated theories of Moscow as the third
Rome. Russians were more anxious to claim their rightful place in a
civilised humanity with common roots in the classical world. Those
young nobles who emulated their Western contemporaries by embarking
on a Grand Tour after 1762 were determined not only to learn from
Western culture but to demonstrate their ability to share in it on equal
terms like the fictional protagonist of Karamzin's *Letters of a Russian
Traveller* (1791–1801):

Everything *national* is nothing before the human. The main business is to be
men and not Slavs. What is good for men cannot be bad for Russians and what
the English and Germans have invented for the use and advantage of man is
mine, because I am a man.[17]

In an age fascinated by comparative sociological development, Russia
naturally became a country worth visiting and studying, especially now
that it was a powerful rival.[18] Uniformly condescending towards the
Muscovite past until late in the eighteenth century, foreigners varied in
their verdicts on their own era. Many lived in expatriate cocoons, understanding little of their Russian surroundings. Some visitors, determined
to define European civilisation in contradistinction to Asiatic savagery,
arrived temperamentally predisposed to paint a picture of barbarity.[19]
Russian backwardness struck even the most charitable: 'Living in
Russia', recorded Gertrude Harris in 1778, '[is] like living in the time of

---

[17] Quoted by A. G. Cross, *N. M. Karamzin: A Study of His Literary Career, 1783–1803*
(Carbondale, IL, 1971), p. 63.

[18] For a new perspective, see G. Goggi, 'The Philosophes and the Debate over Russian
Civilization', in M. Di Salvo and L. Hughes, eds., *A Window on Russia* (Rome, 1996),
pp. 299–305.

[19] L. Wolff, *Inventing Eastern Europe: The Map of Civilization on the Mind of the
Enlightenment* (Stanford, CA, 1994), catalogues the most hostile foreign accounts.

ones Great grandfather to all other civilised European Nations.' Yet positive assessments were not lacking. Even the critical Macartney, could say that by the 1760s Sumarokov had 'regulated the Russian stage and brought it to a state of as much decency, order and magnificence as most others in Europe'.[20]

Beyond a small but growing coterie of proselytisers, Russian culture fared poorly as an export. Though Peter I's Grand Embassy attracted widespread attention, the early notices of Russian publications in European journals were not so much reviews as advertisements inserted by his ambassadors. There was no Western market for Russian art. Russian writers were more often translated at home as a mark of their domestic prestige than abroad in response to foreign demand. They made little impact in the West unless, like Kantemir, they were also diplomats assured of an entrée to polite society. Russian salons in Europe, such as Princess Dashkova's in Edinburgh in the 1770s, did more to demonstrate their hosts' cosmopolitanism than to discuss Russian affairs. Russian themes began to figure in Western literature and music from the 1780s as part of the fashion for historical and topical plots. But they were not popular. C. G. Hempel's turgid opera *Peter the Great, Emperor of Russia* (Leipzig, 1780), celebrating his victory over the Turks, fared only marginally better than William Shield's flop, *The Czar* (Covent Garden, 1790), based on Peter's work at Deptford dockyard.

Of course, this was largely a question of Western ignorance. European dealers bought few Russian-language books because hardly any of their customers knew Russian: Kroll's *Commercial Dictionary, in the English and Russian Languages* did not appear in London until 1800, and only in the 1820s did language primers become readily available. Public interest in Russia had been growing in Britain since the 1790s, and the tsar's visit to London in 1814 stimulated it further. It was the Russian soldiery, especially the romantic Cossacks, who sparked the British literary imagination. Indeed, the Russian troops' fame spread right across Europe. Little more than a century after Peter I had decreed that one in ten members of his military bands must be foreign, a log-hut Russian colony was built at Potsdam in 1826 for the Russian musicians employed by the First Guards Regiment and crack Prussian regiments competed for the honour of having members of the Russian imperial family as honorary colonels-in-chief.

By 1800, the Russian élite's successful internalisation of Western

[20] Quoted by A. Cross, *By the Banks of the Neva: Chapters from the Lives and Careers of the British in Eighteenth-Century Russia* (Cambridge, 1997), p. 372, and Cross, *Anglo-Russica: Aspects of Cultural Relations Between Great Britain and Russia in the Eighteenth and Early Nineteenth Centuries* (Oxford and Providence, RI, 1993), p. 32.

ideas requires us to think of their own cultural sphere as 'largely indigenous and autonomous'.[21] Yet, although the Russians had arrived, they still felt insecure. Abandoning their earlier quest to catch up with the Western vanguard, nationalists now set out instead to distinguish their own culture from allegedly inferior rivals. Newly inspired by the Romantic quest for the Russian soul, the intelligentsia became obsessed with the ambiguities of Russia's place in Europe. As Lieven claims, 'the pull between national traditions and alien cultures' helped to stimulate artistic creativity.[22] However, like the Irish in our own century – another emergent nation 'struggling to distinguish between sterile imitation and productive cultural transfer' – the Russians discovered that 'learning is hard work. It is slow. It is purgative. It is a process, not an event.'[23]

Centre and periphery

By 1721 the St Petersburg Construction Chancellery was spending almost 5 per cent of total state revenue. By contrast, only a decade after the zenith of Moscow baroque, Moscow had descended into desuetude. But, bright as the light from St Petersburg shone, the old capital was never eclipsed. Even at its nadir in the 1710s, many nobles trapped in the quagmire of a bleak northern building-site longed to return to 'the Native Place which the *Russes* are fond of, and where they have their Friends and Acquaintance about them'.[24] As the site of the tsars' coronation, Moscow retained its symbolic significance as the nation's heart and became an icon of anti-cosmopolitan conservatism in modern Russian culture.

Yet there was more to Moscow than this stereotype suggests. Following the foundation there of Russia's first university in 1755, promising writers experimented between 1760 and 1762 on *Useful Entertainment* (*Poleznoe uveslenie*), edited by the university curator, Kheraskov. Eleven out of eighteen major government departments still kept their head office in Moscow in 1763. *Moscow News* (*Moskovskie vedomosti*), first issued in April 1756, was one of two titles with a strong sense of place published by Novikov, who acquired the lease to the Moscow University Press in 1779, the other being the journal *Moscow Monthly* (1780). Karamzin followed with his *Moscow Journal* (1791–2), a literary compilation whose contents were far from parochial. Karam-

---

[21] R. Bartlett, 'Russia and the Enlightenment', in R. Reid, J. Andrew, and V. Polukhina, eds., *Structure and Tradition in Russian Society, Slavica Helsingiensia*, 14 (1994), p. 3.

[22] D. Lieven, *The Aristocracy in Europe, 1815–1914* (London, 1992), p. 19.

[23] J. J. Lee, *Ireland 1912–1985: Politics and Society* (Cambridge, 1989), p. 629.

[24] J. Perry, *The State of Russia Under the Present Czar* (London, 1716, reprinted 1967), p. 262.

zin's very presence attracted other writers to the city. Even during the press's difficult years, the emergence of a regular Muscovite market, based on the popularity of leisure books, stimulated the book trade as a whole though prices were 25 per cent higher than in St Petersburg. Theatrical life also flourished after several false starts. It was in Moscow that Peter I opened the first public theatre in 1702, and though neither this nor a 3,000-seat successor built on Red Square in 1731 survived, a more modest venture managed by an Englishman, Michael Maddox, was central to Russian repertory from 1776 until 1805.

Released from compulsory service in 1762, many nobles returned to their rural estates. Previously, there seems to have been little provincial society to speak of: nobles were diverted by the court, whilst fluctuating merchant fortunes could no longer sustain the competitive patronage that subsidised masterly ecclesiastical decoration down to the 1680s. Yet in the wake of the provincial reform, estates (*usad'by*) near the two capitals became the focus of noble attempts to reproduce court culture for themselves.[25] Savants such as Prince D. A. Golitsyn might retire to pursue a life 'campagnarde et philosophique'.[26] More typical were the Kulomzins, a venerable but unpretentious family whose house at Kornilovo lacked both a library and a park. However, since status was measured by display, magnates such as the Gagarins and the Iusupovs vied to build classical palaces surrounded by individually designed landscape gardens, some modelled on English 'natural' principles admired by the Grand Tourists. Many also built theatres. Of the 173 known between 1780 and the 1840s, fifty-three were in Moscow alone (with a further ten in Moscow province) and twenty-seven more in St Petersburg. Here the trained serfs we encountered in chapter 4 performed rôles played at court by foreigners. Expensive sets and costumes characterised the best establishments: Count P. B. Sheremet'ev, who introduced Gluck's *Alceste* and *Iphigénie en Tauride* to the Russian stage, even employed a Parisian agent to supply the latest technology for his theatre at Kuskovo.

Apart from these rural oases, towns spearheaded the penetration of metropolitan culture into the provincial desert. Theatres, schools, and seminaries were generally urban phenomena. So was the book trade.

---

[25] P. R. Roosevelt, *Life on the Russian Country Estate: A Social and Cultural History* (New Haven, CT, 1995), is beautifully illustrated. See also Iu. A. Tikhonov, 'Dvorianskaia sel'skaia usad'ba bliz Moskvy i Sankt-Peterburga v XVIII veke', *Otechestvennaia istoriia* (1998, no. 2), pp. 37–59, and the bibliography in *Russkaia usad'ba: Sbornik Obshchestva izucheniia russkoi usad'by*, vol. III (Moscow, 1997), pp. 380–6.

[26] G. Dulac and L. Evdokimova, 'La correspondance de Dmitri A. Golitsyn (1760–1784)', *Dix-huitième Siècle*, 22 (1990), p. 372, quoting a letter of 11 December 1778.

Progress was slow and profits tiny. Novikov hoped that provincial merchants would both sell and read his journals but, in a country with fewer bookshops than eighteenth-century Ireland, the plan was premature. No one in the provinces subscribed to *The Painter* (1772), though later journals circulated in more than a dozen towns and the provincial proportion of subscribers had outgrown both Moscow's and St Petersburg's by 1800.

Towns themselves became a visible symbol of central ideals as Catherine II's Commission for the Construction of St Petersburg and Moscow, formed under Betskoi in December 1762, extended urban planning to the provinces. The commission approved 306 new plans before being disbanded by Tsar Paul in 1796. Copies of the plans for Tver', the first town to be redesigned in 1763, served as models in Archangel after 1765 and in Kazan' in the mid-1770s. The majority followed in the decade after the provincial reform. As in St Petersburg in the late 1730s, geometric street plans were to replace 'disorderly' medieval centres; buildings were to be zoned both in height and quality, houses becoming taller and better built towards the centre. This rational aim proved Utopian. Though planners were sensitive to history and to natural features – so that Uglich, on the upper Volga, preserved part of its medieval concentric pattern – the principal restraint was financial. In 1804, twenty-six years after Ladoga's plan was approved, the governor of St Petersburg province confessed that the indigence of its inhabitants limited the number of stone houses to four. Local inertia was a lesser obstacle to central direction than in Britain, where vested interests found greater room for chicanery. But Velikii Ustiug's final shape was not determined until thirty years – and some ten different projects – after the fires of 1772 created the need for a new plan. A few rapidly constructed monuments to national triumphs, such as the cathedral at Kherson (1781–6), built to commemorate the annexation of New Russia and the Tauride, therefore broke the rule of slow progress. Much remained to be done in 1806 when William Hastie, who had come to Russia in 1784 as one of Cameron's Scottish stonemasons, was appointed architect to a revived Construction Committee.

The incongruous exception to this picture of provincial torpor was Siberia, whose towns profited from the presence of Swedish prisoners captured during the Great Northern War, Poles transported after the partitions, and Russian political prisoners despatched there since the seventeenth century. In concert with local bureaucrats, these exiles contributed immeasurably to cultural development. At the gateway to Siberia lay the former Tatar stronghold of Kazan', whose Peter and Paul Cathedral survives as a fine example of Petrine provincial baroque –

European in form, yet lavishly decorated in brash, Asiatic colour. The pupils of Kazan''s *gymnazii* (1758–88) gave public performances of allegorical plays originally written (and perhaps even performed) in German by the school's director, Julius von Canitz. Later, Esipov's repertory company, founded there in 1800, offered original Russian plays in almost half their productions. Further east, Tobol'sk supported the only two provincial journals to which readers subscribed in any number before 1800 (*Biblioteka uchenaia*, 1793–4, and *Irtysh*, 1790–1, which published articles on Voltaire and Condorcet, and an abridged translation of Lord Kames). Seminary pupils performed in the town square, adding *Ermak*, a play by a local priest commemorating the cossack who led the conquest of Siberia, to their repertoire of conventional school drama in the 1770s. In 1791–4, a 560-seat public theatre was built with the co-operation of the governor, A. V. Al'iabev, whose son became a notable composer. The writer August von Kotzebue, exiled in 1800, found boxes adorned with flowers, giving the theatre an Asiatic appearance; but the repertoire was a conventional mixture of tragedies, comedies, and comic operas, about half written by Russians (including Fonvizin, Kheraskov, and Plavil'shchikov) and half by foreigners (among them Molière, Goldoni, and Lessing) in 1802.

As the Siberian example suggests, provincial culture benefited less from encouragement at the centre than from prohibition. This was especially true under Tsar Paul, whose enforcement of his mother's 1796 edict, decreeing the closure of private printing presses in the two capitals, redirected their owners towards Vladimir (where Vasilii Sankovskii, a pioneer private publisher in Moscow in the 1760s, operated as early as 1784), Voronezh, and Nikolaev instead. Although these presses drew on local talent, their output reflected wider interests. The press at Nikolaev, a small Black Sea port, included amongst the thirty or so titles published between 1798 and 1803 the second Russian translation of Kant's *Groundwork on the Metaphysic of Morals* (1803) and three translations of English works of naval interest, thanks to its anglophile director, Vice-Admiral N. S. Mordvinov (1754–1845). But provincial presses produced less than 5 per cent of the books published in eighteenth-century Russia, and once Alexander I relaxed his father's censorship most declined or closed as the initiative returned to the capitals. By 1825, of a total of sixty-one presses, twenty-two were in St Petersburg and ten more in Moscow. Of the remainder, few published more than three or four books each year.

Cosmopolitan culture filtering out into the provinces through the prism of St Petersburg met foreign influences radiating in direct from abroad. After 1721 the Baltic provinces, the fount of German

Protestantism, came to rival Ukraine, the funnel of Polish Catholicism. In Odessa (f. 1794), where Italian – the *lingua franca* of the Mediterranean business community – was used on street signs, relative ease of access allowed an Italian opera company to begin in 1811 a series of annual visits broken only by the war of 1812–14. As Pushkin wrote in 1823: 'Odessa is a European town – so there are no Russian books here.'[27]

There were parts of the empire, especially in the far north, where traditional icon-painting and wood-carving skills either survived or escaped the Western onslaught. Local variations have yet to be fully explored. But it is already clear that in Russia, as elsewhere, élite interest in such traditions was largely a byproduct of the revival of national consciousness. Consequently, many of the 'folk songs' published c. 1800 were stylised adaptations that bowdlerised the original text. State-sponsored ethnographic and geographical expeditions contributed to a growing awareness of local cultures. Siberian travel accounts by P. S. Pallas (1741–1811) acted as sources for localisms defined in the Russian Academy's dictionary. M. M. Ivanov (1748–1823), having studied at the Academy of Arts in the 1760s and then in Paris and Rome, was sent with Potemkin's army to the Crimea (1780–4) and later to Georgia and Armenia, whose scenery inspired his development as one of Russia's first landscape artists. It was the literary example of Sir Walter Scott and Lord Byron that encouraged Russian writers in the 1820s to emulate Pushkin's *Prisoner of the Caucasus* (*Kavkazskii plennik*, 1822) and create a new poetic image of the periphery as sublime wilderness. Later their work helped to generate a potentially subversive Romantic regionalism in the Russian empire. Before 1825, however, Russia remained almost as centralised in cultural terms as it was politically.

This is not to say that the provinces contributed no talent: the opposite is true. Trediakovskii came from Astrakhan', Lomonosov from Archangel. But like the actor-manager Fedor Volkov, who had originally set up his theatre in Iaroslavl', and the host of talented Ukrainians who flocked to St Petersburg, they were attracted by the capital's magnetism. Thus were the provinces bled dry. French cities supported flourishing provincial academies; economic growth boosted a thriving cultural market in the English counties and Scottish cities; German culture blossomed in university towns. Russia could boast none of these achievements. Samuel Bentham was as surprised as he was delighted to discover the *Encyclopédie* at M. M. Pokhodiashin's Ural copper mines in

---

[27] *Pushkin on Literature*, selected, tr., and ed. by T. Wolff (London, 1971), p. 71, Pushkin to Viazemskii, 4 November 1823.

1781; outside the principal noble libraries, about which surprisingly little is known, such finds were probably few and far between.

Science and superstition

Although Peter I had been a convinced propagandist of science and technology, they remained the preserve of a few. The achievements of the Academy of Sciences – greater in theoretical than experimental fields – were recorded, from 1728, in Latin journals which found almost no native subscribers. Parallel Russian texts appeared fleetingly in the 1750s, and again in the 1770s, but were soon abandoned for lack of demand: interested Russians could read the originals. Under Catherine II, private publishers tried to popularise science, but since Novikov 'gave Russians all the lore on Paracelsus' alchemy at a time when he could have informed them of Lavoisier's systematisation of modern chemical knowledge, Priestly's isolation of oxygen (1774–5), and Cavendish's *Chemical Experiments on Air* (1784)', they apparently had no specific syllabus in mind.[28] They were, in any case, working against the grain. In 1752 the Moscow Synodal press had pulped hundreds of copies of unsold scientific books to bind Bibles which remained in heavy demand; works on scientific and technological subjects accounted, even in 1800, for only 5 per cent of the total published.

It would be wrong, however, to suppose that the impact of the natural sciences was limited to readers of learned journals. Euler, following a European pattern from c. 1690, was amongst the academicians who advised the state on the practical uses of their work.[29] Debates on the applicability of rational methods infused every scholarly activity, not least literature. And though there was no Russian equivalent of the peripatetic English scientific lecturer – secular rivals to itinerant evangelical preachers – Princess Dashkova inaugurated public lectures in mathematics, geometry, and natural history at the Academy of Sciences in 1793. Ten years later a course introducing galvanism and gases proved the most popular of four new lecture series offered to the public at the University of Moscow.

From mid-century, mechanical gadgetry found as willing a reception in Russia as it did in the West. Maddox made his name by exhibiting musical clocks which changed scenes, whilst Pierre du Moulin

---

[28] A. Vucinich, *Science in Russian Culture: A History to 1860* (London, 1963), p. 178, sets the sciences in their educational context without giving a wholly satisfactory account of either.

[29] Cf. R. Briggs, 'The *Académie Royale des Sciences* and the Pursuit of Utility', *P&P*, 131 (1991), pp. 38–88.

triumphed in 1759 with a mechanical peasant doll that could waggle its head and blink its eyes. Yet it proved impossible to convert this fascination for automata into a productive interest in technology. Because managers found it safer to rely on cheap serf labour, little use was made of machines such as the 'fire-engine' (steam engine) designed in 1763 by I. I. Polzunov (1729–66) to enable the Ural metallurgical furnaces to operate away from rivers, the principal source of water power, and nearer to mineral deposits.

It is a commonplace that, while both Descartes and Newton believed in God, their work inadvertently undermined the credibility of revealed religion. Since reason explicitly challenged revelation, it is equally conventional to portray obscurantist churchmen as enemies of science. Many clerics no doubt shared Pososhkov's belief that Copernicus and Luther were in league with the devil and that science was (as indeed it became in the nineteenth century) a rival faith. Ecclesiastical resentment was released whenever the foundations of Orthodoxy seemed threatened: Dmitrii Anichkov's treatise on the natural origins of religion was denounced in 1769 as a condemnation of Christianity. But the Synod did more to suppress schismatic than scientific literature, and not all churchmen were prejudiced against science since it remained an inseparable part of the unity of intellectual enquiry in which they still shared. The first known clock in Russia, an astronomical one, had been built by a Serbian monk in the Kremlin in 1404. By 1700, many monasteries – their daily regimen more strictly disciplined by time than that of most Russian peasants – had built turret clocks. Monastery libraries acquired scientific manuscripts and books which helped to sustain a lasting ecclesiastical interest, particularly in meteorology. Feofan (Prokopovich) studied astronomy; as bishop of Pskov, Semen (Todorskii) was among several who collected works on medicine, physics, and mathematics. Evgenii (Bolkhovitinov) ordered Schmidt's *Kosmografiia*, which incorporated Newtonian cosmology, to be translated and used at Voronezh seminary, though he omitted all references to Newton in his own translation of Pope's *Essay on Man*. In the 1760s, Metropolitan Platon (Levshin) was a prominent advocate of inoculation against smallpox.

Inoculation, or variolation, shows how populationist concerns combined with military needs to promote the eradication of communicable disease. Here Russia conformed to the European pattern instead of lagging behind it. Though the first Russian treatise was published in 1755, widespread adoption of the new technique awaited the decisive royal initiative, just as it did elsewhere. Catherine II and her son were inoculated by the English physician Thomas Dimsdale (1712–1800) in

1768, the same year as Maria Theresa who herself followed the example of George III. Inoculation continued at special hospitals in St Petersburg (1768), Kazan' (1771), and Irkutsk, where 3,784 patients were inoculated between 1772 and 1775. Of these, it was claimed, only twenty-eight perished. Most patients at St Petersburg were children of nobles and officers, though Matthew Halliday (1732–1809) was still treating the poor without charge in the 1790s. Although some lords forced their serfs to accept treatment, it was imposed by neither the army nor the medical college. In part this was because inoculation offended not only reactionaries but also some of the Enlightened since it initially seemed as rational to reject it on grounds of fear of infection as to advocate it in the hope of restricting contagion. There was no Russian equivalent of the Western pamphlet war, but illiterate Russians were more likely to be influenced by popular engravings or allegorical ballets such as *Prejudice Overcome* (1768), in which Minerva was inoculated and persuaded Ruthenia, in the Temple of Ignorance, to follow her example.

Unlike variolation, the plague that devastated Moscow in 1771 prompted a series of treatises which stimulated the growth of medical literature. Between 1761 and 1800 some 203 medical titles were published in Russian by comparison with only five in the preceding sixty years. Most interpreted the plague in contagionist terms and consequently emphasised the need for quarantine. When cholera struck Orenburg in 1829–30, valuable time was lost whilst officials devised effective procedures to combat a different disease. Since public health was central to cameralism, fountains, water pipes, and drainage featured in town plans as early as the 1760s and waste-dumping was prohibited. Achievements, however, were modest: even the rich lived in insanitary conditions.

Whatever its limitations, military and populationist concerns combined to give public health a high priority. By 1809, the ratio per head of population of all branches of the medical profession was approximately 1:3,730. Yet despite the 1775 provincial reform's provision for medical boards in provincial towns (reinforced by Tsar Paul in 1797), services remained heavily concentrated in the army, as they were elsewhere in Europe. The need was clear enough: 60 per cent of the 25,000 deaths in the Turkish campaign of 1737 were attributable to disease, and so were 80 per cent of the 12,000 deaths in just one year (1757) of the Seven Years War. Diderot derided clinics offering no more than planks for a bed. But Joseph II, who knew more about it, declared Moscow's military hospital superior to Vienna's in 1780. Expansion of medical provision during the Napoleonic wars created ninety-five base hospitals by 1825, and 1,213 military doctors responsible for the treatment of around

800,000 men. Services for the rest of the population were haphazard. Although St Petersburg's hospitals impressed the English philanthropist John Howard in the 1780s, professional medicine remained unknown to most civilians; there was only one hospital in Olonets province in 1786, treating twenty-five patients at Petrozavodsk. Even where medicine was available, the crude techniques of some inebriated practitioners (not to mention their extortionate fees) led many to seek an alternative.

For the literate, self-help was one option. Printed handbooks sold well in the 1780s and 1790s, complementing manuscript *travniki* (herbals) and *lechebniki*, corresponding to German leechbooks from which some may have been translated (though it seems just as likely that they were the product of a universal popular need). Yet faith never lost its powers of solace. One of Anna Labzina's earliest memories was of tending the sick on her family's small estate between Ekaterinburg and Cheliabinsk in the 1760s. She and her mother knelt before their dying patients, comforting them with stories of Christ's suffering: 'My mother, not needing the aid of medicine, treated all disease herself, and God helped her.'[30] Lacking such loving care, peasants turned to quacks (*znakharki*), usually older women. Some of their potions did no harm and were probably beneficial: vodka infused with herbs had anaesthetic properties; rhubarb, though few peasants had access to it, was valued throughout Europe as a cathartic and an astringent, and seeds exported from Russia made the career of several visiting foreign doctors.[31] However, the value of the more ambitious remedies attempted by these quacks is doubtful. Their spells (often transpositions of simple prayers recorded alongside herbal remedies) rashly purported to guarantee anything from improved health to invigorated sexual performance.

Science and superstition thus overlapped. Though it seems improbable that it was beneficial to wash in a trough from which a horse had just drunk, a generous view of water's cleansing power was not unreasonably shared by respected European medics. The seawater that fascinated them was inaccessible to most Russians.[32] Steam was more promising. A former pupil of Herman Boerhaave at Leiden, Antonio Ribeiro Sanches, a baptised Portuguese Jew who had served as physician to Elizabeth, defended it in his treatise *On Russian Steam Baths*, published in Russian translation in 1779; others extended its powers to

[30] *Vospominaniia Anny Evdokimovny Labzinoi, 1758–1828*, ed. B. L. Modzalevskii (St Petersburg, 1914), p. 5.

[31] See C. M. Foust, *Rhubarb: The Wondrous Drug* (Princeton, 1992), esp. chs. 3 and 7, and J. H. Appleby, '"Rhubarb" Mounsey and the Surinam Toad – a Scottish Physician Naturalist in Russia', *Archives of Natural History*, 11, 1 (1982), pp. 137–52.

[32] See A. Corbin, *The Lure of the Sea: The Discovery of the Seaside, 1750–1840*, tr. J. Phelps (Harmondsworth, 1995), ch. 3.

a cure for smallpox. The communal bathhouse – a subject of lasting fascination to foreigners[33] – was also the focus of a wide range of wholly unscientific legends. Indeed, Russian popular culture drew on a reservoir deep enough to fill a volume much larger than Chulkov's compendious *ABC of Russian Superstitions, Idolatrous Sacrifices, Folk Wedding Rituals, Sorcery, Shamanism, etc.* (1786).

Though the very word 'superstition' irritates scholars anxious not to patronise the peasantry, their efforts to explain the credibility of popular beliefs rather than stigmatise the 'irrational' are still at an early stage. We know, however, that since much depended on the whim of a cruel climate, many popular convictions were linked to the seasonal rhythms of agriculture. As late as 1832, bailiffs on the Gagarin estate at Petrovskoe had peasants flogged for failing to pray for rain. In less anxious form, such preoccupations reached far beyond the peasantry. Especially after 1750, astronomical calendars predicting the weather sold well, and divinatory literature (virtually all translated from German or French) was also in demand, forming an innocent pastime for both sexes until polite society repudiated it in the 1840s.

At the height of the 1771 plague, Metropolitan Amvrosii (Zertis-Kamenskii) was dragged from a choir-loft at Moscow's Don monastery and dismembered by a mob outraged by his ban on their traditional practice of kissing a revered icon in search of a miracle cure. Though this incident is famous, demonstrative piety permeated Russian culture at all levels of society more comprehensively than historians have generally allowed. Icons of the Holy Mother of God, St Nicholas the miracle-worker, and a myriad of local saints credited with direct powers of intervention against mental and physical afflictions remained a magnetic focus for believers into the Soviet period. Nineteenth-century French peasants whipped the statues of saints who let them down. Whether Orthodox were so vengeful seems doubtful (for one thing, they had no statues to flog). Some priests tolerated deviations from canonical norms as the price of popular loyalty to the church. Others contemplated reform. Prompted partly by an Enlightened impulse to increase conscious awareness of revealed dogma and partly by the challenge of denominational rivals, the Orthodox hierarchy set out in the 1760s to reshape the religion of the people by invigorating the church's teaching rôle. However, Russian catechisers encountered in the conservatism of rural piety no less stubborn an obstacle than did contemporary Protestant *Aufklärer*, and Orthodox bishops were doubly hampered by the

---

[33] A. G. Cross, 'The Russian *Banya* in the Descriptions of Foreign Travellers and in the Depictions of Foreign and Russian Artists', *OSP*, NS, 24 (1991), pp. 34–59.

reluctance of an already overburdened parish clergy to embrace intensive pastoral methods.[34]

Religion and secularisation

The late seventeenth century saw the belated impact of Renaissance humanism begin to transform Muscovy's élite religious culture from within. Preaching, neglected since the fifteenth century, was revived. At the court of Aleksei Mikhailovich, sermons with secular overtones stressed the individual's earthly virtue, charity, and humility. The fashion for the *parsuna* – easel portraits depicting likenesses of both the dead and the living in a style reminiscent of the icon – spread from men to women. Secular authors began to explore not only profane humour, but also the individual personality. Some, like the author of the *Tale of Frol Skobeev, a Russian Nobleman*, displayed a degree of satire and cynicism. Peter I forced the pace of change. His simplified secular alphabet, introduced between 1708 and 1710, marked a cultural caesura. Initially used for technical works, the *grazhdanskii shrift*, easier to print than the Church Slavonic alphabet, became after Peter's death the vehicle for a burgeoning secular literature.

Yet the impact of secularisation is easily overstated. The rigid conventions of the *parsuna* did as much to inhibit the development of portraiture as to stimulate it; the interdependence of Russian society, in which self-awareness was long subordinated to collective needs, retarded the development of biography as a genre to the extent that Belinskii could describe memoirs as rare as late as the mid-1830s;[35] and not only treatises on versification, but also widely used literacy primers preserved the Church Slavonic legacy, not least because it had become a symbol of Russian national consciousness. Indeed, Russia stood in 1825 on the brink of a period characterised by a nationalist, religious Romanticism diametrically opposed to the spirit of cosmopolitan secular empiricism that dominated the French Enlightenment. In the 1830s and 1840s, cultural Westernisation in the form of German metaphysics, so far from

---

[34] Compare G. L. Freeze, 'The Rechristianization of Russia: The Church and Popular Religion, 1750–1850', *Studia Slavica Finlandensia*, 7 (1990), pp. 101–35, with N. Hope, *German and Scandinavian Protestantism, 1700 to 1918* (Oxford, 1995), pp. 256–315.

[35] A recent study, doubting that we shall add many to the 153 known eighteenth-century memoirs and diaries (111 of which date from after 1762), notes that several key eighteenth-century figures, including G. S. Vinskii and Princess Dashkova, wrote their memoirs after 1800: A. G. Tartakovskii, *Russkaia memuaristika XVIII–pervoi poloviny XIXv.: ot rukopisei k knige* (Moscow, 1991), esp. pp. 21, 25–6.

being synonymous with Russian modernisation, served rather to curb and restrain it.

On one reckoning, only six secular titles were published in the seventeenth century, and the psalter remained the book in greatest popular demand throughout the eighteenth. Though manuscripts preserved religious culture longer and more widely than the printed book, Vasilii Grigorovich-Barskii's *Journey to the Holy Places of Europe, Asia and Africa, Undertaken in 1723 and Concluded in 1747* (1778) proved to be the harbinger of a genre for which readers had a growing appetite. More than twelve times as many pilgrim accounts were published between 1800 and 1914 as the hundred that appeared in the eighteenth century. Before the advent of the railway and the steamship, few pilgrims could reach Jerusalem (as Pugachev falsely claimed to have done). But communes regularly released families in spring and autumn to journey not only to nearby monasteries but also to more distant holy places in Russia, including the Kiev monastery of the caves (*Pecherskaia lavra*) and the Trinity–St Sergius monastery at Sergiev Posad, outside Moscow. Only in winter did peasants ride: to do so would have constituted a lapse of asceticism and deprived their communes of invaluable beasts of burden.

The growth of pilgrimages reflects a broader spiritual revival within the Orthodox church, and particularly within its monastic tradition. The revival was fostered by ascetic monks, notably St Tikhon of Zadonsk (1724–82), who became a cult figure in the nineteenth century when his relics were a famous shrine. Tikhon's education and reading, which drew heavily on Western theology, were characteristic of the post-Petrine church, though his work was nonetheless infused by Orthodox patristics. The Ukrainian Paisii (Velichkovskii) (1722–94) came still closer to Byzantine hesychasm, learned on Mount Athos, the Greek monastic centre where he spent most of his life. It was from Athos that the practice of spiritual direction by monastic elders (*startsy*) spread into Russia, led by Serafim of Sarov (1759–1833), canonised in 1903.

Since this monastic revival coincided with the closure of many houses at the secularisation of church lands, it was often forced to find informal expression, notably in the 217 unofficial women's communities (*zhenskie obshchiny*) founded between 1764 and 1907. By responding to (and in turn stimulating) local demand, these laid the foundations of another important nineteenth-century phenomenon – the feminisation of religion.[36] However, many Russians, alienated either by the formalism of

---

[36] See B. Meehan, 'Popular Piety, Local Initiative, and the Founding of Women's Religious Communities in Russia, 1764–1907', in S. K. Batalden, ed., *Seeking God: The Recovery of Religious Identity in Orthodox Russia, Ukraine and Georgia* (DeKalb, IL, 1993), pp. 83–105.

the liturgy or by the inadequacy of their priests, sought spiritual comfort and moral perfection outside the Orthodox church. New sects, some characterised by sexual deviance, appeared after 1750, attracting the unsophisticated in growing numbers. Educated men were more likely to turn instead to freemasonry, which provided Novikov and others with an outlet for philanthropy through an appropriately hierarchical form of secularised Christianity.

Private and public, amateur and professional

Just as increasingly sophisticated government prompted specialisation among officials, so cultural complexity fostered incipient professionalisation. Whilst composers became more demanding of their amateur patrons – courtiers performed Bortnianskii's opera *The Falcon* at Pavlovsk in 1786 and Count Nikolai Golitsyn commissioned three string quartets from Beethoven in 1822 – the amateur's rôle was restricted by the growing intricacy of musical instruments and the extravagant orchestral resources demanded by the symphony. The preference for second-rate German composers expressed by Prince A. M. Belosel'skii-Belozerskii (1752–1809) in his *Dialogues sur la musique* (1790/1) is revealing: Mozart, whom he met whilst ambassador in Dresden in 1789, was not only said to be incapable of writing a good tune, but dismissed as 'très savant, très difficile'.[37] Russian professionalisation was nevertheless restrained in two ways: one economic and one political.

The economic limitation was imposed by Russia's underdeveloped market. Far from having been suppressed, as was once supposed, Novikov's earliest journals needed Catherine II's sponsorship to stay solvent. The two charity schools he founded in 1777 and 1778, planning to support them from the proceeds of his masonic periodical *Morning Light* (*Utrennyi svet*), instead came to subsidise the journal. The prominent St Petersburg book dealer J. J. Weitbrecht sold only in winter in the late 1770s. The concert season was confined to Lent, and the French virtuoso violinist Paisible committed suicide in 1781 after a series flopped and plunged him into debt. Only in Britain could the commercialisation of leisure thrive on public purchasing power; elsewhere artists teetered on the precipice between private patronage, which many now found humiliating, and a public market which as yet could barely

---

[37] J. Chailley, 'Les *Dialogues sur la musique* d'Alexandre Belosel'sky', *Revue des Etudes Slaves*, 45 (1966), p. 102.

support them. Mid-century Russian writers might, like Chulkov, advertise that their pens were 'for sale', but for most it was a hollow claim. Protected by the first Russian copyright legislation of 1828, Pushkin looked back on the 'baseness' of eighteenth-century writers, distinguishing himself from them on the grounds that he wrote 'for money' rather than 'for the smile of the fair sex'. Pushkin believed that, by the 1820s, public taste, which he affected to despise, had become sufficiently influential to dictate Russian theatrical fashion. Yet, even then, jobs remained a mainstay of most performers' income. Painters might be encouraged by a growing demand for portraits, but the era of huge merchant fortunes lay in the future. Noble patronage, about which surprisingly little is known, remained a supplement rather than an alternative to the principal source of jobs – the court – which had yet to be transformed from perfidious patron to contractual employer.

The second obstacle to professionalisation was therefore the overweening influence of the state. To say that Peter I 'patronised' the building of St Petersburg is scarcely an adequate way to describe the elemental force with which he decreed and dictated it. In the same way, he conceived of the press as an instrument of state control. The state dominated cultural education, first through the St Petersburg Academy of Sciences and then through the Imperial Academy of Fine Arts (f. 1757), and monopolised the theatre through the Administration of Imperial Theatres (f. 1766). Yet this influence was not only coercive but inspirational: Karamzin could not contemplate writing his history of the Russian state from outside state service and returned to it expressly in order to begin the work. Whilst Russians displayed the same growing concern for specialised training and careers as their Western contemporaries – and in the realm of pure scholarship polymaths such as Lomonosov and Pallas achieved international standards of distinction – their professionalisation was slow and tentative. No Russian profession in this period developed a sense of autonomy; all remained dependent on the state which had done so much to create them. Indeed, so significant was the rôle of the state that we must now devote a separate chapter to its conceptual history.

BIBLIOGRAPHICAL NOTE

Students of literature, a subject that I have neglected, will need V. Terras, ed., *Handbook of Russian Literature* (New Haven, CT, 1985); Terras, *A History of Russian Literature* (New Haven, CT, 1991); and C. L. Drage, *Russian Literature in the Eighteenth Century* (London,

1978). S. Karlinsky, *Russian Drama from Its Beginnings to the Age of Pushkin* (Berkeley, CA, 1985), is lively and idiosyncratic; M. V. Shchedrovitskaia, ed., *Starinnye teatry Rossii: XVIII–pervaia chetvert' XIXv* (Moscow, 1993), presents some interesting recent research. Much Soviet writing was handicapped by chauvinism and a numbing insistence on the (largely fabulous) social content of culture, pitting supposedly progressive democratisers against the forces of reaction. However, the series *XVIII vek*, which reached vol. XX in 1996, is invaluable, and G. J. Marker, *Publishing, Printing and the Origins of Intellectual Life in Russia, 1700–1800* (Princeton, 1985), develops Russian work on the history of the book pioneered by S. P. Luppov. On music, everyone will begin with S. Sadie, ed., *The New Grove Dictionary of Music and Musicians*, 20 vols. (London, 1980). A. Bird, *A History of Russian Painting* (Oxford, 1987), is marred only by naïve historical commentary. G. H. Hamilton, *The Art and Architecture of Russia*, 3rd edn (Harmondsworth, 1983), should be supplemented by T. G. Stavrou, ed., *Russian Art and Society, 1800–1850* (Minneapolis, 1983); W. C. Brumfield, *A History of Russian Architecture* (Cambridge, 1993), is well illustrated.

R. A. Houston, *Literacy in Early Modern Europe: Culture and Education, 1500–1800* (London, 1988), sets the context; B. N. Mironov, 'The Development of Literacy in Russia and the USSR from the Tenth to the Twentieth Centuries', *HEQ*, 31 (1991), synthesises specialist work, which now includes G. Marker, 'Faith and Secularity in Eighteenth-Century Russian Literacy', in R. P. Hughes and I. Paperno, eds., *Christianity and the Eastern Slavs*, vol. II, *California Slavic Studies*, 17 (Berkeley, CA, 1994). In the absence of a comprehensive guide to education, start with M. J. Okenfuss: 'The Jesuit Origins of Petrine Education', in J. G. Garrard, ed., *The Eighteenth Century in Russia* (Oxford, 1973); 'Education and Empire: School Reform in Enlightened Russia', *JfGO*, 27 (1979); and 'From School Class to Social Caste: The Divisiveness of Early-Modern Russian Education', *JfGO*, 33 (1985). See also the special edition of *CASS*, 14, 3 (1980). Okenfuss's stress on ideas complements the institutional emphasis of I. de Madariaga, 'The Foundation of the Russian Educational System by Catherine the Great', *SEER*, 57 (1979), and J. M. Hartley, 'The Boards of Social Welfare and the Financing of Catherine II's State Schools', *SEER*, 67 (1989). G. Marker, 'Who Rules the Word?: Public School Education and the Fate of Universality in Russia, 1782–1803', *RH*, 20 (1993), takes an unusually positive view. J. V. H. Melton, *Absolutism and the Eighteenth-Century Origins of Compulsory Schooling in Prussia and Austria* (Cambridge, 1988), is good on Felbiger. On the church, see R. L. Nichols, 'Orthodoxy and Russia's Enlightenment, 1762–1825', in Nichols and

T. G. Stavrou, eds., *Russian Orthodoxy Under the Old Régime* (Minneapolis, 1978). J. T. Flynn, *The University Reform of Tsar Alexander I* (Washington, DC, 1988), complements the outstanding D. Beauvois, *Lumières et société en Europe de l'Est: l'université de Vilna et les écoles polonaises de l'empire russe (1803–1832)*, 2 vols. (Paris, 1977). For education under Alexander I, see J. C. Zacek, 'The Lancastrian School Movement in Russia', *SEER*, 45 (1967); D. W. Edwards, 'Count Joseph Marie de Maistre and Russian Educational Policy, 1803–1828', *SR*, 36 (1977); and F. A. Walker, 'Popular Response to Public Education in the Reign of Tsar Alexander I (1801–1825)', *HEQ*, 24 (1984).

For conceptual approaches to cultural hierarchies, see Ju. M. Lotman and B. A. Uspenskij, *The Semiotics of Russian Culture*, ed. A. Shukman (Ann Arbor, MI, 1984), and A. M. Panchenko, *Russkaia kul'tura v kanun petrovskikh reform* (Leningrad, 1984). M. Burgess is amusing on 'Fairs and Entertainers in Eighteenth-Century Russia', *SEER*, 38 (1959); A. F. Nekrylova, *Russkie narodnye gorodskie prazdniki, uveseleniia i zrelishcha: konets XVIII–nachalo XX veka*, 2nd edn (Moscow, 1988), is attractively illustrated. C. Kelly, *'Petrushka': The Russian Carnival Puppet Theatre* (Cambridge, 1990), is first-class. N. A. Minenko, 'The Living Past: Daily Life and Holidays of the Siberian Village in the Eighteenth and First Half of the Nineteenth Centuries', *Soviet Anthropology and Archaeology*, 30 (1991), offers a sequel to H. Dewey and K. B. Stevens, 'Muscovites at Play: Recreation in Pre-Petrine Russia', *CASS*, 13 (1979). On the popular prints, see I. Danilova, ed., *Narodnaia graviura i fol'klor v Rossii, XVII–XIX vv.* (Moscow, 1976), and D. Farrell, 'Medieval Popular Humour in Russian Eighteenth-Century *Lubki*', *SR*, 50 (1991). W. F. Ryan and F. Wigzell, 'Gullible Girls and Dreadful Dreams: Zhukovskii, Pushkin and Popular Divination', *SEER*, 70 (1992), gloss a fascinating subject, developed by Wigzell's forthcoming *Reading Russian Fortunes: Gender, Print Culture and Divination in Russia from 1765* (Cambridge, 1998). Though M. Glants and J. Toomre, eds., *Food in Russian History and Culture* (Bloomington, IN, 1997), offer appetising *hors d'oeuvres*, R. E. F. Smith and D. Christian, *Bread and Salt: A Social and Economic History of Food and Drink in Russia* (Cambridge, 1984), is still a more satisfying *entrée*.

H. Rogger, *National Consciousness in Eighteenth-Century Russia* (Cambridge, MA, 1960), and P. K. Christoff, *The Third Heart: Some Intellectual-Ideological Currents and Cross-Currents in Russia 1800–1830* (The Hague, 1970), still have value, though both now show signs of age. More recent work includes L. Greenfeld, *Nationalism: Five Roads to Modernity* (Cambridge, MA, 1992). I. Reyfman, *Vasilii Trediakovsky: The Fool of the 'New' Russian Literature* (Stanford, CA, 1990), takes an original approach to Russian classicism. Though technical, A. P. Vlasto, *A Linguistic History of Russia to the End of the Eighteenth Century* (Oxford, 1988), and especially the brilliant V. M. Zhivov, *Iazyk i kul'tura v Rossii v XVIII vek* (Moscow, 1996), are crucial for the cultural historian. L. R. Lewitter, 'Poland, The Ukraine and Russia in the Seventeenth Century', *SEER*, 68–9 (1948–9), remains essential on pre-Petrine Westernisation. For the later period, see M. Bassin, 'Russia Between Europe and Asia', *SR*, 50 (1991), and J. M. Hartley, 'Is Russia Part of Europe?: Russian Perceptions of Europe in the Reign of Alexander I', *CMRS*, 33 (1992). An important topic is sketched by L. Schulze, 'The Russification of the St Petersburg Academy of Sciences and Arts in the Eighteenth Century', *British Journal of the History of Science*, 18 (1985).

The German dimension is charted by L. Kopelew, ed., *Rußen und Rußland aus deutscher Sicht: 18. Jahrhundert, Aufklärung* (Munich, 1987), and C. Scharf, *Katharina II., Deutschland und die Deutschen* (Mainz, 1996). There is no comparable study of the French connexion, though A. Lortholary, *Le mirage russe en France* (Paris, 1951), remains indispensable and N. A. Kopanev, *Frantsuzskaia kniga i russkaia kul'tura v seredine XVIII veka* (Leningrad, 1988), is also important. F. Venturi explores Italian contacts in *The End of the Old Regime in Europe, 1768–1776: The First Crisis* (Princeton, 1989), and *The End of the Old Regime in Europe, 1776–1789: II Republican Patriotism and the Empires of the East* (Princeton, 1991), both translated by R. B. Litchfield. A. G. Cross, *'By the Banks of the Thames': Russians in Eighteenth-Century Britain* (Newtonville, MA, 1980), and Cross, *By the Banks of the Neva* (above, n. 20), together form the most detailed and impressive study of any country's links with Russia. Works of distinction on Anglo-Russian literary relations include M. P. Alekseev, *Russko-angliiskie literaturnye sviazi (XVIII vek–pervaia polovina XIX veka)*, *Literaturnoe nasledstvo*, vol. 91 (Moscow, 1982), and Iu. D. Levin, *Vospriiatie angliiskoi literatury v Rossii* (Leningrad, 1990).

R. E. Jones surveys 'Urban Planning and the Development of Provincial Towns in Russia, 1762–1796', in Garrard, *The Eighteenth Century in Russia*. On Siberia, see A. Kopylov, *Ocherki kul'turnoi zhizni Sibiri XVII–nachala XIXv* (Novosibirsk, 1974); R. P. Bartlett, 'Culture and Enlightenment: Julius von Canitz and the Kazan' *Gimnazii* in the Eighteenth Century', *CASS*, 14 (1980); and M. G. Al'tshuller, 'Literaturnaia zhizn' Tobol'ska 90-kh godov XVIIIv.', in V. I. Shunkov, *et al.*, *Osvoenie Sibiri v epokhu feodalizma XVII–XIXvv.* (Novosibirsk, 1968). D. Saunders, *The Ukrainian Impact on Russian Culture, 1750–1850* (Edmonton, 1985), is especially wide-ranging. S. Layton, *Russian Literature and*

Empire: Conquest of the Caucasus from Pushkin to Tolstoy (Cambridge, 1994), points to a developing Romantic regionalism.

J. S. Carver, 'A Reconsideration of Eighteenth-Century Russia's Contributions to European Science', *CASS*, 14 (1980), is a good synthesis. The stress of V. Boss, *Newton and Russia: The Early Influence, 1698–1796* (Cambridge, MA, 1972), on the dichotomy between 'Newtonianism' and 'Cartesianism' is challenged by R. W. Home, 'Leonhard Euler's "Anti-Newtonian" Theory of Light', *Annals of Science*, 45 (1988). Home's edition of *Aepinus's Essay on the Theory of Electricity and Magnetism*, tr. P. J. Connor (Princeton, 1979), is prefaced by a monograph developing his study of 'Science as a Career: The Case of F. V. T. Aepinus', *SEER*, 51 (1973). H. Woolf, *The Transits of Venus: A Study of Eighteenth-Century Science* (Princeton, 1959), describes Russian involvement in attempts to measure the solar parallax. For science's broader impact, see M. P. Alekseev, 'Pushkin i nauka ego vremeni', in his *Pushkin: sravnitel'no-istoricheskie issledovaniia* (Leningrad, 1984). On fashionable superstition, see F. Wigzell, 'Reading the Future: Women and Fortune-Telling in Russia (1770–1840)', in R. Marsh, ed., *Gender and Russian Literature: New Perspectives* (Cambridge, 1996). The Western craze for the history of madness has yet to reach Russia (where it was long discouraged for political reasons), though H. Dewey outlines 'Some Perceptions of Mental Disorder in Pre-Petrine Russia', *Medical History*, 31 (1987). J. T. Alexander, *Bubonic Plague in Early Modern Russia: Public Health and Urban Disaster* (Baltimore, 1980), a first-class study of the 1771 epidemic, is the nearest we have to a social history of medicine. A pioneer was R. E. McGrew, *Russia and the Cholera, 1823–1832* (Madison, WI, 1965). D. Willemse, *Antonio Nunes Ribeiro Sanches, Elève de Boerhaave, et son importance pour la Russie* (Leiden, 1966), is more antiquarian. Compare R. P. Bartlett, 'Russia in the Eighteenth-Century Adoption of Inoculation for Smallpox', in Bartlett, et al., eds., *Russia and the World of the Eighteenth Century* (Columbus, OH, 1988), with P. Mathias, 'Swords and Ploughshares: The Armed Forces, Medicine and Public Health in the Late Eighteenth Century', in J. M. Winter, ed., *War and Economic Development* (Cambridge, 1975).

The greatest virtue of J. Billington, *The Icon and the Axe: An Interpretive History of Russian Culture* (New York, 1966), is to take religion seriously. By comparison, D. Treadgold, *The West in Russia and China: Religious and Secular Thought in Modern Times*, vol. I, *Russia, 1472–1917* (Cambridge, 1973), is rather bland. Focusing on élites, P. Bushkovitch, *Religion and Society in Russia: The Sixteenth and Seventeenth Centuries* (Oxford, 1992), argues that the way to secularisation under Peter I was laid long before; focusing on the people, H. Rothe, *Religion und Kultur in den Regionen des russischen Reiches im 18. Jahrhundert* (Opladen, 1984), stresses the lasting religiosity of manuscript culture. W. G. Jones, 'Biography in Eighteenth-Century Russia', *OSP*, NS, 22 (1989), and Jones, *Nikolay Novikov: Enlightener of Russia* (Cambridge, 1984), are indispensable.

A. G. Cross, 'The Great Patroness of the North: Catherine II's Role in Fostering Anglo-Russian Cultural Contacts', *OSP*, NS, 18 (1985), is more penetrating than A. McConnell, 'Catherine the Great and the Fine Arts', in E. Mendelsohn and M. S. Shatz, eds., *Imperial Russia, 1700–1917: State, Society, Opposition* (DeKalb, IL, 1988). The transition between patronage and professionalism is sketched by E. L. Perkins, 'Noble Patronage, 1740s–1850', *CASS*, 23 (1989), and Perkins, 'Mobility in the Art Profession in Tsarist Russia', *JfGO*, 39 (1991). W. Rosslyn, 'Anna Bunina's "Unchaste Relationship with the Muse": Patronage, the Market and the Woman Writer in Early Nineteenth-Century Russia', *SEER*, 74 (1996), adds a gendered dimension to W. G. Jones, 'The Image of the Eighteenth-Century Russian Author', in Bartlett and Hartley, *Russia in the Age of the Enlightenment* (above, n. 1), and Jones, 'Familiar Solidarity and Squabbling: Russia's Eighteenth-Century Writers', in F. Wigzell, ed., *Russian Writers on Russian Writers* (Oxford, 1994). S. Jüttner, 'The Status of the Writer', *SVEC*, 264 (1989), suggests contrasts and comparisons.

7   Ideology

It seemed obvious to nineteenth-century intellectuals obsessed with Hegel that the state had been the driving force of Russian history. Not all of them thought its rôle had been beneficial: some were sure that it was malign whilst others, like Pushkin in *The Bronze Horseman* (1833), were uncomfortably ambivalent, admiring the state's awesome achievements but dismayed by their social costs. Still, whether they idolised or execrated the state, few hesitated to ascribe to it the dominant rôle. So, having already discussed the state's institutional apparatus, now we must probe its ideological foundations.[1]

This chapter approaches the subject from three angles. First, it shows that, just as the monarch continued to play a central rôle in government, so traditional notions of personal rulership continued to coexist alongside abstract conceptualisations of the state until after 1825; secondly, it shows that this duality delayed the emergence in Russia of a political nation self-consciously opposed to the state and its ruling dynasty; finally, it suggests that, in the absence of coherent opposition, the greatest weakness in tsarist rule lay in the alienation of what might have been its firmest bastion of ideological support, the Russian Orthodox church.

Tsar and state

The period between c. 1350 and 1700 marked a crucial transition in Western political thought, for it was then that the dominant modern notion of the state emerged. At stake was a shift from thinking about rulership in terms of personal allegiance to an individual prince to the abstract notion of loyalty to 'the state' – an impersonal entity above and distinct from both the ruler and his subjects. Here lay the origins of Max Weber's classic definition of the state as the sole source of law and

---

[1] By 'ideology', I mean simply a series of beliefs used to justify the Russian old régime. For more explicitly pejorative usages, see D. Kettler, 'Ideology', in D. Miller, ed., *The Blackwell Encyclopaedia of Political Thought* (Oxford, 1991), pp. 235–8.

legitimate force in its own territory and the sole appropriate object of its citizens' loyalties.

Muscovy knew no such concept. Having been relatively insulated, until comparatively late, from both Renaissance and Reformation, it was isolated from most of the intellectual resources on which Western notions of the state depended. It could, of course, draw on the Byzantine Christian–imperialist legacy. But it has often been remarked that, although elements of Byzantine influence on Muscovite ideology are evident, not least in its iconography and architectural symbolism, it is hard to identify ways in which Muscovite writers drew on Byzantine concepts of imperial power. Whilst it has taken scholarship of a high order to reveal Muscovite debts to a few texts, notably Agapetus' *Hortatory Chapters*, written for the Emperor Justinian sometime between AD 527 and 548, what is more immediately striking about both the form and the language in which Muscovites wrote about government is the degree to which philosophical abstractions remained foreign to them. As Western thinkers strove to determine the conditions in which liberty could be preserved, their Muscovite contemporaries were still preoccupied with the struggle between good and evil. Their vocabulary was predominantly biblical in origin, the Old Testament, in particular, providing an abundant reservoir of apocalyptic imagery with which to apportion responsibility for the disasters that had befallen their land. It was not that these writers were unsophisticated: on the contrary, their complex rhetoric wove intricate epic narratives, still admired as literary masterpieces in much the same way as N. M. Karamzin's twelve-volume *History of the Russian State* (1818–29, incomplete), which maintained and developed the conception of history as a moral tale of virtue's triumph over vice.[2] But Russian texts relied not so much on philosophical argument as on literary techniques of characterisation. In these circumstances, it was only to be expected that their conception of the state would be but little developed by comparison with that of their Western contemporaries.

In Muscovy the word 'state' – in Russian, *gosudarstvo* – carried a number of different meanings. It was used to describe either the people or the territory governed by the tsar, sometimes both. In this sense, it is best translated as 'realm' or 'dominion'. Alternatively, it might signify only part of the tsar's kingdom: Siberia, for example, was often referred to as *gosudarstvo Sibiri*. In all these cases, the state was conceived not as a political agent in its own right, to which all subjects owed allegiance and

---

[2] For a sophisticated appreciation of Karamzin's treatment of a crucial episode, see C. Emerson, *Boris Godunov: Transpositions of a Russian Theme* (Bloomington, IN, 1986), pp. 30–87.

which the tsar had himself a duty to maintain, but rather as an object, itself under the control of the tsar – it was 'his' state to use as he pleased, the state which he upheld in order to maintain his own position. It would be wrong to underestimate the tenacity of this image, which far outlasted Peter the Great's reforms. Dictionaries are notoriously slow to respond to etymological change. But it is striking that, as late as 1806, the second edition of the Russian Academy's definitive Russian dictionary still carried only these traditional meanings.

Such antiquated notions survived in spite of Peter's efforts to replace them with a more impersonal notion of the state as an active political force to which both the monarch and his subjects owed an obligation in the cause of a greater good. The notion of 'state affairs' (*gosudarstvennye dela*) had come into use under Tsar Fedor. Peter set out to give it a central place in the Russian political vocabulary. Not content with declaring his own devotion to the 'common good', he exhorted others to adopt the same philosophy. Though Peter does not seem explicitly to have referred to himself as 'a servant of the state', he did delete the phrase 'the interests of His Tsarist Majesty' from a draft reform of the army, inserting instead 'the interests of the state' as the proper object of his soldiers' allegiance. The same impulse was crucial to his economic policy, which produced new industrial enterprises, belonging to 'the state' and exploiting institutionally administered labour (christened the 'state peasantry') in the cause of the 'common good'. Of course, in trying to develop an awareness of the impersonal state, Peter had no intention of encouraging Dutch- or English-style liberties. He was instead attracted to the notion of an initial social contract granting irrevocable, absolute power to the ruler. But this too depended on the introduction into Russia of a conceptual vocabulary in which such ideas could be expressed.

That vocabulary was drawn from Western political thought. Though his library contained a number of classic texts, it seems improbable that Peter himself had read widely in this literature: whatever his extraordinary qualities, the tsar was no intellectual. But among his advisers there were men of learning on whom he could depend not only for his own introduction to political ideas but also for their translation and propagation in Russia. Of these, the most prominent was the Ukrainian cleric, Feofan (Prokopovich), who left the Kiev academy in 1716 to work alongside the tsar and eventually became archbishop of Novgorod and Pskov. He, in turn, patronised others – notably A. D. Kantemir, the diplomat and satirist of Muscovite manners, and the scholar-administrator, V. N. Tatishchev (1686–1750) – fellow members of a so-called learned host (*uchenaia druzhina*) devoted to spreading the new thinking in Russia after Peter's death.

In turning to the West for a new political vocabulary these men naturally discovered not one but many ways of thinking about government. Not all of these were alien to Muscovy by c. 1700, but it was only then that their usefulness in the Russian context began to be fully exploited. In that context the most significant intellectual tradition derived from Aristotle, for whom monarchy was the best form of government. Aristotle was not unknown in medieval Rus', but only a handful of scholars were familiar with any more than the fraction of his scientific work that filtered into the Alexander stories. Not until after the annexation of Ukraine in 1654 did Aristotelian politics make an impact. They owed their appearance then to Jesuit theology which spread them in the form of St Thomas Aquinas's scholastic synthesis of Augustinian and Aristotelian ideas, the greatest monument to the European rediscovery of Aristotle from the Arabs in the thirteenth century. Feofan had himself been reared on these ideas, first at Jesuit colleges in Poland and then in Rome itself. But it was not in its Polish Catholic form that the natural law tradition – based on a belief in a set of divinely ordained and universally applicable principles of social and moral behaviour, natural to man and accessible to him through his capacity to reason – made its greatest impact in Russia. Instead, it was to the version espoused by contemporary German Protestants that Feofan and Peter turned. To both the tsar and his adviser, the attraction of the writings of Samuel Pufendorf (1632–94), Christian Thomasius (1655–1728), and Christian Wolff (1679–1754) was their stress on the duties and obligations of the subject to the state, and their view of the political philosophy of Thomas Hobbes (1588–1679), which they interpreted as a straightforward justification of unlimited sovereign power. Russians also found in these German texts an emphasis on regulation (*Polizei/Policey*) which could readily be expressed in mechanical similes. This, too, was attractive to a monarch who recognised that the changes he wanted to make in Russia would have to be stimulated – initially, indeed, coerced – from above.

Important as the German natural law absolutist tradition came to be in Russian thinking, it was not unique in its influence. By the time of Catherine the Great, when it was partly restated in the school textbook, *On the Duties of Man and Citizen* (1783), it had been challenged, and perhaps surpassed, by the works of the French *philosophes* whose political ideas are less easily classified: Diderot explicitly told Catherine that he did not like to treat serious subjects systematically.[3] But we can postpone discussion of their significance until later in the chapter. For the

---

[3] Diderot, *Mémoires pour Catherine II*, ed. P. Vernière (Paris, 1966), p. 199.

moment let us simply note that a feature of the Russian texts which tried to develop the notion of the impersonal state devoted to the common good was the way that these abstractions sat uneasily alongside traditional images of tsarist rule. Peter and his advisers may have intended to strengthen the monarchy by making 'the state' an additional source of legitimacy, but they succeeded more immediately in dividing the focus of loyalty of their people. One reason why a coherent theory remained elusive was the awkward way in which Western concepts had to be expressed in what was then a poorly formed Russian language. Problems of translation are still a formidable obstacle to the interpretation of Russian political ideas.[4] But a more significant difficulty arose from an unanticipated paradox.

In advocating loyalty to an impersonal state, Peter had no intention of abandoning 'the power and dignity of the tsar', to quote the title of Feofan's panegyric sermon on Palm Sunday 1718. However, he can scarcely have foreseen the degree to which his efforts to develop a wider consciousness of 'the state' would contribute simultaneously to a growing reverence for the individual monarch. Far from being displaced, the tsar's charismatic authority was strengthened, since the new 'state' was inseparably associated with the indomitable person of Peter himself. Though successive rulers encouraged the conduct of political argument in ever more secular terms, their recourse to classical imagery had unintended consequences. In vain did the prefect of the Moscow Slavonic Academy insist that comparisons of Peter with classical deities were not to be taken literally because they came 'not from sacred texts, but from secular histories, and are not sacred icons but figures invented by poets'.[5] Part of the problem lay in the fact that, alongside the references to classical Rome, the tsars' power was increasingly symbolised by overtly Christian imagery previously reserved for sacred subjects. This transition depended in part on Byzantine imagery of the perfect ruler as the 'image and likeness' of God, but it was also a corollary of the contemporaneous political sidelining of the Orthodox hierarchy, which began in the reign of Aleksei Mikhailovich and was completed by Peter's abolition of the patriarchate in 1721. Religious imagery is particularly marked in the banners and medallions produced to celebrate Peter's military prowess. Around 1700, when the last patriarch (Adrian) died, images of Peter himself replaced traditional

---

[4] An erudite attempt to show that *samoderzhavie* meant simply 'sovereignty' rather than 'autocracy' has not found widespread support: see I. de Madariaga, 'Autocracy and Sovereignty', *CASS*, 16, 3-4 (1982), pp. 369–87.

[5] Quoted in R. S. Wortman, *Scenarios of Power: Myth and Ceremony in Russian Monarchy*, vol. I, *From Peter the Great to the Death of Nicholas I* (Princeton, 1995), p. 48.

saintly images on regimental banners, though until the victory at Poltava in 1709 the tsar was more inclined to hide his own person behind heraldic representations of St Andrew, whom he adopted as his patron. Literature provided another vehicle for Christ-like imagery of the tsars. By the middle of the eighteenth century, the panegyric ode (later joined by the Utopian novel) had become the standard genre in which Russian writers proclaimed the tsars' divine status and portrayed Russia as an icon of the heavenly world. Even allowing for formulaic literary conventions, readers could be left in no doubt that these works were intended to declare the sacral status of the tsars. One of Peter I's henchmen, Ivan Kirillov, worshipped a portrait of Peter as an icon, keeping a candle burning in front of it, and by the time of Alexander I, consistently portrayed in angelic imagery, the epithet 'holy' was applied to everything connected with the tsar, so that Metropolitan Platon could even speak of the 'holy blood' flowing in the imperial family's veins.

At a popular level, evidence of the identification of power with the person of the ruler rather than with an abstract conception of the state is provided by the frequent incidence of pretenders. Twenty-three are known from the seventeenth century, and forty-four from the eighteenth, of whom twenty-six appeared in the reign of Catherine the Great alone. Among them were illiterate peasants, Cossacks, and *odnodvortsy*. There were doubtless others about whom we know nothing. Eight pretended to be Peter I's executed son, Aleksei, and sixteen more impersonated the murdered Peter III. But the importance attached to real individuals did not stop there: Pugachev even named his henchmen after Catherine's courtiers. Pretenders based their claim to the throne on a supposed distinction between true and false tsars. If the ruler was impious, then he could not be the true tsar. (Similar logic gave credence to a legend that would have pleased W. S. Gilbert: the true tsar had been substituted, when an infant, by the impostor on the throne.) Pretenders claimed not only the tsar's political power, but also his sacral status. They believed the true tsar to be identifiable as divinely preordained; the scars on Pugachev's body, for instance, were taken to be 'royal signs'. If religious notions lay at the heart of the phenomenon, the popular tradition of the Tsar-Deliverer helps us to understand why so many people believed in pretenders. In part we may see here simply a reflection of the impact of official propaganda, which represented the tsars as the fount of impartial justice. But there was also a deep-seated, Utopian popular belief – which some maintain was punctured only by the massacre of the crowd who petitioned the Winter Palace on 9 January 1905 – in the innate benevolence of the tsar, as opposed to the malevolence of the evil boiars from whom he would deliver his subjects if only he knew of their suffering. Folklore was dominated by images of Ivan the Terrible and Peter the Great. Not surprisingly, in view of their actual achievements, there is a striking ambivalence in the recorded legends about both: revered as conquerors, they were feared as cruel despots. But even the tyrannical motifs in the stories about them mark an acceptance rather than a rejection of cruelty as a complement to firm rule.[6] And that firm rule was identified not with some abstract notion of the state, but with the two most extraordinary Russian tsars, transposed from their mere earthly existence to sacral status by the mythology of popular monarchism.

Alongside the new impersonal state, therefore, old notions of personal monarchy not only survived but were vigorous enough to undergo renewal both among élites and among the mass of the peasantry. When speaking of the state we are really speaking of a dual conception of state and tsar. Neither is readily detached from the other, though their relative importance varied over time. One could show this in several ways. The persistent failure to distinguish between the tsar's own funds and the state treasury is one. But since we have already discussed institutional matters, let us investigate here two related theoretical notions: treason (*izmena*) and the oath of loyalty (*prisiaga*) taken by Russian subjects to each new tsar on his accession.

Until the promulgation of Peter's Military Regulation, the law on political crime was defined by chapter II of the *Ulozhenie* which gave unprecedented prominence to treachery. Significantly, the chapter was entitled 'On the Sovereign's dignity, and how to protect His Sovereign health'. (The sole mention of 'the state' – in the phrase *Moskovskoe gosudarstvo* – employs the territorial sense mentioned above.) A traitor thus betrayed not an impersonal abstraction but the tsar in person, typically by pledging allegiance to a rival individual, as in the case of the defection of Prince A. M. Kurbskii from Ivan the Terrible to King Sigismund of Lithuania in 1564. The only impersonal notion of treason known in Muscovy was apostasy, which survived along with personal betrayal into the Petrine period. Conversely, converts to Orthodoxy were taken to have become Russian subjects, and seventeenth-century prisoners-of-war who had been accepted into the Russian church were excluded from exchanges of prisoners following peace settlements. Iakov Jansen, a Dutch bombardier in Russian service who deserted to the Muslim Turks during the first Azov campaign, was recaptured, tried

---

[6] See M. Perrie, *The Image of Ivan the Terrible in Russian Folklore* (Cambridge, 1987). Related studies include Perrie's *Pretenders and Popular Monarchism in Early Modern Russia* (Cambridge, 1995), which concentrates on the seventeenth century, and D. Field, *Rebels in the Name of the Tsar* (Boston, 1976), which focuses on the nineteenth.

in Moscow for treason in 1696, and broken on the wheel after being convicted of betraying 'the Russian tsar and the Orthodox faith'. The most notorious case, however, was the Ukrainian *hetman* Mazepa's defection to the Swedes in 1708. Like Bogdan Khmel'nitskii in the seventeenth century, Mazepa interpreted his relationship with the tsar as that of a vassal to his sovereign; he owed fealty to Peter, not to any Russian 'state'. His loyalty therefore depended on the maintenance of Peter's personal protection. When it seemed that this had been withdrawn, Mazepa had no compunction about seeking it from the Protestant Charles XII instead. In his propaganda against Mazepa, and still more in the anathema ceremonies he invoked against his Ukrainian followers, an outraged Peter dwelt heavily on Mazepa's 'betrayal of Orthodoxy'. But even this concept could be personalised, as Bishop Feofan (Lopatinskii) showed by representing Peter as Christ and Mazepa as Judas. There is surely more evidence here of the survival of traditional notions than of any shift towards the conception of treason to the secular state.

The same patrimonial motifs long persisted. The dread formula under which political crime was known was 'the Sovereign's word and deed' (*slovo i delo Gosudarevo*), a blanket charge which encompassed the slightest verbal offence against the person or policies of the tsar. By claiming that he knew of some statement or action that went against the sovereign's interest, a man could denounce his fellows, initially to the Preobrazhenskii prikaz and later to its sinister successors which dealt exclusively with cases of this kind. It was a charge which allowed for no distinction between treason and *lèse-majesté*. Not until 1762 was this 'hateful expression' abolished, though records show that prosecutions later continued (for example, in the Ural mines) in still greater secrecy than before. Catherine II's *Nakaz* was typically ambiguous. Though it warned that laws should punish only 'overt acts' (art. 477) and that 'words are never imputed as a crime unless they prepare, or accompany, or follow the criminal action' (art. 480), it nevertheless declared that 'Slanderers ought to be punished' (art. 485). Catherine understood by high treason 'all crimes against the safety of the sovereign and the state' (art. 465). But, even in 1825, the distinction between the two was imperfectly understood.

Consider the plethora of stories about the secret hanging of the five Decembrist ringleaders in 1826. Some said they went to the gallows wearing placards identifying them as 'state criminals', others that they were labelled 'regicides'. The truth remains elusive, but if such placards were indeed worn, it seems likely that 'regicides' would have been the appellation: the interrogations at the Investigatory Commission and the prominent rôle played in it by Nicholas I himself leave no room for doubt about the intensely personal way in which he interpreted the Decembrist threat. Even if the stories are apocryphal, their very existence stands as evidence on the present point: that during our period the notion of an abstract, impersonal state as the principal focus of a subject's loyalty never replaced in Russian minds traditional allegiances to the person of the monarch.

It will be remembered that the occasion of the abortive revolt on 14 December 1825 was the ceremony at which the troops swore allegiance to the new tsar, Nicholas I. The power of the verbal oath in an overwhelmingly illiterate society that still endowed the spoken word with such significance scarcely needs to be stressed. Oaths and vows were criticised as one-sided and primitive by Enlightened thinkers who wanted to substitute sophisticated mutual contracts. But these critics made little impact in Russia, where oaths remained the obverse of denunciations under the charge of *slovo i delo*. It is true that the troops seem to have been quick enough to swear fealty to Catherine II in June 1762, less than a year after they had taken an oath to her deposed husband. But oath-breaking was not taken lightly. It had been one of the most heinous Muscovite crimes, and the lasting reverence in which the oath was held was doubtless enhanced by the penalty of ten years' excommunication for oath-breakers. Exploiting these religious associations, the leading Decembrist K. F. Ryleev planned to spread a rumour that, having taken the oath to Constantine in November, rank-and-file soldiers would sin by swearing allegiance to Nicholas in December.

The confusion between tsar and state was enshrined in the oath formulated by Peter the Great who, in keeping with his drive to distinguish between the two, had decreed that a separate oath should be taken to each. From 1722, the oath taken by civilian officials ran as follows:

What I should both by duty wish, and will in every possible way try to do is to be a true, good and obedient servant and subject of my natural and true Sovereign, the most-powerful Peter the Great, Emperor and Sovereign, etc. [the tsar's titles were listed here] and Her Majesty, Most-Merciful Empress Catherine Alekseevna; to protect, defend, uphold all the rights, prerogatives and privileges belonging to His Majesty's power and authority, and not to spare my life in circumstances requiring it; and to try to help in all which may concern His Majesty's true service and usefulness to the state and Church, with all possible diligence and zeal.[7]

It seems likely that the penetration of this distinction in the minds of

[7] Quoted in G. L. Freeze, *The Russian Levites: Parish Clergy in the Eighteenth Century* (Cambridge, MA, 1977), pp. 29–30.

many who took the oath was limited. Subsequent petitions for retirement submitted simultaneously to the tsar in person and to the servitor's institution support Brenda Meehan-Waters's contention that 'a modernised nobility served a centralised state' whilst simultaneously 'a network of favourites, patrons and kin served both sovereign and servitor'.[8] In view of the relative emphasis in the text of the oath, we can see why officials continued to believe that they were primarily 'in the service of Your Tsarist Majesty'. If this was true of the tsar's noble officers, how much more so of his common soldiers. On the eve of Poltava, Peter reminded his troops that they were fighting not for him but for the state entrusted to him. But bearing in mind their conditions of service, the stoicism of the ill-equipped Russian soldiery is more convincingly explained by a reverence for the person of the *tsar'-batiushka* and his Russia – father and fatherland – than by any loyalty to 'the state'.

What were the consequences for Russian rulership? It is sometimes claimed that tsar and state were mutually supportive, combining to form a distinctively supple Russian absolutism. But it is more convincing to argue that the persistence of personal Russian rulership retarded rather than accelerated the development of a modern notion of the state. This in turn implies a further crucial point. If Habermas can claim that in western Europe 'civil society came into existence as the corollary of a depersonalised state authority',[9] then we can argue that personal conceptions of rulership helped to delay the emergence of a Russian civil society. In one sense, the consequences for the monarchy were not promising: we know how successive reform initiatives foundered on the lack of an educated popular response. But there was also reassurance here. For whilst Russia had no recognisable civil society, there could be no alternative focus of loyalties to rival the tsars. It is no coincidence that the first distinct notion of the state as separate from the tsars was conceived by the Decembrists in an era when state and nation diverged for the first time.

State and nation

Everything said in chapter 6 about the slow development of an educated Russian public should make us wary of predating the formation of a Russian political nation self-consciously opposed to the state, or even of

---

[8] B. Meehan-Waters, *Autocracy and Aristocracy: The Russian Service Elite of 1730* (New Brunswick, NJ, 1982), p. 70.
[9] J. Habermas, *The Structural Transformation of the Public Sphere: An Inquiry into a Category of Bourgeois Society*, tr. T. Burger (Cambridge, 1989), p. 19.

one supportive of the monarchy. Peter undoubtedly sought to foster a small élite of active subjects, working in concert to promote his own conception of the greater good. But the frustration experienced by those few who tried shows what little impact they had. Tatishchev, for example, was disgusted by the failure of his contemporaries to co-operate. Peter's efforts to encourage conscious participation in state affairs degenerated into a struggle simply to enforce rules. It was not until the mid-century that there were the first signs of a broader-based discussion of politics. Even then, it was literary in form and accessible to few. Whilst in the West a vigorous interest in political ideas had long spawned hundreds of political pamphlets, ranging from philosophical theology to pornography, Russians were fed comparatively thin gruel (what little pamphleteering there was was designed primarily to assert Russia's international status abroad, as in the case of Shafirov's treatise on the just causes of the war against Sweden, mentioned in chapter 5). Many important issues were discussed behind the scenes in bureaucratic 'projects'. Most texts familiar to us were read at the time only by those for whom they were written.

Consider Prince M. M. Shcherbatov's critique, *On the Corruption of Morals in Russia*, 'destined to remain hidden in my family'.[10] Written between the end of 1786 and the end of 1787, it lay neglected until published in London in 1858 by the émigré radical, Alexander Herzen. Karamzin's *Memoir on Ancient and Modern Russia*, written for Alexander I in 1810–11 at the instigation of his sister, the Grand Duchess Catherine, was not published in Russia until the twentieth century, though Karamzin's political ideas were earlier propagated through his historical writing and journalism. *Russkaia pravda*, by the radical De-cembrist, Colonel P. I. Pestel', was by nature a secret document known only to co-conspirators; following their arrest, many Decembrists under-standably claimed never to have read it. The most widely known text in our period was doubtless Catherine's *Nakaz*, which was explicitly intended to be propagated. But by 1818, copies were being sold off by weight for pulp.

An initially underdeveloped political awareness was natural in a society in which, only a few decades earlier, foreign visitors to Muscovy had been stunned by the degree of subservience to which even the greatest boiars were subjected by the tsar. Boiars were surely less self-abasing than foreigners supposed. But since Catherine II's predecessors took pleasure in humiliating even their highest-ranking courtiers, the tendency to narrow the social chasm must not be taken too far. Even

[10] Prince M. M. Shcherbatov, *On the Corruption of Morals in Russia*, tr. and ed. A. Lentin (Cambridge, 1969), p. 235.

Diderot, whose Russian experiences confirmed his move towards a theory of popular sovereignty, shared the common Enlightenment view that it would take a long time to lead a politically immature people to liberty. As late as 1801, Count S. R. Vorontsov's belief that the Russian nation was still 'ill-prepared, ignorant, and corrupt' counted against any limitation on monarchical powers.

Evidently it would be naïve to suggest that this harmony of interests between monarch and politically aware subjects was achieved without conflict: it must partly be ascribed to the ruthless suppression of dissent. But this remark applies more to the first half of the eighteenth century than to the period 1762–1825. In practice, if not in theory, until the 1790s Catherine's censorship was as generous as those of her Enlightened neighbours Frederick the Great and Joseph II. She not only tolerated but participated in debate in Russian journals; far from deriding the rôle of writers, she sought their approval, notably in her correspondence with Voltaire. And in case she needed a reminder of their value, native writers were eager to provide it. Fonvizin, in his *Discourse on the Recovery of Pavel Petrovich* (1771), stressed the need for wise advice from a philosopher (which elsewhere he contrasted with the evil counsel of an irresponsible favourite) whilst in his periodical of 1795, *Athenian Life (Afinskaia zhizn')*, Karamzin praised the didactic and moral rôle of ancient Greek rhetoricians and poets. In return, writers and journalists fulfilled their part of the informal contract by eulogising the monarch. Some ideas remained beyond the pale. For instance, Rousseau's *Emile* was banned in 1763, probably on the grounds that it was offensive to Orthodoxy. The motivation for other restrictions is more obvious. The French Revolution alarmed the ageing Catherine and prompted her to impose much stricter limits on what could be published. Radishchev was exiled to Siberia; Voltaire's work was burned; all foreign literature became suspect, and most was banned. But such a reaction is scarcely surprising. Anyone who believes that Catherine's policy was uniquely severe should consider the censorship imposed in Revolutionary France itself by Robespierre's Committee of Public Safety. Tsar Paul strengthened the repression, but, in the more relaxed circumstances of Alexander's reign, political debate was not only resumed but enriched. As tsarevich, Alexander had himself provided financial backing for the *St Petersburg Journal (Sankt-Peterburgskii zhurnal)* of 1798, in which radical writers such as Ivan Pnin found a rare opportunity to publish under Paul. Far from falling into two mutually exclusive and hostile camps, writers and censors, many *literati* of the Alexandrine period, performed both rôles simultaneously.

The tsars and the small group of nobles who thought about politics were united in their acceptance of monarchy as the best form of government; united, too, by the belief that vigilance was required to prevent monarchy from degenerating into despotism. Their common problem, therefore, was to decide how monarchy might best be preserved. Two broad approaches to this problem have been identified in political theory since the Renaissance. The first argues that institutions play the vital rôle in preserving government from corruption; the second that no institution will succeed in this task if those who control it are themselves corrupt.[11] In Russia, it was this second approach that predominated. With a few significant exceptions, to which we shall shortly return, it was generally agreed that if tsarist despotism were to be prevented, it would not be by checks and balances but rather by monarchical self-restraint and by virtuous behaviour on the part of the monarch's leading subjects.

This preoccupation with the way power was *used* rather than with the way it was *constituted* derived largely from the fact that Russians wrote and thought in the shadow of the greatest political treatise of the century, *The Spirit of the Laws* (1748), the masterpiece of the *philosophe* Montesquieu (1689–1755). Montesquieu proposed a tripartite classification of governments – republics, monarchies, and despotisms. To each he assigned a 'principle', or motive force. In republics that principle was 'virtue', in monarchies 'honour', and in despotisms 'fear'. For Montesquieu, republican virtue was 'a very simple thing': love of one's country. In stressing this, he wanted not so much to advocate republican constitutions, which he thought workable only in very small states, as to stress the value of patriotism for any government, including monarchy, the form most appropriate to countries of moderate size. When Catherine II declared that she had 'a republican soul', she wanted only to show that she too appreciated the rôle that virtue might play in government. There was, however, one apparently insuperable obstacle facing anyone who tried to apply Montesquieu's maxims in a Russian context. The master himself had consigned Russia to the ranks of the world's despotisms, and despotism was the eighteenth century's dirtiest word. As we shall see, Montesquieu's association of Russian rule with caprice and corruption offered a well-taken opportunity to critics of the tsars, and the force of his argument was not lost on the empress. When young, Catherine had casually referred to the need for despotic rule in Russia; once she became more closely acquainted with *The Spirit of the Laws* – she had certainly read it by 1760 and later referred to it as her prayer book – she changed her tune. In the *Nakaz* of 1767, which drew

[11] See Q. Skinner, *The Foundations of Modern Political Thought*, 2 vols. (Cambridge, 1978), vol. I, pp. 44–5.

294 of its 655 articles directly from her mentor, she sought to prove that Russia's need for absolute monarchy did not automatically make her a despot in Montesquieu's sense of the word. Not all her contemporaries were convinced. Diderot, for one, reacted scornfully in his unpublished *Observations on the 'Nakaz'* (1774). But Diderot knew little of Russian reality. Those who knew more, though they remained suspicious of Catherine's motives, nevertheless shared many of her basic assumptions.

Had they been concerned to justify constitutional restraints on the monarchy, Russian thinkers might have turned to representative institutions from the past, notably the *veche* of medieval Novgorod and the Muscovite Zemskii sobor. But in most Russian texts, representative institutions play the part of the dog that failed to bark in the night: the striking thing about them is their absence. Nowhere during the succession crisis of 1730 was the Zemskii sobor so much as mentioned. For one thing, these institutions lacked a theoretical justification to rank with the legal-humanist tradition used to legitimise the constitutional rôle of the French *parlements*. For another, it was easy to tar them with the brush of weakness and anarchy. Looking back on the Novgorod city-state in 1761, the historian G. F. Müller associated freedom with bad leadership, an argument already made three years earlier by Lomonosov, whose history made no reference to the *veche* and justified Ivan III's subjugation of the city by the need to restore order. When Radishchev tried to revive memories of the Novgorod republic and in turn to denounce Ivan, Catherine retorted that he made no mention of the cause of Ivan's actions, Novgorod's surrender to the Polish Republic, which accounted for the tsar's punishment of 'the apostates and traitors', though she acknowledged that Ivan had exceeded reasonable limits.[12] Karamzin's *Memoir*, written to refute Speranskii's constitutional proposals, epitomises the denigration of representative institutions in order, by contrast, to reflect glory on the stability associated with unlimited royal power. The few who did turn to institutions as guarantors of liberty thought of them, in a characteristically Russian way, not as constitutional restraints but as administrative channels. When an influential group of senators led by Counts A. R. Vorontsov and P. V. Zavadovskii tried in 1801–3 to restore the collective responsibility of the Senate, they did so not in order to *limit* the powers of the monarchy, but to *increase* them by standardising bureaucratic procedure and limiting ministerial interference (see chapter 5).

In the absence of constitutional restraints, Russians concentrated instead on the need for monarchical self-discipline. Believing that only

---

[12] A. N. Radishchev, *A Journey from St Petersburg to Moscow*, tr. Leo Wiener, ed. R. P. Thaler (Cambridge, MA, 1958), p. 241.

virtue limited a monarch, Sumarokov set out to show in his tragedies that it was by behaving justly, with humility and virtue, that the sovereign identified himself as the representative of divine power on earth. As this example implies, virtue in the Russian context not only carried the secular associations of republican patriotism, but also acquired the Christian overtones of German Pietism, still prominent in the education of many Russian nobles. In this composite form, virtue long remained the cornerstone of political argument in Russia. As late as 1818–21, members of the Union of Welfare, which spawned the two Decembrist groups, the Northern and Southern Societies, believed that the moral and spiritual self-improvement of the Russian nobility was a prerequisite for social or political reform. In 1818, the introduction to the Union's Constitution declared that 'virtue, i.e. the people's good habits, always has been and will be the pillar of the state: should virtue cease, no government, no laws will prevent its fall'.[13]

So far, I have stressed the way in which the tsars and their leading subjects agreed both that monarchy was the ideal form of government and that it could be prevented from degenerating into despotism only by virtuous conduct on the part of both ruler and ruled. All the more important, therefore, to stress that there *were* genuine attempts at constitutional change in the first quarter of the nineteenth century, when several key figures improvised variations on the theme of representative government. Most did so vaguely. Derzhavin dreamed of a Spanish-style 'Cortes'; inspired by the French revolutionaries' Declaration of the Rights of Man, the tsar's 'Young Friends' began blithely to echo its conceptual language. Speranskii, however, was more specific in his 'Introduction to the codification of state laws' (1809). Had his plans been implemented, they would have transformed the theoretical foundations of the Russian old régime. Long portrayed as a benign conservative, Speranskii is now recognised as a genuine liberal, a believer in limited monarchy and the separation of the powers who considered a participative element in law-making essential. Because he knew that their only chance of success lay in a voluntary renunciation of absolute power on the part of the tsar, Speranskii initially disguised the radicalism of his proposals by omitting crucial controversial passages. As we saw in chapter 1, it was this strategy that ultimately precipitated his downfall. Though it did not mark the end of the tsar's interest in constitutionalism, Speranskii's dismissal in March 1812 sealed the fate of his scheme.

Even before Speranskii, there were those, including the aristocratic

---

[13] M. Raeff, *The Decembrist Movement* (Englewood Cliffs, NJ, 1966), p. 70.

constitutionalist, Shcherbatov, who remained unconvinced that Catherine had achieved what she proclaimed and who continued to think her
despotic. But in turning to examine the grounds for their criticism, it is
important to realise that neither serfdom nor the lack of a constitution
was prominent among them. Instead, the most significant cause of
discontent was extravagance, and here Russians could draw on the
support of Western authorities.

Though eighteenth-century thinkers were united in ascribing to
'luxury' a wider meaning than mere extravagance, they were unable to
agree on its significance. A new 'commercial' school greeted the pursuit
of private 'luxury' as a welcome contribution to a thriving economy and
hence to the public benefit. But the older, republican identification of
'luxury' as a harbinger of corruption and decay – a notion derived from
classical Rome, revived in the Renaissance, and perpetuated by Montesquieu – had not yet lost its force.[14] Russian discussions of luxury all
fell into this latter category: court extravagance was condemned because
it was believed that it would lead to the collapse of the Russian state. It is
difficult to know how far, say, Shcherbatov, who subjected the 'voluptu-
ousness' and 'luxury' of Catherine's court to a blistering critique, was
consciously trying to associate himself with any particular theoretical
tradition by referring to classical example, and how far he was simply
displaying his own learning, derived mostly second-hand from the
philosophe Baron d'Holbach (1723–89). Karamzin's classical knowledge
was more sophisticated: on the very first page of his *Memoir on Ancient
and Modern Russia*, he asserted that 'Rome, once strong with valour, had
weakened from luxury, and collapsed.'[15] Yet in his earlier *Letters of a
Russian Traveller* (1791–1801), religious motifs were more prominent,
since it was the 'unspoilt morals and piety' of Zurich that were contrasted with the excessive luxury of the French. Again, the combination
of the religious with the secular is striking. As so often, one faces a
difficulty in interpreting political ideas expressed in literary form: how
much of what is said represents the view of the individual author, and
how much is simply a stylistic feature of the genre in which he wrote?
Perhaps the most plausible conclusion is that Russians concerned about
court excess approached Western sources already convinced from their
own experience of the damaging effects of extravagance and in search of
authoritative support. If this is true, what is striking in retrospect is that
it mattered little where they turned, be it to the classical republicans, to

---

[14] See C. J. Berry, *The Idea of Luxury: A Conceptual and Historical Investigation* (Cambridge, 1994).
[15] R. Pipes, *Karamzin's Memoir on Ancient and Modern Russia: A Translation and Analysis*
(New York, 1972), p. 103.

German Pietism, or even to their own Orthodox tradition: all would confirm their own association of asceticism with virtue and of luxury with corruption and decay.

The related question of war and expansion proved still more contentious. Drawing on the doctrine of the 'just war' revived by Christian Wolff and on Fénelon's widely read *The Adventures of Telemachus, Son of Ulysses* (1699), which argued that a wise and virtuous ruler was one who protected his subjects from the ruinous consequences of a destructive military campaign, Russian writers preached the virtues of peace and stability. Corresponding vices were associated with the corruption of court favourites. Panin, supplanted at court by Potemkin, contrasted a patriotic attachment to peace with the extravagant wastefulness likely to result from self-interested foreign policy; Sumarokov used predominantly military monarchs to represent rulers whose ambitions were unchecked by restraints. Such arguments were not the sole preserve of critics. Montesquieu, prompted by his dislike of Louis XIV's foreign policy, had stressed the need for restraint in military affairs on the grounds that aggressive wars laid waste to productive provinces. Catherine accepted the lesson: 'Peace is necessary to this vast empire', she wrote in one of her notebooks: 'We need population, not devastation.'[16] There was therefore a broad measure of common ground between the empress and her critics, even if they differed over the proper balance of achievements. Since the monarch's rightful search for posthumous 'glory' had to be measured against its immediate costs to her contemporaries, it is hardly surprising that Russians were divided in their view of the golden mean.

The realisation that monarchs and their critics had so much in common helps to explain why, despite the virulence of their criticisms, none of Catherine's Russian detractors found monarchy itself sinister, and only Fonvizin, the mouthpiece for the Panins and other acolytes of Grand Duke Paul, flirted with the notion of legitimate resistance in his *Discourse on Permanent Laws of State* (c. 1782–3). Kheraskov, in his epic *Rossiada* (1779), had the tsar reflect that his title of monarch depended on his sharing power with the people and accepting their laws. Radishchev's dream sequence in his *Journey* condemned flatterers and lauded an idealised monarch, conscious of his own responsibilities and capable of accepting criticism. Neither author, however, contemplated any form of government other than monarchy. Both displayed a staunch faith in the appearance of a just monarch. Even Shcherbatov, having regaled his reader with a litany of appalling royal behaviour, limply

---

[16] Quoted in D. L. Ransel, *The Politics of Catherinian Russia: The Panin Party* (New Haven, CT, 1975), p. 53.

concluded that 'we must only beg God that this evil may be eradicated by a better reign'.[17]

Why this apparent timidity? In part, the answer lies in the available intellectual vocabularies. Russians educated in the German cameralist–natural law school, for example, would find no constitutional safeguards against tyranny and no justification for deposing a tyrant. All preached obedience to the monarch. No doubt the psychology of a service nobility also played its part. But the acceptance of strong monarchy was equally a matter of self-interest. Unlimited monarchy could bolster the cause of reform because it alone guaranteed swiftness of action. That was why even Vasilii Popugaev (b. 1778/9), the most radical member of the Free Society of Lovers of Literature, Sciences, and the Arts (1801–25), was convinced that monarchy was the best form of government. The more widely shared corollary was that a relaxation of monarchical power would in turn weaken the state. There was still little disagreement with Catherine II's declaration in article 11 of the *Nakaz* that any other than absolute government 'would not only have been prejudicial to Russia, but would even have proved its entire ruin'.

The crucial concept encapsulating the association between monarchs and their politically aware subjects was 'the fatherland' – *otechestvo*. The notion of the monarch as 'Father of the Fatherland' – *otets otechestva/pater patriae* – originated as part of the secular Petrine myth propagated first by Feofan (Prokopovich) and later, among others, by Lomonosov in his *Ancient Russian History* (1760). Catherine the Great fostered the same unifying concept of patriotism – love for herself as maternal empress – and found in Novikov a skilled publicist who propagated the image of 'true sons of the fatherland' and their contemptible anti-models in journals produced under her patronage in the early 1770s. There was still no sense in which love for the ruler and love of country could be set against each other. Until 1796 the only way in which the concept of the fatherland was used in an oppositional sense was by those in Panin's entourage who tried, obliquely, to identify patriotism with the person of Grand Duke Paul in contradistinction to the private interests of Catherine and her favourites. Radishchev made a similar point in the dream sequence of his *Journey*, condemning Potemkin as 'the traitor and violator of the public trust'.[18] But the fatherland had not yet been formulated as an abstract concept to which appeal might be made to subvert the authority of the state. Nor could it have been, since I have already suggested that such state authority was still not understood in

[17] Shcherbatov, *On the Corruption of Morals*, p. 259.   [18] Radishchev, *Journey*, p. 75.

Russia in wholly impersonal terms. Karamzin, indeed, believed that nations were the products of their rulers' genius: both state and political nation were still umbilically linked to their progenitors, the tsars.

Not until the late 1790s did the first menacing cracks in this relationship appear. So successful had Catherine been in fostering a sense of public-mindedness that several members of the political nation she had helped to create began to long for an active, rather than merely reactive, rôle in Russian government. Yet they did so when Tsar Paul was least inclined to offer it to them. The thaw in the first years of the reign of Alexander I served only to deepen the sense of betrayal when later, under Arakcheev, his régime abandoned any sense of liberality. By then, however, the censorship law of 1804 had begun to allow the dissemination of radical ideas in Russia, and an incipient network of literary societies and salons – in which the ties of personal friendship were strong – provided a forum, independent of the state, where they could be discussed. Whilst Montesquieu remained seminal, his work was now read in a more radical light. The French *idéologue*, Destutt de Tracy, remarked in his *Commentary* (1817) on Montesquieu's famous treatise, that 'every system where the state is headed by just one person, particularly where the office is hereditary, will inevitably end in despotism'.[19] Tracy had his sights set on Napoleonic pretensions. But Russians were swift to see the wider implications of his remarks. Significantly it was to Tracy that Pestel' referred when interrogated on the inspiration of his political beliefs. He also pointed to his course in political thought at the Cadet Corps in St Petersburg, where he had been asked to read not only Montesquieu, but, among others, Locke, Mably, and Rousseau. The later *philosophes* no longer thought of society solely in terms of Montesquieu's emphasis on hierarchical estates. The Romantic emphasis on individualism had begun to disturb the social conservatism of the Enlightenment. Both Rousseau and Schiller prompted Russian poets to yearn for individual freedom. A new generation of noble bureaucrats searched for a new spiritual identity based on moral integrity: what their parents had accepted as natural – serfdom – they began to think of as inhumane and dishonourable.

Although it now seems that the Revolutionary and Napoleonic wars drew fewer future Decembrists than was once thought into personal contact with the West, Russia's greater involvement in European affairs certainly brought with it a growing awareness of different methods of government. Some thought that, if only European models could be reshaped into a form appropriate to Russian circumstances, they might

---

[19] Quoted in P. O'Meara, 'The Decembrist Pavel Ivanovich Pestel: Some Questions of Upbringing', *Irish Slavonic Studies*, 9 (1988), p. 15.

bear fruit there too. Moderates were encouraged by the generosity accorded to the Finns on their incorporation as a grand duchy in 1809 and by the constitution Alexander I granted to the congress kingdom of Poland in November 1815. This not only introduced press freedoms and civil rights, including habeas corpus, but also decreed that a parliament should meet every two years for thirty days. Although in 1818 the tsar instructed Nikolai Novosil'tsev (1761–1836) to draft a constitution for Russia itself, the resultant federal proposals, based principally on the Polish precedent but also influenced by the constitution of the United States, came to nothing and were revealed only when published by Polish rebels in 1831. Meanwhile, radicals were inspired not so much by constitutions as by revolutions in Naples, Portugal, and Spain, which prompted Pestel' to think in terms of a universal spirit of opposition. Riego's Spanish rising in 1820 was particularly influential among the future Decembrists: it offered a model of military heroism, rather than popular revolution; it warned against trusting a king to act constitutionally; and it inspired Sergei Murav'ev-Apostol of the Southern Society to adopt the use of political catechisms as a means of political propaganda.

In combination, these circumstances prised state and nation apart for the first time. Faith in the coming of a just monarch evaporated; the fatherland was no longer thought inseparable from the monarchy. Instead, the Decembrists associated it, as had Radishchev, with liberty and freedom. But Decembrism was not a unitary movement. Its division into two Societies, the Northern and the Southern, reflected a crucial ideological split. The Northern Society's proposals, encapsulated in the Constitution drawn up by Nikita Murav'ev, advocated a liberal–constitutional state with a loose federal structure inspired by the American example but adapted to Russian conditions. Whilst Murav'ev was preoccupied with the defence of individual liberty, however, the Southern Society followed Pestel' in proposing an interventionist state, owing much to French Jacobinism, in which individual liberty was to be sacrificed, in a way that was to become characteristic of the Russian intelligentsia, to the alleged greater happiness of the whole.

The part of the political nation that turned against the state which had created it was neither united nor large; it had no social roots. It is hard to see how it could have been otherwise. Though civic consciousness was the hallmark of the Decembrist movement, the notion of the town as a political community had little resonance in Russia. Most towns were little more than garrisons, administrative centres, and market-places: they offered no echo of the glorious past of either ancient Rome or medieval Novgorod. The related notion of civility promised an equally restricted response. Indeed, no other was expected. Far from regretting their exclusiveness, contemporary intellectuals revelled in it. Zhukovskii, in a translation of a German essay published in Karamzin's journal *Messenger of Europe* (*Vestnik Evropy*), went so far as to define society as 'a circle of select people – I will not say the best – pre-eminent in wealth, education, dignity, descent; it is a republic with its own laws ... where the evaluation of virtue and talent takes place'.[20]

It was the reaction of Russian rulers – especially Paul I and Nicholas I – that made Russian public opinion more subversive than it might otherwise have been. Accustomed to being courted by Catherine the Great, Russia's political nation was jilted just as its political sophistication was beginning to develop and its social composition beginning to expand beyond the nobility to a broader range of *raznochintsy*. Here were the first signs of a nascent intelligentsia – a group who broke the bounds of the estates, being united neither by social and economic nor by juridical ties, but by their mutual commitment to the power of ideas. But before 1825, only among the most radical Decembrists – in Keep's formulation, neither a pure intelligentsia nor simply a group of discontented officers, but rather a hybrid of the two[21] – did the yearning for liberty, action, and civic-mindedness find conscious expression in the form of a theory exalting a state founded on the authority of a political nation consciously opposed to the monarchy. And the Decembrists, lacking roots in society, were easily put down. Paradoxically, the emphasis the tsars placed on personal devotion was both a source of weakness and a strength. In fact, their position was more secure than they themselves realised. A more flexible approach by Nicholas I might have been all that was needed to reconcile state and nation in Russia. But Nicholas was not the man, and Restoration Europe was not the place, for monarchical flexibility.

Church and state

This cannot be the last word. Whilst in 1825 the menace of an alienated radical intelligentsia lay in the future, leaving state and nation still potentially compatible, even before 1676 a damaging rift between church and state had widened irreparably.

It can easily be made to seem, by reference to the legal record, that Peter I's church reforms created a successful form of Russian absolutism

---

[20] Quoted in W. M. Todd, III, *Fiction and Society in the Age of Pushkin* (Cambridge, MA, 1986), p. 17.

[21] See J. L. H. Keep, *Soldiers of the Tsar: Army and Society in Russia 1462–1874* (Oxford, 1985), pp. 231–72.

in which, in return for supporting it against its schismatic and sectarian rivals, the state mobilised the Orthodox church as the pillar and preacher of the tsarist state. According to this argument, once Peter's successors had softened the blow of his innovations they were able to achieve a reconciliation with the church, thereby disarming what was potentially an alternative focus of allegiance. It is, of course, true that there was little open conflict between church and state before 1825. But it is more important that there was no longer any real sense of identification between them. Instead there was a legacy of profound mistrust. Still more ominously, the only way for the state to placate the church was to support its attempts to extirpate its rivals – the non-Russians within the Russian empire (Jews, Tatar Muslims, Baltic Protestants, Polish Catholics, and so on), and the schismatic and sectarian Russians. Yet any tsar who chose to pursue so intolerant a policy risked alienating in turn the heterodox. Since this dilemma remained unresolved before 1917, religion could never be a reliable force for political and social unity in Russia. Despite all appearances to the contrary, the union between the Orthodox church and the Russian state was an uncertain one.

Though the full implications of this point became clear only in the nineteenth century, the roots of the dilemma lay firmly in the seventeenth. To understand why this was so, we need to know something about the nature of the Orthodox church and its faith. Orthodoxy's claim to unique apostolic authority relies on its related claim to have preserved intact the tradition of the early church. This is a tradition canonised not by the Scripture alone, which in Orthodox eyes left too many questions open, but rather by the resolutions of seven great ecumenical councils (AD 325–787) at which both the church's doctrine and its conciliar government were definitively shaped. Whilst the Catholic church is said by Orthodox to have deviated from this ideal in the Great Schism of 1054, when it succumbed to papal pretensions to superior authority, the Protestants are suspect because of their excessively liberal belief in justification by faith. No church is insensitive to liturgical and doctrinal change. But it will be clear, even from this bald summary, that the Orthodox church is peculiarly vulnerable to it. For much of its existence, it has coped with incremental change by virtue of the fact that its authority relies not on juridical interpretation of doctrine but instead on the propagation of 'right' imagery. By contrast, the two periods in which it was thrown into turmoil – the seventeenth and nineteenth centuries – are those in which, under pressure from rivals, it was forced to define its doctrines more carefully in order the better to defend them.

It is vital to understand that *both* parties in the schism claimed to be faithful to Byzantine Christianity. Patriarch Nikon wanted to correct the church's service books and ritual to realign them with the Greek practice from which he believed the Muscovite church had deviated; his Old Believer opponents branded Nikon's reforms as innovative because they broke with the customs with which they had grown up. Subsequent scholarship has suggested that the Old Believers were right to think that some Muscovite practices were of more ancient origin than those of the Greeks. But this fact is historically less important than the consequences of the schism.

By dividing it, the schism irreparably weakened the church, leaving it ill prepared to withstand the pressures of reforming tsars who wanted to exploit Orthodoxy's spiritual and material resources. In this sense, Peter's abolition of the patriarchate and his creation of the Holy Synod in 1721 marked not so much a revolution as part of the continuum in the state's policy towards the church which began under Aleksei Mikhailovich and culminated with the secularisation of the church lands in 1764 (see chapter 3). That is not to underestimate Peter's personal impact. In the first place, he rubbed salt in the wounds of Old Believers, horrified first by the portrayal of Aleksei Mikhailovich in sacred imagery and no less offended when Peter I declared himself 'Imperator'. This was a title that they believed ought to be reserved exclusively for Christ himself, and Peter's arrogation of it joined his changes to the calendar and his poll-tax census in a trinity of ghastly symbols that the Old Believers used to justify their identification of the tsar with Antichrist. Other titles Peter adopted were equally abhorrent to them. That he called himself 'Peter the First' implied a sacrilegious claim to pre-eminence, whilst the phrase 'Father of the Fatherland', so successful in cementing links between state and nation in the secular sphere, was interpreted by schismatics as a usurpation of the patriarchal title with which, in Russia, it had traditionally been associated. Ironically, the same panegyric odes in which Lomonosov glorified the divine image of the monarchy were quoted in Old Believer manuscripts as evidence confirming Peter as Antichrist. Secondly, Peter's reforms offended the larger body who remained faithful to the Nikonian church. They finally destroyed any remaining vestige of the traditional Muscovite fusion (the Byzantine term is 'symphony') of church and state. To be granted a separate spiritual sphere of influence, parallel to the secular one, was not what the church wanted and almost certainly not what its believers expected of it. In consequence, many clergy remained only lukewarm in their support of the state, and some never recovered from a sense of betrayal. The liturgy was adapted to incorporate a prayer for the tsar. Some priests omitted it in protest; most conformed, but few showed enthusiasm for overt tsarist propaganda. This did not, however, prevent the clergy from becoming identified in the popular mind with unwelcome state intervention in village life.

Since the tsar could enjoy the full support of either the Orthodox church or the schismatics only by repudiating the other, it is a moot point which of the two did more damage to him in the long term. Bishops who resented the abolition of the patriarchate had few arguments of their own with which to defend continued ecclesiastical involvement in affairs of state. They relied primarily on the Catholic political thought towards which Orthodox had gravitated, since the middle of the seventeenth century, as the result of a combination of their own meagre intellectual resources (even the Greeks sent their best men to Italian universities) and the need to stem the challenge of the Catholic Counter-Reformation in Ukraine. Arguments first used in medieval Europe to defend the authority of the pope against Imperial incursion were now deployed in Russia in the cause of Orthodoxy's temporal power. But they were impotent because the hierarchy itself was dominated by Ukrainian bishops who shared Feofan (Prokopovich)'s absolutist convictions. That was why it was so easy for Catherine the Great to denounce 'the absurd principle of the two powers' to a delighted Voltaire, soon after her accession.[22] She made short work of Arsenii (Matseevich), bishop of Rostov, who alone repudiated secularisation and even questioned the legitimacy of Catherine's rule. Charged in 1763 with *lèse-majesté*, after a ceremony in the Kremlin during which he was publicly disgraced, he was exiled first to a monastery, where he continued to protest, and finally to the castle at Reval where he died a prisoner in 1772.

Not least among the indignities which traditionalist bishops were obliged to suffer was the toleration by which Catherine took the political sting out of the schism. Even the enlightened Metropolitan Platon – more *philosophe* than priest, according to Joseph II – could never quite reconcile himself to it, whilst others hankered after persecution. But they were powerless to prevent Catherine's rational policy, which was continued, after a brief interval under Paul, by Alexander I. This policy marked a sharp break with the past. Like the Jansenists in France, another case where the politicisation of a theological dispute helped to undermine the legitimacy of the monarchy, the Old Believers had been transformed into subversives by state support for the anathema pronounced upon them in 1667. Convinced of their treachery, Peter the Great used his Preobrazhenskii prikaz to investigate and torture those

---

[22] W. F. Reddaway, ed., *Documents of Catherine the Great* (Cambridge, 1931), p. 5, Catherine to Voltaire, 11 August 1765.

who identified him with Antichrist. Both Anna and Elizabeth zealously revived his attempt to extirpate the schism. In Smolensk province, where the *popovtsy* (those Old Believers who accepted the authority of their own priests) had spread by the mid-1740s, posses of soldiers were sent out to hunt down offenders and clap them in irons. Yet despite successive tsars' worst fears – perhaps it would be more accurate to say despite their best efforts – Old Believer resentment was never converted into coherent opposition. True, the imagery of martyrdom dominates the texts of even the relatively moderate *pomortsy* (those who lived 'by the sea') community at Vyg. A martyr's death as a soldier of Christ in militant action against Antichrist was not ruled out, as demonstrated by schismatic participation in peasant rebellions, including Bulavin's and Pugachev's. But like those discontented nobles who preferred to leave Russia rather than suffer a régime with which they had lost sympathy, most Old Believers preferred escape to resistance. Escape took many forms. The most extreme committed self-immolation rather than come into contact with the tainted world of Antichrist. Others fled if not the world then at least St Petersburg, eventually forming a diaspora reaching into Poland. Still others sought salvation in a mythical golden age, in which Ivan the Terrible stood as the symbol of true Muscovite Orthodoxy.

Such people posed little threat to the régime. During his visit in 1773–4, Diderot, mindful of the split between Jansenists and Jesuits and of the damage done by the expulsion of the Protestants after Louis XIV's revocation of the edict of Nantes in 1685, warned Catherine of the danger of creating martyrs by persecution. Catherine hardly needed to be told. Even before her accession she had been convinced of the advantages of toleration. In 1763, exiled schismatics were allowed to return from Poland to Siberia and to the south, where, permitted to practise their own religion and even to build their own churches provided that they formed separate rural colonies, they helped to populate newly settled areas. Yet Catherine by no means granted complete religious liberty: not until 1905 would it become legal for a Russian to subscribe to the faith of his choice. Neither could toleration eliminate religious conflict at a stroke. It could only submerge it, thereby postponing the worst consequences for the state.

Even if neither the Orthodox church nor the schism became the focus of real political menace, by alienating both the state denied itself what might have been its firmest bastion of ideological support. To take the church first, it remained demoralised and ineffective, relatively weak in its pastoral influence and resentful of the state's use of clerical pupils as a pool of educated labour to supply its own need for teachers, doctors, and lawyers. Ironically, the Orthodox revival which began during the early years of the nineteenth century, and later flourished in the top echelon of the ecclesiastical schools system – the four theological academies at Moscow, St Petersburg, Kiev, and eventually Kazan' (f. 1842) – served further to undermine the church–state alliance in the long term. In an ambitious enterprise fuelled by the nationalist fervour of 1812, and motivated by the dual desire to distinguish true Orthodoxy from Westernising accretions and defend it from rival faiths within the empire, the church's scholars naturally turned to both Patristic and early Russian sources for normative guidance in their attempt to recover the authentically Muscovite and Byzantine foundations of their faith. Paradoxically, the emphasis on the conciliar basis of Orthodoxy that they discovered in the early church and its Muscovite descendant implicitly undermined the legitimacy of the artificially created Petrine Synodal bureaucracy. A campaign that had set out to defend and define Russian Orthodoxy ended, in the eyes of sceptical statesmen, in potential subversion. Radicalism among ecclesiastical scholars seemed merely to confirm suspicions that the church schools turned out priests who were too ready to participate in and organise peasant disorders. It made for a very uneasy relationship between church and state.

Even in the eighteenth century there were already those who doubted the wisdom of this sacrifice, not all of them churchmen. Karamzin, who argued for a more authoritative episcopal hierarchy and a Synod with a broader 'sphere of action', remarked presciently in his *Memoir* that the clergy's use to the state was 'proportionate to the general respect it enjoys among the people'.[23] He recognised that, so long as Russia's priests were a despised caste, socially indistinguishable from the peasantry and reliant on them for their income, such respect was bound to remain negligible.

We shall probably never know how many Orthodox believers were lost to the schism: estimates range from around 5 per cent, probably too low, to as much as 30 per cent of the population, surely too high. Despite the system for registering schismatics, worked out in 1716–21, loopholes were numerous. Some avoided trouble (and the double poll tax) by claiming that they were registered in a former place of residence. Others came to an arrangement with local Orthodox priests, either by bribing them or by appealing to their better natures against persecution. Most simply disguised themselves as Orthodox.

If it is impossible accurately to quantify the schism, then we can at least be certain that this was a segment of society which was effectively

---

[23] Pipes, *Karamzin's Memoir*, p. 203.

lost to the state. Modern scholars are not alone in their ignorance of the Old Believers. Neither the Orthodox church nor the government knew much about them. The secret committee formed to investigate them in 1820 owed its origins not to Orthodox zeal but to the schismatics' own request for state intervention to resolve an internal economic dispute. The minutes of its meetings reveal neither omnipotence nor omniscience. Kochubei, minister of the interior, confessed that he was utterly confused by schismatic affairs.[24] For years, ignorance remained the principal obstacle to either a reconciliation between church and state, or a properly effective conversion campaign. There is not much evidence that the tentacles of the 'well-regulated state' ever enclosed the schism.

And yet there is reason to think such a sacrifice on the part of the state unnecessary. Although the extremist wing of the Old Belief – the priest-less Theodosians and the *beguny* – consistently refused to pray for the tsar in their services, the more moderate *pomortsy* had been brought round to it as early as the 1730s in the Vyg community. In part this was a tactical response to government pressure, but as that community's leader, Andrei Denisov, had suggested as early as the 1720s, the Old Believers, far from being disloyal, preserved the best of Russian traditions and were faithful subjects of the tsars. Despite rumours that the Moscow Old Believers offered hospitality to the French invaders in 1812, the classic case of betrayal was actually that of Varlaam, Orthodox bishop of Mogilev, who took the oath to Napoleon. In the nineteenth century, as the state turned away from cosmopolitan rationalism towards particularist nationalism, it came grudgingly to see the force of Old Believer advocacy that they above all could act as a conservative, Russian bastion against revolution. But in doing so, it only offended still further the Orthodox church, now in turn alarmed by sectarian and schismatic growth during the long period of relative toleration.

The much vaunted alliance between the tsarist state and the Orthodox church rested on shaky foundations. In 1825, the weakness remained hidden, since the tsars had not yet been forced to rely on it. But as the challenge of the radical intelligentsia became more intense in the course of the nineteenth century, the weakness at the ideological heart of the Russian old régime would be cruelly exposed.

Although the tsars strove to alter popular expectations of their rulers in the eighteenth century – deliberately shifting the emphasis of the monarch's function from 'the preservation of religious morality and

---

[24] See P. Pera, 'The Secret Committee on the Old Believers: Moving away from Catherine II's Policy of Religious Toleration', in R. Bartlett and J. M. Hartley, eds., *Russia in the Age of the Enlightenment* (London, 1990), p. 229.

Orthodoxy to the inculcation of a work ethic and civic virtue'[25] – it proved harder to execute this design than they expected. Propagandists might preach devotion to the common good rather than to the traditional Muscovite image of 'the most pious tsar', but in a society still governed by people rather than by institutions, the personal element in absolute monarchy stubbornly refused to recede. The corollary was that corporate opposition was slow to develop. Until the advent of radical Decembrism, most critics of the régime shared their rulers' fundamental assumption that Russia was best governed by monarchy. Tolerant censorship under Catherine II initially allowed differences over the way the monarch's power should be exercised to be defused without overt hostility. Ultimately, however, when the Russian régime proved insufficiently flexible to accommodate the intelligentsia it had done so much to create, an articulate, critical minority within educated society became vocal enough to begin to undermine the régime. Yet this handful of radical critics would never have been enough to subvert the tsars had their ideological underpinnings not already been shaky. In this sense, the crucial weakness of the Russian old régime was its failure to achieve a mutually satisfactory compromise with an established church aggrieved by the state's failure to protect it not only from secular bureaucrats, but, still more significantly, from confident religious rivals able, unlike many Orthodox priests, to practise what they preached.

BIBLIOGRAPHICAL NOTE

On grounds of originality, scarcely any Russian text belongs in the pantheon of European political thought. Most are derivative, and the authorship of even some of the most famous is in question. J. Cracraft asks 'Did Feofan Prokopovich Really Write *Pravda Voli Monarshei?*', *SR*, 40 (1981), suggesting that he was not the sole author. P. Dukes, ed., *Russia Under Catherine the Great*, vol. II, *Catherine the Great's Instruction (NAKAZ) to the Legislative Commission, 1767* (Newtonville, MA, 1977), offers a contemporary translation with a good introduction. Catherine's sources are available in translation: Montesquieu, *The Spirit of the Laws*, tr. and ed. A. Cohler, B. Miller, and H. Stone (Cambridge, 1989), and Beccaria, *On Crimes and Punishments and Other Writings*, ed. R. Bellamy, tr. R. Davies (Cambridge, 1995). Diderot's sceptical *Observations on the 'Nakaz'* are translated in *Diderot's Politics*, ed. J. H. Mason and R. Wokler (Cambridge, 1992). A. M. Wilson, 'Diderot in Russia, 1773–1774', in J. G. Garrard, ed., *The Eighteenth Century in Russia*

[25] C. H. Whittaker, 'The Reforming Tsar: The Redefinition of Autocratic Duty in Eighteenth-Century Russia', *SR*, 51, 1 (1992), pp. 83–4.

(Oxford, 1973), covers the visit. P. Zaborov, *Russkaia literatura i Vol'ter: XVIII–pervaia tret' XIXvv.* (Moscow, 1978), and Iu. M. Lotman, 'Russo i russkaia kul'tura XVIII veka', in M. P. Alekseev, ed., *Epokha prosveshcheniia* (Leningrad, 1967), document the Russian reception of Voltaire and Rousseau respectively. For an important Russian writer, see W. Gleason, ed., *The Political and Legal Writings of Denis Fonvizin* (Ann Arbor, MI, 1985). Gleason's *Moral Idealists, Bureaucracy and Catherine the Great* (New Brunswick, NJ, 1981) overstates the debt owed by Fonvizin, Sumarokov, and others to German ideas. On Shcherbatov, start with A. Lentin, '*A La Recherche du Prince Méconnu*: M. M. Shcherbatov (1733–90) and His Critical Reception Across Two Centuries', *CASS*, 28 (1994). Commentaries on Radishchev include F. Venturi, 'A Portrait of Alexander Radishchev', in Venturi, *Studies in Free Russia* (Chicago, 1980), and A. McConnell, *A Russian Philosophe: Alexander Radishchev, 1749–1800* (The Hague, 1964). J. L. Black, *Nicholas Karamzin and Russian Society in the Nineteenth Century: A Study in Russian Political Thought* (Toronto, 1975), ranges widely. Two collections of extracts in translation remain useful: M. Raeff, ed., *Russian Intellectual History: An Anthology* (New York, 1966), and Raeff, *Plans for Political Reform in Imperial Russia, 1730–1905* (Englewood Cliffs, NJ, 1966). Speranskii's political writings are in M. M. Speranskii, *Proekty i zapiski*, ed. S. N. Valk (Moscow and Leningrad, 1961). The classic work of radical Decembrism is P. Pestel', *Russkaia pravda*, which occupies vol. VII (Moscow, 1958) of the invaluable series in progress, *Vosstanie dekabristov: dokumenty*. Translated extracts from this and from other Decembrist writings are introduced by M. Raeff, *The Decembrist Movement* (above, n. 13).

The secondary sources on the subject are fragmentary and controversial. I know of no study covering the same ground as this chapter, though there are suggestive accounts of the later years in A. Walicki, *A History of Russian Thought from the Enlightenment to Marxism* (Oxford, 1980), and L. Schapiro, *Rationalism and Nationalism in Russian Nineteenth-Century Political Thought* (New Haven, CT, 1967). The following suggestions relate to the sections of the chapter above.

On the rise of the impersonal state, start with Q. Skinner, 'The State', in T. Ball, *et al.*, eds., *Political Innovation and Conceptual Change* (Cambridge, 1989). J. H. Shennan, *The Origins of the Modern European State, 1450–1725* (London, 1974), links political theory to power politics; a short but sophisticated sequel, Shennan, *Liberty and Order in Early Modern Europe: The Subject and the State, 1650–1800* (London, 1986), contrasts state development in Russia and France. M. Cherniavsky, *Tsar and People* (New Haven, CT, 1961), is a provocative study of kingship;

C. Whittaker, 'The Reforming Tsar' (above, n. 25), and Whittaker, 'The Idea of Autocracy Among Eighteenth-Century Russian Historians', *RR*, 55 (1996), herald a forthcoming book. G. G. Weickhardt, 'Political Thought in Seventeenth-Century Russia', *RH*, 21 (1994), ascribes an implausibly high degree of modernity to Kotoshikhin, Krizhanich, and Simeon Polotsky. J. Cracraft, 'Empire Versus Nation: Russian Political Theory Under Peter I', *HUS*, 10 (1986), refers to earlier work, among which B. Syromiatnikov, *'Reguliarnoe' gosudarstvo Petra Pervogo i ego ideologiia* (Moscow, 1943), has been particularly influential. Its thesis, stressing German influence, has been developed by M. Raeff, *The Well-Ordered Police State: Social and Institutional Change Through Law in the Germanies and Russia, 1600–1800* (New Haven, CT, 1983), and challenged by I. de Madariaga, who argues that, by the time of Catherine II, French thinkers were more important: see her 'Catherine and the *Philosophes*', in A. G. Cross, ed., *Russia and the West in the Eighteenth Century* (Newtonville, MA, 1983), and her 'Catherine II and Montesquieu: Between Prince M. M. Shcherbatov and Denis Diderot', in *L'età dei lumi: studi storici sul settecento europeo in onore di Franco Venturi*, 2 vols. (Naples, 1985). On sacralisation, see V. M. Zhivov and B. A. Uspenskii, 'Tsar' i bog: semioticheskie aspekty sakralizatsii monarkha v Rossii', in B. A. Uspenskii, ed., *Iazyki, kul'tury i problemy perevodimosti* (Moscow, 1987). Different perspectives on pretenders appear in K. V. Chistov, *Russkie narodnye sotsial'no-utopicheskie legendy XVII–XIXvv.* (Moscow, 1967), a provocative account; B. A. Uspenskii, 'Tsar and Pretender: *Samozvanchestvo* or Royal Imposture in Russia as a Cultural-Historical Phenomenon', in Ju. M. Lotman and B. A. Uspenskij, *The Semiotics of Russian Culture*, ed. A. Shukman (Ann Arbor, MI, 1984); and P. Longworth, 'The Pretender Phenomenon in Eighteenth-Century Russia', *P&P*, 66 (1975). O. Subtelny, 'Mazepa, Peter I and the Question of Treason', *HUS*, 2 (1978), is important. A. M. Kleimola, 'The Duty to Denounce in Muscovite Russia', *SR*, 31 (1972), offers a longer perspective.

On the development of a political nation, J. L. H. Keep, 'The Muscovite Elite and the Approach to Pluralism', *SEER*, 48 (1970), argues that Muscovite society was not politically passive. K. A. Papmehl, *Freedom of Expression in Eighteenth-Century Russia* (The Hague, 1971), emphasises the liberality of Catherine II's censorship. R. E. Jones, 'Opposition to War and Expansion in Late Eighteenth-Century Russia', *JfGO*, 32 (1984), shows that these issues ranked higher than serfdom in critics' eyes. Soviet scholarship is reviewed by M. Raeff, 'Between Radishchev and the Decembrists', *SR*, 26 (1967); S. C. Ramer offers further insights in 'The Traditional and the Modern in the Writings of Ivan Pnin', *SR*, 34 (1975), and Ramer, 'Vasilii Popugaev, The Free Society of Lovers of Literature, Sciences and the Arts, and the Enlightenment Tradition in Russia', *CASS*, 16 (1982). For a debatable approach to a crucial subject, see A. Kahn, 'Readings of Imperial Rome from Lomonosov to Pushkin', *SR*, 52 (1993). On Alexander I's reign, compare the psychological interpretation of M. Raeff, 'Andrei Turgenev and His Circle', in A. Rabinowitch and J. Rabinowitch, eds., *Revolution and Politics in Russia: Essays in Memory of B. I. Nicolaevsky* (Bloomington, IN, 1972), with D. Christian, 'The "Senatorial Party" and the Theory of Collegial Government, 1801–1803', *RR*, 38 (1979). A. Martin, *Romantics, Reformers, Reactionaries: Russian Conservative Thought and Politics in the Reign of Alexander I* (DeKalb, IL, 1997), appeared too late to be discussed.

Amongst the vast literature on the Decembrists, see J. Gooding, 'The Liberalism of Michael Speransky', *SEER*, 64 (1986), and Gooding, 'Speransky and Baten'kov', *SEER*, 66 (1988). Gooding dissects Soviet historiography in 'The Decembrists in the Soviet Union', *Soviet Studies*, 40 (1988). P. O'Meara, *K. F. Ryleev: A Political Biography of the Decembrist Poet* (Princeton, 1984), is a careful study; Ju. M. Lotman, 'The Decembrist in Everyday Life', in Lotman and Uspenskij, *The Semiotics of Russian Culture*, is inspired. I. de Madariaga, 'Spain and the Decembrists', *European Studies Review*, 3 (1973), probes a special relationship. Also stimulating is F. A. Walker, 'Christianity, the Service Ethic and Decembrist Thought', in G. A. Hosking, ed., *Church, Nation and State in Russia and Ukraine* (London, 1991).

M. Malia, 'What Is the Intelligentsia?', in R. Pipes, ed., *The Russian Intelligentsia* (New York, 1961), and M. Confino, 'On Intellectuals and Intellectual Traditions in Eighteenth-Century and Nineteenth-Century Russia', *Daedalus* (1972), are still required reading. D. M. Griffiths, 'In Search of Enlightenment: Recent Soviet Interpretation of Eighteenth-Century Russian Intellectual History', *CASS*, 16 (1982), warns against pre-dating a proto-intelligentsia. N. V. Riasanovsky, *A Parting of Ways: Government and the Educated Public in Russia, 1801–1855* (Oxford, 1976), has a long chapter on the eighteenth century.

To the work on the church listed under chapter 6, add S. A. Zenkovskii, 'The Russian Church Schism: Its Background and Repercussions', *RR*, 16 (1957), and M. Cherniavsky, 'The Old Believers and the New Religion', *SR*, 25 (1966). N. S. Gur'ianova, *Krest'ianskii antimonarkhicheskii protest v staroobriadcheskoi eskhatologicheskoi literature perioda pozdnego feodalizma* (Novosibirsk, 1988), expands on the discussion of prayers for the tsar in R. O. Crummey, *The Old Believers and the World of Antichrist: The Vyg Community and the Russian State, 1694–1855*

(Madison, WI, 1970). There is much on Old Believers in R. G. Pikhoia, *Obshchestvenno-politicheskaia mysl' trudiashchikhsia Urala (konets XVII–XVIIIvv.)* (Novosibirsk, 1987), but the most significant modern work is by P. Pera, 'Dispotismo illuminato e dissenso religioso: i Vecchi Credenti nell'età di Caterina II', *Rivista Storica Italiana*, 97 (1985), and A. I. Mal'tsev, *Starovery-stranniki v XVIII–pervoi polovine XIXv.* (Novosibirsk, 1996).

8   The economy

Many textbooks begin with the economy. Here it has been left until last – not because it is unimportant, but because economics is best understood in the context of society, politics, and culture. It is fortunate that economic history is more than a matter of numbers since Russia's surviving statistical record is thin. So sparse are the sources in some sectors that one cannot 'put the numbers in' without making many of them up: the beginner is faced with a bewildering array of those mutually incompatible multipliers with which scholars lay snares for the unwary. Be it a question of population, production, or price series, the lack of standardised contemporary measures is not the least obstacle to a universally acceptable quantitative methodology. Yet it would be perverse not to acknowledge the advances that cliometricians have made. Their conclusions inform much of what follows.

One further difficulty is worth stressing at the start. The national state ranks amongst the least appropriate units for the purposes of economic analysis. Whilst long-term change is probably best assessed on a continental or even global scale, short-term regional variations deprive many national aggregates of meaning. If this be true of Britain, how much more so of the Russian empire, whose vast territory encompassed almost every climatic and ecological variable except the tropical swamp. At its north-eastern tip lay volcanic Kamchatka, where Mount Kliuchevskaia erupted five times in the eighteenth century – over 8,000 miles across the Siberian taiga and more than six months' travelling time from the bleak bog surrounding St Petersburg. Between lay the Ural mountains, only gradually accepted as the division between Europe and Asia. A more important (though invisible) boundary within European Russia separated the forested marsh-land to the north and west of Moscow from the grassy steppe to the south and east, where fertile black soil provided the mainstay of Russian agriculture. By 1825, expansion had incorporated not only the sun-drenched Caucasian slopes, but also huge tracts of the east European plain. As William Tooke observed in 1799: 'Here are delightful and charming regions, where Nature seems to have dispensed her gifts of every kind with an unsparing hand; while towards others she has acted so like a stepmother that all appears desert and gloomy.'[1] A better appreciation of regional and local geography is a key aim for future research. Meanwhile, it is natural to analyse Russia's economic performance in the context of the state's broad aims and specific policies, which in turn drew on current vocabularies of economic thought.

Economic ideas and economic policy

At the dawn of a new millennium, it is easy to forget how recent is our conception of the primacy of economics in government. We are not helped by a school in the history of economic thought which imputes an artificial modernity to the ideas of Adam Smith (1723–90).[2] According to this anachronistic tradition, Smith was the prophet of liberal capitalism – a critic of the steady-state 'mercantile' system which he himself helped to define in pejorative terms, and an advocate instead of boundless growth driven by individual enterprise freed from the dead hand of state intervention.

At first sight, Russian economic development can be safely accommodated within such a scheme. The Shuvalov reforms of 1754–5, when heavy internal customs duties were lifted, can be seen as presaging the policy of Catherine II which apparently subverted Peter I's *dirigisme* and in turn heralded a fascination with Smith's *laissez-faire* philosophy in Russian government around 1800. This outline contains an important kernel of truth, but also three serious defects. It obscures a crucial continuity in Russian economic policy, which even in its most 'liberal' phases always preserved a central regulatory rôle for the state; it ignores the extent to which political economists, Smith included, understood economics in a wider jurisprudential context; and it overstates their optimism about economic growth, which Smith, as we shall see at the end of this chapter, believed to be limited in the circumstances he was able to foresee.

Though Smith's impact in Russia is not in doubt, its origins are debatable. By one account, S. E. Desnitskii, who heard Smith lecture at the University of Glasgow in 1762–3, transmitted some of his ideas to St Petersburg, allowing their incorporation into Catherine's *Nakaz* nine years before the publication of *An Inquiry into the Nature and Causes of*

---

[1] W. Tooke, *View of the Russian Empire During the Reign of Catherine the Second and to the Close of the Present Century*, 3 vols. (London, 1799), vol. I, p. 69.
[2] For a historical antidote, see D. Winch, *Riches and Poverty: An Intellectual History of Political Economy in Britain, 1750–1834* (Cambridge, 1996), pp. 35–123.

the Wealth of Nations in 1776. Against this, it seems that most of chapter 22 of the *Nakaz* was taken straight from the *Encyclopédie* article on 'Finances'.[3] Still, Smith certainly came to be promoted by Counts A. R. and S. R. Vorontsov, their sister, Princess Dashkova, and Vice-Admiral N. S. Mordvinov, all vocal admirers of Britain. Though Smith was best known through French and German popularisers, H. F. Storch's multi-volume *Historical-Statistical Portrait of the Russian Empire* (1797–1803) not only quoted him but adopted his stress on natural liberty. By the time Storch embarked on his *Course in Political Economy or Exposition of the Principles which Determine the Wealth of Nations* (6 volumes, 1815) for Alexander I's sons, he even ventured to criticise his mentor. N. I. Turgenev's *Essay on the Theory of Taxation* (1818) followed Smith closely, and A. P. Kunitsyn, who had studied in Paris, lauded the great man to his pupils at the lycée at Tsarskoe Selo. In fact, so modish had political economy become by the 1820s that Pushkin listed familiarity with Smith among the pretensions of his dandy, Evgenii Onegin, though so strong was the Russians' dependence on foreign sources that, as N. I. Grech noted, 'not a single book on Political Economy was published in the Russian language' in 1814.[4]

More in hope than expectation, Alexander himself had been encour-aged by his departing Swiss tutor to regard Smith's 'indispensable' masterpiece as 'true classic' whose 'principles, once well grasped, allow you to estimate what happens in matters of manufacture, trades, commerce, and taxation'.[5] But these principles were not initially inter-preted in *laissez-faire* terms. Far from regarding Smith as revolutionary, his first continental readers assimilated his ideas into the cameralist schema.[6] Smith appeared to offer Russians, as he had Germans, a middle way between the anarchy of excessive liberty and the straitjacket of excessive restraint. And by the 1750s, the regulation imposed by Peter I already seemed too restrictive to last.

Peter I inherited a tradition of economic regulation. But whereas

---

[3] Compare A. H. Brown, 'Adam Smith's First Russian Followers', in A. S. Skinner and T. Wilson, eds., *Essays on Adam Smith* (Oxford, 1976), with V. Kamendrowsky, 'Catherine II's *Nakaz*, State Finances and the *Encyclopédie*', *CASS*, 13, 4 (1979), pp. 545–54.

[4] *Sochineniia Nikolaia Grecha*, 3 vols. (St Petersburg, 1855), vol. III, p. 302, 'Obozrenie russkoi literatury v 1814g.'.

[5] For La Harpe's annotated reading list of 6 April 1795, see J.-C. Biaudet and F. Nicod, eds., *Correspondance de Frédéric-César de la Harpe et Alexandre Ier*, 3 vols. (Neuchâtel, 1978–80), vol. I, pp. 111–39, quoted at p. 137. Although La Harpe urged that perseverance would make the grand duke finish Smith's book, it was not long before Alexander confessed that his father's parades had made greater claims on his time.

[6] See K. Tribe, *Governing Economy: The Reformation of German Economic Discourse, 1750–1840* (Cambridge, 1988), mercifully more readable than the texts it digests.

Muscovite supervision had done more to inhibit growth than to stimu-late it, Peter was more ambitious. He set out to goad the rapid industrial development required not only by his immediate military needs but by a perception that Russia's productive capacity needed to be developed if the empire were to achieve its international potential. Industry was driven by a ruthless military-command system even after supervisory responsibilities had passed to the Colleges of Mines and Manufactures, separated in 1722. Always suspicious of profiteers, Peter was never-theless persuaded to sell or lease many state enterprises to the private sector from 1714, and especially after 1720. Privatisation persisted into the 1730s, motivated partly by profit and partly by a desire to develop Russian managerial talent. The policy was justified by results: 86 per cent of private ironworks survived the twenty years after the tsar's death and so did 72 per cent of all textile manufactories. But the workforce remained unreliable. Whilst unskilled labour could be compulsorily drafted, skilled workers remained in short supply despite attempts to attract foreign masters to train native apprentices. Moreover, because Russia had no bank until 1754, because Peter was unwilling to advance credit, and because individuals proved reluctant to risk their own capital, many factories depended either on tsarist monopolies or on protectionist customs duties. Peter I therefore bequeathed, just as he had inherited, what was in many ways a tautly regulated economy.

It would be misleading to stress theory as the motor of Peter's policy. Though mercantilist ideas – emphasising the need for a full treasury, sustained by a favourable balance of trade – might have been expected to attract Muscovites trying to steady an economy upset by civil unrest and war, it is hard to establish a link between theory and practice. The modern editors of Iurii Krizhanich's *Politika* (1666) show that both Aleksei Mikhailovich and Prince V. V. Golitsyn possessed a copy, and note that Peter later implemented some of Krizhanich's economic recommendations. However, they failed to unearth a single contem-porary Russian reference to the Croatian Jesuit's treatise. Indeed, as Gerschenkron remarks, 'a distinctive feature of Russian mercantilism was the almost complete absence in it of general theorising'.[7]

Ivan Pososhkov's *Book of Poverty and Wealth* (1724) is the exception that proves the rule.[8] Significantly, its author died in prison in 1726, jailed for expressing unorthodox views in his unsolicited advice to the

---

[7] J. M. Letiche and B. Dmytryshyn, eds., *Russian Statecraft: The Politika of Iurii Krizhanich* (Oxford, 1985), p. lxxv; A. Gerschenkron, *Europe in the Russian Mirror: Four Lectures in Economic History* (Cambridge, 1970), p. 83.

[8] I. Pososhkov, *The Book of Poverty and Wealth*, ed. and tr. A. P. Vlasto and L. R. Lewitter (London, 1987).

tsar. Pososhkov certainly drew on cameralist ideas, but a search for specific influences would prove pointless since Peter's drive to free Russia from reliance on foreign supplies did not depend on any one individual. In so far as theorists contributed to policy-making before the 1760s, it was not through comprehensive schemes but as 'projectors' offering piecemeal solutions to specific problems. As Panin complained in 1763, this meant that regulation had tended to be applied 'with only the particular need of the moment in mind, and hence without co-ordination in the whole or even part of the whole'.[9]

The 1760s witnessed the search for a more consistent strategy. By then, theory had begun to play a greater part in the formulation of policy. Yet although Catherine II read widely in the burgeoning litera-ture of political economy, she was no less pragmatic than Peter had been. Bielfeld was among the cameralists who led her to transfer large-scale industry from Moscow to provincial towns, and cameralism reinvigorated the governmental interest in urban public health which had lapsed since Peter's time. Sonnenfels shared with the French physiocrats a stress on the primacy of agriculture that Catherine echoed where Peter had not. She continued the relaxation of the Petrine system of regulation begun by Petr Shuvalov in 1754. Her rejection of mono-polies, her lowering of internal tariffs and customs duties (until war against revolutionary France prompted their reimposition at a high rate), and her openly expressed preference for hired labour in industry were all measures compatible with liberal economics, and they were reinforced by periodic statements of confidence in unfettered enterprise.

But this is not to say that Catherine trusted market forces. Indeed, she was careful, in her *Nakaz*, to distinguish liberty of trade 'for the benefit of the state' from freedom of operation for the merchant, defending customs on the grounds that 'What cramps the trader does not cramp the trade' (arts. 321–2). Dismissive of foreign treatises that neglected Russian circumstances, Catherine was most impressed by Necker's *On the Legislation and the Commerce of Grain* (1775), which she read in 1777. Louis XVI's minister drew on his own experience as a speculator to argue that, whilst government intervention in the grain trade was necessary to protect consumers from selfish merchants' attempts to raise prices, arbitrary interference must be avoided. Heeding this warning against the temptation to veer between the extremes of liberty and regulation, Catherine strove for the balance that Necker recommended.

But such a balance could never be stable whilst incipient economic

---

[9] Quoted in V. Kamendrowsky, 'State and Enterprise in the Thought of N. I. Panin', in R. P. Bartlett, *et al.*, eds., *Russia and the World of the Eighteenth Century* (Columbus, OH, 1988), p. 482.

liberalism ran counter to rigid social conservatism. The tension was already apparent in 1766, when a competition sponsored by the Imperial Free Economic Society prompted 162 essays on the extent to which peasants should be granted property rights in land. The winner, Beardé de l'Abaye of Aachen, proposed to introduce landownership for the serfs so gradually and so minimally that they would have remained dependent on rentiers. Second prize went to A. Ia. Polenov, whose native entry (one of only seven written in Russian) was thought too subversive to publish merely because it suggested that peasants might be granted enough land to subsist. In 1770, Prince D. A. Golitsyn, suspected of wishing to *give* peasants the land they worked, was quick to deny that any such 'extravagance' had entered his head. Radishchev's radicalism on this issue was rare indeed.

Since Justi had written in 1760 that 'peasants must be the proprietors of rural land' and that serfdom 'could only have arisen in the most barbarous times',[10] an emphasis also found in Pastor J. G. Eisen's contemporaneous work on the subject in Russia's Baltic lands, it did not need Adam Smith to suggest that economic prosperity and civil liberty went hand in hand. Catherine had herself asserted that 'Agriculture can never flourish there, where no persons have any property of their own' (*Nakaz*, art. 295). Yet widespread suspicion of the social implications of modern economics is indicated by Esther Kingston-Mann's scathing verdict on the Tula landlord, A. T. Bolotov (1738–1833), author of several enlightened treatises in agronomy:

Known to his peers as a trenchant critic of communal backwardness and peasant indolence and as an advocate of improved 'English' and 'German' systems of crop rotation, Bolotov was known to his peasants as a master who taught them to behave more rationally by having them tied hands and feet, thrown into a bath of steaming water, fed salted fish without being permitted to drink, and then stripped, tarred and feathered, and paraded through the streets of their villages.[11]

The tension between social and economic doctrine became more marked in the 1790s as the individualist implications of Smith's ideas sank in. Though Storch's economic advice pointed towards emancipation, his conviction that the poor needed a stricter moral code than the rich tempered his confidence in the economic potential of the individual. Mordvinov, one of Smith's key advocates and president of the Imperial Free Economic Society 1823–40, was equally adamant that property

---

[10] *Foundations of the Power and Happiness of the State*, quoted in M. Walker, 'Rights and Functions: The Social Categories of Eighteenth-Century German Jurists and Cameralists', *JMH*, 50 (1978), p. 242.

[11] E. Kingston-Mann, 'In the Light and Shadow of the West: The Impact of Western Economics in Pre-Emancipation Russia', *CSSH*, 33, 1 (1991), pp. 89–90.

rights could not be separated from 'supreme authority over others'. Whilst such values prevailed, economic liberalism could make only limited headway.

Smith's influence peaked under Speranskii, whose financial plan of 1810 was the first comprehensive Russian economic treatise since Pososhkov's *Book of Poverty and Wealth*. Speranskii's domination was nevertheless brief. Economic liberalism made no impression on Alexander I's last finance minister, Count E. F. Kankrin (1774–1844). Kankrin expressed the classic mercantilist view that the total wealth of the world was a fixed quantity, a principle which governed his whole approach to the economy. In contrast to Speranskii, who wanted to increase the wealth of the revenue producer in order to allow him to pay more to the state, Kankrin insisted that the budget could be balanced only by minimising expenditure and extracting maximum revenue from existing sources. It was to him that Russia owed the stabilisation of its currency after a period of chaos inflicted by the Napoleonic wars. But he was also responsible for enshrining, in the law on corporations of 6 December 1836, the principle of bureaucratic regulation of corporate activity that was to hobble Russian entrepreneurs until 1917.

Economic policy long relied more heavily on *a priori* social assumptions than on economic data, despite a dawning recognition that carefully digested information was a prerequisite of successful policy-making. Whilst British scholars who set out to collect and classify information about the material world were usually private individuals, Russia set up the sort of state-directed expeditions encouraged by German cameralism. The geographical department of the St Petersburg Academy of Sciences sponsored around fifty eighteenth-century expeditions (only Berlin had a similar department and its responsibilities were narrower). Civilian scholars combined with military men to explore and map the expanding empire. Their work has understandably been interpreted as a sign of a modernising scientific culture. But although 'political arithmetic' had been pioneered in England in the middle of the seventeenth century, it was only 200 years later that the various statistical approaches adopted in different European states converged towards 'modern' quantitative analysis. Until then, the principal purpose of many investigations remained descriptive.[12] Soviet scholars used to speak of the 'creative adaptation' of Western cartographic methods from the time of Peter I. But Russians would surely have adopted European models wholesale had they not lacked

---

[12] S. Woolf, 'Statistics and the Modern State', *CSSH*, 31, 3 (1989), pp. 588–604.

instruments and trained personnel. The *Atlas rossiiskii* (1745) acknowledged that some distances had been measured by pacing; surveys were
still completed simply by observation from high ground. Though J. N.
DeLisle's 1728 instructions for map-makers stressed the need for
accurate data, evidence continued to be gathered by inquisitorial
rather than geodetic methods. Much information was never converted
into cartographic form, remaining in textual appendices to the maps.
This was the classic German method, understandably adopted by
Russian expeditions led by scholars of German origin, notably G. F.
Müller and P. S. Pallas.

In one sense, the record of these expeditions is impressive. The
general survey proposed by the Academy of Sciences in the 1760s began
in Moscow province from 1766 to 1781, and twenty-three provinces
had been surveyed by the end of the century. Yet it was one thing to
collect information, another to make intelligent use of it. Fearing
misrepresentation abroad, the tsars proved reluctant, as inquisitive
foreigners such as Diderot discovered, to divulge much beyond published laws and edicts. Though a goldmine for historians, the data
gleaned by eighteenth-century expeditions were often ignored at the
time. Until the 1760s, central government tended simply to charge
provincial officials with incompetence or sabotage when things went
wrong (a habit which persisted into the twentieth century). However,
the Legislative Commission's subcommittee on the 'middling sort of
people' recognised the need for knowledge of what actually happened in
towns and the Commission on Church Lands was bound to deal in
numbers, though its efforts paled into insignificance by comparison with
the achievements of the Austrian Geistliche Hofkommission (1782), 'a
kind of Domesday Survey of the Austrian church' which has prompted
the claim that under Joseph II 'rigorously compiled statistics became an
essential tool of enlightened absolutism'.[13]

Only in demography were quantitative methods fully endorsed in
Russia. Here the motive was clear: as Lomonosov stressed to Catherine
II in 1764, Russia needed to develop its natural resources in order to
compete with the West and there was no more important resource than
people. When A. L. Schlözer was commissioned to undertake statistical
work on the population of St Petersburg in 1764, populationism was at
its zenith. So long as backward economies depended on manual labour,
manpower was deemed vital. Count Z. G. Chernyshev had written in
1763 that a state could 'support its army not through the extensiveness
of lands, but only in proportion to the people living in them and the

---

[13] P. G. M. Dickson, 'Joseph II's Reshaping of the Austrian Church', *HJ*, 36, 1 (1993),
pp. 92–3.

revenues collected there'.[14] Indeed, the conviction that a country's strength, happiness, and progress depended on the size of its population was widely shared in a Europe yet to be warned by Thomas Malthus (1766–1834) that 'the power of population is indefinitely greater than the power in the earth to produce subsistence for man'.[15] Whereas Malthus would argue in 1798 that an 'unchecked' population could be expected to increase in geometrical ratio whilst subsistence lagged behind in arithmetical ratio, mid-century thinkers still believed that the world's population was a finite resource for which there was bound to be competition. And in a fiercely competitive world, Russians were far from certain that they would triumph.

In his *Observations Concerning the Increase of Mankind* (1751), Benjamin Franklin suggested that the combination of abundant land with a shortage of labour and the high frequency of marriage at a low age all augured well for the rapid growth of America's population. Although there could scarcely have been a closer parallel to Russia's situation than the one Franklin described (see chapter 4), no echo of his optimism was heard there. Instead, Russians were more easily persuaded by those, like Montesquieu, who believed that population had declined from its peak in virtuous ancient times, and they were especially vulnerable to the charges made by d'Amilaville, in his *Encyclopédie* article 'Population', that 'men are not born where servitude awaits them'. In his treatise *On the Preservation and Increase of the Population*, presented in the form of a letter to I. I. Shuvalov on 1 November 1761 and deemed too sensitive to publish until 1871, Lomonosov criticised forced marriages and warned that peasant youths must not be permitted to marry infertile old women.[16] As I have suggested in chapter 4, it seems unlikely that either evil was as prevalent as Lomonosov thought. Nevertheless, Catherine herself flagged the dangers of underpopulation in the *Nakaz*, seeking to counter them by settling foreigners, admitted by legislation of 1762 and 1763, in agricultural colonies on the Volga. But whilst she strove to find ways of increasing what she believed to be a diminishing resource, the population defied all contemporary predictions. In Russia, as in western Europe, the second half of the eighteenth century marked the onset of uninterrupted demographic growth.

[14] Quoted in W. C. Fuller, Jr, *Strategy and Power in Russia, 1600–1914* (New York, 1992), p. 128.

[15] T. R. Malthus, *An Essay on the Principle of Population*, ed. A. Flew (Harmondsworth, 1970), p. 71. See also F. G. Whelan, 'Population and Ideology in the Enlightenment', *History of Political Thought*, 12, 1 (1991), pp. 35–72.

[16] M. V. Lomonosov, *Polnoe sobranie sochinenii*, 11 vols. (Moscow, 1950–83), vol. VI, pp. 381–403, discussed by V. P. Lystsov, *M. V. Lomonosov o sotsial'no-ekonomicheskom razvitii Rossii* (Voronezh, 1969), pp. 197–250.

Population and natural resources

Muscovy's population in 1678 has been estimated at 10.5 million. Since the seven censuses conducted between 1719 and 1817 counted only males and differed in their methods, eighteenth-century totals are also a matter of educated guesswork. Still, the general trend is clear. The adult male population increased from 7,791,063 in 1719 to 18,617,650 by 1795, giving putative aggregate figures of 14 million in 1724 and 36 million in 1796. Much the greater part of the increase came after 1750. The Russian population in 1817 is estimated at 45 million and by 1835 it had recovered from the Napoleonic wars to reach 60 million. Relying on similar figures, Urlanis derives a percentage rate of increase for Russia of 66.3 between 1750 and 1800 and 156.7 between 1750 and 1850, a spectacular rate thrown into relief by the sluggish figures for France – 28.6 per cent and 58.6 per cent respectively. Only Britain experienced a rate of increase comparable to Russia's in this period.

Annexation accounted for only one-third of eighteenth-century growth. Much new land in the south was underpopulated, whilst the Baltic lands devastated by the Great Northern War recovered only in the 1760s. Of Russia's acquisitions, only Poland and Ukraine were relatively densely inhabited. Demographic expansion therefore depended primarily on natural increase. In the current state of research, we can only speculate on the balance between fertility and mortality rates, though there is clear evidence that the latter fell only in the late nineteenth century.

If it cannot account for growth itself, the availability of new land does much to explain why population increase did not force Russia into the jaws of a Malthusian trap. Overall population density remained low. Between 1719 and 1795, it rose only from 3.5 to 7.2 people per square kilometre in European Russia, just under ten times lower than the British average. The regional breakdown is naturally more complex. As late as 1897, 40 per cent of the empire's total population occupied only 6 per cent of its area. Relatively speaking, the south-eastern steppe gained population at the expense of the north-western forest, through a process of internal migration that lasted more than four centuries from the middle of the sixteenth century without displacing most Russian peasants from the borders of the pre-Petrine state.[17] Even in the Muscovite heartland, however, the average number of people per square kilometre by 1795 was no more than thirty.

Sensible of Russia's land mass and understandably inclined to stress

[17] D. Moon, 'Peasant Migration and the Settlement of Russia's Frontiers, 1550–1897', *HJ*, 40, 4 (1997), pp. 865–67.

the pressing demand for labour, historians have been reluctant to acknowledge a shortage of land before 1800. Yet contemporaries in the central provinces were by then convinced of it. Though the proportion of ploughed land in European Russia, stable at around 20 per cent throughout the seventeenth century, increased to only 31 per cent between 1696 and 1796, responses to the Senate's 1767 inquiry into rising grain prices (the first to ask about land shortage) suggest that in the longest-settled areas there was already a perceptible lack of *usable* land measured by the need, as defined by contemporaries, for 2–3 *desiatiny* per person. By 1795, two-thirds of the land was cultivated in the most densely populated province, Tula, more than enough to exhaust the soil. And this was despite the fact that southern acquisitions had provided much-needed breathing space. Indeed, scarcity of land in some parts of New Russia prompted the government in 1804 to try to restrict foreign immigration to those deemed capable of making the best use of limited resources.

Demographic increase and soil exhaustion stoked up pressure which was not released until the railway opened up Siberia to mass migration in the 1890s. Nevertheless, for most Russians in 1825, land shortage still lay in the future. In our period, it was the contrast between the potential of Russia's resources and the performance of its native cultivators that struck commentators most forcibly. As the Hanoverian envoy in the time of Peter I remarked:

Russia abounds in Merchandize, but not in ready Money, and considering the vast Extent of its Empire, it is justly a matter of Surprize, that there is such a Disproportion between its Extent and Revenues, there being many Provinces, which yield to none in the world in Fruitfulness and the plentiful Produce of all that is necessary for human life.[18]

Korb, the Austrian envoy, had a sarcastic solution to this paradox: 'the land is naturally fertile enough, if it were not left in uncultivated sterility by the laziness of the people'.[19] This view persisted. La Harpe reminded the young grand duke Alexander that the variety and fertility of the Russian soil promised *une opulence solide* if only agriculture could be 'brought to the same degree of perfection that one sees in England, in Germany and elsewhere'.[20] Yet Storch complained in 1801 that nowhere in Europe was agriculture practised so negligently. Native critics joined the chorus. Pososhkov blamed peasant poverty on a

---

[18] F. C. Weber, *The Present State of Russia*, 2 vols. (London, 1723, reprinted 1968), vol. I, p. 48.

[19] J.-G. Korb, *Diary of an Austrian Secretary of Legation at the Court of Czar Peter the Great*, 2 vols. in 1 (London, reprinted 1968), vol. II, p. 222.

[20] Biaudet and Nicod, *Correspondance de la Harpe et Alexandre Ier*, vol. I, p. 161, La Harpe to Alexander, 28 April 1796.

mixture of idleness and harsh treatment by indifferent masters. Lords, in turn, berated peasant apathy. Peasants on *obrok* estates certainly neglected their land once it had satisfied their own needs because proto-industrial occupations were more profitable; peasants on *barshchina* estates had little incentive to work harder solely on behalf of their lords and the undernourished were prone to lethargy. Yet idleness alone cannot account for the waste of resources that dogged the economy.

Two things applied a brake. The first was the interdependence of society. So long as the three-field system enforced co-operative methods, it was almost impossible for individuals to experiment with either tools or techniques. Reliance on the household's resources to farm strips of land miles apart limited the functional specialisation of labour. Popular beliefs further retarded the adoption of new methods. Animals were so valuable that peasants proved reluctant to slaughter even diseased livestock and the potato was discredited because the first concerted attempt to introduce it coincided with the cholera epidemic of 1830 (though pioneers such as Sievers had attempted to promote the crop as early as the 1760s).

Paradoxically, the second reason why resource husbandry was little developed lay in the country's prodigious natural wealth. Whilst demographic pressure forced smaller states, notably Prussia, to experiment with productive new techniques, Russians, like the early American colonists, saw little reason to invest in intensive methods. So long as land remained freely available, reliable extensive cultivation was at least as rational as risky innovation. Shcherbatov complained in 1788 of complacent lords who shunned agricultural development. But few petty nobles could risk investments that would have inflicted immediate losses without guaranteeing long-term gain. Only those who were already profiting from the established system could afford to experiment, and there was little incentive for them to do so.

Members of the Imperial Free Economic Society who filled its journal with earnest exhortations to improve were preaching to the converted. Outside their charmed circle, whose radius barely penetrated the provinces, their advice fell on deaf ears. Only two noble petitions in 1767 proposed the formation of local committees to promote agriculture. Russians rejected the wisdom propagated by the students Catherine II sent abroad to learn British methods. The school of agriculture formed in 1798 under the supervision of A. A. Samborskii, formerly Orthodox chaplain to the London embassy, was closed along with its model farms in 1803. By then, progressive methods were suspect as a Western import incompatible with Russian conditions. Crop rotation, allowing regeneration of the soil, remained as rare as the use of green fallow, which could be used for pasture. Over 30 per cent of arable lay in bare fallow even in the 1870s. As late as 1881 only 0.9 per cent of the sown area was planted with clover, though it had been introduced into Russia in the 1760s and was in widespread European use by the 1780s. Manuring was rarer still since contemporaries thought the black earths so fertile as to render further treatment pointless. Incipient attempts at conservation show a dawning awareness that resources were not infinite. The need to replenish reserves for the court to plunder prompted periodic restrictions on hunting, and there were also attempts to preserve fish stocks. But it is timber that offers the best evidence of ambivalence over conservation.

Timber played a part in the life of every Russian. Punishment books show how much peasants were prepared to risk by stealing this crucial construction material. A range of industrial enterprises consumed timber in their furnaces. Salt was produced by boiling brine for six hours or more; the Demidov ironworks alone was said to burn 400,000 logs per annum in the 1760s. By then the state silver mines at Kolyvan had depleted the surrounding forest so severely that the smelting process had been transferred elsewhere. 'Greedy distilleries', as Bolotov lamented, 'reduce to ashes in the course of one summer something which takes a hundred years to grow.'[21] By 1800, up to 500,000 trees were felled each year to build river craft. Though the rôle of forest products was marginal in the totality of exports compared with that played by flax and hemp, exports accounted for further deforestation since timber was required by all eighteenth-century navies: 23 of Peter I's 178 manufactories were sawmills. Foreigners sensed an opportunity to profit. The English merchant William Gomm, having purchased in 1756 the right to exploit the Onega basin forests, was alone permitted to export up to 600,000 trees a year in the decade after 1764. Expanding agriculture further damaged the forests: in the north, slash-and-burn cultivation (*podseka*) persisted into the nineteenth century, whilst an estimated 32 million hectares were felled between 1725 and 1796 to make way for arable and pasture. Cumulatively, these demands put pressure on even abundant Russian resources. The last alone reduced the forested area by more than 10 per cent.

Since wood was lucrative for the landowner, nobles were aware that it was a diminishing asset. Though conservationist sentiments had earlier been expressed, for example by Pososhkov, it would be anachronistic to suppose that they outweighed self-interest in the motivation of most nobles at the Legislative Commission of 1767. Only two petitions

---

[21] Quoted in D. Eeckaute, 'La législation des forêts au XVIIIe siècle', *CMRS*, 9, 2 (1968), p. 195.

advocated a state conservation programme for timber; most simply wanted to limit its industrial use and to ban exports. Neither state nor private forest land was replanted, though a litany of legislation from Peter I to Paul strove to define reservations where felling was banned and access prohibited. Despite surveillance by the Admiralty, the state remained powerless to enforce its edicts. By 1740, it was sufficiently alarmed to ban the export of beams and restrict the operation of sawmills around Vyborg, and in 1756 Elizabeth banned timber exports from Narva. But these measures were localised and temporary. Though she herself wrote a memorandum on the need for conservation, Catherine II wanted to maximise rather than limit exports, as her generosity to Gomm shows. Indeed, by 1800 the state was once again competing with foreigners, making timber shortages common even in previously copiously wooded areas. As Tooke observed in 1799, 'the proper culture of timber, in many, or even in most parts of the empire, is still to be reckoned among the unusual matters of office; and that too even when a sensible scarcity calls aloud for the utmost care'.[22] A century later, deforestation would expose the land to drought and desiccating winds (*sukhovei*). As yet, however, their seemingly inexhaustible resources persuaded Russians that they could afford to be profligate with what God had given them.

Not even divine wrath could deter them, though it continued to reveal itself in mysterious meteorological ways. 'When you have seen how dreadful the climate is in Muscovy', quipped Montesquieu, 'you would never believe that to be exiled from it is a punishment.'[23] For farmers, however, Russia's continental climate was no joke. Whilst Western producers might hope for a growing season of up to eight months, steppe cultivators could expect no more than six in a good year. Further north the season lasted only three and a half months; in eastern Siberia it was shorter still. Agriculture was handicapped by severe winters, early frosts, and flooding characteristic of the 'little ice age'. Though the worst was over by the 1760s, expansion into fertile southern lands later brought its own problems, including variable precipitation to which wheat was especially vulnerable. Freak conditions inflicted havoc. At Tulchyn in Ukraine, hail 'the size of bantams' eggs' was reported just before the harvest in 1824, a year which also suffered from one of the plagues of locusts which periodically infested the south. Ignorant of any more effective prophylactic, even German settlers resorted to banging crockery at them in the hope of scaring them off. Amongst the officials

---

[22] Tooke, *View of the Russian Empire*, vol. I, p. 77.
[23] Montesquieu, *Persian Letters*, tr. and ed. C. J. Betts (Harmondsworth, 1973), p. 111.

sent to investigate their failure was Pushkin, who, just before resigning, filed his dismissive report in rhyme:

> The locusts flew on and flew on, then alighted
> To stay,
> They sat and they sat and ate everything up, then
> Were off and away.[24]

The strength of the chain linking natural disasters to poor economic performance is less certain than Pushkin's sardonic verdict would allow, though he was not alone in stressing their impact. Shcherbatov, for one, ranked natural calamity high among the causes of famine in the 1780s, a decade blighted by the cumulative effects of drought and low yields in successive summers. The most authoritative historian of the subject suggests that 'a frequency of natural calamities in the neighbourhood of every second year can be associated with a lower-than-average population growth rate'.[25]

Though it is hard to define either the location of natural disasters or the scope of their effects, 1760–1810 marked years of relative respite between two more seriously affected periods, 1700–60 and 1810–60. Within this broad outline, local variations deserve emphasis. The plague of 1770–2 may have killed about 100,000 in central Russia, half of them in Moscow, and about 20,000 more elsewhere in the empire. But, as Catherine II predicted in 1775, Moscow was 'a Phoenix which will be born again from its ashes': natural increase and in-migration recouped the city's demographic losses within a decade.[26] On *barshchina* estates, where peasants were less mobile, the consequences of natural calamity were more devastating. At Petrovskoe in Tambov province, children aged five to nine in 1827, infant survivors of the difficult winter of 1822, constituted only 10.7 per cent of the population by comparison with an average of 14.6 per cent between 1813 and 1824. Though the severe winters of 1709, 1729, and 1730 caused shortages throughout most of Russia, partial but recurrent local famines were just as serious. Data from the 1767 Senate inquiry suggest that each district suffered famine on average once every seven or eight years; cattle plague struck roughly as often. So the governor of Lithuania was probably right to claim in 1805 that there was a partial crop failure in some part of his province every year.

Sensitivity to local variation is equally desirable in the calculation of

---

[24] *Pushkin on Literature*, selected, tr., and ed. by T. Wolff (London, 1971), p. 33; this translation by Henri Troyat.

[25] A. Kahan, 'The Tsar "Hunger" in the Land of the Tsars', in Kahan, *Russian Economic History: The Nineteenth Century*, ed. R. Weiss (Chicago, 1989), p. 137.

[26] *SIRIO*, 23 (1878), p. 15, Catherine to Grimm, 30 January 1775.

yields. Until recently, historians argued that uniform conditions of soil and climate generated uniform yields over a wide area. There is something in this. But rye and wheat regularly did better in the black-soil than in the non-blacksoil zone, not only because the earth was naturally more fertile, but also because in some parts grazing cattle, *en route* to market in Moscow, manured the fields for years before they were broken up for cropping. In Blanchard's words, 'extensive pastoralism ... supported an intensive agricultural regime'.[27] Parts of Ukraine, the Don valley, and the land between Penza and Ufa all benefited in this way. Elsewhere, the long-held assumption that Russian output/seed ratios were universally abysmal is open to question. Most scholars have accepted an average Russian ratio of 3 to 3.5:1, and ratios of 1:1 were not uncommon on poor land. Arguing that official averages, on which the conventional view depends, were too low (since landlords concealed the size of their harvest lest profits be depleted by military requisitioning), Hoch, referring to the period 1811–60, stresses instead both sharp annual fluctuations and marked local differences within the same region at any one time.[28]

If he is right, then the fragility of the Russian economy lay less in inherently low productivity than in its inability to compensate for temporary, localised shortages. This, in turn, implies that Russia suffered more from problems of distribution than from the problems of production that most contemporary economists strove to solve. There is plenty of evidence to support such a view. Although, in total, Russians produced more grain than they could eat, we know that some peasants starved whilst foreign travellers described tables laden with produce close by. This underlines the importance of Sen's warning that 'starvation is the characteristic of some people not *having* enough to eat. It is not the characteristic of there *being* not enough to eat. While the latter can be a cause of the former, it is but one of many *possible* causes.'[29]

First among these was inadequate damage limitation. Until the foundation of Count M. S. Vorontsov's First Transport Insurance Company in 1823, cover was largely confined to policies offered to Russian merchants by Dutch agents. Riga's civic societies, offering cover against fire, were not emulated until the 1860s, despite the predominance of wooden buildings in Russian cities. The State Bank founded by Catherine II in 1786 offered policies for Russia's few stone buildings but

[27] I. Blanchard, *Russia's 'Age of Silver': Precious-Metal Production and Economic Growth in the Eighteenth Century* (London, 1989), p. 228, a powerful revisionist work.

[28] S. L. Hoch, *Serfdom and Social Control in Russia: Petrovskoe, A Village in Tambov* (Chicago, 1986), pp. 28–36.

[29] A. Sen, *Poverty and Famines: An Essay on Entitlement and Deprivation* (Oxford, 1982), p. 1; emphasis in original.

business was too weak for its Insurance Section to survive beyond 1822. Though Tsar Paul had meanwhile attempted to encourage transit and storage insurance for the commodity market, his project failed for lack of demand. Villages remained scarcely protected, relying on primitive measures such as the allotments advocated by Pososhkov as fire-breaks. In 1722 Peter I decreed that dwellings must be built in pairs separated by a gap of at least 60 metres and by 70 metres from livestock. This edict remained the most detailed law of its kind until provincial governors were empowered to impose still more elaborate symmetry in 1830. Judging by the volume of laws alone, Russian rulers stove earnestly to control village construction. But a plethora of legislation implies proportionate problems of enforcement. Model villages were few, confined to the main post-roads. Russian achievements pale by comparison with Scottish landlords' efforts to transform their villages into attractive and profitable centres of production and consumption, which resulted between 1730 and 1830 in the reconstruction of more than 130 villages, many in the Highlands.[30]

If more estates had produced a surplus, hoarding might have proved a problem. Yet many were satisfied with subsistence, which left them exposed when crops failed. Even on market-oriented estates, prohibitive storage costs and shortage of capital forced both lord and peasant to sell cheap in times of plenty, opening the way for speculators in a bad year. At the height of the 1787 shortage, St Petersburg's governor-general complained that the city's grain trade was in the hands of nine greedy profiteers. It took a tragedy on the scale of the Napoleonic invasion to prompt the government to intervene. At the governor's instigation, devastated Kaluga province (where Napoleon had only a few months earlier noticed 'the great abundance of everything') was granted a state loan of 1 million rubles to buy grain from Orel and Tula provinces. The state presumably regarded intervention as exceptional since, from the time of Peter I, it had followed a common European pattern by legislating to provide reserves in time of need. Had this system operated as well as it did in Prussia, the government might have exerted a measure of price control by requisitioning grain when it was plentiful and releasing it when it was short (though it is hard to believe that it could have controlled the inflation in grain prices, which increased 630 per cent over the course of the century). Even when stone granaries

---

[30] Compare J. Pallot, 'Continuity and Change in Village Planning from the Eighteenth Century', in L. Holzman and J. M. Knapp, eds., *Soviet Geography Studies in Our Time* (Milwaukee, WI, 1987), pp. 319–49, with T. C. Smout, 'The Landowner and the Planned Village in Scotland, 1730–1830', in N. T. Phillipson and R. Mitchison, eds., *Scotland in the Age of Improvement* (Edinburgh, 1970), pp. 73–106.

were built to replace rotting wooden ones under Catherine II, the system remained vulnerable to corrupt officials.

No account of economic problems would be complete without a consideration of the impact of Russian culture. Just Juel, Danish envoy to Peter I, remarked that by the end of the seven-week Lenten fast many Russians looked 'half-dead', so great was their weight-loss. Granted a special dispensation by the patriarch of Constantinople, Peter allowed his troops meat during campaigns. Though he knew of this edict, Field Marshal Apraksin declined to enforce it in 1757: by the time the Synod renewed permission for meat to be distributed, the great fast was already over and 11,000 men – a fifth of Apraksin's army in East Prussia – had collapsed from malnutrition. In St Petersburg's state factories, fasters worked one day fewer (three rather than four) in the week before Easter in 1731. Lomonosov, claiming that fasting was more appropriate to warmer climes, later linked a sharp seasonal rise in the death rate to the privations of the fast on which Russians embarked towards the end of their harsh winter. Those tempted (wrongly) to counter that fasters were few might be reminded of Bossy's judgement on western Europe, where 'the compromises of the lax were balanced by the austerities of those who fasted more than they were obliged to do'.[31]

Damage inflicted by accident, waste, and custom was compounded by war and rebellion. Though the economic consequences of war are debatable, and were hotly disputed by contemporaries (see chapter 7), the immediate destruction of the productive lands at the southern and western periphery is clear. In the late 1760s, William Richardson included among the 'dreadful features of Russian and Tatarian warfare' the sight of 'fertile provinces rendered desolate; towns and villages in flames; numerous herds of cattle rapaciously driven away'.[32] This was no exaggeration. When Napoleon razed Smolensk in 1812, only 350 out of 2,250 buildings survived and losses were estimated at more than 6 million rubles. The year 1812 apart, few pitched battles took place on Russian soil, but the empire faced the consequences of destruction by its own troops. Before Poltava, Peter I scorched a broad swathe of productive land between Pskov and Cherkassk. In 1740, officers returning the Turkish campaign were shocked by the devastation in Ukraine, where up to seventy-five regiments had been quartered *en route* to the front at a cost of ten times the hetmanate's annual budget. Bailiffs at Count M. S. Vorontsov's estate near Vitebsk estimated the total damages of the

---

[31] J. Bossy, *Christianity in the West 1400–1700* (Oxford, 1985), p. 52.
[32] Quoted in Fuller, *Strategy and Power*, p. 106, where Richardson, tutor to Lord Cathcart's children in St Petersburg and subsequently professor of humanity at Glasgow, is mistakenly identified as a diplomat.

Napoleonic wars at over 110,000 rubles, of which almost half was said to have been caused by Russian soldiers. No less destructive were peasant revolts south-east of Moscow, perfectly placed to disrupt trade with the Orient. Pugachev's revolt halted the Volga salt caravans (though it indirectly stimulated production in Perm' to compensate for shortages) and hastened the decline of the Ural mines and foundries. The total damage to industry was estimated at 2.5 million rubles. Elsewhere, countless smaller, localised disputes probably did as much as Bulavin and Pugachev to retard the productivity of individual estates.

These human failings help to explain why potentially sufficient levels of production were never translated into consistently satisfactory levels of consumption. Two features of the distribution network merit special attention: transport and market mechanisms.

Transport and technology

If 'the real dimensions of a state are given by the ratio between its linear dimensions and area, on the one hand, and, on the other, the time taken to travel over it',[33] then the already elephantine Russian empire begins to defy measurement. Even whilst its economy remained overwhelmingly agricultural, the southern grain-producing areas lay far from centres of consumption around Moscow and St Petersburg. The empire was plentifully endowed with salt, but its concentration in the northern Urals impeded efficient supply. Once intensive industrialisation began in the nineteenth century, difficulties of distribution multiplied: the overwhelming majority of mineral deposits were located in Asiatic Russia. If Russians were to dominate the space at their disposal, they needed to develop an efficient transport system. In this they were only partially successful.

Based on the model of the Mongol Tatars, who had drawn on Chinese experience, the Muscovite postal system (*iam*) gave the tsars a network safer and faster than anything in sixteenth-century Europe. No doubt it encouraged coachmen to know that a one-hour delay was punishable by death. The system was designed to improve military communications and to speed the journey of foreign embassies, primarily in an effort to prevent their seeing anything. (Even in the 1680s, the tsar still ritually washed his hands after meeting foreign embassies to purge any lingering taint of infection.) The successor to the Muscovite Postal Chancellery (1550–1711) maintained a fast service at great cost: the St Petersburg to Moscow route alone employed nearly 13,000 *iamshchiki* in the 1760s.

[33] R. E. Mousnier, *The Institutions of France Under the Absolute Monarchy 1598–1789: Society and the State*, tr. Brian Pearce (Chicago, 1979), p. 686.

Whatever its merits, however, the *iam* could not cope with the needs of an expanding commodity market.

For this purpose, Russian roads were even less adequate than their miserable European counterparts. Nobles resented the state's conscription of their peasants as navvies, and serfs in turn strove to bribe their way out of one of their most hated obligations. Thirty-five noble instructions to the Legislative Commission argued that the work should be done at the state's expense. Yet not until 1816 did the state begin to construct metalled roads, and even then progress was slow, the highway from St Petersburg to Moscow being completed only in 1834. By 1843 there were no more than 7,700 miles of metalled road – a third the length of British trunk roads and one-twentieth the length of those in France. Until then, Russia's thirteen principal 'tracts', radiating outward from Moscow, were constructed from tree-trunks (another drain on forestry resources) covered with gravel or sand. These primitive roads languished in a condition that made the traveller fortunate to average more than two or three miles per hour, even in good weather. Progress was often slower: not for nothing are the Russian spring and autumn called *rasputitsa* – the 'wayless' time of bad roads. Though bridges helped to reduce the journey time from Moscow to St Petersburg from five weeks to one over the course of the eighteenth century, improvements failed to keep pace with travellers' expectations. The situation in Siberia was worse. Traders struggled for up to three months along the track from Iakutsk to Okhotsk. The journey might have taken two weeks had not predators and perilous terrain left the road strewn with the skeletons of pack-horses (the route annually required between 6,000 and 10,000 animals by 1800). In the circumstances, it seems a sign of sophistication rather than backwardness that pre-Petrine maps measured distances by travelling time rather than in linear terms.

By the 1760s, the government was uncomfortably aware of shortcomings in land transport. N. E. Murav'ev (1724–70), appointed to the newly created Chancellery for the Construction of State Roads in 1764, had declared in his *Dissertation on Commerce* the previous year that 'there can be no commerce without communications'.[34] Murav'ev's stint as Russian representative on the French general staff during the Seven Years War had convinced him of the utility of such great highways as the road from Lyons to Turin and reminded him of Roman glories. But, as so often, it was easier to diagnose the Russian problem than to solve it. Charged by Catherine with improving communications, provincial gov-

[34] S. M. Troitskii, 'Zapiska Senatora N. E. Murav'eva o razvitii kommertsii i putei soobshcheniia v Rossii (60e gody XVIIIv.)', in A. L. Narochnitskii, ed., *Istoricheskaia geografiia Rossii XII–nachalo XXv* (Moscow, 1979), p. 237.

ernors were bewildered even when they were industrious. Sievers
reported that Novgorod officials knew nothing of roads between towns.
Systematic change remained negligible before the time of Paul I.

The inadequacy of land transport laid a heavy burden on waterways.
As part of his plan to make Russia the main conduit of East–West trade,
Peter the Great dreamed of a 'union of rivers' – a system of canals to
link the Baltic, the Black Sea, and the Caspian by way of the Neva, the
Volga, and the Don. His vision was realised only under Stalin. The
problem was not so much one of distance – the proximity of river
headwaters required relatively short connecting canals – as one of
technology. In our period this meant manpower rather than machine
power, just as it had in the sixteenth century when Suleiman the
Magnificent first contemplated, only rapidly to abandon, the idea of
linking the Volga with the Don. Since the state took the initiative, the
provision of manpower depended on the absence of more pressing
demands. By 1701, John Perry had worked on the Volga–Don canal for
three years with less than half the workforce he needed. In 1700 the tsar
had had to lay him off, 'having about this time lost the Battel of *Narva*,
and the War with *Sweden* being like to continue, which required more
immediate Supplies of Men and Money'.[35] Progress was therefore slow.
Though the first part of Peter's scheme, the vital Vyshnyi–Volochek
system, was finished in 1720, it was not until 1810–14 that the
Marinskii and Tikhvinskii systems completed a network linking the
Caspian to the Baltic.

Even then it was vulnerable to the climate. In winter, ice trapped the
autumn caravan from the Volga to St Petersburg, whilst in summer the
water table was often too low to allow craft to pass. These hazards
restricted navigation on even the lower Volga, below Kazan', to about
two hundred days in the year. In the north, the Msta – whose rapids not
only sank unstable laden craft on the journey downstream but made the
system impassable upstream – was never navigable for more than
seventy-seven days a year between 1801 and 1812, and once for as few
as thirty-three days. Since the expense of returning a wooden bark was
prohibitive (Sievers reported in 1783 that it would cost twice the price
of a new barge to haul an old one back to Novgorod), it was more
profitable, on completion of a single downstream journey from Rybinsk
to the capital, to break up craft for firewood.

Whilst a bark with a following wind might make seven miles an hour,
one hauled upstream by the legendary Volga boatmen (*burlaki*) – a
skilled workforce supplemented by a larger pool of serfs – could manage

[35] J. Perry, *The State of Russia Under the Present Czar* (London, 1716, reprinted 1967),
p. 5; emphasis in original.

only seven miles a day. This tortuous rate was in itself a stimulus to improvement, but it was reinforced by government incentives from the time of Peter I. In response to a Senate order of 1757, forty craft were built to ply salt up the Volga between Saratov and Nizhnii Novgorod. Propelled by a complicated winch and anchor mechanism, and intended to carry 50,000 poods of freight, each was supposed to need only a quarter of the crew of its less sophisticated predecessors (one man per thousand poods). In the event, they could carry no more than 40,000 poods, had a working life of only half the projected ten years, and were prohibitively expensive. The scheme was abandoned in 1761. In 1782, a still more ambitious operation, this time using horses as the motive force, also came to grief. Characteristically, its inventor, a former serf, Ivan Kulibin, established his reputation by making intricate mechanical toy eggs for Catherine II: when transferred to a grand scale, such ingenuity proved unworkable. Samuel Bentham was more successful. He spent 1784–7 on Potemkin's estate at Krichev in Mogilev province developing a system of barge chains allowing craft to negotiate bends in the river, and helping to clear the channel of a common obstacle created by profit-hungry owners, inclined to overload.

Not until 1810 were the first successful horse-powered craft introduced – by a Frenchman, Jean-Baptiste Poidevard. These were cheaper to man, requiring only a fifth of the crew of a standard barge. But the ten-year privilege granted to Poidevard in 1814 delayed their widespread adoption. Only in the early 1840s did their number grow significantly, by which time horse-powered barges provided almost half the Volga traffic. The first steamships had appeared on the Volga in 1815–17, followed in 1823 by the first on the Dnepr. This was not significantly later than their advent in the United States, but, whereas the American traffic burgeoned rapidly, it was only in the 1850s that steam travel on Russian rivers developed.

Thus it was only when defeat in the Crimea prompted a belated investment in railways that the grain-producing black-earth region was brought nearer to the capital than India was to England in terms of the time needed to haul freight. Until then, transport costs made it more profitable to convert grain into alcohol than to sell it for human consumption. Even in the famine-hit 1780s, grain was imported into both Voronezh and Khar'kov provinces to supply the distilleries. Perhaps as little as a third of the grain produced in 1788 was consumed by humans. Since grain was commonly transported in bulk, covered only by matting, much valuable produce rotted in transit. Unseasonable thaws damaged a country dependent on natural deep freeze. As Tooke noted, the capital's food supply was badly disrupted during the abnormally mild winter of 1789–90, when 'several provinces suffered great injury' and 'great quantities of the provision bought for the supply of St Petersburg was so spoilt that it was thrown away'.[36]

As so often in Russian history, however, the achievements outweighed even these drawbacks. Despite a shocking rate of loss and damage, the increase in freight passing through the Vyshnyi–Volochek system was spectacular. It rose a hundred times between its creation in 1712–19 and the 1750s, when it carried a maximum of 216,000 tons a year. Not the least benefit of this system of waterways was the work it provided, though this was a mixed blessing to employers in other sectors whose hired labourers drifted away in the spring thaw. Estimates of the water-borne workforce range from fewer than 60,000 in c. 1700 to more than 220,000 in 1800, of whom three-quarters were employed on the Volga. Thanks to restrictions on mobility, the Russian waterways never offered the passenger service that made the Dutch *trekvaart* network such a thriving concern. But the availability of compulsorily transferable cheap labour compensated for the transport system's many expensive defects. It thus came to offer a means of provisioning St Petersburg and boosting both domestic and foreign trade, markets to which we now turn.

Trade and commerce

In 1700 Muscovy was still profiting from the fur trade which had not only enriched but empowered the medieval princes who controlled it. Furs had always been exchanged for valuable goods – silver, silks, and herbs – and this trend persisted after 1689, when the treaty of Nerchinsk confirmed a Chinese market supplied by the Russian conquest of Kamchatka. Here, careless of the ecological cost, adventurers slaughtered some 24,000 sables, more than 5,000 foxes, and 460 sea otters between 1707 and 1715 alone. Though most of the profits were pocketed by entrepreneurs who bribed officials to turn a blind eye, a combination of reprisal and reform allowed the government to penetrate the trade in 1727–8, thus establishing a monopoly. It was a Pyrrhic victory. The value of a trade worth as much as 2.25 million rubles a year in the mid-1720s fell to a mere 30,000 rubles a decade later. Though the Chinese trade continued, particularly in medicinal herbs, it languished until the 1770s. Meanwhile, the acquisition of the Baltic lands in the Great Northern War signified a decisive shift in the balance of Russian foreign trade from overland to overseas.

Whereas c. 1650 roughly three-quarters of Russian overseas trade

[36] Tooke, *View of the Russian Empire*, vol. I, p. 28.

passed through Archangel (f. 1584), this icy northern outpost suffered rapid decline when challenged by warm-water ports on the Baltic. Riga and Reval were in turn eclipsed by St Petersburg, a point which supports the argument that capital cities which were also ports were economically the period's most successful urban centres.[37] St Petersburg's dominance, initially induced by legislation, was soon self-propelled by the demands of its own population. Together, the capital and Riga accounted for over 80 per cent of Russia's overseas commodity trade by 1800. During the eighteenth century, this trade had increased approximately fifteenfold, as first iron and later grain supplemented the list of exports traditionally dominated by flax and hemp.

The importance of the Anglo-Russian trade qualifies it for special attention. In volume it rose steadily from 1700, so that by the 1730s the British had supplanted the Dutch as the Russians' most significant trading partners. By 1764–5, the value of their business probably stood at more than £1 million, twice that of 1734, the year of the Anglo-Russian trade treaty renewed in 1766, which consolidated the British merchants' dominant position. The British became the biggest consumers of Russian products, a few still hoping that trade with Russia might give access to the East. They bought around two-thirds of flax and hemp exports, which together accounted for about 40 per cent of Russia's total, and profited in turn from the sudden demand for woollen cloth to make uniforms for Russia's expanding army (a trade which contributed to the English export boom of the 1700s and foundered only when the Prussian Cloth Company won a contract for the 1730s from Russians disgusted by poor-quality English products). From the 1750s, the British found a niche as principal suppliers of colonial luxuries which helped to satisfy the increasingly sophisticated tastes of Russian nobles. By 1793–5 sugar, at nearly 6 million rubles, accounted for over a fifth of the value of Russia's total imports, more than four times the value of wine.

If trade in the North at the time of Peter the Great was nearly balanced, then Britain's dependence on Russian naval stores subsequently tipped the scales in Russia's favour. To some extent this advantage was offset by charges the British could recoup for carrying the cargo. Until the 1760s, virtually the whole trade was carried in British ships, which by virtue of their reliability and economy still accounted for 63 per cent of goods exported from St Petersburg in 1804. Alexander I's

---

[37] J. de Vries, *European Urbanization 1500–1800* (London, 1984), pp. 140–2. For a dissenting voice, see J. V. Th. Knoppers, *Dutch Trade with Russia from the Time of Peter I to Alexander I: A Quantitative Study in Eighteenth-Century Shipping*, 3 vols. (Montreal, 1976), vol. I, pp. 151–60.

commitment to Napoleon's blockade of British ships in 1807 was therefore highly damaging to the Russian economy. By then, however, the
Russians had developed their own merchant marine, which increased
eight times between 1775 and 1787 alone. Discounting the low starting
point and the foreign ships flying Russian flags in an attempt to evade
customs duties, this was a spectacular advance which supported the
expansion of Russian trade in the Black Sea and the eastern Mediterranean.

As these new markets opened up after 1760, boosted by interruptions
to the Atlantic trade during the War of American Independence
(1775–83), so the composition of Russia's exports began to change:
naval stores channelled through the Baltic gradually yielded in significance to grain shipped through the Black Sea. An embryonic Muscovite
grain trade, based on small surpluses from the provinces of Novgorod
and Pskov, had begun to pass through Narva and Archangel before
1700. But it was profitable only when international prices were high and
it collapsed during the Great Northern War. In the 1720s and 1730s,
surpluses were diverted to provision St Petersburg by protectionist
governments anxious to prohibit exports. Yet when restrictions were
lifted in the 1740s, the Russian market rapidly responded. When
European famine in the winter of 1772–3 prompted Catherine II,
encouraged by the Free Economic Society, to permit the export of grain
to Holland and the Rhineland, the Tuscan newspaper *Notizio del Mondo*
claimed that 'free export has made the fortune of many Russian
provinces, where grain was abundant'.[38] Even then, grain remained a
small percentage of gross product value. In the mid-1780s, before the
foundation of Odessa in 1794, the Black Sea ports handled only 2–3 per
cent of the country's foreign trade. By 1802, grain (almost exclusively
wheat) accounted for 17.5 per cent of total exports, and in the first half
of the nineteenth century, as the southern lands came into their own,
grain exports rose by fifteen times, to 35.7 million bushels in 1850 (3.5
per cent of the total grain crop).

The significance of foreign, and especially British, merchants in the
Russian economy extended beyond international trade. Deterred by
punitive tariffs from trading inland, they indirectly stimulated the
domestic market by advancing credit to indigenous merchants and
making deposits against promised supplies. It was only in this way that
Russian dealers were able to fund their own mutual transactions.

Cash shortages conspired with huge distances to delay the fusion of
local and regional trading networks into a single national market. The

---

[38] Quoted in F. Venturi, *The End of the Old Regime in Europe 1768–1776: The First Crisis*,
tr. R. B. Litchfield (Princeton, 1989), p. 94.

time-scale remains contentious. Mironov's claim to detect a unified, all-Russian market by 1800 is disputed by Milov, prepared to concede its formation only under the impact of the railways a century later. Shaw convincingly argues that in our period it was proximity to the markets of Moscow and St Petersburg, or access to them via the waterways, that mattered most in market integration.[39] Feeble links to the national market were not necessarily detrimental to local economies. Indeed, both in Siberia and on the steppe, market penetration benefited Russians at the expense of native traders unaccustomed to monetary transactions, whilst in Ukraine money-lending for the market aggravated anti-Semitism. But whatever view one takes of the advance of an all-Russian market, a topic which has preoccupied Russian historians more than their Western colleagues, few now question the trend towards integration or doubt that its crucial links were fairs.

Only after 1840 did the balance of domestic trade shift from the periodic to the permanent. Meanwhile, fairs not only grew in number but spread more evenly over the empire: there were 224 towns with bazaars and fairs in the 1760s, 555 by the 1850s. A striking proportion (36 per cent in 1760, and 51 per cent in 1800) were held in villages on noble estates. Most happened between May and September, when dry roads made them easier to reach, clement weather allowed them to be held outdoors, and the widest variety of produce was available. The uneven distribution of religious festivals in the calendar also mattered since 80 per cent of fairs took place on such *prazdniki*, most lasting between one and three days. Specialisation remained rare: merchants and trading peasants sought security by operating both as retailers and as wholesalers of a wide range of goods. There were, however, a few specialist wholesale fairs lasting for up to a month. Much the greatest was at Nizhnii Novgorod, where goods worth 28.2 million silver rubles were traded in 1829. By 1863, this 'Makarevskii' fair (named after the miracle-working saint, Makarii Zheltovodskii (d. 1444), who founded the monastery where it was first held in 1624) alone accounted for a quarter of the turnover of Russia's fair trade.

Few could compete at this level, though some first-guild merchants made exorbitant profits. In the mid-1760s, Savva Iakovlev turned over 500,000 rubles a year on the Moscow and St Petersburg alcohol monopoly he purchased in 1750. The ennobled Iakovlev owned 9 per cent of all the shops in St Petersburg in the 1780s. By contrast, most

[39] J. Pallot and D. J. B. Shaw, *Landscape and Settlement in Romanov Russia, 1613–1917* (Oxford, 1990), pp. 193–215. Cf. B. N. Mironov, *Vnutrennyi rynok Rossii vo vtoroi polovine XVIII–pervoi polovine XIXv* (Leningrad, 1981), and I. D. Koval'chenko and L. V. Milov, *Vserossiiskii agrarnii rynok: XVIII–nachalo XX veka* (Moscow, 1974).

registered merchants traded on an insignificant scale. In 1764, even the Zvenigorod magistracy in relatively advanced Moscow province confessed that the town's 335 merchants had no trade or handicrafts 'of any kind and only for their subsistence do they from time to time sell goods to travelling persons and this in the smallest [amount]'.[40] A study of trading peasants around Nizhnii Novgorod in the early eighteenth century found that only 5–6 per cent of its sample operated beyond their own village, though these, all from large estates, made major gains plying the Volga. The same pattern persisted a century later. A list of 346 peasants commanding capital on a Sheremet'ev estate in Tver' province in 1803 credited almost half with less than 1,000 rubles. But five men had accumulated 100,000–160,000 rubles by supplying grain to St Petersburg and thirty-two owned their own boats.

Since fortunes were made by only a tiny minority of adventurers, the safest route to security was to bypass the market by establishing regular relationships and fixing prices in advance. Shcherbatov offered two of Russia's most successful textile entrepreneurs, I. D. Zatrapeznov in Iaroslavl' and A. S. Ashastin in Kostroma, both a regular supply of semi-finished linen and a ready source of seasonal labour from serfs who would otherwise have lain idle in the winter. In return, Ashastin provided Shcherbatov with capital which enabled him to invest in his weaving sheds at Kuzmodem'ianskoe and increase the revenues of the estate by more than 400 per cent between 1771 and 1793.[41] Those unable to establish networks of this kind were most likely to prosper by winning government contracts. A study of merchant fortunes in the Pereiaslavl'–Riazan' region in the 1730s showed that each one of the handful of men who stayed solvent depended on state contracts for his survival.

The integration and growth of Russian internal markets must be kept in perspective. Turnover was small, access to the market uneven, and the level of commercialisation limited. The proportion of marketed goods remained low: Hermann's contemporary calculations put it at only 6 per cent, excluding grain, in 1788. It could hardly have been otherwise whilst almost 90 per cent of Russia's labour remained preoccupied by mere subsistence. Whilst demand for other goods and services remained relatively feeble, the market absorbed agricultural produce faster than it redistributed proto-industrial products. However, as we shall now see, we cannot separate urban industry from rural agriculture.

[40] Quoted in W. Daniel, 'The Merchants' View of the Social Order in Russia as Revealed in the Town *Nakazy* from *Moskovskaia Guberniia* to Catherine's Legislative Commission', *CASS*, 11, 4 (1977), p. 506.
[41] See W. Daniel, 'Conflict Between Economic Vision and Economic Reality: The Case of M. M. Shcherbatov,' *SEER*, 67, 1 (1989), esp. pp. 60–4.

Agriculture and industry, town and country

Forty-one of the fifty-seven urban petitions to the 1767 Legislative Commission pleaded for more land. Whilst Kargopol' reported townsmen who 'live by farming on their own rural parcels of land, like peasants', Moscow complained that as a result of urban expansion 'such a small part of the meadow land remains that it is almost impossible to feed cattle in the summer'.[42] Profiting from local demand, market gardening developed in towns after 1750 to the extent that, from a sample of 209 towns in European Russia in the 1760s, Mironov calculates that no fewer than 128 (61 per cent) ought to be classified as 'agrarian' on the grounds that the majority of their populations were engaged in some way in agriculture. Only nine towns (4 per cent) would then have qualified as 'industrial'; by the 1850s the proportion had risen to 43 per cent.

Just as towns retained an interest in agriculture, so the countryside was an important location for industry. Even before 1700 there is evidence of rural handicrafts. Subsequently, villages in market-oriented provinces began to specialise. By 1800, three loose networks of rural industry had formed in the non-blacksoil region where agricultural yields were insufficient to satisfy lords' demands for profit and *obrok* repaid nobles better than *barshchina*. To the north and east of Moscow, surplus peasant labour was diverted into weaving silk, cotton, and linen. The provinces of Vladimir and Kostroma formed a second textile region, where cotton dominated linen by the nineteenth century. Further east, Nizhnii Novgorod lay at the centre of a network of villages, almost all on Sheremet'ev estates, specialising in tanning and metalwork. By 1825, a few villages were becoming small centres of commerce. In Mstera, a Panin village in Vladimir province, linen manufactories which had employed 800 in 1828 had disappeared by mid-century leaving the manufacture of mass-produced icons as the dominant occupation of the population.

The advantage of small-scale rural industry lay in its flexibility: low fixed costs and small overheads allowed it to undercut factories hampered by high production and transport costs. Consumption was also significant. Whereas large-scale manufactories depended on mass demand and consumer concentration in highly populated areas – both at a premium – smaller-scale enterprises were better placed to supply what little the majority wanted (and could afford) to buy. In consequence, cottage industries prospered by supplying provincial and rural markets, whereas large-scale manufacturing did better where its product

---

[42] Quoted in J. M. Hittle, *The Service City: State and Townsmen in Russia 1600–1800* (Cambridge, MA, 1979), p. 154.

could be exported, sent direct to Moscow or St Petersburg, or delivered in bulk under government contract.

The precious- and ferrous-metal industries were classic beneficiaries of economies of scale, but each faltered after an initial boom. So low-grade were the ores at Nerchinsk in the Amur valley, where silver mining began in 1704, that production was marginal before a chance discovery of higher-grade ores at Kolyvan, more than 5,000 miles to the west, opened up a market for Nerchinsk's surplus lead in 1747. The Demidovs had been mining copper at Kolyvan for twenty years. But once lead from Nerchinsk could be used to extract silver from Kolyvan's argentiferous copper ores, the two Siberian mines, taken into state control, generated a combined output of some 2.2 million rubles at the peak of production in the 1770s (the annual equivalent of 40,000 kg of silver). At this point Russia produced more precious metals than the rest of Europe put together. The bonanza, however, was brief. In the 1770s the supply of ores began to run low, Pugachev caused chaos, and labour legislation of 1779–83 restricted the exploitation of the ascribed peasantry. More significant still was the revival of Latin American silver production in the 1760s. This eclipsed the European industry, including Russia's, until its second precious-metal boom, this time in gold, began in the mid-1830s.

It was not so much foreign competition as changing demand that eventually crippled the iron industry. Opened in the 1630s by foreign entrepreneurs, Russia's ironworks were transformed by Peter I, who started production in the Urals from scratch. Seeking self-sufficiency in arms, forty of Peter's 178 manufactories made armaments or iron. By 1725, however, they were producing more than the state required and would have faced crisis had not low labour costs enabled them to undercut European competitors. By mid-century, Russia, a net importer in 1700, had become the world's largest iron producer, displacing Sweden as Britain's principal supplier. Mid-century annual output of 2 million poods rose to 9.9 million in 1800, by which time the Urals and Siberia were responsible for 82 per cent of production. So long as European markets continued to demand basic bar iron rather than wrought iron or steel, primitive technology and serf labour were well equipped to supply it. In the middle of the nineteenth century, however, when the market began to require quality rather than quantity, Russian industry proved incapable of responding.

Economic growth

Twenty years ago, the consensus on Russia's economic performance would have been clear. Steady growth from 1725, based on small-scale industry, serf labour, and primitive technology, looked more like stagnation when compared to rapid developments in the West, especially when set alongside the British industrial revolution. It was precisely this comparison that led Gregory to conclude that 'the immediate post-Petrine period witnessed the beginning of the relative economic decline of Russia vis-à-vis Western Europe, which accelerated after 1800'.[43]

Confidence in this verdict has since been undermined. On the one hand, some historians of the British economy are no longer persuaded that a revolutionary interpretation of their subject is appropriate, arguing instead for gradual change which alone makes Russia's performance look more impressive. On the other hand, Newman and Blanchard argue that the Russian position has itself been understated and that eighteenth-century Russia underwent an 'agricultural revolution' generating growth more rapid and more extensive than has hitherto been realised.

Though neither hypothesis is beyond question, it is striking that recent work starting from a variety of methodological standpoints concurs on dynamic Russian growth after 1750. Government played its part by relaxing regulatory constraints, but economic expansion owed more to autonomous developments over which the state had only limited control and of which its knowledge was uncertain. Access to fertile land in New Russia was a safety valve for population growth and yielded abundant harvests at a time when rising grain prices boosted commercial production for foreign and domestic markets. Cheap labour compensated for expensive transport, allowing domestic turnover to rise and trading networks in provinces close to the waterways to fuse. These markets were supplied by proto-industrial products from estates in the infertile non-blackearth provinces whose lords had subordinated their paternalist instincts to the profits they could make from diversification. All this took place in a period in which large-scale natural disasters were fewer than in the previous half-century and when the dislocation caused by frequent wars had impressed on European states the need for international restraint and internal recovery. According to Blanchard, this favourable conjunction of circumstances gave Russia 'an almost five-fold increase in national income' between c. 1720 and c. 1807, an achievement which put it alongside Britain 'at the very top of the national-income league table'.[44]

Growth was achieved by a *combination* of an international credit economy with a servile domestic economy – predominantly subsistence-

---

[43] P. R. Gregory, 'Russian Industrialization and Economic Growth: Results and Perspectives of Western Research', *JfGO*, 25 (1977), p. 204.

[44] Blanchard, *Russia's 'Age of Silver'*, pp. 281–2.

based yet linked, if feebly, to a network of increasingly integrated, partially cash-based, local, regional, and perhaps national markets. Instead of succeeding one another in stages as modernisation theory prescribes, these modes of production and exchange existed alongside each other in a mutually reinforcing relationship. Though it could not match the scale of Prussia's production for the market, Russia's economic growth in the eighteenth century was no less firmly rooted in serfdom. To quote Blanchard again:

At best the role of the so-called 'modern' sector, including manufactories producing luxury wares, was passive in the growth process ... At worst, excluding the production of luxury wares, its impact was a negative one ... Growth came from within peasant society not from without.[45]

Serfdom was therefore not an inbuilt brake on growth in the way that emancipationists would later claim, just as, by extension, its abolition could never be an economic panacea. Demand for a product was more significant than the type of labour used to manufacture it.

Since the traditional economy long incorporated the very dynamic elements which might have helped permanently to transform it, the question must be: why did they not do so? For, despite the phenomenal growth of the eighteenth-century economy, Russia relapsed into poverty after c. 1810. Explanations of why something did *not* happen are always hazardous, and in this case we are further handicapped by is relatively poor knowledge of the economy between 1800 and 1861. But it is possible to suggest provisional explanations for abject economic failure after the Napoleonic wars. The most plausible hypothesis, advanced by Peter Gatrell, is that all those circumstances which had previously combined to stimulate the boom coalesced after 1810 into a vicious circle of restraint.[46] Declining yields in the black-soil provinces prompted nobles to reimpose *barshchina* on peasants loath to surrender the relative autonomy of *obrok*. But the crisis in productivity probably owed more to the cumulative effects of overcropping on exhausted soil than it did to inadequate supervision of the peasantry. The consequences of a century of careless resource-husbandry were at last beginning to bite. Their impact was the more grievous for coinciding with the French invasion of 1812 and the depression which struck Europe after the Napoleonic wars. To make matters worse, a new sequence of natural

---

[45] *Ibid.*, p. 254.
[46] P. Gatrell, 'Russian Economic History: The Legacy of Arcadius Kahan', *SR*, 50, 1 (1991), pp. 176–8. See also Gatrell, 'The Meaning of the Great Reforms in Russian Economic History', in B. Eklof, *et al.*, eds., *Russia's Great Reforms, 1855–1881* (Bloomington, IN, 1994), pp. 85–90.

disasters inflicted cholera on lands which could no longer easily absorb an expanding population.

Russia, in other words, found itself in precisely the predicament predicted by Smith in *The Wealth of Nations*: by 1800 it was 'a country which had acquired that full complement of riches which the nature of its soil and climate, and its situation with respect to other countries, allowed it to acquire'. This was a ceiling from which it 'could, therefore, advance no further' unless the structure of its organic economy were subsequently to be transformed.[47] Smith could foresee no such transformation. When, late in the nineteenth century, the Russian state tried forcibly to induce one on the basis of newly discovered mineral resources, railways, and technological transfer from the West, it faced the resilience of a population inured by centuries of bitter experience to value security higher than enterprise. Only foreigners and natives with nothing to lose could afford to take chances. Since no one had less to lose than schismatics outlawed by the régime, Old Believers remained disproportionately prominent among Russia's entrepreneurs. By contrast, most Russians shrank back into a risk-averse search for stable subsistence from which it still remains to be seen whether they will fully emerge.

BIBLIOGRAPHICAL NOTE

A. Kahan, *The Plow, the Hammer and the Knout: An Economic History of Eighteenth-Century Russia* (Chicago, 1985), is a sophisticated account of market penetration within the servile economy. B. N. Mironov, 'Consequences of the Price Revolution in Eighteenth-Century Russia', *Economic History Review*, 45 (1992), summarises the most stimulating Russian historian's conclusions, though it seems doubtful that so broad a spectrum of economic change can convincingly be attributed to a single cause as Mironov seeks to claim. Without saying much directly about Russia, E. L. Jones, *The European Miracle: Environments, Economies and Geopolitics in the History of Europe and Asia* (Cambridge, 1981), and Jones, *Growth Recurring: Economic Change in World History* (Oxford, 1988), cast much light on its economic problems over the long term.

On mercantilism, start with D. C. Coleman, *Revisions in Mercantilism* (London, 1969). S. Blanc, 'The Economic Policies of Peter the Great', in W. L. Blackwell, ed., *Russian Economic Development from Peter the Great to Stalin* (New York, 1974), survives a poor translation. Reprinted

---

[47] Quoted in E. A. Wrigley, 'Why Poverty Was Inevitable in Traditional Societies', in J. A. Hall and I. C. Jarvie, eds., *Transition to Modernity: Essays on Power, Wealth and Belief* (Cambridge, 1992), p. 102.

in the same volume is A. Kahan's influential 'Continuity in Economic Activity and Policy During the Post-Petrine Period in Russia', *JEcH*, 25 (1965), to be supplemented by W. Daniel, 'Entrepreneurship and the Russian Textile Industry: From Peter the Great to Catherine the Great', *RR*, 54 (1995). Daniel explores the links between economic and social policy in 'The Merchantry and the Problem of Social Order in the Russian State: Catherine II's Commission on Commerce', *SEER*, 55 (1977), and 'Grigorii Teplov and the Conception of Order: The Commission on Commerce and the Role of the Merchants in Russia', *CASS*, 16 (1982). W. M. Pintner, *Russian Economic Policy Under Nicholas I* (Ithaca, NY, 1967), also bears on the reign of Alexander I.

For a contemporary statistician, see R. E. McGrew, 'Dilemmas of Development: Baron Heinrich Friedrich Storch (1766–1835) on the Growth of Imperial Russia', *JfGO*, 24 (1976). L. Bagrow, *A History of Russian Cartography up to 1800* (Wolfe Island, Ont., 1975), survives criticism by L. A. Goldenberg and A. V. Postnikov, 'Development of Mapping Methods in Russia in the Eighteenth Century', *Imago Mundi*, 37 (1985). Also relevant is D. J. B. Shaw, 'Geographical Practice and Its Significance in Peter the Great's Russia', *Journal of Historical Geography*, 22 (1996). R. P. Bartlett, *Human Capital: The Settlement of Foreigners in Russia 1762–1804* (Cambridge, 1979), stresses populationism. B. Hollingsworth, 'A. P. Kunitsyn and the Social Movement in Russia Under Alexander I', *SEER*, 43 (1964), introduces Russian views of British political economy.

The key authority on demography remains V. M. Kabuzan: *Narodonaselenie Rossii v XVIII–pervoi polovine XIXv.* (Moscow, 1963), and *Izmeneniia v razmeshchenii naselenii Rossii v polovine XIXv.* (Moscow, 1971). A sense of what we are missing comes from E. A. Wrigley and R. S. Schofield, *The Population History of England 1541–1871: A Reconstruction* (London, 1981). W. H. Parker, *An Historical Geography of Russia* (London, 1968), synthesises contemporary foreign accounts. R. A. French touches on resource management in 'Russians and the Forest', in J. H. Bater and R. A. French, eds., *Studies in Russian Historical Geography*, 2 vols. (London, 1983), vol. I; A. V. Dulov, *Geograficheskaia sreda i istoriia Rossii: konets XV–seredina XIXv* (Moscow, 1983), is more comprehensive, though he makes it hard to see the wood for the trees. P. J. Best, 'Insurance in Imperial Russia', *JEurEcH*, 18 (1989), is appropriately pessimistic.

R. A. French, 'Canals in Pre-Revolutionary Russia', in Bater and French, *Studies in Russian Historical Geography*, vol. II, R. E. Jones, 'Getting the Goods to St Petersburg: Water Transport from the Interior, 1703–1811', *SR*, 43 (1984), and especially G. Istomina, *Vodnye puti*

Rossii vo vtoroi polovine XVIII–nachale XIX veka (Moscow, 1982), all make Kahan's chapter in *The Plow, the Hammer and the Knout* seem too sanguine. R. M. Hayward, 'The Development of Steamboats on the Volga River and Its Tributaries, 1817–1856', *Research in Economic History*, 6 (1981), complements F. N. Rodin, *Burlachestvo v Rossii* (Moscow, 1975). On problems of distribution and access in Siberia, see J. R. Gibson, *Feeding the Russian Fur Trade: Provisionment of the Okhotsk Seaboard and the Kamchatka Peninsula, 1639–1856* (Madison, WI, 1969).

The longest part of Kahan's *The Plow, the Hammer and the Knout* summarises a lifetime's work on international trade. A. Attman, 'The Russian Market in World Trade, 1500–1860', *Scandinavian Economic History Review*, 29 (1981), is a concise survey. D. W. Jones, *War and Economy in the Age of William III and Marlborough* (Oxford, 1989), has much to say on Anglo-Russian trade, innovatively discussed by J. Newman, 'The Russian Grain Trade, 1700–1779', in W. Minchinton, ed., *The Baltic Grain Trade* (Exeter, 1985); Newman, 'The English Contribution to the Economic Revolution in Russia in the Eighteenth Century', in Minchinton, ed., *Britain and the Northern Seas* (Pontefract, 1988); and Newman, '"A very delicate Experiment": British Mercantile Strategies for Financing Trade in Russia, 1680–1780', in I. Blanchard, A. Goodman, and Newman, eds., *Studies in the Industrial and Financial History of Early Modern Europe* (Stuttgart, 1990). See also the survey by H. H. Kaplan, *Russian Overseas Commerce with Great Britain During the Reign of Catherine II* (Philadelphia, 1995). W. Kirchner, 'Ein Beitrag zur deutsch–russischen Wirtschaftsgeschichte des 18. Jahrhunderts', *JfGO*, 38 (1990), is concise. C. M. Foust, *Muscovite and Mandarin: Russia's Trade with China and Its Setting, 1727–1856* (Chapel Hill, 1969), is detailed and informative. On Siberia, V. A. Aleksandrov, 'The Beginnings of the Irbit Fair', *Soviet Geography*, 31 (1990), and R. F. Drew, 'The Siberian Fair: 1600–1750', *SEER*, 39 (1960–1), and works listed under chapter 2. G. E. Munro, 'Feeding the Multitudes: Grain Supply to St Petersburg in the Era of Catherine the Great', *JfGO*, 35 (1987), contributes to the history of the capital.

M. Confino, *Systèmes agraires et progrès agricole: l'assolement triennal en Russie aux XVIIIe–XIXe siècles* (Paris, 1969), sets agriculture in its social context. W. Daniel, 'Conflict Between Economic Vision and Economic Reality: The Case of M. M. Shcherbatov' (above, n. 41), is a first-class study of estate management. J. Blum, *The End of the Old Order in Europe* (Princeton, 1978), and W. Abel, *Agricultural Fluctuations in Europe: From the Thirteenth to the Twentieth Centuries* (London, 1980), offer comparisons. M. Falkus, *The Industrialisation of Russia, 1700–1914* (London,

1972), is less sophisticated than O. Crisp, 'Labour and Industrialisation in Russia', in *The Cambridge Economic History of Europe*, vol. VII (Cambridge, 1978).

On the urban economy, and much more besides, see B. N. Mironov, *Russkii gorod v 1740–1860 gg.* (Leningrad, 1990), partly summarised in Mironov, 'Les villes de Russie entre l'Occident et l'Orient (1750–1850)', *Annales: Economies, Sociétés, Civilisations*, 46 (1991). Individual cities are analysed by J. H. Bater, *St Petersburg: Industrialization and Change* (London, 1976); P. Herlihy, *Odessa: A History 1794–1914* (Cambridge, MA, 1986); and J. T. Alexander, 'Catherine II, Bubonic Plague and the Problem of Industry in Moscow', *AHR*, 79 (1974). See also A. V. Koval'chuk, 'Moskva kak krupneishii tekstil'nyi tsentr Rossii vo vtoroi polovine XVIII veke', *Otechestvennaia istoriia* (1996, no. 6). E. A. Wrigley, 'City and Country in the Past: A Sharp Divide or a Continuum?', *Historical Research*, 64 (1991), interprets a complex historiography. G. Rozman, *Urban Networks in Russia, 1750–1800, and Premodern Periodization* (Princeton, 1976), sacrifices too much to his model. F. F. Mendels, 'Proto-Industrialization: The First Phase of the Industrialization Process', *JEcH*, 32 (1972), spawned a huge literature charted by S. Ogilvie and M. Cerman, eds., *European Proto-Industrialization* (Cambridge, 1996). Stimulating essays on Russia include E. Melton, 'Proto-Industrialization, Serf Agriculture and Agrarian Social Structure: Two Estates in Nineteenth-Century Russia', *P&P*, 115 (1986), and R. L. Rudolph, 'Agricultural Structure and Proto-Industrialization in Russia: Economic Development with Unfree Labour', *JEcH*, 45 (1985).

Conclusion

By 1825, educated Russians had stood for so long before the mirror of Western culture, and reinvented themselves so many times in its kaleidoscopic image, that their history may seem to offer more scope to a post-modernist investigation than to one informed by the earthier concerns of modernisation theory. Indeed, at first sight, what is most striking about the modernisation model in the Russian case is its limited applicability. Russia in 1825 was by no means a modern state. Nowhere in Europe was popular participation in politics so severely discouraged; nowhere was subsistence agriculture so widely practised; nowhere did the workings of the world remain so mysterious to so many. Behind the façade of its rationally ordered bureaucratic hierarchy, and beneath the level of the cosmopolitan nobility, the Russian empire remained a peasant society ruled by autocrats who never relinquished their personal grip on the impersonal state authority they were so anxious to develop.

Yet if the Russian experience warns against any simple, linear theory of modernisation, the concept nevertheless helps to bring into focus crucial interrelationships between government, economy, and society. Russia's kinship-dominated peasant communities were not the casual detritus of government-led modernisation: they were its direct consequence. As the state counted the cost of its new standing army, its extensive multi-national territories, its administrative institutions, and its glittering cosmopolitan capital, the people paid the price. Risk-averse peasants relapsed into intensified collective responsibility as the only safe way to meet the government's increasing fiscal demands. The more Russian rulers tried to modernise their state, the more backward their empire became.

So long as the world was judged by eighteenth-century standards, that was not a handicap. The multi-ethnic nobility coalesced into a fiercely loyal, highly cultured, and resourceful imperial élite. Serf labour successfully supplied the demands of a huge army reserve, domestic agricultural productivity, and an international market dependent upon pig iron and naval stores. The problem came when, elsewhere, new technology and the rise of the nation-state made Russia's dynastic empire look increasingly anachronistic and inflexible. Everywhere in Europe, the revolutionary occupation helped to stimulate nationalism; only in Russia did French troops serve to discredit the cause of rational reform. In the Italian peninsula, Napoleonic government bequeathed even to the benighted Papal States a legacy of toleration and rational bureaucracy that could be exploited in the cause of national liberation from Austrian supremacy. In Russia, rationalism after 1825 was tarred with the brush of Decembrist subversion. Nicolaevan Russia was not a stagnant pool. Beneath its placid surface, reformist ideas circulated in the chancelleries of St Petersburg and the theological academies of the Orthodox church, just as much as in the underground circles of the radical intelligentsia. But the tsar himself had set his face against change. Only after Russia had been humiliated in the Crimea (1854–6) – barely forty years after its triumph over Napoleon – was it feasible to launch a further bout of state-led modernisation prompted by the need to defend its imperial pretensions.

Index

NEW APPROACHES TO EUROPEAN HISTORY